Shaping Inclusive Educational Policies and Practices With Generative AI

Gürhan Durak
https://orcid.org/0000-0003-2944-3713
The Open University, UK

Serkan Çankaya
https://orcid.org/0000-0002-3951-9809
İzmir Democracy University, Turkey

IGI Global
Scientific Publishing
Publishing Tomorrow's Research Today

Vice President of Editorial	Melissa Wagner
Director of Acquisitions	Mikaela Felty
Director of Book Development	Jocelynn Hessler
Production Manager	Mike Brehm
Cover Design	Jose Rosado

Published in the United States of America by
IGI Global Scientific Publishing
701 East Chocolate Avenue
Hershey, PA, 17033, USA
Tel: 717-533-8845 | Fax: 717-533-7115
Website: https://www.igi-global.com E-mail: cust@igi-global.com

Library of Congress Cataloging-in-Publication Data

LCCN: 2025032420 (CIP Data Pending)
ISBN13: 979-8-3373-3745-6
Isbn13Softcover: 979-8-3373-3746-3
EISBN13: 979-8-3373-3747-0
British Cataloguing in Publication Data
A Cataloguing in Publication record for this book is available from the British Library.

Table of Contents

Preface x

Chapter 1
The Role of Generative AI in Redefining Inclusive Education Practices 1
Mustafa Kayyali, Maaref University of Applied Sciences, Syria

Chapter 2
Ethical Implications of AI in Promoting Equity and Access in Education 29
Mustafa Kayyali, Maaref University of Applied Sciences, Syria

Chapter 3
Rethinking Artificial Intelligence Implementation for Inclusive and Equitable Quality Higher Education in South Africa 55
Godwin Kaisara, Namibia University of Science and Technology, Namibia
Khulekani Yakobi, Mangosuthu University of Technology, South Africa
Kabiru Ishola Genty, Namibia University of Science and Technology, Namibia & Lagos State University, Nigeria
Sulaiman Olusegun Atiku, Namibia University of Science and Technology, Namibia & Walter Sisulu University, South Africa

Chapter 4
Reworlding Inclusion: Speculative Futures of STEM Education in the Age of Generative AI 79
Masud Ahmmed, Victoria University, Australia
Janine Arantes, Victoria University, Australia

Chapter 5
AI-Driven Approaches to Inclusive Science Teaching in a Liberal Arts Context 105
Nicole Simon, SUNY Nassau CC, USA

Chapter 6
Assistive Technologies for Learners With Disabilities Using GenAI 139
Tary Hadani, Universitas Esa Unggul, Indonesia
Chrisella Natasia Tanujaya, Universitas Esa Unggul, Indonesia
Binastya Anggara Sekti, Universitas Esa Unggul, Indonesia

Chapter 7
Empowering Special Education Through Generative AI With Opportunities, Challenges, and Case Studies 171
O. Bhaskaru, Vignan's Foundation for Science, Technology, and Research, India
K. Lalitha, Santhiram Engineering College, India

Chapter 8
Generative AI for Inclusive Special Education: Case Studies in Accessibility, Personalization, and Ethical Design 205
S. Prabagar, Alliance School of Advanced Computing, Alliance University, Bengaluru, India
Rashmi Mothkur, Alliance University, Bengaluru, India
C. B. Swetha, Alliance University, Bengaluru, India
Asha Kurian, Alliance University, Bengaluru, India
K. Pavithra, Christ University, Bengaluru, India
S. Aarthi, Marwadi University, Rajkot, India

Chapter 9
AI, Impostor Syndrome, and Emotional Resilience: Rethinking SEL and Student Well-Being in Inclusive AI-Enhanced ESL Classrooms 237
Maria Arjie Tobias Domingo, Independent Researcher, Philippines

Compilation of References 269

About the Contributors 305

Index 311

Detailed Table of Contents

Preface x

Chapter 1
The Role of Generative AI in Redefining Inclusive Education Practices 1
Mustafa Kayyali, Maaref University of Applied Sciences, Syria

Generative AI is transforming the very foundations of inclusive education—shifting the focus from reactive accommodations to proactive, personalized learning ecosystems. This chapter examines how AI can adapt content, pedagogy, and assessment to meet the needs of learners across diverse linguistic, cultural, and cognitive backgrounds. It explores real-world applications, from AI-assisted translation and adaptive tutoring to tools that enhance accessibility for students with disabilities. At the same time, it addresses the ethical imperatives of bias mitigation, transparency, and cultural respect. By weaving together technological potential with policy frameworks, the chapter offers a roadmap for educational systems seeking to embed inclusion not as an afterthought, but as a core design principle in the AI era.

Chapter 2
Ethical Implications of AI in Promoting Equity and Access in Education 29
Mustafa Kayyali, Maaref University of Applied Sciences, Syria

Generative AI is reshaping the educational landscape, offering unprecedented possibilities for personalization, resource creation, and access to learning. Yet its integration into classrooms and policy frameworks raises pressing ethical questions: Will AI narrow the educational divide or deepen existing disparities? This chapter critically examines the intersection of AI ethics, equity, and access in education, exploring how algorithmic design, data governance, and institutional choices influence outcomes for marginalized learners. Drawing on global perspectives, it discusses both the transformative potential and the risks of exclusion embedded in AI-driven systems. The chapter proposes guiding principles for designing and implementing generative AI tools that uphold fairness, cultural responsiveness, and accessibility. In doing so, it argues for a proactive, policy-driven approach to ensure that AI serves as a bridge—rather than a barrier—to inclusive, equitable education for all.

Chapter 3
Rethinking Artificial Intelligence Implementation for Inclusive and Equitable Quality Higher Education in South Africa 55
Godwin Kaisara, Namibia University of Science and Technology, Namibia
Khulekani Yakobi, Mangosuthu University of Technology, South Africa
Kabiru Ishola Genty, Namibia University of Science and Technology, Namibia & Lagos State University, Nigeria
Sulaiman Olusegun Atiku, Namibia University of Science and Technology, Namibia & Walter Sisulu University, South Africa

Generative Artificial Intelligence (GenAI) is rapidly transforming global higher education, offering both unprecedented opportunities and complex challenges. In South Africa, where the legacy of apartheid has entrenched deep educational inequalities, the strategic implementation of GenAI holds the potential to either bridge or widen existing divides. This chapter critically examines how GenAI can be harnessed to promote inclusive and equitable quality higher education in South Africa, while addressing the structural, ethical, and practical challenges that accompany its adoption. Drawing insights from a comprehensive synthesis of the existing literature on GenAI and education, this chapter argues that the AI revolution has the potential to either narrow or intensify existing educational inequalities in South Africa. If not implemented equitably, GenAI may further widen the gap between historically privileged and marginalised universities. The chapter suggests the need for critical dialogue to ensure that GenAI catalyses an inclusive and equitable higher education in South Africa.

Chapter 4
Reworlding Inclusion: Speculative Futures of STEM Education in the Age of Generative AI... 79
Masud Ahmmed, Victoria University, Australia
Janine Arantes, Victoria University, Australia

This chapter argues that inclusion in STEM education must be reimagined in the age of Generative AI (GenAI). Drawing on speculative fabulation and feminist theories of epistemic justice, we examine how GenAI reshapes knowledge production, assessment, and representation, often reinforcing bias and exclusion. Through three speculative scenarios, we explore divergent futures of STEM learning and Initial Teacher Education (ITE), showing how AI can either entrench dominant norms or foster pluralistic, relational pedagogies. We propose that inclusion must shift from representational fixes to a radical, justice-oriented reworlding of education, where AI is governed transparently, designed with care, and co-created with those historically marginalised.

Chapter 5
AI-Driven Approaches to Inclusive Science Teaching in a Liberal Arts Context 105
Nicole Simon, SUNY Nassau CC, USA

This chapter explores AI-Driven Approaches to Inclusive Science Teaching in Liberal Arts Contexts, emphasizing how generative artificial intelligence (AI) can enhance inclusivity through Universal Design for Learning (UDL) principles. Drawing on CAST's framework for AI and UDL, we examine how generative AI tools support personalized learning pathways, improve access, and reduce barriers in science education for diverse learners. Recent findings (Francis, Jones, & Smith, 2025) highlight the importance of balancing AI innovation with academic integrity, while Haroud and Saqri (2025) underscore the varying digital literacies and attitudes of students and faculty toward AI integration. Building on Schreffler et al.'s (2019) review of UDL in STEM for students with disabilities, this chapter illustrates how AI can align with inclusive pedagogies to better serve liberal arts students often underrepresented in science disciplines. We propose practical, ethical, and pedagogical strategies for higher education faculty to implement AI inclusively in science classrooms.

Chapter 6
Assistive Technologies for Learners With Disabilities Using GenAI 139
Tary Hadani, Universitas Esa Unggul, Indonesia
Chrisella Natasia Tanujaya, Universitas Esa Unggul, Indonesia
Binastya Anggara Sekti, Universitas Esa Unggul, Indonesia

Generative Artificial Intelligence (GenAI) is revolutionizing education by providing personalized learning experiences for students with disabilities. This chapter explores the role of GenAI and assistive technologies, such as screen readers and mobility devices, in enhancing educational accessibility. GenAI enables real-time adaptation of learning materials, making them more suitable for students with cognitive, physical, and sensory disabilities. While the potential is significant, challenges such as accessibility, educator training, and data privacy must be addressed. The chapter emphasizes the need for infrastructure development and training to fully integrate GenAI into inclusive education systems.

Chapter 7
Empowering Special Education Through Generative AI With Opportunities, Challenges, and Case Studies 171
O. Bhaskaru, Vignan's Foundation for Science, Technology, and Research, India
K. Lalitha, Santhiram Engineering College, India

Generative Artificial Intelligence (GenAI) is transforming special education by delivering personalized, accessible, and inclusive learning experiences for students with diverse cognitive, sensory, communication, and behavioral needs. Unlike traditional technologies, GenAI can dynamically create content, adapt learning pathways, and simulate social-emotional scenarios, opening new opportunities for engagement and independence. This chapter explores GenAI's multifaceted applications in special education—ranging from augmentative communication and adaptive assessments to emotion-sensitive interventions—supported by real-world case studies. It also critically addresses ethical, technical, and policy challenges, including data privacy, algorithmic bias, and accessibility. Emphasizing the value of co-design with educators and disability advocates, the chapter offers balanced insights and actionable guidance for educators, researchers, policymakers, and AI developers working to create inclusive educational environments.

Chapter 8
Generative AI for Inclusive Special Education: Case Studies in Accessibility, Personalization, and Ethical Design 205
S. Prabagar, Alliance School of Advanced Computing, Alliance University, Bengaluru, India
Rashmi Mothkur, Alliance University, Bengaluru, India
C. B. Swetha, Alliance University, Bengaluru, India
Asha Kurian, Alliance University, Bengaluru, India
K. Pavithra, Christ University, Bengaluru, India
S. Aarthi, Marwadi University, Rajkot, India

This chapter explores the transformative role of Generative AI in special education, emphasizing its ability to personalize learning, enhance accessibility, and support neurodiverse learners. Grounded in Universal Design for Learning (UDL) and inclusive pedagogy, it analyzes how tools like GPT, DALL·E, and Whisper enable individualized instruction through text simplification, visual storytelling, and real-time captioning. Case studies illustrate improved reading comprehension, classroom participation, and emotional development among students with dyslexia, hearing impairments, and autism. Ethical challenges including algorithmic bias, data privacy, and the digital divide are critically discussed. The chapter provides actionable recommendations for educators, developers, and policymakers to ensure human-centered, ethical AI integration. It advocates for co-design frameworks, inclusive

UX, and equity-focused policies to promote scalable, responsible AI use in diverse educational contexts.

Chapter 9
AI, Impostor Syndrome, and Emotional Resilience: Rethinking SEL and Student Well-Being in Inclusive AI-Enhanced ESL Classrooms 237
Maria Arjie Tobias Domingo, Independent Researcher, Philippines

This book chapter explores the emotional impact of generative artificial intelligence (AI) on tertiary-level ESL learners, drawing on a mixed-methods case study conducted at a Philippine state university. While AI tools offer linguistic support and academic efficiency, they also introduce emotional risks such as doubt, dependency, and diminished self-authorship, collectively identified as AI-Induced Impostor Syndrome (AI-IIS). Through the lens of Social-Emotional Learning (SEL), the chapter analyzes how AI use affects learners' confidence, identity, and ethical decision-making. It argues that SEL is essential for fostering emotionally inclusive and psychologically safe AI integration. Practical strategies for reflection, dialogue, mentorship, and policy co-creation are offered to help educators address the emotional dimensions of AI use. By embedding SEL into design, instruction, and institutional policy, the chapter promotes a model of AI-enhanced learning where students do not merely perform well with AI, but thrive alongside it.

Compilation of References 269

About the Contributors 305

Index 311

Preface

Generative Artificial Intelligence (GenAI) represents a paradigm shift in the way education is designed, delivered, and experienced (Fırat & Kuleli, 2024). Unlike earlier waves of educational technology that primarily digitized existing practices, GenAI introduces fundamentally new possibilities: the ability to generate text, images, simulations, and adaptive learning pathways in real time (Durak & Cankaya, 2024). This shift is not merely about efficiency or automation—it is about reimagining what inclusion means in education. Historically, inclusive education has often been framed as an effort to retrofit systems for marginalized learners, providing accommodations after structures were already in place. GenAI, by contrast, opens the door to designing systems that are inclusive by default (Öncü, Gevher, & Erdoğdu, 2025).

At the core of this book lies the recognition that inclusion is multi-dimensional: linguistic, cultural, cognitive, socio-economic, and emotional. GenAI can generate multilingual content, support learners with disabilities through personalized assistive technologies (Durak et al., 2025), create culturally responsive examples, and adapt instructional strategies to different cognitive needs. Equally important, it forces educators and policymakers to engage with pressing ethical issues such as bias, transparency, and accessibility (Nayır, Sarı, & Bozkurt, 2024). This book therefore explores both the opportunities and challenges of embedding GenAI into inclusive educational policies and practices, presenting conceptual discussions, empirical studies, case-based insights, and systematic reviews (Orak & Turan, 2024). The subject matter is not confined to classrooms. It spans educational policies, curriculum frameworks, higher education practices, special education, STEM and liberal arts teaching, social-emotional learning, and even broader policy domains such as data science for equity planning (Durak, Çankaya, Özdemir, & Can, 2024).

The rise of GenAI coincides with unprecedented global challenges and transformations in education. On one hand, the COVID-19 pandemic accelerated the digitalization of learning, highlighting both the potential and the inequities of technology-mediated education. On the other, international policy frameworks such as the United Nations' Sustainable Development Goal 4 (SDG4) emphasize inclusive and equitable quality education for all. GenAI sits at the intersection of these realities (Kaleci, 2025). In today's world, education systems face a dual imperative: to provide equitable access to diverse learners and to prepare individuals for rapidly evolving digital economies. Generative AI tools—such as ChatGPT, Claude, and Bard—are already being used by millions of learners and educators globally. They enable adaptive feedback, language translation, personalized tutoring, and creative problem-solving. Yet, these same tools carry risks: algorithmic bias, cultural insensitivity, privacy concerns, and the potential to widen digital divides if not implemented thoughtfully (Durak & Cankaya, 2024).

Against this backdrop, the conversation around GenAI in education has moved beyond technological fascination. Policymakers, institutions, and communities now ask fundamental questions: How do we ensure that AI supports diversity rather than uniformity? How can AI be governed to promote fairness and transparency? What policies and practices are needed to safeguard vulnerable learners while enabling innovation? This book positions itself within these global debates, offering a roadmap that balances technological potential with social responsibility (Öncü et al., 2025). In short, the topic of shaping inclusive educational policies and practices with GenAI is at the heart of contemporary educational reform and digital transformation. It responds directly to the urgent need to harness emerging technologies in ways that are ethically grounded, contextually sensitive, and future-oriented.

The audience for this book is intentionally broad, reflecting the cross-disciplinary nature of Generative AI and inclusive education. It is written for educators and practitioners in K–12 and higher education who are seeking ways to integrate GenAI tools into their classrooms in ways that enhance inclusivity through practical frameworks, pedagogical models, and case studies (Fırat & Kuleli, 2024); for policymakers and educational leaders in government agencies, and institutions who will benefit from the book's examination of equity, governance, and ethical frameworks that can guide national and international policy decisions (Nayır et al., 2024); for researchers and academics in fields such as educational technology, instructional design, computer science, and the social sciences who will find conceptual insights, empirical contributions, and identified gaps for future research (Durak et al., 2025); for technology developers and EdTech industry professionals who increasingly recognize that inclusivity is both an ethical responsibility and a design challenge, and will find guidance on building AI systems that prioritize accessibility, cultural responsiveness, and equity (Kaleci, 2025; Orak & Turan, 2024); and for students and lifelong learners, the ultimate end-users of these technologies, who will gain a deeper understanding of both the possibilities and the limitations of GenAI in education (Durak et al., 2024).

The book is organized into 25 chapters, and the subsequent paragraphs present concise overviews of their key contributions.

CHAPTER OVERVIEW

Chapter 1: The Role of Generative AI in Redefining Inclusive Education Practices

Generative AI is transforming the very foundations of inclusive education—shifting the focus from reactive accommodations to proactive, personalized learning ecosystems. This chapter examines how AI can adapt content, pedagogy, and assessment to meet the needs of learners across diverse linguistic, cultural, and cognitive backgrounds. It explores real-world applications, from AI-assisted translation and adaptive tutoring to tools that enhance accessibility for students with disabilities. At the same time, it addresses the ethical imperatives of bias mitigation, transparency, and cultural respect. By weaving together technological potential with policy frameworks, the chapter offers a roadmap for educational systems seeking to embed inclusion not as an afterthought, but as a core design principle in the AI era.

Chapter 2: Ethical Implications of AI in Promoting Equity and Access in Education

Generative AI is reshaping the educational landscape, offering unprecedented possibilities for personalization, resource creation, and access to learning. Yet its integration into classrooms and policy frameworks raises pressing ethical questions: Will AI narrow the educational divide or deepen existing disparities? This chapter critically examines the intersection of AI ethics, equity, and access in education, exploring how algorithmic design, data governance, and institutional choices influence outcomes for marginalized learners. Drawing on global perspectives, it discusses both the transformative potential and the risks of exclusion embedded in AI-driven systems. The chapter proposes guiding principles for designing and implementing generative AI tools that uphold fairness, cultural responsiveness, and accessibility. In doing so, it argues for a proactive, policy-driven approach to ensure that AI serves as a bridge—rather than a barrier—to inclusive, equitable education for all.

Chapter 3: Rethinking Artificial Intelligence Implementation for Inclusive and Equitable Quality Higher Education in South Africa

Generative Artificial Intelligence (GenAI) is rapidly transforming global higher education, offering both unprecedented opportunities and complex challenges. In South Africa, where the legacy of apartheid has entrenched deep educational inequalities, the strategic implementation of GenAI holds the potential to either bridge or widen existing divides. This chapter critically examines how GenAI can be harnessed to promote inclusive and equitable quality higher education in South Africa, while addressing the structural, ethical, and practical challenges that accompany its adoption. Drawing insights from a comprehensive synthesis of the existing literature on GenAI and education, this chapter argues that the AI revolution has the potential to either narrow or intensify existing educational inequalities in South Africa. If not implemented equitably, GenAI may further widen the gap between historically privileged and marginalised universities. The chapter suggests the need for a critical dialogue to ensure that GenAI catalyses an inclusive and equitable higher education in South Africa.

Chapter 4: Reworlding Inclusion: Speculative Futures of STEM Education in the Age of Generative AI

This chapter argues that inclusion in STEM education must be reimagined in the age of Generative AI (GenAI). Drawing on speculative fabulation and feminist theories of epistemic justice, we examine how GenAI reshapes knowledge production, assessment, and representation, often reinforcing bias and exclusion. Through three speculative scenarios, we explore divergent futures of STEM learning and Initial Teacher Education (ITE), showing how AI can either entrench dominant norms or foster pluralistic, relational pedagogies. We propose that inclusion must shift from representational fixes to a radical, justice-oriented reworlding of education, where AI is governed transparently, designed with care, and co-created with those historically marginalised.

Chapter 5: AI-Driven Approaches to Inclusive Science Teaching in Liberal Arts Context

This chapter explores AI-Driven Approaches to Inclusive Science Teaching in Liberal Arts Contexts, emphasizing how generative artificial intelligence (AI) can enhance inclusivity through Universal Design for Learning (UDL) principles. Drawing on CAST's framework for AI and UDL, we examine how generative AI tools support personalized learning pathways, improve access, and reduce barriers in science education for diverse learners. Recent findings (Francis, Jones, & Smith, 2025) highlight the importance of balancing AI innovation with academic integrity, while Haroud and Saqri (2025) underscore the varying digital literacies and attitudes of students and faculty toward AI integration. Building on Schreffler et al.'s (2019) review of UDL in STEM for students with disabilities, this chapter illustrates how AI can align with inclusive pedagogies to better serve liberal arts students often underrepresented in science disciplines. We propose practical, ethical, and pedagogical strategies for higher education faculty to implement AI inclusively in science classrooms.

Chapter 6: Assistive Technologies for Learners with Disabilities Using GenAI

Generative Artificial Intelligence (GenAI) is revolutionizing education by providing personalized learning experiences for students with disabilities. This chapter explores the role of GenAI and assistive technologies, such as screen readers and mobility devices, in enhancing educational accessibility. GenAI enables real-time adaptation of learning materials, making them more suitable for students with cognitive, physical, and sensory disabilities. While the potential is significant, challenges such as accessibility, educator training, and data privacy must be addressed. The chapter emphasizes the need for infrastructure development and training to fully integrate GenAI into inclusive education systems.

Chapter 7: Empowering Special Education Through Generative AI with Opportunities, Challenges and Case Studies

Generative Artificial Intelligence (GenAI) is transforming special education by delivering personalized, accessible, and inclusive learning experiences for students with diverse cognitive, sensory, communication, and behavioral needs. Unlike traditional technologies, GenAI can dynamically create content, adapt learning pathways, and simulate social-emotional scenarios, opening new opportunities for engagement and independence. This chapter explores GenAI's multifaceted applications in special education—ranging from augmentative communication and adaptive assessments to emotion-sensitive interventions—supported by real-world case studies. It also critically addresses ethical, technical, and policy challenges, including data privacy, algorithmic bias, and accessibility. Emphasizing the value of co-design with educators and disability advocates, the chapter offers balanced insights and actionable guidance for educators, researchers, policymakers, and AI developers working to create inclusive educational environments.

Chapter 8: Generative AI for Inclusive Special Education- Case Studies in Accessibility, Personalization, and Ethical Design

This chapter explores the transformative role of Generative AI in special education, emphasizing its ability to personalize learning, enhance accessibility, and support neurodiverse learners. Grounded in Universal Design for Learning (UDL) and inclusive pedagogy, it analyzes how tools like GPT, DALL·E, and Whisper enable individualized instruction through text simplification, visual storytelling, and real-time captioning. Case studies illustrate improved reading comprehension, classroom participation, and emotional development among students with dyslexia, hearing impairments, and autism. Ethical challenges including algorithmic bias, data privacy, and the digital divide are critically discussed. The chapter provides actionable recommendations for educators, developers, and policymakers to ensure human-centered, ethical AI integration. It advocates for co-design frameworks, inclusive UX, and equity-focused policies to promote scalable, responsible AI use in diverse educational contexts.

Chapter 9: AI, Impostor Syndrome, and Emotional Resilience - Rethinking SEL and Student Well-Being in Inclusive AI-Enhanced ESL Classrooms

This book chapter explores the emotional impact of generative artificial intelligence (AI) on tertiary-level ESL learners, drawing on a mixed-methods case study conducted at a Philippine state university. While AI tools offer linguistic support and academic efficiency, they also introduce emotional risks such as doubt, dependency, and diminished self-authorship, collectively identified as AI-Induced Impostor Syndrome (AI-IIS). Through the lens of Social-Emotional Learning (SEL), the chapter analyzes how AI use affects learners' confidence, identity, and ethical decision-making. It argues that SEL is essential for fostering emotionally inclusive and psychologically safe AI integration. Practical strategies for reflection, dialogue, mentorship, and policy co-creation are offered to help educators address the emotional dimensions of AI use. By embedding SEL into design, instruction, and institutional policy, the chapter promotes a model of AI-enhanced learning where students do not merely perform well with AI, but thrive alongside it.

Taken together, the chapters in this volume illustrate how GenAI is a transformative force that compels educators, policymakers, and researchers to rethink the very foundations of inclusion in education. By combining theoretical insights, practical frameworks, empirical evidence, and forward-looking reviews, the book contributes a perspective that bridges pedagogy, policy, and technology. Its impact lies in demonstrating that inclusive education in the age of AI must be designed intentionally, ethically, and collaboratively—ensuring that innovation advances equity rather than worsening divides. In doing so, this book contributes an approach for supporting educational systems that are equitable, adaptable, and learner-centered..

REFERENCES

Durak, G., & Cankaya, S. (2024). Are alarm bells ringing in academia? ChatGPT as a sample of using chatbots in education. *Turkish Online Journal of Distance Education, 25*(3). Advance online publication. DOI: 10.17718/tojde.1353737

Durak, G., Çankaya, S., Esinbay, E., Yaman, H. E., Can, S., Özdemir, D., İkizler, Z., & İncemen, S. (2025). The critical role of structured training in GenAI adoption: A longitudinal case study on student perceptions and skills development. *International Journal of Technology and Design Education*. Advance online publication. DOI: 10.1007/s10798-025-10025-y

Durak, G., Çankaya, S., Özdemir, D., & Can, S. (2024). Artificial intelligence in education: A bibliometric study on its role in transforming teaching and learning. *International Review of Research in Open and Distance Learning*, *25*(3), 219–244. DOI: 10.19173/irrodl.v25i3.7757

Fırat, M., & Kuleli, S. (2024). GPT vs. Google: A comparative study of self-code learning in ODL students. *Journal of Educational Technology & Online Learning, 7*(3), 308–. https://doi.org/DOI: 10.31681/jetol.1508675

Kaleci, D. (2025). Integration and application of artificial intelligence tools in the Moodle platform: A theoretical exploration. *Journal of Educational Technology & Online Learning*, *8*(1), 100–111. DOI: 10.31681/jetol.1595079

Nayır, F., Sarı, T., & Bozkurt, A. (2024). Reimagining education: Bridging artificial intelligence, transhumanism, and critical pedagogy. *Journal of Educational Technology & Online Learning*, *7*(1), 102–115. DOI: 10.31681/jetol.1308022

Öncü, S. E., Gevher, M., & Erdoğdu, E. (2025). Exploring the potential use of generative AI for learner support in ODL at scale. *Journal of Educational Technology & Online Learning*, *8*(1), 80–99. DOI: 10.31681/jetol.1559442

Orak, C., & Turan, Z. (2024). Using artificial intelligence in digital video production: A systematic review study. *Journal of Educational Technology & Online Learning*, *7*(3), 286–307. DOI: 10.31681/jetol.1459434

Chapter 1
The Role of Generative AI in Redefining Inclusive Education Practices

Mustafa Kayyali
https://orcid.org/0000-0003-3300-262X
Maaref University of Applied Sciences, Syria

ABSTRACT

Generative AI is transforming the very foundations of inclusive education—shifting the focus from reactive accommodations to proactive, personalized learning ecosystems. This chapter examines how AI can adapt content, pedagogy, and assessment to meet the needs of learners across diverse linguistic, cultural, and cognitive backgrounds. It explores real-world applications, from AI-assisted translation and adaptive tutoring to tools that enhance accessibility for students with disabilities. At the same time, it addresses the ethical imperatives of bias mitigation, transparency, and cultural respect. By weaving together technological potential with policy frameworks, the chapter offers a roadmap for educational systems seeking to embed inclusion not as an afterthought, but as a core design principle in the AI era.

INTRODUCTION

In recent years, education has entered a transformative era where the boundaries between pedagogy, technology, and human experience are being redefined. Among the emerging forces shaping this evolution, generative artificial intelligence (AI) stands out as both a disruptor and an enabler, challenging long-held assumptions about how learning can—and should—be delivered (Challoumis, 2024). For decades, the pursuit of inclusive education has been guided by a vision of equity: a world in

DOI: 10.4018/979-8-3373-3745-6.ch001

which learners, regardless of their physical abilities, linguistic backgrounds, cultural heritage, or socio-economic conditions, have equal access to meaningful educational opportunities. Yet, despite significant progress, the reality has often fallen short. Traditional approaches to inclusion, while well-intentioned, have frequently been reactive—seeking to accommodate differences after systems have already been designed for a presumed "standard" learner.

Generative AI presents an opportunity to rewrite this paradigm entirely (Radanliev, 2024). Rather than adapting pre-existing content or retrofitting teaching methods, AI can proactively design educational experiences that account for diversity from the very beginning. Its capacity to analyze vast amounts of data, model individual learning needs, and generate tailored instructional materials has opened the door to unprecedented personalization—personalization that is not confined to academic ability, but extends to language, cultural context, learning style, and even emotional state. In this sense, generative AI is not merely a tool; it is a catalyst for reimagining inclusion as an embedded, dynamic, and evolving feature of the educational landscape.

However, this transformation is not without complexity. The integration of generative AI into education raises pressing questions: How can we ensure that personalization does not become a form of digital segregation? What safeguards are needed to prevent the amplification of existing biases under the guise of adaptation? How can educators maintain the human dimension of teaching when increasingly sophisticated AI systems can produce content, assessments, and feedback at a scale no human could match? These questions are not peripheral—they are central to whether generative AI will become a force for genuine inclusion or a technological veneer masking deeper inequities (Alasadi & Baiz, 2023).

The urgency of these considerations is amplified by the broader societal shifts that accompany the adoption of AI technologies (Sakubu, 2025). In a globalized, hyper-connected world, learners are not only navigating their own local educational contexts but are also increasingly exposed to diverse cultural and intellectual frameworks. Generative AI, with its ability to translate, contextualize, and reinterpret content, has the potential to bridge these divides in ways no previous technology could (Chen, 2024). Yet, the same tools that can democratize access to knowledge can also create new forms of dependency, where learners rely heavily on algorithmically curated experiences and lose opportunities for critical engagement.

This chapter positions generative AI not simply as an emerging innovation but as a pivotal turning point in the evolution of inclusive education. It will examine the ways in which AI is reshaping our understanding of equity, explore real-world applications that demonstrate both its promise and its pitfalls, and propose ethical, pedagogical, and policy frameworks that can help ensure that inclusion remains the guiding principle in its deployment. In doing so, it seeks to move the conversation beyond technological capability toward a deeper consideration of values, intentionality, and the shared responsibility of educators, policymakers, and technologists.

FROM ACCOMMODATION TO INCLUSION: HOW GENERATIVE AI REFRAMES EDUCATIONAL EQUITY

For much of modern educational history, "inclusion" has been framed through the language of accommodation. The system is built first, its rules and structures laid down, and only later—almost as an afterthought—does it turn toward those who don't fit the mold. The adjustments are often well-meaning: a longer exam time for a student with dyslexia, a translated version of a worksheet for someone learning the language of instruction, a note-taker assigned to a classmate who cannot see the board. But these measures, however essential, rarely unsettle the underlying architecture of the system itself. They patch holes in a ship that was never designed with all passengers in mind.

Generative AI invites us to think differently—not merely about adding ramps to the stairs but about designing the building so that ramps and stairs are no longer separate, so that everyone enters through the same doorway without the feeling of being accommodated (Kaplan, 2024). The technology's ability to produce, adapt, and contextualize content on demand means that the educational experience need not be static (Kayyali, 2025 A). It can change in real time, responding to the learner's pace, linguistic background, or sensory preferences without marking those changes as special exceptions.

This shift is subtle but radical. Accommodation says, "We've made the standard for most people, and here's your tailored fix." Inclusion says, "There is no single standard—only a flexible ecosystem that adjusts to whoever walks in." Generative AI gives that philosophy teeth. With the right design, it can produce multiple versions of a concept simultaneously: a rich textual explanation, a visual storyboard, a simplified language summary, an audio narration with adjustable speed and tone—all generated in moments, without burdening the educator with hours of manual preparation (Villena et al, 2024). Suddenly, the notion of a "default" learner begins to dissolve.

But here's where it gets complicated. Technology doesn't arrive as a neutral guest. It brings with it the biases of its training data, the assumptions coded into its algorithms, and the power dynamics of those who control it. We've seen what happens when AI systems, trained on skewed data, produce outputs that inadvertently reinforce stereotypes or exclude marginal voices. In education, where every nuance in tone, language, or cultural framing can shape how a learner perceives themselves, such biases can wound as much as they assist (Essa, 2024). So while the promise of generative AI is dazzling—the ability to make learning experiences genuinely bespoke—the danger is equally real. We risk producing the digital equivalent of "accommodations" all over again, but this time at algorithmic speed.

To avoid that trap, inclusion must be embedded not just in the outputs AI creates but in the very design of the systems themselves. That means involving diverse stakeholders—students with disabilities, multilingual learners, educators from marginalized communities—not as afterthoughts in testing but as co-architects of the technology. It also means that developers must think beyond the efficiency metrics that dominate Silicon Valley and attend to the slow, messy realities of human learning. A platform that generates beautifully personalized content in milliseconds is worthless if that content subtly alienates or misrepresents the learner's culture, identity, or lived reality.

The reframing of educational equity through generative AI also forces us to confront an uncomfortable truth: the idea of the "average" student, long used as a benchmark for curriculum design, was always something of a fiction. It smoothed over differences to make mass education manageable, but at the cost of invisibilizing vast swaths of learners. Generative AI erodes the necessity of that fiction. If an algorithm can adapt reading materials to multiple comprehension levels instantly, the logic for a single, standardized version begins to crumble. This isn't just a pedagogical shift—it's a philosophical one.

Some might worry that removing the "average" will fragment the classroom, that every student on their own path will make shared learning experiences impossible. Yet this fear misunderstands what inclusion can be. The point is not to isolate learners in algorithmically tailored bubbles but to create shared spaces where diversity of access methods is normalized. Two students can be reading the same text—one with simplified vocabulary and visual annotations, another with complex thematic analysis—and still discuss the same core ideas together. The shared intellectual journey remains; the route each takes is simply more responsive to their needs.

Generative AI amplifies this possibility through its fluidity. A teacher no longer needs to preemptively prepare multiple versions of a lesson (Butler-Ulrich et al, 2024). They can, in the moment, request an alternative explanation for a concept that's not landing, or generate practice questions calibrated to a specific student's error patterns. This immediacy transforms responsiveness from a rare act of pedagogical heroism into a standard feature of the learning environment.

And yet, one can't ignore the human side of this. Education is not only about the transmission of knowledge; it's also about affirmation, belonging, and identity formation. A learner who feels seen will often persist longer, take greater risks, and engage more deeply. Here's where AI, for all its capacity, meets its limit. It can mimic empathy in tone and phrasing, but it cannot truly know the lived experience of the child in front of it. That's why the reframing of equity must be twofold: generative AI can handle the adaptive scaffolding, while educators, peers, and communities handle the human connection. The danger comes when we imagine the scaffolding can replace the structure itself.

Figure 1. Inclusive Affordances Enabled by Generative AI

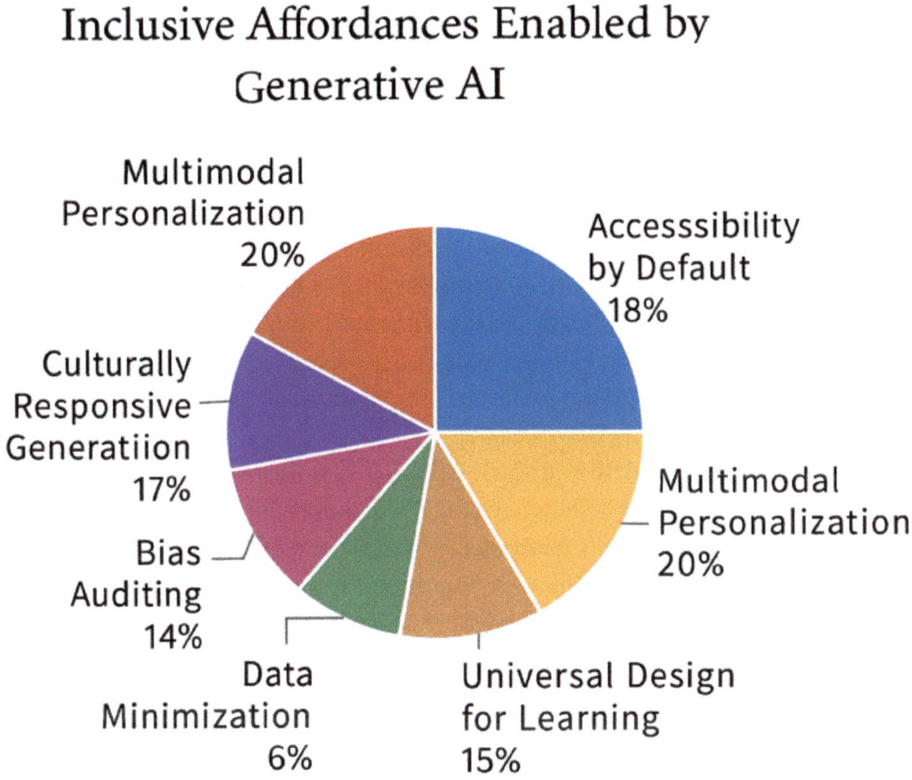

The reframing also nudges us to consider equity not as a static goal but as an evolving practice. Contexts change—linguistic landscapes shift, new disabilities are recognized, socio-economic divides morph under new technologies. Generative AI, if designed with agility and ethical grounding, can adapt alongside these shifts (Wamba et al, 2025). Imagine a system that learns not only from academic data but from sociocultural signals: noticing that a refugee influx has changed the dominant languages in a district, or that a local crisis has altered the emotional climate of the classroom, and adjusting its support materials accordingly. This is not science fiction; the pieces already exist. What's lacking is the political and institutional will to integrate them in ways that are equitable and respectful.

A thornier issue emerges when we think about power. Who owns the AI systems that will define the future of inclusion? If they are proprietary, controlled by a handful of corporations, the definition of "inclusive" will inevitably be shaped by corporate priorities. This could mean privileging certain languages, curricular standards, or pedagogical styles that align with the company's target markets. True inclusion requires decentralization—a willingness to let communities adapt and govern the systems themselves. Without that, we risk replacing the old centralized educational model with a new, shinier, but equally narrow one.

Then there's the question of access to the technology itself. Inclusion is hollow if only the wealthiest schools can afford the systems that make it possible. The digital divide isn't just about internet access anymore; it's about access to high-quality AI models, the computing infrastructure to run them, and the expertise to integrate them meaningfully into pedagogy (Ortiz et al, 2025). Generative AI could very well deepen inequalities if its benefits accrue disproportionately to already advantaged institutions. Reframing equity in this context means advocating for policy measures that ensure broad access, perhaps through open-source models, public funding, or shared infrastructure.

There's a paradox worth acknowledging: the more adaptive and personalized AI becomes, the less visible its work will be. If it does its job perfectly, the learner may never notice that their version of the lesson was different from anyone else's. This invisibility can be a virtue—reducing stigma and normalizing diversity of need—but it can also make it harder to monitor and evaluate equity. How do we ensure fairness when the system's responses are uniquely tailored and thus harder to compare? This calls for new forms of transparency, not in the sense of showing every line of code to every user, but in communicating the principles, boundaries, and safeguards that guide the AI's decisions.

What makes generative AI different from earlier educational technologies is its generativity itself—the capacity to create, not just retrieve. A search engine can find you a resource; a generative model can build you one from scratch, adapted to the exact context you specify. This creative flexibility is both its strength and its liability. It can offer a dyslexic student a phonics-rich retelling of a complex text, or it can inadvertently strip away the cultural nuance that makes that text meaningful. The reframing of equity here requires a shift from seeing AI as a mechanical helper to seeing it as a collaborator whose output must be critically engaged with, not passively accepted.

In reframing educational equity through generative AI, the conversation inevitably circles back to values (Mohammed, 2025). What do we mean by "fair"? Is it about giving everyone the same materials, or about giving each person what they specifically need to flourish? The latter feels intuitively right, yet it raises endless complexities about measurement, accountability, and societal expectations. A student given highly simplified content might meet short-term success but be underprepared for the demands of higher education or the workplace. Here, the educator's role is irreplaceable: to calibrate support so that it scaffolds without limiting, to use AI's adaptability as a ladder rather than a cage.

The danger in any technological revolution is that the rhetoric of possibility runs ahead of the messy, granular realities of implementation. Generative AI is no exception. We can already see prototypes that dazzle—instant translations, adaptive quizzes, immersive simulations—but translating those into sustained, equitable practice across diverse classrooms is a different challenge altogether (Pratschke, 2024). Equity is slow work. It resists the quick-fix mentality that technology often promises. The reframing, then, is less about imagining AI as a magic wand and more about weaving it into the long, patient labor of building systems that honor the breadth of human difference.

In this way, the movement from accommodation to inclusion is not merely a matter of adopting a new toolset; it's about altering the mental architecture through which we see learners. Generative AI offers us the scaffolding to do so, but the blueprint still comes from us. The question is whether we will use that scaffolding to build something genuinely new—or simply to shore up the old structures with a fresh coat of paint.

Personalization at Scale: AI-Driven Learning Pathways for Diverse Learners

The idea that education should adapt to each learner's unique profile has been whispered in pedagogical circles for decades, yet in practice it has often been little more than a polite fiction. Classrooms, bound by timetables and curricular mandates, move like trains on fixed tracks—pausing only briefly to let those who struggle catch their breath before the whistle blows again. The most ambitious efforts at personalization have tended to be artisanal, crafted laboriously by committed educators working late into the night to differentiate worksheets or prepare alternative assessments for a handful of students. Beautiful in intention, brittle in scale.

Generative AI shifts that equation—not by making the teacher work faster, but by reshaping the very mechanics of adaptation (Baskara, 2023). The notion of "personalization at scale" used to sound like a contradiction in terms. How can something be both deeply individual and mass-produced? The answer, it turns out, is that generative AI doesn't mass-produce in the old sense at all. It doesn't stamp identical objects from a mold; it spins infinite variations from a common fabric, weaving threads differently for each recipient.

Picture a mathematics lesson on quadratic functions. One student receives a symbolic derivation with annotated steps, another gets a narrative framing of parabolas through the lens of sports trajectories, and a third sees the concept animated visually, the curve bending in real time as variables change (Polverini, 2022). Each pathway is generated in the moment, not pulled from a dusty repository, but conjured to match what the system believes will resonate with that particular learner at that particular juncture. The personalization isn't bolted on; it's intrinsic.

Yet the real shift isn't just in the variety of output—it's in the pace and fluidity of adaptation. Traditional differentiated instruction often freezes once it's delivered. The teacher makes three levels of a worksheet; the students work through them; the cycle repeats next week. AI-driven pathways, by contrast, are alive. They can recalibrate mid-lesson, responding to signals that a student has mastered a skill sooner than expected, or that they've misunderstood a foundational step and need a detour. In this sense, personalization stops being an act of prediction and becomes a dance with the present moment.

Of course, scale is a double-edged word here. Scaling personalization implies reach, but reach without depth risks superficiality. A perfectly tailored learning sequence that's generated in seconds is still worthless if it's designed around the wrong assumptions. The algorithms will only ever be as insightful as the data that feeds them, and educational data—despite the big claims—remains patchy, context-dependent, and messy. We're not talking about the controlled variables of a physics experiment; we're talking about human lives, with all their unpredictability, contradictions, and quiet disruptions.

The seductive danger is to equate scale with universality: to imagine that because a system can generate millions of adaptive lesson fragments, it has captured the diversity of learners. But diversity isn't a statistical spread—it's a lived texture. Two students with identical scores on a diagnostic test might differ profoundly in how they interpret a problem, how cultural references land, how language wraps itself around their thinking. An AI system worth trusting in this space must be sensitive not just to performance metrics but to signals of identity, context, and emotional state—things that are harder to quantify but impossible to ignore (Kaur et al, 2022).

Personalization at scale, then, is not about pressing a button and watching a billion bespoke lessons bloom; it's about building a responsive ecosystem where each learner's pathway is co-authored by human judgment and machine generation. The teacher's role doesn't vanish—it shifts. Instead of spending hours preparing static materials, educators might spend their time shaping the parameters and guardrails of the AI's output, vetting its cultural resonance, and integrating its adaptations into the messy social dynamics of the classroom.

This, in turn, reframes what "diverse learners" even means. In the old discourse, the phrase tended to refer to those at the margins: students with disabilities, language learners, those performing far above or below the median. With AI, the scope widens. Diversity is no longer a label for a subgroup; it becomes the default state (Chi et al,

2021). Every learner—every human—engages with material differently, filters it through personal experience, carries cognitive patterns and emotional rhythms that defy standardization. The promise of personalization at scale is that it makes room for this reality without the stigma of exception.

And yet, there's a haunting question: will this personalization deepen connection to learning, or will it create a landscape where students never encounter friction, never have to stretch into ways of thinking that feel alien? Struggle, after all, isn't always a flaw; sometimes it's the soil where understanding takes root. An AI system that trims away every moment of difficulty risks producing learners adept at comfort but ill-prepared for ambiguity. True personalization, paradoxically, might mean knowing when *not* to adapt, when to let a learner wrestle with complexity a little longer.

Figure 2. Reach vs Equity-Gap Reduction by GenAI Interventions

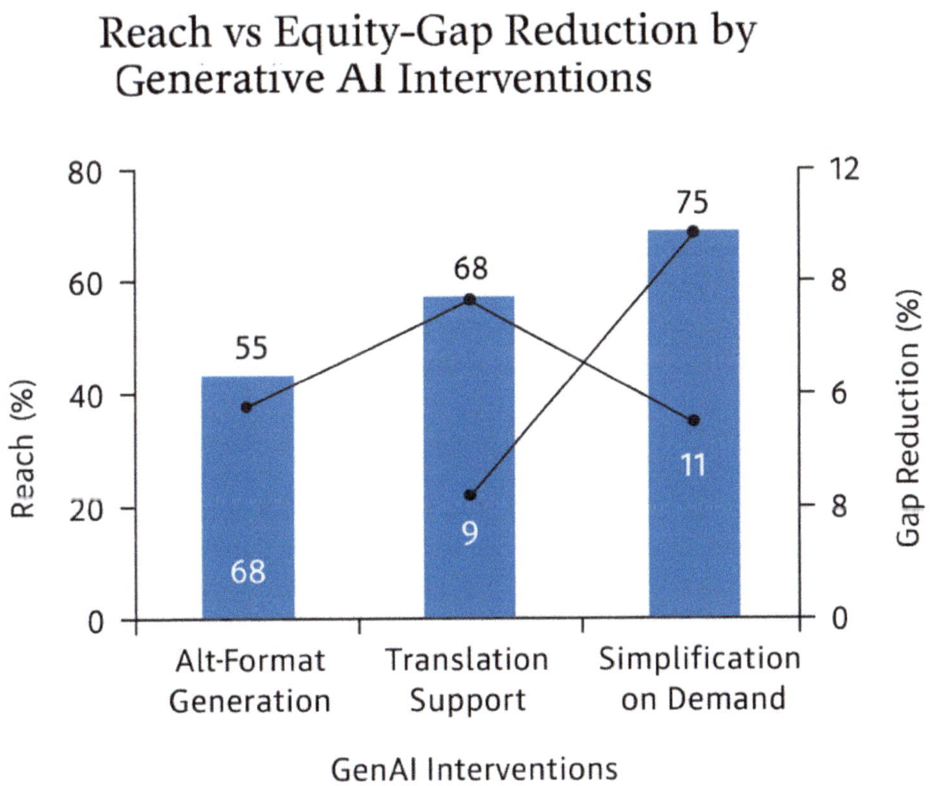

The scaling of personalization also brings into play the politics of whose knowledge is deemed worth embedding. AI models trained predominantly on Western curricula, for example, may generate pathways that assume certain cultural touchstones, modes of reasoning, or linguistic idioms (Ghimire, 2025). A "personalized" history lesson for an Indigenous student might still carry the framing of a settler narrative unless deliberate steps are taken to decolonize the data and the generation process. This is why personalization at scale cannot be left solely to engineers; it demands collaborative stewardship among technologists, educators, cultural historians, and the learners themselves.

One might imagine a future in which each learner's pathway is not just a private stream but part of a larger learning commons. The AI doesn't merely generate for an individual; it learns from the patterns across individuals, identifying which narrative hooks work for certain profiles, which visual metaphors unlock comprehension for certain communities. This creates a feedback loop: personalization becomes smarter as the collective experience grows, but only if that collective is truly representative. If the training data is drawn from a narrow slice of humanity, the "scaled" personalization will merely replicate the same narrowness—only now dressed in the clothing of individualized care.

Scaling also complicates assessment. If every learner's path is different, how do we know they've met the same essential thresholds? AI can certainly produce dynamic assessments tailored to each path, but the temptation will be to collapse these back into comparable metrics for institutional convenience. Here lies a tension: personalization seeks to honor difference, but institutional systems often seek to normalize it. If we're not careful, AI-driven pathways could end up as an elaborate detour that still funnels everyone back to the same narrow definitions of success (Angel, 2024).

There's a quieter, more human risk too: the erosion of shared moments. Part of the magic of learning together is grappling with the same text, the same experiment, the same problem—each in our own way, but together. When personalization is hyper-individualized, those common reference points can thin out, leaving learners on parallel tracks that rarely intersect. The challenge is to design AI pathways that branch and flex but still circle back to shared spaces where perspectives can collide and cross-pollinate.

It's tempting to see all this as a purely technical puzzle—better data, better algorithms, better interfaces—but the heart of personalization at scale is not technology at all. It's a philosophy of respect: respect for the learner's starting point, for their pace, for the forms of knowledge that shape them. AI simply gives us new tools to practice that respect at a scope we've never had before (Daugherty & Wilson, 2024). The question is whether we will choose to use those tools in ways that deepen human learning or merely accelerate the industrial efficiency of schooling.

And perhaps the most startling thing about scaling personalization through AI is that it reveals how much sameness we've tolerated in education—not because it was pedagogically sound, but because it was administratively convenient. Rows of desks, identical textbooks, synchronized bell schedules—these were logistical solutions masquerading as educational necessities. Generative AI doesn't demand that we keep those patterns; it invites us to dismantle them. Whether we accept that invitation is another matter entirely.

Bridging Cultural and Linguistic Gaps Through AI-Mediated Communication

One of the quiet truths of education is that language is never just a tool for conveying information—it's a landscape, a vessel of culture, identity, memory. When two people speak, they aren't merely exchanging words; they're navigating a terrain shaped by idioms, historical echoes, and unspoken norms. To cross from one linguistic landscape into another is not just to swap vocabulary but to step into a different way of seeing the world. For learners whose education is delivered in a language not their own, this crossing can be exhilarating, exhausting, or, more often, both at once.

Generative AI enters this space like an unexpected bridge-builder—unlike the rigid, one-way translation tools of the past, it can not only convert sentences but also reshape them in ways that preserve tone, intent, and cultural resonance (Banda, 2024). At its best, it operates less like a mechanical interpreter and more like a perceptive mediator, aware that the same phrase, dropped into two different cultural soils, can bloom into entirely different meanings. The technology can be tuned to spot where a literal rendering would fall flat, where a metaphor beloved in one culture might misfire in another, and where silence itself speaks volumes.

Of course, this is where the fascination and the peril intertwine. The bridge AI builds is only as sound as the materials it draws from. If its training diet is dominated by certain linguistic norms—over-representing the voices of the Global North, under-representing oral traditions, privileging standard registers over dialects—then the bridge will be uneven. It may carry some travelers across with grace while leaving others feeling as if their language, their way of speaking, is somehow less legitimate. The very same system that promises to make education more accessible could quietly reinforce the hierarchy of languages and dialects that has existed for centuries.

Yet, when designed with care, AI-mediated communication can do something profoundly human: it can act as a listener that never tires, a translator that never mocks the learner's accent, a patient guide through the labyrinth of meaning (Wang, 2024). For a refugee student entering a classroom where the dominant language feels alien, the ability to summon an instant, context-sensitive explanation in their mother tongue can be the difference between sinking and swimming. Not just a dictionary definition, but an explanation wrapped in familiar imagery, aligned with their cultural frame of reference.

Still, this goes beyond translation. Communication across cultures involves more than finding equivalent words—it's about carrying the rhythm, the implied etiquette, the subtle cues that tell someone whether a statement is a joke, an invitation, or a challenge. A teacher might praise a student by saying, "You're getting there," intending encouragement, but in another cultural lens, that phrase could sound faintly condescending, as if the progress were grudgingly acknowledged. AI systems capable of adjusting these nuances in real time could spare learners from the small, accumulating misinterpretations that erode confidence (SWARGIARY, 2024).

But perhaps the more radical possibility lies in how AI can facilitate bidirectional cultural exchange. In the traditional model, the burden of adaptation falls heavily on the learner from the minority language group: they must conform, adjust, translate themselves. What if AI could distribute that effort more evenly? Imagine a classroom where the teacher can instantly see a learner's question rendered in their own language, along with cultural annotations that explain the phrasing choices, allowing the teacher to meet the learner halfway (Kayyali, 2025 D). The technology could act as a two-way cultural lens, not just a one-way converter.

Such a shift would demand a rethinking of educational authority. When AI mediates language, it inevitably shapes meaning, deciding—often invisibly—what to keep, what to smooth over, what to adapt. This makes it not just a bridge but a filter. And filters have politics. In global education, where histories of colonization and cultural suppression still ripple, the politics of language choice can never be treated as neutral. The question isn't simply whether AI can translate, but whether it can do so in a way that honors the dignity of every voice it touches.

One might worry that overreliance on AI mediation will create a crutch, preventing learners from developing fluency in the target language (Graham & Milan, 2025). There's some truth in that danger. But the opposite risk is equally real: denying students these tools for fear of dependency may simply leave them stranded on the far bank, staring across a river they cannot yet cross. The balance lies in designing AI as a scaffold—present at the moments of steep difficulty, gradually fading as competence grows, never removing the challenge entirely but cushioning it just enough to keep the learner moving forward.

It's also worth considering that AI's role here is not confined to high-stakes moments of instruction. Informal, hallway-level communication—the small talk that cements belonging—often matters just as much as the formal lesson. A student who can join in a lunchtime joke or respond to a passing comment from a peer is more likely to feel part of the community. These micro-moments, too, can be mediated by AI, offering discreet prompts or cultural explanations in the background, so that learners can participate without the sting of feeling perpetually one step behind.

There's another dimension here that rarely gets discussed: AI's potential to restore languages that have been sidelined or endangered. In a classroom that has, for generations, taught only in the dominant national language, an AI system could make it feasible to incorporate parallel instruction in a heritage language without demanding that the teacher be fluent. This isn't just a technical fix—it's an act of cultural repair. It signals to learners that their language is not a liability to be shed but a resource to be cultivated.

The tension, of course, is that AI's fluency can sometimes feel too smooth (Napitupulu & Dalimunte, 2025). Communication stripped of all friction can lose the rough edges where human connection often happens. Misunderstandings, hesitations, the slightly awkward search for a word—these moments are part of the texture of cross-cultural interaction. They remind both sides that communication is a joint act, requiring patience and imagination. If AI becomes so seamless that we no longer need to wrestle with difference, we might lose something of the mutual vulnerability that fosters genuine understanding.

At the same time, one cannot romanticize difficulty when it comes at the cost of participation. A student who remains silent because the linguistic leap feels too dangerous will not magically acquire confidence through struggle alone. Here, AI can serve as a kind of rehearsal space, allowing learners to practice expressing themselves, test unfamiliar structures, and experiment with tone before stepping into public interaction. In this private dialogue with a machine, the fear of judgment falls away, making room for risk-taking (Gimmler, 2024).

In its most ambitious form, AI-mediated communication could help shift the educational environment from one where difference is accommodated to one where it is actively leveraged. Instead of being a barrier to overcome, linguistic diversity could become a source of insight, a way for the whole class to see concepts refracted through multiple cultural lenses. The AI doesn't just translate the dominant narrative outward—it brings alternative perspectives inward, enriching the shared discourse.

This is perhaps the most underappreciated aspect of AI in this domain: its ability to surface equivalences and metaphors that might not occur to a human teacher bound by their own linguistic habits (Kayyali, 2025 E). A physics principle explained through the imagery of a snow-covered pine in one culture could be rendered through the metaphor of monsoon rains in another. Neither is more "correct," but each is more alive in its own context. Such cross-pollination doesn't just bridge gaps—it changes the shape of the landscape entirely.

The promise is immense, but so is the responsibility. Every AI-mediated interaction is a tiny act of interpretation, a decision about what meaning to privilege and what to leave unsaid (Bozdağ, 2024). At scale, these micro-decisions can tilt entire narratives, subtly shifting the cultural balance of the classroom. Transparency—about how the AI works, whose voices it was trained on, and what biases it may carry—is essential if educators are to wield it responsibly.

The dream of perfect communication across languages and cultures has always been haunted by the fear of homogenization: that in making everything mutually intelligible, we might flatten the richness of difference into a bland, globalized vocabulary. AI will not resolve that tension—it will intensify it. The challenge is to use the bridge not to erase the river beneath it, but to make crossing possible while still feeling the currents that shape each shore.

In the end, AI-mediated communication is not a neutral conduit (Sahebi & Formosa, 2025). It's an active participant in the conversation, a silent co-author shaping what passes between speaker and listener. Whether that role becomes one of erasure or enrichment depends on the choices we make now—choices about design, about governance, about whose knowledge we choose to encode. It's not enough for the bridge to be sturdy; it must also be honest about where it leads.

Ethical Guardrails: Ensuring Fairness, Transparency, and Cultural Sensitivity

The more sophisticated generative AI becomes in shaping educational experiences, the more urgently we must wrestle with a truth that's easy to sidestep: no technology is neutral. The data that feeds it, the logic that structures it, the hands that design it—none of these emerge from a vacuum. They are shaped by histories, by worldviews, by power. And when we introduce such a system into a classroom, we are not merely adding a tool to the teacher's kit; we are importing a set of values, often invisibly. Without guardrails, that import can carry quiet harm in its wake.

Fairness is the word people like to lead with. It sounds straightforward, almost procedural (Burke & Leben, 2024). But fairness in the context of generative AI is slippery—it isn't only about whether the system treats everyone the same; it's about whether it responds to differences in ways that protect dignity. In education, "equal treatment" can be the wrong goal. Two learners might both need scaffolding, but the nature of that support—the tone, the cultural frame, the pacing—will differ if it is to be truly equitable. An AI model that applies identical adjustments across the board risks committing a subtler kind of injustice: smoothing over the very differences that equity seeks to respect.

The challenge lies in the invisible edges. Bias in AI is often portrayed as something obvious, a glaring prejudice that leaps off the screen (Klaassen, 2024). More often, it seeps in quietly, in patterns of omission and framing. A history lesson generated for a global classroom might mention European explorers as central actors while relegating Indigenous narratives to a footnote (Kayyali, 2026). A science example might unconsciously default to Western measurement systems, or an economics problem might assume familiarity with banking structures common only in affluent economies. None of these are overt slurs, yet together they tilt the learning environment toward certain cultural norms, leaving others perpetually peripheral.

To set meaningful guardrails, transparency has to run deeper than the occasional technical disclosure. Transparency in education is about making visible not just the "how" of an algorithm but the "why" of its decisions. If a reading comprehension passage is adjusted for complexity, the learner and teacher alike should know what the system changed, why it judged that change necessary, and what trade-offs came with it. Without that visibility, trust erodes, and trust is the foundation on which both learning and inclusion rest.

Cultural sensitivity is perhaps the most delicate strand of all (Ungar et al, 2023). It's one thing to strip a lesson of overt bias; it's another to design it in a way that resonates with the learner's lived reality. A metaphor that works beautifully for one audience can land as irrelevant or even insulting for another. Generative AI is capable of tailoring cultural references—but only if it has access to data that authentically represents those cultures, and only if the system has been built with mechanisms for community feedback. The old model of technology deployment—design in a lab, distribute globally—will not suffice.

Yet cultural sensitivity is not the same as cultural essentialism (Xu et al, 2023). One of the risks of well-meaning adaptation is that it can freeze people into stereotypes. Not every student from a rural area wants their math problem wrapped in farming scenarios; not every student from a particular linguistic background connects with the same idioms. Guardrails must leave room for individuality, not just group identity. That means the system has to be flexible enough to learn from the learner—not merely about them.

The ethical dimension deepens when we consider how AI's "explanations" will be perceived (McDermid et al, 2021). In some cultures, questioning the teacher's choice of material might be discouraged; in others, it might be encouraged as a sign of engagement. If the AI offers an explanation that contradicts or reframes a teacher's approach, how is that handled? Does the AI defer to local norms, or does it challenge them? Each choice carries implications, and each must be considered deliberately rather than left to the defaults of a developer's own cultural background.

It's tempting to think that ethical guidelines can be written once and applied universally. In practice, ethical guardrails for AI in education will have to be both stable and adaptive. Stable enough to uphold non-negotiable commitments—respect for human dignity, the avoidance of harm, protection of privacy—and adaptive enough to respond to shifting cultural, political, and pedagogical landscapes. A phrase that is innocuous today might acquire charged meaning tomorrow; a teaching approach that is inclusive in one context might be exclusionary in another. Guardrails must be living things, revisited and renegotiated as contexts evolve.

Table 1. Ethical Risk Mitigation Matrix for Inclusive GenAI

Challenge	How it Shows Up	Potential Harm	Mitigations (Illustrative)	Priority
Cultural Bias in Outputs	Examples center dominant norms; marginalize local narratives	Alienation; stereotype reinforcement	Diverse training data; community review boards; prompt libraries including local frames	High
Accessibility Gaps	Inconsistent captions/alt text; no dyslexia-friendly modes	Exclusion of disabled learners	WCAG-aligned defaults; auto-captions; alt text generation with human check	High
Opaque Adaptations	Leveling not explained to learners/teachers	Distrust; learned helplessness	Explain adjustments; show options; allow teacher/learner override	Medium–High
Data Over-Collection	Unnecessary behavioral/ emotion tracking	Privacy harms; chilling effects	Data minimization; consent dashboards; deletion by default	High
Language Dilution	Literal translations miss cultural tone/idiom	Misinterpretation; disengagement	Human-in-loop on key artifacts; culturally tuned glossaries	Medium
Over-Automation	AI replaces teacher judgment	Deprofessionalization; brittle systems	Escalation rules; reflection checkpoints; co-assessment	Medium

Fairness in AI also demands honesty about limitations (Barocas et al, 2023). There will be moments when the technology simply does not have enough cultural or linguistic grounding to adapt appropriately. Pretending otherwise is a disservice. Far better to have the system acknowledge its uncertainty—perhaps even invite the human teacher to guide the adaptation—than to fabricate authority. This humility is itself an ethical stance, a way of refusing the illusion of omniscience that AI systems often project.

One area where ethical reflection is especially urgent is in the treatment of sensitive historical or political content. Generative AI may be called upon to generate explanations of contested events or to present multiple perspectives on a polarizing issue (Kayyali, 2025 B). Without guardrails, the system might default to the most represented viewpoint in its training data, effectively marginalizing dissenting or minority narratives. A commitment to fairness here means designing the system to flag such topics explicitly, offering multiple perspectives and clarifying their sources, rather than collapsing them into a single, seemingly neutral account.

The role of human oversight cannot be overstated. No matter how advanced AI becomes, the responsibility for its ethical use will rest with the humans who deploy it (Holzinger et al, 2025). Guardrails are not just code—they are policies, training protocols, feedback loops. Teachers must be empowered to question, override, or supplement AI outputs. Students, too, should be encouraged to approach AI-generated content critically, not as gospel but as one contribution in a larger conversation.

Privacy threads through all of this as a quiet but potent concern. To personalize learning, AI systems collect and process vast amounts of data—performance metrics, behavioral patterns, even inferred emotional states. Without stringent safeguards, this data can become a liability, exposing students to risks they cannot fully grasp. Ethical guardrails here are not optional; they are the boundary between AI as an ally and AI as a surveillance apparatus. This means minimizing data collection to what is genuinely necessary, anonymizing wherever possible, and making clear to learners what is being tracked and why.

Perhaps the most easily overlooked element of ethical design is sustainability—not in the environmental sense (though that matters too), but in the social sense. An AI system that dazzles in its first year but becomes obsolete or unmaintainable in its third is not ethical in any meaningful sense. Sustainability here means building systems that can be updated, localized, and adapted without requiring prohibitively expensive interventions from proprietary vendors. It means ensuring that the guardrails themselves are not locked behind corporate firewalls but can be shaped by the communities that use the technology.

Cultural sensitivity, in this vision, is not just a "feature" of the AI—it's a relationship. A relationship between the technology and the community, between the designer's intent and the learner's reception. And like any relationship, it will require ongoing care, the willingness to listen, and the humility to admit when it has gone wrong. AI will make mistakes—sometimes small, sometimes glaring. What matters is how quickly and transparently those mistakes are acknowledged, and how sincerely the system is improved in response.

In the rush to innovate, there's a temptation to treat ethics as a hurdle to clear so that development can proceed. But in education, the stakes are too high for that mindset. Here, ethics is not the brake; it is the steering wheel (Baker & Baker, 2022). Without it, we might move quickly, but we have no guarantee we are moving in a direction worth reaching. Guardrails are not about limiting possibility; they are about channeling it toward outcomes that expand, rather than constrict, the horizons of learners.

This is where cultural sensitivity intersects with fairness and transparency in the deepest sense: by refusing to see learners as data points to be optimized and instead seeing them as participants in a shared human endeavor. An ethical AI in education should not only adapt to the learner's cognitive needs but also affirm their place in the world, reflect their realities back to them in ways that are neither distorted nor diminished, and invite them to engage with perspectives beyond their own without erasing the ground beneath their feet (Yambal & Waykar, 2025).

It is not a small task. It will not be finished in a single policy document or a one-off training session. But the absence of these guardrails leaves us vulnerable to something far more damaging than technical glitches: a slow erosion of trust, a creeping normalization of bias, an education system that appears more inclusive on the surface while replicating the same old exclusions under a veneer of algorithmic objectivity.

If there is one principle that might serve as the bedrock for all the others, it is this: the ethical use of AI in education should leave learners more empowered, not more dependent; more aware, not more managed; more connected, not more isolated. Every guardrail—whether it's about fairness, transparency, or cultural sensitivity—should be measured against that standard. And if it doesn't hold up, it's not a guardrail at all.

Future Horizons: Sustaining Inclusion in the Age of Intelligent Systems

Projecting forward into a world saturated with intelligent systems, one is struck by a tension that refuses to resolve neatly: the more capable these technologies become, the more precarious the human decisions surrounding them. It's easy to romanticize the idea of a future where every learner, anywhere, is enveloped in a cocoon of perfectly tuned, AI-driven instruction (Kayyali, 2024). That picture is seductive, but it risks masking the real question: what happens when inclusion is no longer something we strive for, but something we assume the system has already handled? Complacency is as dangerous as scarcity.

Inclusion, to be sustained, cannot rely on the illusion of permanence. A system that works equitably today may stumble tomorrow, not because its code rotted, but because the world shifted under its feet. Demographics change. Political climates tilt. Languages evolve in unpredictable directions, blending, borrowing, bending the grammar that yesterday's models considered fixed. The communities we serve will not hold still long enough for an algorithm to perfect its craft once and for all. Sustaining inclusion, then, means designing systems that are not monuments but living organisms—capable of adaptation, aware of their own limits, and responsive to signals that something in the social terrain has moved.

There's a strange paradox here. As AI grows more sophisticated, it can handle increasingly complex personalization, yet the human structures around it—school policies, curricula, funding streams—often remain stubbornly rigid (Gulson et al, 2022). We could, in theory, have an AI that offers a dozen culturally resonant pathways through the same content, but if standardized testing insists on one narrow representation of knowledge, those pathways collapse back into a single lane by the time they're assessed. Sustaining inclusion means pushing beyond the technical achievements to reshape the institutional frameworks that decide what counts as learning, who decides that, and how those decisions can be contested.

The "future horizon" isn't just technological; it's political and ethical. Intelligent systems will not arrive in an untouched educational wilderness. They will enter a landscape shaped by decades, even centuries, of uneven access, linguistic hierarchy, and cultural bias. If we simply drop AI into that environment without challenging its foundations, the technology will take on the shape of the vessel that contains it (Kayyali, 2025 C). In that sense, sustaining inclusion is not a matter of keeping the AI "fair" in isolation, but of ensuring the broader ecosystem into which it is deployed does not quietly nullify its inclusive potential.

One can imagine a more fluid model of education, where learning pathways are not dictated by geography, funding, or the happenstance of birth, but are orchestrated dynamically between human mentors, peer communities, and adaptive systems. The AI would not be a single, monolithic presence, but a constellation of interconnected agents, each fine-tuned to specific contexts (Sapkota et al, 2025). Some would specialize in linguistic bridging, others in accessibility for neurodiverse learners, others in real-time feedback tuned to a student's emotional state. Yet such a network would only be as inclusive as the governance that shapes it. Who sets the parameters? Who decides what "inclusive" even means in contexts that may have conflicting values?

The horizon is not just about scaling out; it's also about deepening in. Intelligent systems could eventually move beyond content delivery into the realm of fostering critical capacities—helping learners evaluate competing narratives, navigate ambiguity, and understand not only the "what" of knowledge but the "how" and "why" of its construction (Moustaghfir & Brigui, 2024). Inclusion in this deeper sense is not about everyone receiving the same opportunity to absorb facts, but about everyone having the tools to interrogate, remix, and contribute to the collective body of knowledge. Sustaining this form of inclusion would require AI to be less of an oracle and more of a companion in inquiry—one that invites dissent as readily as it offers guidance.

Table 2. 12-Month Roadmap for Inclusive GenAI Adoption

	Focus	Key Activities
Q1	Governance & Voice	Form inclusive AI council incl. students w/ disabilities & multilingual reps; publish data policy; risk register
Q2	Pilots & Capacity	Run 2 pilots (translation + alternative formats); PD on UDL + prompt design; set KPIs incl. equity metrics
Q3	Audit & Iterate	Bias and accessibility audits; learner/parent focus groups; adjust models/prompts; publish changes
Q4	Scale & Sustain	Institutionalize guardrails; budget for access funds/devices; longitudinal evaluation & public dashboard

It's tempting to believe that once the right safeguards are in place, inclusion will take care of itself. But inclusion is not an end state; it's a habit, a posture toward the world. It must be renewed constantly, especially in an era where intelligent systems can evolve faster than the policies meant to regulate them. Imagine an AI that starts perfectly aligned with inclusive values but slowly, subtly, drifts as it ingests new data streams—shifting its recommendations toward the preferences of the most vocal users, or adjusting its cultural framing to match dominant media narratives (Johnsen, 2024). Without continual auditing and recalibration, such drift can undo years of progress before anyone notices.

Sustaining inclusion will demand new forms of vigilance—some automated, others resolutely human. Automated monitoring could scan for patterns of exclusion in real time: which students are dropping out of certain learning paths, whose voices are underrepresented in generated examples, which dialects are consistently mistranslated or "corrected" toward a standard. Human oversight, however, will remain irreplaceable for interpreting those patterns, for asking whether the signals point to technical flaws, cultural blind spots, or larger structural inequities that the AI alone cannot solve.

There's also the matter of agency. An inclusive system is not one that simply adapts to the learner's profile; it's one that lets the learner shape the adaptation (Petrachenko, 2024). Too often, personalization is imagined as something done to the learner—an invisible process in which the system decides what's best. The future worth working toward is one where learners can peer into that process, tweak it, even reject it. This doesn't mean burdening them with technical minutiae, but giving them real levers to influence how their learning unfolds. Inclusion that cannot be actively co-authored is, at best, a polite form of control.

Looking further ahead, the very definition of "inclusion" may stretch under the pressure of emerging realities. As AI-mediated classrooms become commonplace, geographic boundaries will matter less, but other forms of exclusion might grow sharper: disparities in computational resources, in teacher training for AI integration, in the ability of communities to localize systems to their cultural needs. There's a risk of creating a new digital elite—not defined by internet access alone, but by access to the highest-quality intelligent systems, the ones tuned most closely to the learner's world. Sustaining inclusion will mean anticipating these new fault lines before they harden.

We may also need to grapple with inclusion across temporal boundaries. Intelligent systems can archive and resurface a learner's past interactions indefinitely. Done well, this could enable deeply personalized learning trajectories that span years, even decades, revisiting concepts in ways that reflect the learner's evolving context. Done poorly, it could trap learners in the shadows of their earlier performance, making it harder to escape the inertia of past struggles. The future horizon will test our ability to design systems that remember without imprisoning, that adapt without predetermining.

The cultural dimension cannot be overstated. As intelligent systems become co-authors of educational experiences, they will inevitably contribute to shaping cultural norms (SELVI, 2024). An AI that consistently frames environmental issues through a Western lens, or that defaults to examples from urban life, will leave its imprint on the worldview of millions. Sustaining inclusion requires an intentional multiplicity—deliberately weaving diverse cultural narratives into the system's expressive range, not as token alternates but as equally valid defaults. This is not a decorative gesture; it is a defense against the slow erasure that can occur when one cultural frame becomes invisible through ubiquity.

There's also a subtler, almost philosophical horizon to consider: what happens to inclusion when the learner's counterpart is not another human, but a machine? Will the ease of AI-mediated understanding make human-to-human differences feel more jarring, or will it train us to be more patient with one another? Will students accustomed to perfectly tuned feedback struggle in environments where misinterpretation and negotiation are the norm? Sustaining inclusion in such a future might mean designing systems that occasionally, deliberately, let misunderstanding stand—reminding learners that not every exchange can, or should, be frictionless.

The future will also ask us to rethink the social fabric of education itself. Intelligent systems could, paradoxically, make inclusion more solitary if the focus remains solely on tailoring the individual's pathway (Almufareh et al, 2024). We will need to find ways to braid those pathways together, ensuring that diversity of approach does not collapse into isolation. Inclusion, after all, is as much about belonging as it is about access. The AI must not only help each learner see themselves reflected in the material; it must help them see themselves as part of a shared enterprise, connected to others who are learning alongside them in their own distinct ways.

In the end, the horizon is not a finish line. It's a shifting edge, always receding as we approach. Sustaining inclusion in the age of intelligent systems will be less about "getting there" and more about cultivating the capacity to navigate—together—the constant movement of that edge. It will require humility from technologists, courage from educators, and participation from learners themselves. And it will demand a collective refusal to let the convenience of automation dull our attentiveness to the human complexities that make inclusion worth sustaining in the first place.

CONCLUSION

The emergence of generative AI in education marks a moment of both extraordinary possibility and profound responsibility. It offers us the tools to break free from the constraints of one-size-fits-all education, to dismantle systemic barriers that have long excluded certain learners, and to create personalized pathways that respect the full spectrum of human diversity. At its best, generative AI can reframe inclusion not as an afterthought or a remedial measure, but as the very foundation upon which educational systems are built. This is not a minor shift—it is a redefinition of what it means to provide equitable education in a complex, interconnected, and fast-changing world.

Yet, as this chapter has underscored, technological potential does not automatically translate into social progress. The same algorithms that can adapt a reading passage to a student's language level can also reproduce cultural biases hidden in their training data. The same tools that enable real-time translation can inadvertently prioritize dominant linguistic norms over minority voices. Without careful design, transparent governance, and inclusive policymaking, generative AI could risk reinforcing the very inequities it seeks to address—only now, under the guise of innovation.

Moving forward, the challenge is to ensure that the development and deployment of generative AI are guided by an ethical compass rooted in fairness, cultural sensitivity, and learner empowerment. This means more than technical safeguards; it calls for continuous human oversight, diverse stakeholder participation, and a willingness to interrogate the social consequences of AI-enabled decisions. Educators must remain not only facilitators of learning but also critical mediators between students and the technologies that shape their educational journeys.

Importantly, the work of building inclusive education in the AI era is not a task for educators alone. It demands collaboration across sectors: policymakers who can craft frameworks that protect equity while fostering innovation; technologists who design systems with accessibility and cultural responsiveness as core requirements, not optional features; and researchers who monitor, evaluate, and refine AI applications in real educational contexts. Only through such partnerships can generative AI's transformative potential be fully realized in ways that serve all learners.

In the end, the question is not whether generative AI will change education—it already is. The real question is whether we will shape that change intentionally, ensuring that the systems we build reflect the values we hold. Inclusion, in this context, is not simply about granting access; it is about creating environments in which every learner can thrive, contribute, and find belonging. If we succeed, the integration of generative AI into education could stand as one of the most significant advances in the pursuit of equity in our time—a testament to our ability to harness innovation in the service of humanity. If we fail, it will be yet another reminder that technology, without vision and responsibility, can magnify the very divides it promises to bridge. The choice is ours, and the time to act is now.

REFERENCES

Alasadi, E. A., & Baiz, C. R. (2023). Generative AI in Education and Research: Opportunities, concerns, and solutions. *Journal of Chemical Education*, *100*(8), 2965–2971.

Almufareh, M. F., Kausar, S., Humayun, M., & Tehsin, S. (2024). A conceptual model for inclusive technology: Advancing disability inclusion through artificial intelligence. *Journal of Disability Research*, *3*(1), 20230060.

Angel, B. (2024). *The Wolf is at the Door: How to Survive and Thrive in an AI-driven World*. Entrepreneur Press.

Baker, D. L., & Baker, R. L. (2022). Knowledge and wisdom: High stakes testing and learning outcomes. In *Neuroethical Policy Design: A Lifetime's Exploration of Public Policy and Human Brains* (pp. 101–118). Springer International Publishing.

Banda, R. (2024). Building Social Equity with AI.

Barocas, S., Hardt, M., & Narayanan, A. (2023). *Fairness and machine learning: Limitations and opportunities*. MIT press.

Baskara, F. R. (2023). Navigating pedagogical evolution: The implication of generative AI on the reinvention of teacher education.

Bozdağ, A. A. (2024). The AI-mediated intimacy economy: A paradigm shift in digital interactions. *AI & Society*, •••, 1–22.

Burke, K., & Leben, S. (2024). Procedural fairness: A key ingredient in public satisfaction. *Ct. Rev.*, *60*, 6.

Butler-Ulrich, T., Hughes, J., & Morrison, L. (2024). Creativity and Generative AI for Preservice Teachers. In *Contemporaneous Issues about Creativity*. IntcchOpen.

Challoumis, C. (2024). The dawn of artificial intelligence. In *XIX International Scientific Conference*. London. Great Britain (pp. 169-205).

Chen, Y. (2024). Generative Artificial Intelligence Empowering Translation: Current Status, Challenges, and Prospects. The Educational Review, USA, 8(12).

Chi, N., Lurie, E., & Mulligan, D. K. (2021, July). Reconfiguring diversity and inclusion for AI ethics. In Proceedings of the 2021 AAAI/ACM Conference on AI, Ethics, and Society (pp. 447-457).

Daugherty, P. R., & Wilson, H. J. (2024). *Human+ Machine, Updated and Expanded: Reimagining Work in the Age of AI*. Harvard Business Press.

Essa, H. (2024). *The Consciously Unbiased Educator*. ASCD.

Ghimire, A. (2025). Utilizing ChatGPT to integrate world English and diverse knowledge: A transnational perspective in critical artificial intelligence (AI) literacy. *Computers and Composition*, *75*, 102913.

Gimmler, A. (2024). Exploring the Possibilities of Dramatic Rehearsal as a Framework for the Evaluation of Digital Technologies in Education. In *Framing Futures in Postdigital Education: Critical Concepts for Data-driven Practices* (pp. 163–179). Springer Nature Switzerland.

Graham, O., & Milan, Y. (2025). The Influence of AI Tools on the Student Writing Process and Compositional Fluency.

Gulson, K. N., Sellar, S., & Webb, P. T. (2022). *Algorithms of education: How datafication and artificial intelligence shape policy*. U of Minnesota Press.

Holzinger, A., Zatloukal, K., & Müller, H. (2025). Is human oversight to AI systems still possible? *New Biotechnology*, *85*, 59–62. PMID: 39675423

Johnsen, M. (2024). *AI Alignment*. Maria Johnsen.

Kaplan, J. (2024). *Generative Artificial Intelligence: What Everyone Needs to Know*. Oxford University Press.

Kaur, D., Uslu, S., Rittichier, K. J., & Durresi, A. (2022). Trustworthy artificial intelligence: A review. *ACM Computing Surveys*, *55*(2), 1–38.

Kayyali, M. (2024). Future possibilities and challenges of AI in education. In *Transforming education with generative AI: Prompt engineering and synthetic content creation* (pp. 118–137). IGI Global Scientific Publishing.

Kayyali, M. (2025a). Ethical Implications of Generative AI in Education: Privacy, Bias, and Integrity. In Transformative AI Practices for Personalized Learning Strategies (pp. 185-218). IGI Global Scientific Publishing.

Kayyali, M. (2025b). Generative AI and Education: Transforming Teaching and Learning Through Collaborative Intelligence. In Humans and Generative AI Tools for Collaborative Intelligence (pp. 25-52). IGI Global Scientific Publishing.

Kayyali, M. (2025c). The Future of AI in Education: Predictions and Emerging Trends. Next-Generation AI Methodologies in Education, 367-406.

Kayyali, M. (2025d). AI in Higher Education: Revolutionizing Curriculum and Administration. In AI Adoption and Diffusion in Education (pp. 31-62). IGI Global Scientific Publishing.

Kayyali, M. (2025e). Ethical Implications of Generative AI in Education: Privacy, Bias, and Integrity. In Transformative AI Practices for Personalized Learning Strategies (pp. 185-218). IGI Global Scientific Publishing.

Kayyali, M. (2026). The Impact of AI on Classroom Dynamics in Higher Education: Shifting Roles for Professors and Students. In Responsible AI Integration in Education (pp. 151-180). IGI Global Scientific Publishing.

Klaassen, G. (2024). Confronting bias in artificial intelligence: building transparent, diverse, and ethical AI systems.

McDermid, J. A., Jia, Y., Porter, Z., & Habli, I. (2021). Artificial intelligence explainability: The technical and ethical dimensions. *Philosophical Transactions of the Royal Society A*, *379*(2207), 20200363. PMID: 34398656

Mohammed, R. R. (2025). Generative AI in the Academy: Analysis of Stakeholders' Experiences in US Higher Education Organizations (Doctoral dissertation, Arizona State University).

Moustaghfir, S., & Brigui, H. (2024). Navigating critical thinking in the digital era: An informative exploration. International Journal of Linguistics. *Literature and Translation*, *7*(1), 137–143.

Napitupulu, M. F., & Dalimunte, A. A. (2025). A study of students' perception of character AI in practicing English speaking fluency. Celtic: A Journal of Culture, English Language Teaching. *Literatura y Lingüística*, *12*(1), 384–404.

Ortiz, E. A., Vergara, N. C., Pabón, T. F., Gambi, G. D. N., Giambruno, C., Alfaro, M. P., & Segura, D. R. (2025). AI and Education: Building the Future Through Digital Transformation.

Petrachenko, J. (2024). Dwelling in the In-Between: A Self Study of Moving into a Classroom with Unconventional Learners.

Polverini, G. (2022). Exploring interdisciplinarity between physics and mathematics: the design of a linguistic and an epistemological tool for analysing texts about the parabolic motion (Doctoral dissertation, Master thesis in Physics, Alma Mater Studiorum–University of Bologna).

Pratschke, B. M. (2024). *Generative AI and education: Digital pedagogies, teaching innovation and learning design*. Springer Nature.

Radanliev, P. (2024). Artificial intelligence: Reflecting on the past and looking towards the next paradigm shift. *Journal of Experimental & Theoretical Artificial Intelligence*, •••, 1–18.

Sahebi, S., & Formosa, P. (2025). The AI-mediated communication dilemma: Epistemic trust, social media, and the challenge of generative artificial intelligence. *Synthese*, *205*(3), 1–24.

Sakubu, D. (2025). *Challenges of Artificial Intelligence today and future implications for society and the world*. World Journal of Advanced Research and Reviews.

Sapkota, R., Roumeliotis, K. I., & Karkee, M. (2025). Ai agents vs. agentic ai: A conceptual taxonomy, applications and challenges. arXiv preprint arXiv:2505.10468.

SELVI, B. (2024). Artificial Intelligence in Higher Education: Transforming Internationalization at Home. Shanlax Publications Book Chapters, 1-17.

SWARGIARY. (2024). *K*. Addressing Maladaptive Behaviors from AI Integration in Learning. EdTech Research Association.

Ungar, M., Theron, L., & Höltge, J. (2023). Multisystemic approaches to researching young people's resilience: Discovering culturally and contextually sensitive accounts of thriving under adversity. *Development and Psychopathology*, *35*(5), 2199–2213. PMID: 37128831

Villena, F., Véliz, C., García-Huidobro, R., & Aguayo, S. (2024). Generative artificial intelligence in dentistry: Current approaches and future challenges. arXiv preprint arXiv:2407.17532.

Wamba, S. F., Queiroz, M. M., Randhawa, K., & Gupta, G. (2025). Generative artificial intelligence and the challenges to adding value ethically. *Technovation*, *144*, 103235.

Wang, Q. (2024). Mutual theory of mind for human-AI communication in AI-mediated social interaction (Doctoral dissertation, Ph. D. Dissertation. Georgia Institute of Technology).

Xu, Y., Wen, F., Zuo, B., & Rhodes, M. (2023). Social essentialism in the United States and China: How social and cognitive factors predict within-and cross-cultural variation in essentialist thinking. *Memory & Cognition*, *51*(3), 681–694. PMID: 35419740

Yambal, S., & Waykar, Y. A. (2025). Future of Education Using Adaptive AI, Intelligent Systems, and Ethical Challenges. In Effective Instructional Design Informed by AI (pp. 171-202). IGI Global Scientific Publishing.

KEY TERMS AND DEFINITIONS

Accessibility by Default: captions, alt text, dyslexia-friendly layouts, keyboard navigation, and screen-reader structure generated automatically.

Bias Auditing: systematic checks of model outputs for stereotype patterns and subgroup performance gaps before and during deployment.

Culturally Responsive Generation: prompts and models that adapt examples, metaphors, and contexts to local languages and lived realities.

Data Minimization: collecting only the least data needed to personalize learning, with consent dashboards and deletion by default.

Explainable Adaptation: transparent notes that show what the AI changed (level, format, pacing) and why, with human override.

Multimodal Personalization: on-demand generation of text, audio, visuals, and simplifications so each learner gets the same concept in a form that works for them.

Universal Design for Learning (UDL): a framework that designs flexible goals, methods, materials, and assessments so all learners can access and engage from the start.

Chapter 2
Ethical Implications of AI in Promoting Equity and Access in Education

Mustafa Kayyali
https://orcid.org/0000-0003-3300-262X
Maaref University of Applied Sciences, Syria

ABSTRACT

Generative AI is reshaping the educational landscape, offering unprecedented possibilities for personalization, resource creation, and access to learning. Yet its integration into classrooms and policy frameworks raises pressing ethical questions: Will AI narrow the educational divide or deepen existing disparities? This chapter critically examines the intersection of AI ethics, equity, and access in education, exploring how algorithmic design, data governance, and institutional choices influence outcomes for marginalized learners. Drawing on global perspectives, it discusses both the transformative potential and the risks of exclusion embedded in AI-driven systems. The chapter proposes guiding principles for designing and implementing generative AI tools that uphold fairness, cultural responsiveness, and accessibility. In doing so, it argues for a proactive, policy-driven approach to ensure that AI serves as a bridge—rather than a barrier—to inclusive, equitable education for all.

INTRODUCTION

Artificial Intelligence is no longer a distant technological aspiration—it has quietly embedded itself in the daily realities of education. Among its most influential advancements, generative AI stands out as a tool capable of producing text, images, simulations, and even interactive learning experiences with minimal human

DOI: 10.4018/979-8-3373-3745-6.ch002

prompting (Balaji et al, 2025). This technology offers a vision of education in which learning materials are not fixed commodities but living, adaptive resources that can respond to the needs, language, culture, and pace of individual learners. It invites us to imagine a classroom where a rural student in a low-resource region has access to the same tailored instruction and rich content as a student in a technologically advanced urban center.

Yet, behind this vision lies a more complex truth: access to AI-powered education is uneven, and the systems themselves may embed structural inequities (Ahmed, 2024). Generative AI tools are shaped by the datasets on which they are trained, the design priorities of their creators, and the infrastructure needed to deploy them. These conditions raise fundamental ethical questions: Who gets to shape the narratives that AI delivers? Whose cultural knowledge is prioritized or omitted? Which learners are left behind because their schools lack the bandwidth, the devices, or the institutional support to integrate these technologies?

Equity in education has always been an evolving ideal—contested, redefined, and reframed across different historical and political contexts. The arrival of AI does not automatically resolve inequities; in fact, without deliberate ethical safeguards, it risks reinforcing them. Algorithmic bias, data exclusion, and socio-economic divides can mean that the benefits of AI are unevenly distributed, with privileged students reaping more advantages while disadvantaged learners face digital barriers disguised as progress (Dinker, 2024).

Moreover, the notion of *access* is itself multi-layered. It is not enough to place an AI tool in a school and declare the playing field leveled. True access involves meaningful participation—where learners can engage with AI-generated content in a language they understand, within a curriculum that reflects their lived experiences, and in a way that develops their critical thinking rather than reducing them to passive consumers (Kim et al, 2025). This requires educators, policymakers, and technologists to move beyond a purely technical perspective and to adopt an ethical lens that foregrounds human dignity, cultural inclusion, and social justice.

Generative AI, in its current trajectory, sits at a crossroads. On one path, it could become an unprecedented equalizer, reducing costs, transcending geographical boundaries, and offering every learner a personalized route to knowledge. On the other, it could evolve into yet another mechanism by which the already advantaged surge ahead, while others struggle against new, invisible walls. This chapter seeks to navigate this critical juncture—examining not only the promises of AI but also its potential pitfalls—while advocating for policies and practices that ensure inclusivity is a foundational principle, not a by-product, of technological progress in education.

RETHINKING EDUCATIONAL JUSTICE IN THE AGE OF GENERATIVE AI

Educational justice has always been a restless idea — one that refuses to sit still, forever expanding and contracting as the social, political, and technological landscapes around it shift (Bozkurt et al, 2023). Some eras have defined it narrowly, reducing it to the notion that every child should simply be in a classroom. Others have stretched it into a broader moral horizon, where the quality, relevance, and dignity of the learning experience matter as much as its availability. Now, in the strange and shimmering dawn of generative AI, this old concept has found itself in new territory, forced to contend with a machine intelligence capable of producing essays, explanations, feedback, even artworks — all in seconds.

It is tempting to see this moment as the opening of a golden gate: the instant when the long-promised dream of tailored, resource-rich education for all finally slips from theory into reality. The technology seems almost theatrical in its potential. A student in a remote village with no library can summon a reading list on medieval history. A child struggling with algebra can receive patient, step-by-step guidance at any hour of the day. Lessons can adapt not just to age or grade level, but to personal curiosity, learning style, and even mood. It's the kind of vision that has animated countless reformers and innovators — the promise of collapsing the stubborn distance between the privileged and the underserved.

But the trouble with beautiful visions is that they can dazzle us into overlooking the shadows. Justice in education has never been about handing everyone the same textbook, and it will not be achieved by placing the same AI tool into every student's hands (Kumashiro, 2024). The deeper question — perhaps the more uncomfortable one — is this: *Whose voices, values, and assumptions are woven into the architecture of these systems?* And equally, *who gets left behind in the name of progress?*

Generative AI systems do not spring from nowhere; they are born from data — mountains of text, images, and audio scraped from an imperfect world (Kayyali, 2025 A). That world is riddled with inequalities, silences, and distortions. The data reflects them. And the algorithms, for all their mathematical elegance, tend to reproduce what they are fed. An AI tutor trained primarily on English-language academic sources will, inevitably, privilege certain worldviews over others (Albeihi & Rice, 2025). It might offer a luminous explanation of Newtonian mechanics but falter when asked to contextualize a piece of indigenous oral history, or misinterpret the nuances of a non-Western philosophical tradition.

This is where the language of "access" starts to feel thinner than it ought to. Access, in a purely technical sense, could mean a rural school installing a computer lab with AI-driven software (Tripathi et al, 2025). But true access — the kind that aligns with justice — requires that the content generated is relevant, respectful, and resonant for those learners. It asks whether the AI understands their language in more than a grammatical sense, whether it can navigate the subtleties of their cultural references, whether it avoids the quiet violence of erasure.

And here lies another knot in the fabric: the uneven terrain of infrastructure. AI is computationally hungry. It needs servers, bandwidth, and devices powerful enough to run it — or at least to connect to the clouds where it lives (Prangon & Wu, 2024). For a student in a school with unstable internet, the door to AI's promise swings open only halfway. Even when the connection is there, the licensing costs for premium AI tools can put them out of reach for institutions already struggling to afford basic materials. The irony is bitter: the very communities that could benefit most from flexible, low-cost, high-quality educational content are often those least able to harness it.

Yet the injustice isn't just about the digital divide in a narrow sense; it's also about the *direction* in which AI pushes the educational system itself. If policymakers see AI primarily as a cost-cutting measure — a way to replace, rather than support, human teachers — the results can be corrosive (Rainie & Anderson, 2024). Students may find themselves interacting more with a screen than with a living, breathing educator who can notice when their confidence falters or when a concept sparks unexpected joy. Educational justice has always depended on the presence of mentors, guides, and role models who embody the values they teach. No algorithm, however sophisticated, can model empathy in the same way a committed teacher can.

And yet — to dismiss AI entirely would be to abandon a tool that, in the right hands, could radically reduce the inequities that have plagued education for centuries. The question is not *whether* we integrate it, but *how* we do so without letting it harden existing hierarchies. One way forward is to embed equity into the design stage itself: diversifying the datasets, involving educators and communities in shaping how the AI responds, and making transparency a norm rather than a luxury. Learners should be able to question the AI's output, see where its information comes from, and recognize its limitations. In that way, interacting with AI becomes not just an exercise in consumption, but an education in critical thinking.

Still, ethical integration demands more than just tinkering with the technology. It calls for rethinking the entire ecology of education (Bardone et al, 2024). What counts as "success" when an AI tutor is involved? Is it higher test scores, faster completion of assignments, or something subtler — a deeper curiosity, a greater sense of agency, an ability to connect knowledge to lived reality? If we pursue speed and efficiency as the sole metrics, AI may well deliver them — but at the cost of the reflective, dialogical spaces where genuine learning tends to take root.

Educational justice in the age of AI will also require a kind of moral humility from those designing and deploying these systems (Madaio et al, 2022). AI, for all its seeming omniscience, does not have a stake in justice. It does not feel the sting of discrimination or the relief of opportunity. Those are human experiences. It is we who must decide what "fair" looks like, what compromises are unacceptable, and which communities should be prioritized. And that means resisting the seductive pull of technological determinism — the belief that the mere availability of a tool will inevitably lead to better outcomes.

Consider a school in which the AI is trained to adapt reading materials to each student's proficiency level. At first glance, this seems unquestionably positive (Kayyali, 2025 B). But what if the system quietly lowers expectations for certain students based on historical performance data that itself reflects systemic disadvantage? What if it never challenges them with more complex texts because the algorithm assumes they are unlikely to succeed? Here, the injustice is not in access but in aspiration. The AI's "personalization" may actually cement a ceiling over a learner's potential.

The work of rethinking educational justice in this era, then, is partly about vigilance — not paranoia, but an attentive skepticism toward claims of neutrality and universality. It is about remembering that technology, like policy, is shaped by choices, and those choices carry values. Even decisions that appear purely technical — the choice of training data, the setting of parameters, the weighting of certain outputs — are never value-free. They are moral decisions in disguise.

Some educators have begun to argue that the most ethical use of AI in education is not to outsource teaching tasks but to *expand* the human capacity for connection and creativity (Luckin, 2025). Let the AI handle repetitive, low-level tasks — generating practice problems, summarizing long articles — so that teachers can spend more time in dialogue with their students, facilitating discussions, mentoring, and exploring the messy, unpredictable questions that machines cannot easily process. In this way, AI becomes a servant to the higher aims of education rather than its silent director.

Of course, there is a tension here. The same system that can liberate a teacher from administrative drudgery can also be used by administrators to justify increasing class sizes or reducing staff. The line between augmentation and replacement is thin, and it will not be held by good intentions alone. It will require explicit policy protections, as well as an educational culture that values the irreplaceable work of human educators.

Justice in education, reimagined through the lens of generative AI, might mean something far more demanding than equal access to the same software (Rahimi & Azadmanesh, 2025). It might mean cultivating a learning environment where AI is one voice among many, where its outputs are interrogated rather than passively accepted, and where its presence does not diminish the importance of human relationships, cultural specificity, and moral responsibility.

If there is hope in this moment, it lies in the fact that AI is still malleable — its role in education not yet calcified. We are, collectively, in the position of setting precedents. The standards we choose now — about transparency, inclusivity, data ethics, and the boundaries between machine and human judgment — will shape not only the immediate experience of today's students but also the expectations of the generations that follow. And those choices, subtle as they may seem, will either draw us closer to or further from the deeper meaning of educational justice: the belief that every learner, regardless of where they are born or the resources they inherit, deserves not just a place in the classroom, but the tools, respect, and recognition to flourish within it.

AI AS AN EQUALIZER OR AMPLIFIER OF INEQUITIES?

Few technologies arrive with as much duality baked into their DNA as generative AI. It's a machine that can whisper in the ear of the struggling student at midnight, untangling a math problem line by line. It's also a machine that can spit out an answer so confidently wrong, or so subtly biased, that the learner may not even notice the damage until much later—if at all. To frame AI as either savior or saboteur is too simple, yet the tension between those roles is exactly what makes it such a complicated force in education.

The equalizer narrative is seductive. It paints AI as the great flattening agent in a world of jagged opportunity. Where human resources are scarce, the machine stands ready—tireless, fluent, infinitely scalable. One can almost imagine the headlines: *AI brings Harvard-level tutoring to remote villages*. And, in a way, there's truth in that fantasy. Large language models can generate summaries of complex texts, translate material into multiple languages, and offer a kind of personalized pacing that traditional classrooms, bound by timetables and overworked teachers, rarely achieve (Wang et al, 2024). For a child whose school library consists of a handful of outdated textbooks, such capabilities can feel almost miraculous.

Yet miracles in technology often come with invisible disclaimers. What looks like a universal tool often wears the fingerprints of the contexts in which it was made. The datasets feeding AI models are not a random slice of human knowledge—they are a curated, filtered, sometimes messy patchwork of what has been digitized, archived, and deemed relevant (Cameron, 2021). That patchwork is uneven. Some cultures are overrepresented, others barely a whisper. This means that AI's answers may slide toward certain linguistic norms, historical interpretations, and cultural frames, while marginalizing others without a hint of malice—just the cold momentum of statistical probability.

When educational systems take AI at face value, the risk isn't merely in occasional factual errors; it's in the slow, creeping normalization of a worldview that subtly sidelines the very diversity it claims to serve. A student in Nairobi or Lima may receive an answer shaped by datasets rich in American and European sources, presented as if they were universal truths. The underlying message—that knowledge flows in one direction, from the "center" to the "periphery"—isn't printed anywhere, yet it seeps in all the same.

The amplification of inequities can also happen through the infrastructure that enables AI to function in the first place (Bircan & Özbilgin, 2025). Tools that depend on stable high-speed internet, modern devices, and paid subscriptions are naturally easier to adopt in well-funded schools than in that where even electricity is intermittent. The result? Students in wealthier districts or countries gain routine exposure to AI's benefits, refining their ability to use it critically and creatively, while others encounter it sporadically—perhaps only through stripped-down versions with limited features. Over time, this differential access doesn't just mirror existing educational divides; it stretches them wider.

One of the more insidious forms of amplification comes from how AI interacts with pre-existing performance data (Bridewell et al, 2024). Personalization is a core selling point for many educational AI tools. On the surface, it seems like the ultimate form of fairness: the system adjusts to each learner's needs, pacing, and abilities. But what happens when those needs are inferred from data sets marred by systemic bias? A student from a historically marginalized group, whose earlier academic record reflects years of under-resourced schooling, might be algorithmically steered toward less challenging material—reinforcing the false narrative that they are less capable. In this way, personalization can become a velvet-gloved form of tracking, locking students into ceilings disguised as support.

Still, it would be dishonest to suggest that the technology is doomed to deepen divides. The very same attributes that allow it to amplify inequity—its reach, adaptability, and capacity for scale—can be harnessed in deliberate, equity-centered ways. Imagine an AI system intentionally trained on multilingual, multicultural corpora, co-created with educators from across the globe, and audited regularly by independent bodies for bias and representation gaps (Behera et al, 2024). Imagine open-source AI tools, hosted on lightweight platforms, designed to run even on low-cost devices offline, with periodic updates synced when connectivity allows. These aren't just technical tweaks; they are political choices, statements about whose needs are prioritized.

But that's the rub: AI doesn't choose. People do. And those choices are shaped by the economic and political realities of the moment. Private companies driving AI innovation have shareholders to satisfy; their incentives often lean toward markets that can pay, not necessarily communities that could benefit most. Governments, too, may see AI as a chance to demonstrate modernization without necessarily confronting the deeper structural reforms—funding equity, teacher training, curriculum overhauls—that justice in education actually requires (Kayyali, 2022).

The role of the educator in this equation becomes crucial. AI's promise as an equalizer depends heavily on whether teachers are trained and empowered to use it critically (Agarwal & Bhatnagar, 2025). Without this layer of human mediation, students risk treating AI outputs as gospel, missing the chance to interrogate and contextualize them. In classrooms where teachers themselves are not confident with the technology—or worse, where they fear it will replace them—the relationship between human and machine can quickly tilt toward mistrust or over-reliance, neither of which supports equitable learning.

The psychological dimension deserves attention too. Access to AI isn't just about devices and bandwidth; it's about the confidence to engage with it as a tool rather than a gatekeeper. Students who grow up accustomed to questioning, editing, and remixing AI outputs will inevitably extract more value from it than those who approach it with hesitation, unsure of how—or whether—they're "allowed" to challenge its authority (Helvie, 2025). That confidence, in turn, often correlates with socio-economic background, prior exposure to technology, and the kinds of learning cultures fostered at home and in school.

Perhaps the most unsettling thought is that inequities can be amplified even when the technology is working exactly as designed. AI can't see the wider context of a learner's life: the lack of a quiet study space, the burden of domestic responsibilities, the chronic stress of poverty or displacement. It can adapt to a student's performance in the narrow sense of quiz scores and typed responses, but it cannot address the structural conditions shaping that performance. Without a broader policy framework—investments in infrastructure, social supports, teacher development—AI risks becoming a high-tech veneer over the same old disparities.

At its best, though, AI has the capacity to surface needs that might otherwise remain invisible. Patterns in student interactions could help identify those at risk of disengagement, allowing teachers to intervene sooner. Automated translation could give immigrant or refugee learners access to materials in their home language without waiting for scarce human translators. Adaptive assessments could provide real-time feedback that guides students toward mastery at their own pace, rather than penalizing them for falling behind an arbitrary schedule (Secl, 2025). These possibilities are not science fiction; they exist now. The challenge is making them available and meaningful to all, not just to the already advantaged.

The truth is, AI will likely be both an equalizer and an amplifier, often at the same time (Yahya et al, 2022). Its impact will vary from classroom to classroom, policy to policy, and the same tool that levels a playing field in one context may tilt it in another. The task, then, is not to settle the question once and for all, but to stay in the discomfort of its ambiguity, to keep asking: Who is this serving? Who is being overlooked? And what structural conditions must change for the answer to tilt toward equity rather than exclusion?

If history is any guide, new educational technologies rarely erase inequities on their own. Radio, television, the internet—all were heralded as democratizing forces, yet each was absorbed into the existing architectures of advantage and disadvantage (Ford et al, 2021). AI will be no different unless we make it so. That means coupling technological adoption with deliberate redistribution of resources, ongoing bias audits, participatory design involving the communities most affected, and a willingness to slow down the rollout of tools until they meet ethical thresholds.

In the end, the question of whether AI acts as an equalizer or an amplifier isn't really about the technology. It's about us—our priorities, our policies, and our willingness to see equity not as a side effect but as a non-negotiable aim (Youvan, 2024). Left to its own devices, AI will follow the path of least resistance, flowing along the channels carved by existing power structures. Guided with care, it can be made to cut new ones, irrigating educational deserts that have been dry for far too long.

The future isn't fixed. The same algorithm that parrots bias today could, in a different configuration, become the most vigilant bias detector tomorrow. Whether we get the first outcome or the second will depend less on what's possible and more on what we decide is acceptable. That decision, quietly and urgently, is already being made—in boardrooms, ministries, staff meetings, and classrooms. And its consequences will echo far longer than the current fascination with AI as the latest educational fad.

ETHICAL FRAMEWORKS FOR INCLUSIVE AI INTEGRATION

If generative AI is to enter the classroom as more than a shiny distraction or a budgetary shortcut, it needs an ethical skeleton strong enough to bear the weight of the promises being made. Without such a framework, the technology risks being absorbed into the same old machinery that has, for centuries, rationed opportunity according to lines of wealth, language, geography, and power (Kayyali, 2025 C). Ethics here isn't some ornamental appendix tacked onto a technical process—it is the architecture itself. Strip it away and the whole edifice collapses into expedience.

The trouble is, ethics in AI often arrives prepackaged in the language of glossy corporate responsibility reports: a handful of bullet points about fairness, transparency, and accountability, followed by a photo of smiling children gathered around a tablet (NAKAMURA, 2025). This is not what an ethical framework looks like; it is what marketing looks like when it dresses in moral clothes. Real ethics is slower, less photogenic, more uncomfortable. It involves asking questions that unsettle the momentum of product releases. It means entertaining the possibility that some tools should not be deployed at all—not yet, or perhaps ever.

Inclusive AI integration begins with an admission that the default settings of technology are rarely neutral (Mergen et al, 2025). They tend to reflect the priorities, cultural norms, and blind spots of their creators, who often inhabit the most connected, resourced, and educated pockets of the world. Left unchecked, those defaults can become invisible rules that govern who benefits from AI in education and who merely watches from the edges. The first act of ethical design, then, is deliberate counterweighting—seeking out and embedding perspectives from the margins before the system hardens into place.

This isn't a call for tokenism. Dropping a few translated phrases into a user interface does not constitute cultural inclusivity, just as appointing a single "diversity advisor" does not dismantle structural bias. The framework has to be built so that inclusivity is not an afterthought but a living constraint—something that shapes the earliest design choices and persists through every update, audit, and iteration. For example, if a model is going to serve classrooms in multilingual regions, then the training data needs to encompass not only major global languages but also local dialects, minority languages, and forms of expression that resist neat grammatical categorization.

Transparency is often invoked as the cornerstone of ethical AI, and it matters—but not in the hollow sense of publishing an impenetrable technical report that only a handful of engineers can decode (Puplampu, 2024). In the educational context, transparency has to operate on multiple levels: teachers must be able to see how an AI arrives at its conclusions, students must be equipped to question the authority of its outputs, and policymakers must have access to independent assessments of bias, accuracy, and safety. A system that simply delivers answers without showing its reasoning turns the learning process into a kind of intellectual fast food: quick, palatable, but ultimately hollow.

Another pillar is accountability, though the word tends to deflate the moment it leaves the page. Accountability cannot mean a buried clause in the terms of service stating that the company is not liable for "errors or omissions." Nor can it be reduced to public relations damage control after harm has been done. In a functioning ethical framework, accountability should be proactive—establishing in advance who bears responsibility if an AI's recommendations lead to exclusion, misinformation, or unequal treatment. And this responsibility cannot rest solely on end users. The ecosystem—developers, distributors, school systems, and regulators—must share it.

Ethical inclusivity also demands ongoing, participatory governance (Ahmad & Islam, 2024). Too often, the people most affected by educational technology are consulted only after it has been designed, marketed, and sold. By then, their feedback is treated as optional or is funneled into minor interface tweaks rather than structural change. An authentic framework would invert this sequence: communities, educators, and students would be engaged in shaping the technology from the outset, not merely reacting to it after the fact. This is messy work. It slows the speed of innovation. But innovation without participation is less progress than imposition.

Bias mitigation cannot be treated as a one-time quality-control procedure, checked off before launch and forgotten (Auger et al, 2024). Bias is not static; it mutates as the data shifts, as the patterns of usage change, as the sociopolitical environment evolves. An AI model that performs acceptably in one year can, by the next, begin producing outputs that subtly reinforce stereotypes or neglect emerging realities. Ethical frameworks must therefore build in periodic audits—true audits, not ceremonial ones—conducted by actors independent of the institutions that stand to profit from the tool's success.

There is also the question of *consent*, an often-overlooked principle in AI ethics for education. When students interact with AI, they are not just consuming its outputs; they are feeding it data. This data—questions asked, mistakes made, even the cadence of responses—can be absorbed back into the system, refining it for future users. Without clear, informed consent, the boundary between a learner and a training dataset becomes perilously thin (Harden & Fanfarelli, 2023). Ethical integration means making data practices visible and negotiable: students (and their guardians) should have the ability to understand what is collected, how it is used, and the right to withdraw from that process without forfeiting their access to education.

Affordability and accessibility must also be written into the ethical blueprint (Reddy, 2025). A tool that can dramatically improve learning outcomes but costs more than most schools can afford is not an inclusive tool—it is a boutique product. Similarly, if it requires cutting-edge hardware or uninterrupted high-speed internet, its usefulness will be sharply skewed toward already-advantaged environments. Building for inclusivity means embracing constraints: designing so that the technology runs on older devices, functions in low-bandwidth conditions, and can be distributed under open or low-cost licenses.

But perhaps the most elusive part of an ethical framework for AI in education is cultivating a culture of critical use. No matter how inclusive the design, how transparent the processes, how equitable the distribution—AI remains a fallible, non-human actor (Kayyali, 2026). It should not be positioned as an oracle but as a collaborator whose suggestions are open to challenge. Embedding this ethos into classrooms requires teacher training that goes beyond technical tutorials; it calls for pedagogical strategies that integrate AI into dialogue, analysis, and reflection rather than allowing it to silently dictate answers.

Ethics, in this sense, is less about codifying a perfect set of rules and more about setting the conditions under which human judgment retains primacy (Schuster, 2023). There is no way to predict every scenario in which an AI tool might go wrong or be misused, but a well-constructed framework can create habits of vigilance—teachers asking "why did the system say this?", students comparing outputs with alternative sources, administrators reviewing not only efficiency metrics but also indicators of inclusion and learner agency.

And yet, even the most robust ethical scaffolding will strain under pressure if the surrounding policy landscape is indifferent or hostile to equity (Marrero, 2024). Technology does not operate in a vacuum; it seeps into the cracks of whatever system it enters. If that system tolerates underfunded schools, untrained teachers, and unequal access to basic infrastructure, then AI will replicate and sometimes amplify those deficiencies. This is why ethical AI integration cannot be divorced from the larger struggle for educational justice. The framework must be porous enough to recognize when the barriers lie beyond the machine and into the structures of the society deploying it.

There's a temptation to see ethics as a brake pedal on innovation, but in truth, it is closer to a steering wheel. Without it, the momentum of technological development is as likely to careen into inequity as it is to steer toward inclusion (Taylor et al, 2022). The goal is not to slow AI's integration into education but to direct it, to give it a compass that points toward the dignity of all learners. This compass is built not from a single grand principle but from many small, sometimes fragile commitments: to listen to those at the margins, to keep the workings of the system visible, to share responsibility for its effects, to adapt when harm emerges.

Such commitments are not glamorous. They rarely fit into neat marketing copy. But they are what separate a tool that merely works from one that works *justly*. An AI that dazzles with speed and fluency but leaves certain learners behind has failed, regardless of its technical sophistication. An AI that occasionally stumbles but does so within a structure that detects, corrects, and learns from its failings has a chance to be more than a passing novelty—it can become part of an educational ecosystem in which technology serves humanity, and not the other way around.

POLICY PATHWAYS FOR EQUITY AND ACCESS IN DIGITAL LEARNING

If equity in digital learning is to move from the vocabulary of conference speeches into the grit of everyday reality, it needs more than inspirational language and vague aspirations (Pettitt, 2023). It needs policy—not as a static legalistic document gathering dust in an education ministry's filing cabinet, but as a living, breathing framework capable of bending with technological change while holding fast to human dignity. Without that, digital learning risks becoming a mirror of the inequalities it was supposed to challenge, reflecting them back with greater clarity but no remedy.

Yet policy in this domain often walks a tightrope between the visionary and the pragmatic. Lean too far toward the visionary and you get lofty declarations about “inclusive innovation” without the budget lines or enforcement mechanisms to make them real. Tilt too far toward pragmatism and you risk policies that are technically implementable but ethically hollow—frameworks that ensure devices are distributed but fail to ask what kind of learning culture those devices will inhabit. The balance is delicate, but the stakes are anything but abstract.

One pathway begins with the recognition that access is not a single threshold to be crossed—*now you have internet, now you are included.* Access is layered: infrastructure, affordability, digital literacy, culturally relevant content, and the capacity to participate meaningfully rather than passively. A policy that focuses solely on one layer—say, installing high-speed broadband in schools—without addressing the others, builds a bridge to nowhere. Students may have the connection but not the confidence to navigate it critically, or the resources may be there but loaded with content that erases their histories.

To avoid this pitfall, governments and institutions must design policy with what could be called equity from the ground up (Norman-Major, 2023). This means mapping the digital terrain not just in terms of coverage or hardware but in terms of the lived realities of learners: the languages they speak at home, the cultural references that frame their understanding, the rhythms of their days and seasons, the barriers—visible and invisible—that influence how and when they can learn. Without this grounding, “equity” becomes a word applied from above, as if it were an app you could download onto any device and expect it to run smoothly.

Funding models form the bedrock of such pathways, yet they are too often the silent partner in policy conversations (Pedrazas et al, 2021). Equity in digital learning cannot depend on short-term grants or the philanthropic whims of corporate actors. It requires sustained public investment, distributed according to need rather than political convenience (Kayyali, 2024 A). This is harder than it sounds, especially in systems where wealthier districts or schools wield more political influence. But if policy is to be more than a gesture, resource allocation must be recalibrated toward the peripheries—the rural schools, the refugee learning centers, the urban neighborhoods where internet access is a luxury and not a given.

There is also the matter of *ownership*. Who owns the tools, the platforms, the data generated by millions of digital learning interactions? In too many cases, the answer is not the learners or their communities but private corporations whose business models rely on monetizing data or locking institutions into proprietary ecosystems. A serious policy for equity has to address this asymmetry. This could mean mandating open-source alternatives, negotiating public-interest licensing agreements, or establishing data sovereignty protections so that student information cannot be extracted and commodified without consent. Without such measures, the digital classroom becomes yet another site of extraction, where value flows away from the communities generating it.

Teacher agency is another fault line. Policies that treat educators merely as implementers of centrally procured technologies miss the point (Lee & Lee, 2024). Teachers are not passive conduits; they are interpreters, gatekeepers, and, at times, resistors. For digital learning to serve equity, teachers must be part of the decision-making process—not just in pilot phases but in shaping long-term strategies. This requires policies that invest in teacher training not as a one-off workshop but as an ongoing professional dialogue, integrating pedagogical practice with evolving technology in a way that honors local context.

One often-overlooked dimension is the pace of policy implementation (Kang et al, 2023). There is a temptation to move fast, to announce bold digital rollouts as proof of modernization. But speed without reflection can entrench disparities. Imagine a nationwide deployment of AI-based learning platforms in a country where half the schools have stable internet and half do not. The policy might look like a leap forward on paper, but in reality, it widens the gap—those with connectivity surge ahead while others watch from the sidelines. An equity-centered approach might mean slower deployment, but with the guarantee that each stage addresses readiness gaps before moving to the next.

The content itself is a policy concern, though it often gets left to curriculum departments or outsourced entirely to vendors. Digital learning platforms are not neutral delivery systems; the materials they host embody specific cultural, political, and epistemological assumptions. A truly inclusive policy would require content audits for cultural relevance, linguistic accessibility, and representation—not as sporadic reviews but as part of the quality assurance process. It would also create mechanisms for local content creation, ensuring that students can learn not only *about* the world but also *from within* their own world.

Monitoring and evaluation mechanisms must be designed to capture more than quantitative indicators (Ba, 2021). If a policy's success is measured solely by the number of devices distributed or the percentage of schools with Wi-Fi, it will miss the subtler—and arguably more important—question: is learning becoming more equitable? This calls for mixed-method approaches that combine hard metrics with qualitative insights: student voices, teacher narratives, community feedback. Such measures resist easy standardization, but without them, policymakers risk confusing activity for impact.

Another critical pathway involves forging alliances beyond the education sector. Digital inequities often reflect broader social inequities: poverty, housing instability, gender discrimination, geographic isolation (Helsper, 2021). Policies that address only the school-based aspects of access will struggle against these larger forces. Cross-sector collaboration—with telecommunications, social services, cultural ministries, and community organizations—can help align resources and strategies. For example, a policy might link school connectivity programs with rural electrification projects, or integrate digital literacy initiatives with adult education programs so that learning becomes a community-wide capacity rather than a school-bound service.

International cooperation also has a role, though it carries its own set of tensions. Global partnerships can bring in funding, technical expertise, and access to cutting-edge tools, but they can also impose one-size-fits-all models that flatten local diversity (Voss, 2024). Equity-focused policies should engage with international frameworks selectively, adopting what aligns with local priorities while resisting pressures to conform to external benchmarks that ignore cultural and economic realities.

Accountability must be distributed but clear. A policy that spreads responsibility so widely that no one feels it is theirs to uphold is a policy designed to evaporate under pressure. Lines of responsibility should be explicit: who ensures infrastructure maintenance, who oversees data privacy, who evaluates pedagogical impact. At the same time, accountability should not become punitive to the point of discouraging experimentation. Digital learning is still an evolving space; policies need to protect the space for innovation while guarding against harms.

Perhaps the deepest challenge is philosophical: deciding what kind of digital learning environment counts as "equitable." Is it one where every student has identical resources, or one where resources are distributed according to need? Is it enough to give all students the same digital tools, or must those tools be adapted to different ways of knowing and learning? These questions have no simple answers, but without wrestling with them explicitly, policies will default to the path of least resistance—standardization masquerading as equality.

In the end, policy pathways for equity and access in digital learning are not linear roads but braided streams, intersecting and diverging depending on context (Christanti et al, 2024). They require adaptability without losing ethical direction, collaboration without surrendering local autonomy, ambition tempered by patience. The task is not to design a perfect system—none exists—but to create the conditions under which inequities can be recognized early, addressed deliberately, and prevented from becoming structural features of the digital learning landscape.

Equity is not a destination you arrive at and declare the journey over. It is a posture, a constant recalibration, an openness to hearing from those whose needs are not being met. If digital learning policies can carry that posture forward—embedding it in funding mechanisms, governance structures, teacher development, and content creation—then technology might finally serve as the bridge it has long promised to be, rather than the moat it too often becomes.

NAVIGATING THE HUMAN–MACHINE PARTNERSHIP IN EDUCATION

The conversation about AI in education often gets snagged in a binary: the machine as either the usurper of human roles or the obedient servant (Cant et al, 2024). In reality, neither captures the strange intimacy of what is emerging—a partnership, awkward and uneven at times, between human educators and computational systems that can process more information in seconds than a human could in a lifetime. The trick, if there is one, is not to decide once and for all whether this is "good" or "bad," but to learn how to move within it without losing our footing, to find a rhythm where the machine extends human capacity without hollowing it out.

Partnerships of any kind require boundaries, trust, and the ability to adapt when one side missteps (Faulconbridge et al, 2025). The trouble here is that AI doesn't experience trust or mistrust, nor does it feel the weight of responsibility when something goes wrong (Kayyali, 2024 B). That burden remains human. Which means that the relationship is inherently asymmetrical—the human party is accountable, the machine is not. This alone should temper the current rhetoric about "AI replacing teachers" or "AI being just another tool." It is neither a full substitute nor a simple pencil; it is a force multiplier, and like any multiplier, it amplifies both strengths and weaknesses already present in the system.

To navigate this terrain, we have to think less about "integration" in the technical sense and more about choreography. Where does the human step forward, and where does the machine step back? What is the texture of an interaction where both are involved? Imagine a history lesson: the AI can instantly generate primary sources from multiple languages, offer context, even simulate debates between historical figures. The teacher, meanwhile, can sense when a student's expression flickers with doubt, when a comment carries the weight of personal experience, when the discussion veers into moral territory that requires care (Aldrich, 2025). The machine has reach; the human has resonance. One without the other is incomplete.

And yet, the line between reach and resonance is not always sharp. There will be moments when the AI seems to offer empathy—crafting a response that mirrors the tone of a struggling student—and moments when the teacher delivers information with the precision of a data-driven answer. The boundaries blur. That's where the danger of over-reliance creeps in. If teachers begin outsourcing too much of the cognitive heavy lifting to AI—lesson planning, grading, feedback—their role risks shrinking to that of a supervisor, more focused on overseeing workflow than engaging in the unpredictable, messy act of teaching (Aboodi, 2025).

On the other hand, ignoring AI entirely is its own kind of abdication. Students are already experimenting with it, sometimes privately, sometimes with their peers, discovering both its shortcuts and its flaws (Mickelsen, 2025). If educators retreat from this space, they cede the ground to unmediated use, where the technology's biases, limitations, and seductive efficiencies go unexamined. A partnership implies mutual shaping: the machine influences how we teach and learn, and we, in turn, influence how the machine is used, refined, and even conceived.

The emotional landscape of this partnership is worth noting. For some teachers, AI represents relief—the possibility of shedding repetitive tasks and reclaiming time for deeper engagement with students. For others, it triggers anxiety: about job security, about the erosion of professional identity, about the subtle replacement of human judgment with algorithmic suggestion. Both reactions are valid, and any serious navigation of this partnership has to create space for these tensions rather than brushing them aside with blanket optimism.

There is also the question of authority. In the traditional classroom, the teacher's authority rests on a blend of subject expertise, pedagogical skill, and the personal credibility built over time (Sliwka et al, 2024). Introduce AI into the mix, and suddenly the teacher is no longer the sole—or even the primary—source of certain types of information. Some students may begin to see the machine as a more "objective" authority, especially when it delivers polished, confident answers in seconds. This shifts the teacher's role toward that of an interpreter or mediator, someone who can explain not only the subject matter but also the strengths and blind spots of the machine's reasoning.

And perhaps that's one of the central skills for this era: teaching students how to have a critical conversation with an AI system. Not just how to prompt it effectively, but how to question its assumptions, spot when it is speaking beyond its knowledge, and cross-check its outputs against other sources. This is literacy in its expanded sense—not only the ability to read and write, but to navigate the ecology of human–machine discourse. A partnership in which students become passive recipients of AI output is not a partnership at all; it is a quiet transfer of agency from the learner to the algorithm.

The institutional context shapes this dynamic as much as individual practice does. A school that frames AI as a collaborative tool, offering professional development and encouraging experimentation, will foster a very different partnership than one that adopts AI primarily as a cost-saving measure (Knibbe et al, 2024). In the latter, the pressure to "scale" education can lead to situations where a single teacher, supported by AI, is expected to handle twice the usual number of students. The technology might function well in such a scenario, but the relational fabric of education will thin.

One way to preserve that fabric is to anchor policy and practice in what might be called *pedagogical non-negotiables*—elements of teaching and learning that will not be delegated to machines (Sharma, 2023). This could include mentoring relationships, certain forms of assessment that require human judgment, or the facilitation of sensitive discussions. By making these boundaries explicit, schools send a signal that the human dimension is not an optional luxury but the core around which AI can orbit.

The partnership also demands adaptability over time. AI tools evolve rapidly, and what seems groundbreaking one year can feel obsolete the next (Sridhar et al, 2025). Teachers and institutions must be prepared for the emotional and logistical churn that comes with this pace of change. The machine will not slow down; the human side must decide when to keep pace and when to step out of the race. Sometimes the most ethical decision is not to adopt the latest feature or platform, but to pause, evaluate, and consider its implications for learners who are more than just nodes in a network.

Cultural context weaves another layer into this navigation. In some educational settings, the idea of conversing with a machine about personal struggles might feel alien, even inappropriate (Aslanimehr, 2025). In others, it might be embraced as a safe, low-stakes way to articulate thoughts before sharing them with a human teacher. A successful partnership will have to respect these variations rather than imposing a uniform model of human–machine interaction.

It's also worth acknowledging that the partnership is not evenly matched across the globe. In affluent contexts, "navigating" the partnership may involve fine-tuning the balance between AI support and teacher agency. In under-resourced contexts, the partnership might begin with something far more basic: ensuring that there is any access to the machine at all. The language of partnership must stretch to include both realities, or else it risks becoming the rhetoric of privilege.

Ultimately, navigating the human–machine partnership in education is less about drawing a clean map than about learning to live with shifting terrain (Capel & Brereton, 2023). The goal is not to reach a final equilibrium—there may never be one—but to cultivate an agility that allows both sides to move in ways that keep the learner's growth at the center. Sometimes the human will lead, sometimes the machine will, and sometimes the most important act will be to step aside and let the learner take the lead.

That, perhaps, is the most radical possibility in all this: that the real partnership is not between teacher and machine at all, but between the learner and the constellation of human and technological resources available to them. If we can shape that constellation so that it empowers rather than constrains, challenges rather than flattens, and listens as much as it speaks, then the human–machine partnership in education might become something genuinely worthy of the name.

CONCLUSION

The story of generative AI in education is still being written, and whether it will be remembered as a tool of emancipation or exclusion depends largely on the decisions we make now. As with every educational innovation, the challenge lies not merely in *what* the technology can do, but in *how* and *why* it is deployed. History has shown that new tools can reinforce old hierarchies unless equity is deliberately embedded in their design, distribution, and governance.

The ethical implications are far from theoretical. When AI models replicate societal biases in the content they produce, they risk perpetuating the very inequalities education is meant to dismantle. When access to these tools is gated by infrastructure, cost, or language, they transform from democratizing forces into gatekeepers of opportunity. The responsibility, therefore, does not rest solely on the shoulders of engineers and AI companies; it extends to educators, school leaders, policymakers, and the communities they serve. It is a shared ethical project.

An equitable AI-enabled education system must begin with representation in data and design—ensuring that the diverse realities of learners, especially those from marginalized communities, are reflected in the datasets and ethical frameworks guiding AI development. It must continue with policies that protect against exclusion—investing in infrastructure, teacher training, and open-access resources so that the benefits of AI are not concentrated in a few well-funded institutions. And it must culminate in pedagogical practices that treat AI as a partner in critical inquiry, not as a substitute for human engagement.

The goal is not to slow innovation but to guide it—anchoring technological progress in values that ensure no learner is invisible in the system's eyes. This requires courage to confront uncomfortable truths about bias, power, and privilege in both human and machine decision-making. It demands a shift from reactive policy-making to proactive, ethically grounded strategies that place human flourishing at the center of AI integration in education.

If generative AI is to fulfill its promise as an equalizer, we must see it not as a neutral tool, but as a mirror of our societal choices. A mirror that can either reflect our inequities or our aspirations for justice. The difference will depend on whether we treat equity and access as optional features or as the very foundation of our AI-enabled educational future. In shaping that future, we are not only defining the role of technology in the classroom but also reaffirming what we believe education itself should stand for.

REFERENCES

Aboodi, R. (2025). The Worrisome Potential of Outsourcing Critical Thinking to Artificial Intelligence. *Educational Theory.*

Agarwal, R., & Bhatnagar, A. (2025). Transforming Education: Harnessing the Power of AI to Empower Educators. Productivity, 66(1).

Ahmad, I., & Islam, M. R. (2024). Empowerment and participation: Key strategies for inclusive development. In *Building strong communities: Ethical approaches to inclusive development* (pp. 47–68). Emerald Publishing Limited.

Ahmed, F. (2024). The digital divide and AI in education: Addressing equity and accessibility. *AI EDIFY Journal, 1*(2), 12–23.

Albeihi, H. H. M., & Rice, M. F. (2025). Generative AI and language diversity: Implications for teachers and learners.

Aldrich, T. (2025). Literary Postcritique and American Transcendentalism: Helping Students Practice Community-Building by Rewilding Literature in the Classroom (Doctoral dissertation, University of Arkansas).

Aslanimehr, P. (2025). *Exile as an Educative Engagement: The Dizziness of Recognition*. Taylor & Francis.

Auger, S., Besnier, J. B., van Bijnen, M., Cherqui, F., Chuzeville, G., Clemens, F. H. L., ... & Ugarelli, R. M. (2024). Data management and quality control. Asset Management of Urban Drainage Systems: If anything exciting happens, we've done it wrong!.

Ba, A. (2021). How to measure monitoring and evaluation system effectiveness? *African Evaluation Journal, 9*(1), 953.

Balaji, M. T. M., & Balajiraja, N. UMA, M. P., & Nair, M. S. P. (2025). Generative AI Tools: Concepts, Applications, and Innovations. Academic Guru Publishing House.

Bardone, E., Mõttus, P., & Eradze, M. (2024). Tinkering as a complement to design in the context of technology integration in teaching and learning. *Postdigital Science and Education, 6*(1), 114–134.

Behera, S. K., Ibrahim, A. H., & Romdhani, F. (Eds.). (2024). *Inclusive educational practices and technologies for promoting sustainability*. IGI Global.

Bircan, T., & Özbilgin, M. F. (2025). Unmasking inequalities of the code: Disentangling the nexus of AI and inequality. *Technological Forecasting and Social Change*, *211*, 123925.

Bozkurt, A., Junhong, X., Lambert, S., Pazurek, A., Crompton, H., Koseoglu, S., & Romero-Hall, E. (2023). Speculative futures on ChatGPT and generative artificial intelligence (AI): A collective reflection from the educational landscape. *Asian Journal of Distance Education*, *18*(1), 53–130.

Bridewell, W., Bello, P. F., & Bringsjord, S. (2024). The Technology of Outrage: Bias in Artificial Intelligence. arXiv preprint arXiv:2409.17336.

Cameron, F. R. (2021). *The future of digital data, heritage and curation: in a more-than-human world*. Routledge.

Cant, C., Muldoon, J., & Graham, M. (2024). *Feeding the machine: The hidden human labor powering AI*. Bloomsbury Publishing USA.

Capel, T., & Brereton, M. (2023, April). What is human-centered about human-centered AI? A map of the research landscape. In *Proceedings of the 2023 CHI conference on human factors in computing systems* (pp. 1-23).

Christanti, M. F., Mawangir, M., Arevin, A. T., Ramadhan, I., & Limijadi, E. K. S. (2024). The digital divide in education: Bridging gaps in the era of online learning. *Migration Letters : An International Journal of Migration Studies*, *21*(S4), 1070–1079.

Dinker, N. (2024). Artificial intelligence and inequality: examining the social divides created by technological advancements. International Journal of Innovations in Science, Engineering And Management, 228-236.

Faulconbridge, J., Sarwar, A., & Spring, M. (2025). How professionals adapt to artificial intelligence: The role of intertwined boundary work. *Journal of Management Studies*, *62*(5), 1991–2024.

Ford, B., Bernholz, L., Landemore, H., & Reich, R. (2021). Technologizing democracy or democratizing technology? A layered-architecture perspective on potentials and challenges. Digital technology and democratic theory, 274-321.

Harden, P., & Fanfarelli, J. R. (2023). Boundaries, Informed Consent, and Learning. In Ethical Considerations of Virtual Reality in the College Classroom (pp. 293-304). Routledge.

Helsper, E. (2021). The digital disconnect: The social causes and consequences of digital inequalities.

Helvie, F. C. (2025). *Ghost in the Classroom: A Practical Guide to AI, Pedagogy, and Possibility*. Forrest C. Helvie.

Kang, B., Ma, X., Du, C., Pang, T., & Yan, S. (2023). Efficient diffusion policies for offline reinforcement learning. *Advances in Neural Information Processing Systems*, *36*, 67195–67212.

Kayyali, M. (2022). Equity, Equality, Diversity, and Inclusion as Key Performance Indicators in Higher Education. *Online Submission*, *3*(5), 1–3.

Kayyali, M. (2024). A). Future directions towards sustainable educational equity: Policies and practices. In *Exploring Educational Equity at the Intersection of Policy and Practice* (pp. 81–100). IGI Global Scientific Publishing.

Kayyali, M. (2024). B). Future possibilities and challenges of AI in education. In *Transforming education with generative AI: Prompt engineering and synthetic content creation* (pp. 118–137). IGI Global Scientific Publishing.

Kayyali, M. (2025 A). The Future of AI in Education: Predictions and Emerging Trends. Next-Generation AI Methodologies in Education, 367-406.

Kayyali, M. (2025 B). AI in Higher Education: Revolutionizing Curriculum and Administration. In AI Adoption and Diffusion in Education (pp. 31-62). IGI Global Scientific Publishing.

Kayyali, M. (2025 C). Ethical Implications of Generative AI in Education: Privacy, Bias, and Integrity. In Transformative AI Practices for Personalized Learning Strategies (pp. 185-218). IGI Global Scientific Publishing.

Kayyali, M. (2026). AI in Education: Learning Platforms for Personalized Learning. In Advanced Interdisciplinary Applications of Large Language Models and AI Agents (pp. 83-108). IGI Global Scientific Publishing.

Kim, J. H., Moldavan, A. M., Terry, R., & Massey, C. C. (2025). Enhancing Student Engagement With Generative AI. In *Transformative AI Practices for Personalized Learning Strategies* (pp. 69–106). IGI Global Scientific Publishing.

Knibbe, J., Peschl, R., & Osiyevskyy, O. (2024). Unleashing Creative Potential: The Role of Generative AI in Business Education. In Impacts of Generative AI on Creativity in Higher Education (pp. 399-422). IGI Global.

Kumashiro, K. K. (2024). *Against common sense: Teaching and learning toward social justice*. Routledge.

Lee, S., & Lee, K. (2024). Smart teachers in smart schools in a smart city: Teachers as adaptive agents of educational technology reforms. *Learning, Media and Technology*, *49*(3), 456–477.

Luckin, R. (2025). Nurturing human intelligence in the age of AI: Rethinking education for the future. *Development and Learning in Organizations*, *39*(1), 1–4.

Madaio, M., Blodgett, S. L., Mayfield, E., & Dixon-Román, E. (2022). Beyond "fairness": Structural (in) justice lenses on ai for education. In The ethics of artificial intelligence in education (pp. 203-239). Routledge.

Marrero, A. (2024). In the Crosshairs: Navigating Political Pressures as a New Leader. In Pursuing Equity and Success for Marginalized Educational Leaders (pp. 101-117). IGI Global.

Mergen, A., Çetin-Kılıç, N., & Özbilgin, M. F. (2025). Artificial intelligence and bias towards marginalised groups: Theoretical roots and challenges. In *AI and Diversity in a Datafied World of Work: Will the Future of Work be Inclusive?* (Vol. 12, pp. 17–38). Emerald Publishing Limited.

Mickelsen, S. B. (2025). Exploring the Role of AI and Educators in Shaping Student Creativity.

NAKAMURA, T. M. (2025). ETHICAL AI IN US NEWSPAPER COVERAGE: MEDIA FRAMING AND CORPORATE ACCOUNTABILITY.

Norman-Major, K. (2023). Balancing the four Es; or can we achieve equity for social equity in public administration? In *Social Equity in the Public Administration Classroom* (pp. 27–46). Routledge.

Pedrazas, M. A., Hahm, W. J., Huang, M. H., Dralle, D., Nelson, M. D., Breunig, R. E., ... & Rempe, D. M. (2021). The relationship between topography, bedrock weathering, and water storage across a sequence of ridges and valleys. Journal of Geophysical Research: Earth Surface, 126(4), e2020JF005848.

Pettitt, J. (2023). How Exemplary Female Executive Leaders in Higher Education Use Five Principles of Grit—Courage, Conscientiousness, Long-Term Goals, Resilience, and Excellence Versus Perfection—to Accomplish Extraordinary Results in Their Organizations (Doctoral dissertation, University of Massachusetts Global).

Prangon, N. F., & Wu, J. (2024). AI and computing horizons: Cloud and edge in the modern era. *Journal of Sensor and Actuator Networks*, *13*(4), 44.

Puplampu, R. (2024). *What Everyone Should Know About the Rise of AI: AI Transparency, Privacy, and Ethics Best Practices*. Puplampu Books.

Rahimi, Z., & Azadmanesh, S. (2025). Educational Justice in the Age of Artificial Intelligence through the Lens of Deconstruction Theory. It is under consideration.

Rainie, L., & Anderson, J. (2024). Experts imagine the impact of artificial intelligence by 2040. Imagining the Digital Future Center. *Retrieved*, (December), 15.

Reddy, K. J. (2025). Accessibility and Affordability of Technologies. In *Innovations in Neurocognitive Rehabilitation: Harnessing Technology for Effective Therapy* (pp. 285–304). Springer Nature Switzerland.

Schuster, N. (2023). The skill model: A dilemma for virtue ethics. *Ethical Theory and Moral Practice*, *26*(3), 447–461.

Secl, M. J. (2025). The Educational Perspective of At-Risk Students: How Standards-Based Grading Affects Students in Alternative Education.

Sharma, L. (2023). *Building Culture: A handbook to harnessing human nature to create strong school teams*.

Sliwka, A., Klopsch, B., Beigel, J., & Tung, L. (2024). Transformational leadership for deeper learning: Shaping innovative school practices for enhanced learning. *Journal of Educational Administration*, *62*(1), 103–121.

Sridhar, A., Pesala, B., Radhakrishnan, G., Niezgoda, J., & Gopalakrishnan, S. (2025). Evolution of Artificial Intelligence. In *Artificial Intelligence and Biological Sciences* (pp. 26–37). CRC Press.

Taylor, C., Dewsbury, B., & Brame, C. (2022). Technology, equity, and inclusion in the virtual education space. In *Technologies in Biomedical and Life Sciences Education: Approaches and evidence of efficacy for learning* (pp. 35–60). Springer International Publishing.

Tripathi, A., Yadav, V., & Kumar, S. (2025). Leveraging artificial intelligence for rural education: A systematic review of transforming learning opportunities and bridging the urban-rural divide.

Voss, A. (2024). The Future We're Building: How Today's Innovations Will Shape Tomorrow's World. eBookIt. com.

Wang, S., Xu, T., Li, H., Zhang, C., Liang, J., Tang, J., . . . Wen, Q. (2024). Large language models for education: A survey and outlook. arXiv preprint arXiv:2403.18105.

Yahya, S. I., Alameri, B. M., Jamshidi, M., Roshani, S., Chaudhary, M. A., Ijemaru, G. K., & Roshani, S. (2022). A new design method for class-E power amplifiers using artificial intelligence modeling for wireless power transfer applications. *Electronics (Basel)*, *11*(21), 3608.

Youvan, D. C. (2024). Amplification Through Progression: From Analog Signals to Artificial Intelligence.

Chapter 3
Rethinking Artificial Intelligence Implementation for Inclusive and Equitable Quality Higher Education in South Africa

Godwin Kaisara
https://orcid.org/0000-0002-5684-6764
Namibia University of Science and Technology, Namibia

Khulekani Yakobi
https://orcid.org/0000-0001-7568-5065
Mangosuthu University of Technology, South Africa

Kabiru Ishola Genty
Namibia University of Science and Technology, Namibia & Lagos State University, Nigeria

Sulaiman Olusegun Atiku
https://orcid.org/0000-0001-9364-3774
Namibia University of Science and Technology, Namibia & Walter Sisulu University, South Africa

ABSTRACT

Generative Artificial Intelligence (GenAI) is rapidly transforming global higher education, offering both unprecedented opportunities and complex challenges.

DOI: 10.4018/979-8-3373-3745-6.ch003

In South Africa, where the legacy of apartheid has entrenched deep educational inequalities, the strategic implementation of GenAI holds the potential to either bridge or widen existing divides. This chapter critically examines how GenAI can be harnessed to promote inclusive and equitable quality higher education in South Africa, while addressing the structural, ethical, and practical challenges that accompany its adoption. Drawing insights from a comprehensive synthesis of the existing literature on GenAI and education, this chapter argues that the AI revolution has the potential to either narrow or intensify existing educational inequalities in South Africa. If not implemented equitably, GenAI may further widen the gap between historically privileged and marginalised universities. The chapter suggests the need for critical dialogue to ensure that GenAI catalyses an inclusive and equitable higher education in South Africa.

INTRODUCTION

Artificial Intelligence (AI) has developed exponentially, revolutionizing industries and extending the realms of what is possible for humanity since its first conceptualization in the 1950s. Recent technological advancements, particularly in the domain of neural networks and machine learning, have made Generative AI (GenAI) increasingly play a critical role in contemporary society. The emergence of GenAI is accompanied by a broad range of opportunities and challenges, depending on what GenAI means to different stakeholders. For example, one of the industries that has been significantly transformed by GenAI in recent times is higher education (Zawacki-Richter *et al.*, 2019). As noted by Fontanillas and colleagues, GenAI offers students an opportunity to access more and better-quality education (Fontanillas et al., 2025). As a result, governments all over the world are making significant investments in GenAI to improve the reach and quality of education (Chatterjee & Bhattacharjee, 2020) The global emphasis on quality education for all, as espoused in the United Nation's Sustainable Development Goal 4, ensures that GenAI's potential to increase inclusivity continues to gain attention. Commentators have labeled AI as a "game changer" that can leapfrog development in various industries, including education (Kumar *et al.*, 2023). Recently, there has been a burgeoning body of knowledge illuminating various facets of GenAI in higher education institutions (HEIs). According to the World Economic Forum's (WEF) projections, Global spending on AI in education is estimated to increase from $5.18 billion to about $112.3 billion in 2034 (Haoyang & Towne, 2025).

While Global GenAI adoption continues to increase, the technology's adoption is still in its infancy in Africa. Countries like China, the UK, and the US are leading in GenAI investment and implementation, reporting improved educational experiences and operational impacts. According to Mutambara (2025), GenAI improves personalized learning pathways and educational content generation, enhancing learning outcomes and access in countries with diverse educational challenges. Consequently, students in regions with poor digital development, such as sub-Saharan Africa, often miss out on the benefits of GenAI commonly enjoyed by their peers in developed countries (Hughes et al, 2025).

Nevertheless, countries such as Nigeria, Kenya, Ghana, Rwanda and South Africa have deployed relatively advanced GenAI initiatives. This is unsurprising, given that the foregoing countries have been among the continental leaders in the deployment of educational technology (Kaisara & Bwalya, 2022). South Africa's robust AI ecosystem, in particular, positions it as the continental leader in AI adoption and research (Ade-Ibijola & Okonkwo, 2023). Most of the extant body of knowledge in GenAI in HEIs emanates from the Global North, and the domain area is largely underdeveloped in the Global South. Therefore, there is a need for more discourse advancing the contextual nuances of the Global South. As with any technological innovation, GenAI needs to be aligned with the context in which it is applied. This is further necessitated by the fact that most technological interventions in the Global South largely fail due to an overreliance on Global North know-how, with little emphasis on contextual differences (Kaisara et al., 2021).

The purpose of this chapter is to discuss how GenAI may be implemented for inclusive and equitable quality higher education in South Africa. This is essential given that proactive GenAI implementation strategies can position HEIs as responsible stakeholders that promote educational parity regardless of socio-economic status (Hughes et al. 2025). The chapter is informed by a thorough literature review, drawing insights from various disciplines such as education, information systems, and development. The chapter is structured as follows: Section two provides the background and justification of the theoretical framework underpinning the chapter. Section three reports on the South African HEIs' context, elucidating the historical background and its influence on the modern higher education landscape. Section four discusses the challenges and barriers to equitable AI implementation in South Africa. Section five outlines how GenAI can act as a catalyst for inclusive and quality higher education. The sixth section proposes strategies that could guide policymakers in their quest for inclusive and equitable AI implementation. This is followed by recommendations, limitations, avenues for future research, and conclusions.

BACKGROUND

The theoretical framework underpinning this chapter is a realism-inspired approach, grounded in the work of Lin (2024), who critiques the prevailing ethical frameworks of GenAI, which is based on principlism, rigid formalism, and technological solutionism for their limited applicability to the real-world challenges posed by GenAI technologies.

Principlism, as defined by Lin, involves adherence to abstract, high-level ethical principles such as fairness, justice, transparency, and privacy. While these principles are well-intentioned, Lin argues that they are often too vague and context-insensitive to guide ethical decision-making effectively in dynamic academic environments. Similarly, rigid formalism refers to the strict, literal application of ethical rules without accommodating the specific nuances of context, which can lead to inflexible and impractical outcomes. Technological solutionism, on the other hand, reflects the mistaken belief that ethical problems can be solved solely through more advanced technical tools or model improvements. Lin (2024) argues that this approach neglects the inherently social, cultural, and institutional dimensions of AI deployment.

Lin (2024) emphasizes that traditional frameworks fall short of addressing the complex realities of research practices, especially in academic environments characterized by infrastructural, linguistic, or systemic inequalities. He contends that overreliance on abstract principles like fairness is problematic, as such terms are contested and can vary significantly depending on context. For example, efforts to enhance transparency may conflict with privacy obligations, and different interpretations of fairness may contradict each other (Lin, 2024).

Within the context of GenAI, Lin argues that the proliferation of high-level AI ethics principles has led to a "Triple-Too" problem: too many initiatives, too abstract principles, and too much emphasis on risks rather than benefits. These abstract principles often fail to translate into actionable practices within the nuanced realities of scientific research. Lin's realism advocates that GenAI needs to recognize inherent social and cultural disparity, rather than applying uniform rules or relying solely on technological solutions. Understanding these limitations and functionality is an appropriate way to promote ethical behavior through contextualized strategies especially for Gen AI in HEIs as it is applicable in South Africa.

CURRENT LANDSCAPE OF AI IN SOUTH AFRICAN HIGHER EDUCATION

GenAI is steadily reshaping the landscape of HEIs in South Africa (Aithal & Maiya, 2023), reflecting global innovation trends while simultaneously responding to unique local socio-economic and infrastructural realities (Omodan, 2024). While the transformative potential of GenAI in HEIs is widely acknowledged, its successful implementation within the South African context hinges on addressing protracted structural inequalities, investing in digital infrastructure and skills development for technological integration (Opesemowo & Adekomaya, 2024). Across the HEIs sector in South Africa, it is evident that some universities are beginning to explore and implement AI-driven tools and systems to enhance administrative efficiency, academic delivery, student engagement, and research capabilities (Atiku & Boateng, 2020; Patel & Ragolane, 2024). As such, several South African universities have initiated pilot projects and strategic integrations of AI technologies for teaching and learning, administration, and library services. For example, the University of the Western Cape (UWC), Mangosuthu University of Technology (MUT), the University of Pretoria, and the University of Fort Hare have all made significant strides in adopting AI-enhanced educational practices. An empirical study established that AI research hubs at universities like Pretoria and Witwatersrand support both academic research and operational use cases (Maimela & Mbonde, 2025). This assertion was supported in the work of Funda and Mbageleli (2024), where the scholars argued that AI adoption enhances personalized learning, administrative automation, and student performance analyses. For instance, at UWC, Bayaga (2025) reports the use of GenAI in teaching, learning, and research, particularly within the Faculty of Law. The study surveyed both students and staff, revealing insights into adoption intentions and engendered attitudes towards GenAI in academic contexts. Similarly, a survey conducted by Xulu and colleagues involving 184 students at MUT found that ChatGPT and similar tools were perceived as valuable for learning support, academic writing, and engagement, though concerns about academic integrity and dependency were noted (Xulu et al., 2024).

The University of Pretoria has also incorporated AI into its institutional operations, particularly in library services. Funda and Francke (2024) highlight that the implementation of robotic systems such as the *"Libby"* assistant has shown potential to support educational management functions in the university. *"Libby"* was designed to improve student engagement and information access, offering round-the-clock support for frequently asked questions and library services. By improving the university's responsiveness and information availability, *"Libby"* enhances the service experience of students. Mbangeleli and Funda (2024) confirm an increasing adoption of AI-powered tools for administrative optimization and enhanced student support. Similarly, Maphalala and Ajani (2025) noted the presence of AI learning tools across multiple institutions, reflecting a growing momentum in digital innovation within the South African higher education landscape.

Furthermore, GenAI integration in HEIs has significantly expanded into student-facing technologies, such as learning management systems (LMSs) and virtual support services. These systems are being augmented with AI functionalities to personalize learning experiences, provide real-time feedback, and support adaptive learning pathways (Rane et al., 2023). Chen et al. (2023) postulate that chatbots and virtual assistants are now commonly used to manage routine student inquiries, offer academic support, and provide continuous access to institutional resources. There are some notable efforts made by certain universities in South Africa to introduce GenAI-powered tools. According to SIS Global (2024), the University of the Free State launched *"KovsieChat,"* an AI chatbot powered by GPT-4 in 2024. This tool handles a wide array of student inquiries, ranging from course information to administrative assistance, and supports multilingual interactions across eleven of South Africa's official languages. The tool has processed over 5 million messages from more than 77,000 users since its inception. A study conducted by Mungai et al. (2024) highlights the efforts at Nelson Mandela University to embed GenAI tools within LMS environments to enhance learner engagement and customize content delivery based on individual learner profiles. Similarly, the University of Cape Town (UCT) introduced *"Zizu,"* a chatbot integrated into its Gender-Based Violence (GBV) app *"Kwanele"* to provide confidential support and information to staff and students (University of Cape Town, 2024). At the University of Fort Hare, Funda and Cilliers (2024) reported that over 80% of surveyed students used GenAI tools such as ChatGPT to enhance their academic writing. While 61% indicated improved output quality, the study also highlighted concerns about dependency, digital literacy, and the ethical use of such tools. These findings align with pedagogical reviews, such as that by Mungai *et al.* (2024), which highlight the role of LMS-integrated AI systems in facilitating quizzes, self-paced learning, and instructional feedback through continuous data monitoring.

Research in this domain shows that AI has facilitated significant advancements across disciplines, particularly in data analytics, Natural Language Processing (NLP), and Machine Learning (ML). There is growing interest in interdisciplinary research involving AI applications in sectors such as health sciences, agriculture, and finance. Leading institutions such as the University of Pretoria and the University of the Witwatersrand have established AI-focused research centers and innovation hubs that contribute to both local development and global AI scholarship. At the University of Pretoria, the work of Cassez et al. (2023) illustrated AI applications in NLP, including the development of word embeddings, data augmentation methods, and language datasets for under-resourced African languages. These are essential for tasks such as document classification, Named Entity Recognition (NER), and automated translation.

As demonstrated through multiple case studies, universities in South Africa are progressively integrating GenAI into teaching, learning, administration, and research. However, this evolving landscape calls for a more comprehensive understanding of the systemic enablers and constraints underpinning such transformation. Central to the successful integration of GenAI is the development of robust policy and governance frameworks (Chan, 2023). For this reason, national directives and institutional strategies must coalesce to guide ethical, sustainable, and context-sensitive implementation. Currently, many HEIs are still in the process of aligning GenAI adoption with broader digital transformation strategies under the oversight of the Department of Higher Education and Training (DHET), often without clear operational frameworks. The dearth of AI policies or operational frameworks is not only confined to the higher education space but is prevalent across various industries in Africa.

Simultaneously, concerns regarding ethics and academic integrity have become increasingly prominent (Mahabeer & Pirtheepal, 2019). These challenges are not limited to developing countries, but also in digitally advanced countries such as Estonia (Kalmus & Nikiforova, 2024). According to Hutson (2024), the proliferation of GenAI tools has introduced complex dilemmas around authorship, plagiarism, surveillance, and algorithmic bias. Institutions are beginning to address these concerns by developing internal policies, but there is a need for coordinated sector-wide guidelines to support ethical decision-making and preserve the integrity of academic work (Akande & Atiku, 2022). Furthermore, digital equity and inclusion remain critical challenges. Although some urban and historically advantaged universities have launched sophisticated AI systems, many rural and under-resourced institutions face barriers related to infrastructure, bandwidth, and device access (Yakobi & Yakobi, 2025). This digital divide risks exacerbating educational inequalities unless deliberate efforts are made to ensure inclusive design and equitable access to GenAI tools across linguistic, socio-economic, and geographic lines.

The human element of this transformation necessitates ongoing capacity building and professional development. Faculty readiness and staff competence are foundational to GenAI integration. Institutional investment in digital literacy, AI training, and pedagogical innovation is essential. Specific training on various aspects of GenAI should not only be limited to staff but also extended to students, as it enhances their understanding of different facets of GenAI (Fontanillas et al., 2025). Centers for Teaching and Learning (CTLs) and institutional development offices play a key role in equipping educators with the skills needed to adapt and innovate in AI enabled learning environments. In parallel, the transformation of curricula has become an emergent imperative. Universities are beginning to revise programs to incorporate AI literacy and interdisciplinary competencies, preparing graduates for an AI-driven world of work. The integration of GenAI into curricular design, especially within non-technical disciplines, is gaining momentum and necessitates updated accreditation mechanisms and quality assurance systems. To ensure long-term viability, there is a growing need for systematic monitoring, evaluation, and impact assessment of GenAI initiatives. Beerkens (2020) suggests that institutions must adopt evidence-based practices to measure educational outcomes, user engagement, and administrative improvements, while also capturing unintended consequences and disparities. This will inform iterative development and policy refinement.

Moreover, strategic partnerships and innovation ecosystems are proving instrumental in advancing GenAI capabilities. Faisal et al. (2017) confirmed that collaborations with industry, government, and international research consortia have enabled knowledge transfer, research funding, and technological development. In the pursuit of GenAI in education, collaboration may benefit from engagements with both local actors and international entities such as the United Nations, which has long promoted inclusive and quality education. Furthermore, the emergence of university-based AI hubs and incubators has positioned certain institutions as critical actors in South Africa's digital innovation landscape. The sustainability and scalability of GenAI interventions remain a pressing consideration. While pilot programs have yielded promising outcomes, their broader institutionalization requires strategic investment, leadership commitment, and interoperable systems. Without a coordinated national strategy that supports long-term funding and infrastructure development, many initiatives risk remaining fragmented and unsustainable.

Challenges and Barriers to Equitable AI Implementation

Equitable implementation of GenAI technologies across South African HEIs remains unequal, primarily due to inequalities in institutional resources, digital infrastructure, and overall readiness (Opesemowo & Adekomaya, 2024). As such, many HEIs, particularly those in rural or historically disadvantaged contexts, continue to face technology infrastructural challenges, limited funding, and a lack of coherent policy frameworks (Atiku & Anane-Simon, 2022), which inhibit progress in GenAI integration and widespread uptake of such technologies (Mogoale et al., 2025). Persistent challenges such as the high cost of AI technologies, shortages of technical expertise, and the absence of institutionally embedded governance structures further encumber meaningful adoption (Goos & Savona, 2024). Studies by Molaudzi and Marutha (2024) and Mbangeleli and Funda (2024) highlight the unequal state of GenAI readiness, particularly within university libraries, citing governance challenges, inadequate funding, and ethical concerns related to academic integrity, data privacy, and the digital divide.

Empirical studies consistently show that AI systems often underperform when applied to diverse real-world populations due to dataset bias and representation (Noorale et al., 2021), institutional and infrastructure constraints (Goktas & Grzybowski, 2025), workflow and integration challenges (El-Arab et al., 2025), stakeholder engagement and continuous evaluation (Gurevich et al., 2023), among others. For example, clinical AI models for diagnostics often misdiagnose marginalized groups such as Black, Hispanic, female, and low-income patients because datasets were predominantly homogeneous and unrepresentative of these populations. Yousefi et al (2025) posited that the askNivi chatbot project in Nigeria developed gender-aware auditing to optimize natural language processing for equitable healthcare access, addressing local population needs with sensitivity to demographic differences. Nevertheless, the empirical studies here are more prevalent in the health sector than the educational sector, especially in the South African context. However, some of the key challenges and barriers of GenAI in HEIs in South Africa include digital inequality and infrastructure disparities (Maimela & Mbonde, 2025), ethical and cultural challenges (Maimela & Mbonde, 2025), socioeconomic and academic barriers (Ragolane, 2025), lack of professional development and institutional support (Ragolane, 2025), privacy, data security, and algorithmic bias risks (Guadu et al., 2025), to mention a few.

Despite the increasing recognition of GenAI's potential to transform teaching and learning and administration duties, significant barriers to the effective implementation of AI technologies for inclusive and equitable quality higher education remain a challenge in South Africa. Ethical considerations, especially those involving data protection, algorithmic bias, and the risk of entrenching socio-economic inequalities, often remain critical in a context where access to technology is already uneven (Anane-Simon & Atiku, 2024; Ormond, 2022). While national institutions such as the DHET and the Council on Higher Education (CHE) have acknowledged the importance of integrating AI strategically into higher education, systemic issues continue to undermine equitable implementation. Mehling and Kolleck (2019) argue that the lack of national coordination and fragmented institutional efforts contribute to inconsistencies across the HEIs sector. Such challenges are not unique to South African HEIs, but prevalent across various African countries (Arakpogun et al., 2021), including Rwanda (Sebihi et al., 2025) and Ghana (Asamoah & Amarteifio, 2025). Addressing these challenges requires targeted investment in digital infrastructure, the development of GenAI literacy initiatives, inclusive policy and ethical frameworks, and greater collaboration between government, academia, and industry stakeholders. Such a multi-stakeholder approach is essential to closing the GenAI adoption gap and ensuring that digital transformation in South African HEIs is both inclusive and sustainable.

The implementation of GenAI presents significant opportunities for pedagogical innovation, administrative efficiency, and enhanced research capacity across HEIs. However, the realization of these benefits remains constrained by a range of structural, socio-cultural, and institutional challenges that disproportionately affect historically disadvantaged and rural institutions. While GenAI is being progressively introduced across selected institutions, its adoption is unequal, raising pressing concerns about digital inequality, exclusion, and long-term sustainability. At the forefront of these challenges are infrastructural and resource disparities in many South African HEIs. Many institutions, particularly those situated in underserved regions, such as the Walter Sisulu University, the University of Limpopo, the University of Fort Hare, the University of Venda, and the University of Zululand, face chronic underinvestment in digital infrastructure, unreliable internet connectivity, and limited access to computing hardware (Opesemowo & Adekomaya, 2024; Yakobi & Yakobi, 2025). These conditions undermine the scalability and sustainability of GenAI technologies and create barriers to participation for both students and staff. The high costs of GenAI systems, alongside ongoing budgetary constraints in the sector, further exacerbate these divides.

Equally critical is the shortage of technical expertise and institutional capacity, which is a problem that is prevalent across Africa (Arakpogun et al., 2021). Many HEIs lack the specialized human resources needed to implement, manage, and maintain AI systems. This includes not only data scientists and GenAI specialists but also educators trained in digital pedagogy. In many cases, institutions are unable to provide adequate professional development, leaving staff underprepared to leverage GenAI tools effectively (Mbangeleli & Funda, 2024). Institutional culture and change management processes also play a vital role in shaping GenAI adoption. Resistance to change, uncertainty regarding the pedagogical value of GenAI, and a lack of internal communication strategies can stall progress (Kalmus & Nikiforova, 2025). Without strong leadership and inclusive governance structures, initiatives risk being externally driven, rather than embedded within long-term institutional planning.

The fragmentation of strategic vision across the sector further complicates equitable implementation. Despite the growing recognition of GenAI's potential, there remains no unified national AI strategy for higher education. As noted by Mehling and Kolleck (2019), this lack of coordination results in inconsistent adoption, duplicated efforts, and missed opportunities for collaboration. Many HEIs operate in silos, with limited mechanisms for sharing best practices or pooling resources. Moreover, the regulatory and ethical landscape surrounding GenAI remains underdeveloped. Concerns about data privacy, algorithmic bias, and academic integrity are particularly pronounced in contexts where regulatory compliance (e.g., under the Protection of Personal Information Act) is uneven. Without sector-wide ethical frameworks, institutions are left to navigate these issues independently, raising the risk of misuse and exacerbating mistrust among stakeholders (Ormond, 2022).

The issue of digital equity and inclusion is further compounded by language and cultural challenges. The predominance of English in GenAI platforms can marginalize students who are more proficient in indigenous South African languages, while the lack of localization in GenAI systems impedes cultural relevance and engagement. Similarly, gender and social disparities in access to technology mean that GenAI tools may inadvertently reinforce existing inequalities unless inclusive design principles are prioritized. From the student perspective, digital literacy gaps present a critical barrier. For instance, students from under-resourced backgrounds often lack the foundational digital competencies required to effectively use AI-supported systems (Mathai, 2024). This creates a dual challenge that includes enhancing access while simultaneously building the skills needed for meaningful engagement. In this context, targeted digital literacy programs are essential to prevent the deepening of the digital divide (Arakpogun et al., 2021).

Capacity gaps in GenAI research and innovation mean that only a handful of institutions are actively contributing to the development of locally relevant AI solutions. Without broader support for research funding, interdisciplinary collaboration, and the establishment of innovative ecosystems, many institutions remain positioned as passive consumers rather than active shapers of GenAI technologies. The equitable implementation of GenAI in South African HEIs is constrained by a confluence of factors, including infrastructural inequality, skills deficits, governance fragmentation, ethical ambiguity, and socio-cultural exclusion (Dlamini & Ndzinisa, 2025). Addressing these multifaceted challenges requires a coordinated, multi-stakeholder approach, one that brings together government, academia, and industry to ensure inclusive, contextually appropriate, and sustainable digital transformation across the sector.

GenAI as a Catalyst for Inclusive and Quality Higher Education

The recent and rapid evolution of GenAI has profoundly influenced various sectors, such as health, agriculture, the military, and the educational sector. Education is emerging as a pivotal area of transformation due to its ability to redefine teaching methodologies, learning experiences, and administrative efficiencies (Saragih, 2024). AI is transforming higher education by enhancing inclusivity and quality through personalized learning, accessibility, and operational efficiency. According to Saman et al (2024), GenAI tools like ChatGPT and adaptive platforms have tailored educational experiences that accommodate diverse learning needs while optimizing institutional processes. An empirical study by Nongqwenga and Funda (2024) exploring GenAI usage among South African university students reported that personalized learning plans enhanced by GenAI, continuous feedback, and stakeholder engagement could substantially reduce dropout rates, address diverse learner needs, and improve educational equity. This was corroborated by Smit et al (2025), where students perceived AI-enabled content as comparable in quality to their own work and recognized the need for appropriate institutional policies to govern ethical and effective AI usage in education.

While GenAI promises innumerable opportunities in transforming the inclusivity and reach of higher education, the intersection of GenAI and education faces significant challenges, including disparities in access, ethical concerns, and the lack of standardized frameworks for implementation (Saragih, 2024; Saman et al., 2024).

Therefore, higher-quality education that promotes inclusivity requires ethical considerations around bias, privacy, and academic integrity that are proactive to maximize the benefits of the collaboration. For instance, personalized learning should adapt content that each student needs using AI-driven analytics of learning patterns and performance data. This approach will support diverse learners, including those with disabilities or language barriers, by providing customized resources and feedback using a GenAI language tool assistant to overcome cultural and linguistic challenges. Kalnina et al. (2024) mention AI-enabled systems that identify students' risk at an early stage as well as expand educational access for marginalized groups and non-traditional learners. Similarly, AI-assisted grading frees educators for higher-value mentorship and curriculum development. Thus, operational efficiency gains in higher educational institutions arise from the implementation of AI because it is used in automating administrative tasks such as admissions, scheduling, and using predictive analytics to boost student retention rates (Kalnina et al., 2024; Saragih, 2024; Saman et al., 2024).

The evolution of GenAI is continuously causing a pervasive change in the global higher education landscape. For South African HEIs, GenAI presents significant opportunities to catalyze inclusive and quality education, where systemic barriers and enduring inequalities still interfere with equitable access to higher education (Kunjumuhammed, 2024). When implemented thoughtfully and ethically, GenAI can enhance inclusive and equitable education, pedagogical effectiveness, and expand access to quality education for disadvantaged groups. Additionally, Suliman and colleagues argue that inclusivity in the use of GenAI in HEIs can be cultivated by drawing on the Bantu principles of Ubuntu (Suliman et al. 2004). Ubuntu is grounded in African communalism and emphasizes the importance of collective well-being. The eight principles that underpin Ubuntu are compassion, caring, forgiveness, honesty, love, perseverance, responsibility, and self-control. Considering the importance of Ubuntu to the cultural identity of Africans, Ubuntu may potentially promote inclusive GenAI systems that resonate with the local users, thereby improving its acceptance and reducing the impact of common challenges affecting technological interventions.

While Ubuntu can play a key role in enhancing the success of GenAI in HEIs, key challenges such as ethical risks and academic integrity can also be mitigated through AI strategy policy frameworks. Wang and Si (2024) believe that addressing systemic barriers and inequalities, ensuring local relevance, and embedding critical digital literacies in both policy and practice could improve AI uptake. Improving access for historically marginalized groups is one of GenAI's most important promises for South Africa's higher education system. AI also promises to minimize the chasms between the historically advantaged and disadvantaged segments of the population through the adoption of social justice principles (i.e., equity, access, and participation) within the South African education system. Academic social justice will empower students in remote or underprivileged regions, whereby AI-driven platforms such as adaptive learning technologies, language translation tools, and intelligent tutoring systems can help close the access gap (Cassez et al., 2023).

Furthermore, AI-powered chatbots and virtual assistants can offer round-the-clock academic assistance and administrative direction, minimizing reliance on overworked employees within universities (Funda & Francke, 2024). GenAI can also help make teaching more inclusive by allowing students to learn in ways that are best for their language, cognitive, and social needs (Fitas, 2025). This is especially important in South Africa, where differences in language and socio-economic challenges can have a considerable impact on how well students perform in their academics. AI has the power to change the way academics teach and students learn at universities, not just by giving access to more information. For instance, educators can use predictive analytics to find students who are at risk and create targeted interventions (Choi et al., 2018). GenAI can also help with curriculum review by giving real-time feedback to improve the content and teaching methods over time.

STRATEGIES FOR INCLUSIVE AND EQUITABLE AI IMPLEMENTATION

Aside from AI-use policies and digital literacy training, inclusive and equitable AI implementation requires a multi-faceted approach spanning data curation, algorithmic design, governance frameworks, and cross-sector collaboration. As HEIs continue to strive to harness GenAI for socio-economic development and educational transformation, the challenge will always lie in ensuring that its deployment is inclusive, equitable, and aligned with the country's historical, cultural, and socio-economic contexts. Currently existing digital inequalities in South Africa are a true reflection of past marginalization patterns and legacy systems, with low-income households, rural areas, and historically underprivileged institutions having the least access (Nyahodza & Higgs, 2017). GenAI implementation strategies must address the digital divide across the board by promoting capacity building, ensuring local relevance, and embedding ethical governance frameworks. At this stage, GenAI systems are mostly developed in Euro/American or Westernized contexts, with the risk of reproducing linguistic, epistemic, and cultural biases when applied in African settings. Therefore, South Africa has a huge responsibility to invest in the reengineering and development of GenAI systems that are contextually and culturally relevant. Amongst the chief strategies, there should be a development of multilingual GenAI tools, especially for the 11 official South African languages, to ensure linguistic inclusion and improved educational accessibility (SIS Global,

2024). Effective regulation and policy are essential to ensure that GenAI technologies are implemented in a manner that protects rights, promotes equity, and ensures accountability. Without robust governance, GenAI may exacerbate surveillance, discrimination, and data exploitation. The DHET and the CHE have the responsibility to develop a national AI policy and ethical framework for HEIs, aligned with the African Union's Continental Strategy on AI and global best practices. The proposed framework for inclusive and equitable GENAI implementation in South African higher education systems is provided in Figure 1.

Figure 1. Framework for Inclusive and Equitable GenAI Implementation in South African Higher Education.

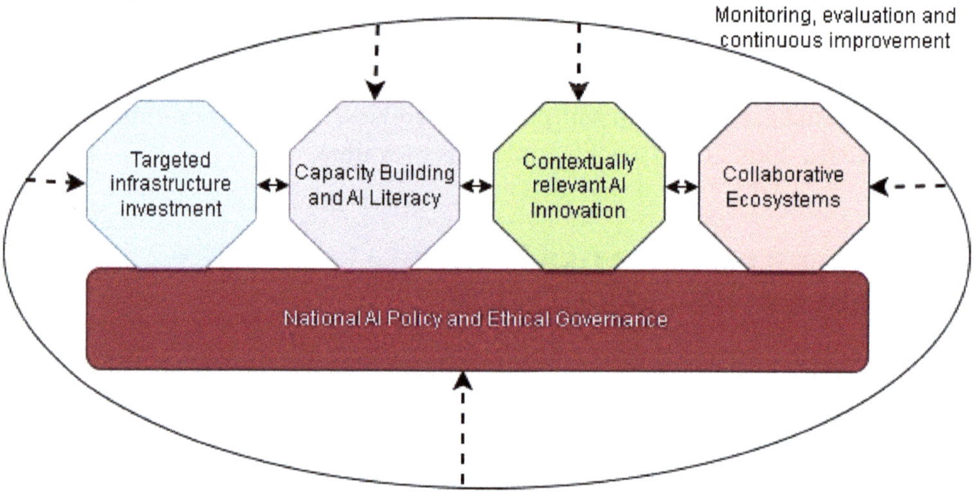

Source: Authors' compilation

The framework (Figure 1) indicates that GenAI implementation in South Africa should be anchored on a robust National AI Policy and Ethical Governance. Policies must inform targeted infrastructure investment, capacity building, and AI literacy initiatives, develop contextually relevant AI innovation, and ensure collaborative ecosystems. All these facets of the framework are linked to each other, as depicted by the bidirectional arrows. The various facets of the framework should also be monitored, evaluated, and continuously improved, given the highly dynamic nature of GenAI.

This framework is designed to address systemic inequalities and foster equitable, sustainable adoption of GenAI technologies in higher education across diverse South African contexts, thereby advancing inclusive quality education and social justice.

Prioritize Targeted Investment: Allocate dedicated funding towards upgrading digital infrastructure in historically disadvantaged institutions, ensuring reliable internet access, hardware availability, and platform interoperability. Financial support should extend to ongoing maintenance and scaling of AI tools to prevent fragmented and unsustainable implementations.
Develop National AI Policy and Ethical Frameworks: Establish comprehensive, enforceable policies that address data privacy, algorithmic fairness, academic integrity, and ethical use of GenAI technologies in higher education. These frameworks should align with international best practices while incorporating South Africa's unique socio-cultural context and the African Union's Continental AI strategy.
Enhance AI Literacy and Capacity Building: Implement nationwide AI training programs for both academic staff and students to develop digital competencies and critical awareness of AI's role and limitations. Institutional Centers for Teaching and Learning must integrate GenAI pedagogy into professional development and curricular design, fostering preparedness to leverage AI for inclusive teaching and learning.
Promote Contextually Relevant AI Innovations: Support research and development of GenAI applications that address local educational needs, including multilingual tools for South Africa's eleven official languages. Encourage interdisciplinary collaborations that integrate Indigenous knowledge systems, such as Ubuntu, to cultivate culturally responsive AI solutions.
Foster Collaborative Ecosystems: Cultivate partnerships among government agencies, academia, industry, and international organizations to promote resource sharing, knowledge transfer, and co-creation of scalable AI interventions. Innovation hubs and research centers should be incentivized to drive localized AI development attuned to socio-economic realities.
Implement Monitoring and Evaluation Mechanisms: Establish systematic processes to assess the impact, inclusivity, and unintended consequences of GenAI initiatives. Evidence-based evaluations will inform iterative policy adjustments and ensure continuous alignment with dynamic equity objectives.

Operationalizing these policy steps within a multi-stakeholder framework, South Africa's higher education sector can leverage GenAI not only to bridge existing educational divides but also to pioneer innovative pathways towards inclusive, quality learning for all. The success of AI integration, like other Information and Communication Technologies, hinges on an in-depth understanding of contextual complexities and embedding social justice as a foundational principle in technological adoption.

RECOMMENDATIONS

Given the entrenched structural inequalities inherited from the apartheid era, South Africa's higher education sector exhibits significant disparities in access to resources, digital infrastructure, and technical expertise. To ensure that GenAI works for inclusive and quality higher education, this study recommends a multi-pronged, context-sensitive approach prioritizing funding for historically disadvantaged institutions to upgrade digital infrastructure, ensuring equitable access to GenAI tools and platforms. This would lead to the development of AI literacy among both academic staff and students, with particular emphasis on under-resourced universities.

Similarly, the development of inclusive policy and ethical frameworks such as formulating national guidelines for AI adoption in higher education, will address issues of equity, data privacy, algorithmic bias, and academic integrity. This will give a mandate that all GenAI initiatives undergo equity impact assessments to prevent the entrenchment of existing inequalities and encourage collaboration between government, academia, and industry to pool resources, share expertise, and develop scalable GenAI solutions tailored to the South African context. Thus, supporting the creation of innovation hubs and research centers that will focus on GenAI applications for local challenges, particularly those affecting marginalized communities. Moreso, the study recommends promoting contextualized and locally relevant GenAI solutions that incentivize the development of AI tools that support local languages and address region-specific educational needs that are adaptable to varied infrastructural realities. This will support interdisciplinary research that integrates AI with local pedagogical practices and cultural contexts. The use of local value indigenous value systems, such as Ubuntu, may help in promoting inclusive and contextually responsive GenAI systems

With these recommendations, South African HEIs and policymakers can harness the transformative potential of GenAI, thereby advancing progress towards inclusive and equitable quality education for all South Africans, rather than widening the educational divide.

LIMITATIONS AND FUTURE RESEARCH

While this chapter illuminates what the authors believe are invaluable insights, it has several limitations. Firstly, the chapter is anchored on an analysis of secondary data. While scholars may draw inferences from a robust synthesis of extant literature, the ability to develop new insights is limited and largely dependent on the quality of the literature analyzed. Furthermore, studies relying on secondary data are largely retrospective, which means that researchers cannot assess causal relationships. More studies are needed to contribute to the nascent yet increasing body of knowledge on AI implementation in South African HEIs and the broader Global South. The focus on South Africa implies that the insights of this chapter, while invaluable, should not be deemed to be universally applicable in the Global South. More studies are needed to enrich the body of evidence, including comparative studies.

CONCLUSION

The integration of GenAI into the South African higher education system presents substantial opportunities to advance inclusive and equitable quality education, while simultaneously confronting significant systemic challenges rooted in historical inequalities. The enduring legacy of apartheid has produced deep disparities in digital infrastructure, institutional resources, and technological expertise across universities, especially those serving in rural areas and historically marginalized communities. Despite notable progress by leading institutions in AI adoption for pedagogical, administrative, and research purposes, the unevenness in AI readiness underscores the urgent need for context-specific, strategic interventions. To harness the transformative potential of GenAI as a catalyst for social justice and educational equity, South African policymakers and higher education stakeholders must pursue a coordinated set of actionable policy measures proposed in this chapter.

REFERENCES

Ade-Ibijola, A., & Okonkwo, C. (2023). Artificial intelligence in Africa: emerging challenges. In Eke, D. O., Wakunuma, K., & Akintoye, S. (Eds.), *Responsible AI in Africa: Challenges and Opportunities* (pp. 101–117). Palgrave Macmillan.

Aithal, P. S., & Maiya, A. K. (2023). Innovations in the higher education industry–Shaping the future. [IJCSBE]. *International Journal of Case Studies in Business, IT, and Education*, *7*(4), 283–311.

Akande, J. O., & Atiku, S. O. (2022). Developing Industry 4.0 accountants: Implications for higher education institutions in Namibia. *Development and Learning in Organizations*, *36*(5), 16–19. DOI: 10.1108/DLO-09-2021-0177

Anane-Simon, R., & Atiku, S. O. (2024). Artificial intelligence and automation for the future of startups. In Baporikar, N. (Ed.), *Ecosystem Dynamics and Strategies for Startups' Scalability* (pp. 133–153). IGI Global Scientific Publishing.

Arakpogun, E. O., Elsahn, Z., Olan, F., & Elsahn, F. (2021). Artificial Intelligence in Africa: Challenges and Opportunities. In Hamdan, A. (Eds.), *The Fourth Industrial Revolution: Implementation of Artificial Intelligence for Growing Business Success* (pp. 375–388). Springer., https://doi.org/https://doi.org/10.1007/978-3-030-62796-6_22

Atiku, S. O., & Anane-Simon, R. (2022). Stimulating Creativity and Innovation Through Apt Educational Policy. In Fields, Z. (Ed.), *Achieving Sustainability Using Creativity, Innovation, and Education: A Multidisciplinary Approach* (pp. 113–133). IGI Global Scientific Publishing., DOI: 10.4018/978-1-7998-7963-3.ch006

Atiku, S. O., & Boateng, F. (2020). Rethinking Education System for the Fourth Industrial Revolution. In Atiku, S. (Ed.), *Human Capital Formation for the Fourth Industrial Revolution* (pp. 1–17). IGI Global Scientific Publishing., DOI: 10.4018/978-1-5225-9810-7.ch001

Bayaga, A. (2025). Leveraging AI-enhanced and emerging technologies for pedagogical innovations in higher education. *Education and Information Technologies*, *30*(1), 1045–1072.

Beerkens, M. (2020). Evidence-based policy and higher education quality assurance: progress, pitfalls and promise. In *Impact evaluation of quality management in higher education* (pp. 38–53). Routledge.

Cassez, F., Fuller, J., Ghale, M. K., Pearce, D. J., & Quiles, H. M. (2023). Formal and executable semantics of the ethereum virtual machine in dafny. In *International Symposium on Formal Methods* (pp. 571-583). Cham: Springer International Publishing.

Chan, C. K. Y. (2023). A comprehensive AI policy education framework for university teaching and learning. *International Journal of Educational Technology in Higher Education*, *20*(1), 38.

Chatterjee, S., & Bhattacharjee, K. K. (2020). Adoption of artificial intelligence in higher education: A quantitative analysis using structural equation modeling. *Education and Information Technologies*, *25*(5), 3443–3463. DOI: 10.1007/s10639-020-10159-7

Chen, Y., Jensen, S., Albert, L. J., Gupta, S., & Lee, T. (2023). Artificial intelligence (AI) student assistants in the classroom: Designing chatbots to support student success. *Information Systems Frontiers*, *25*(1), 161–182.

Choi, S. P., Lam, S. S., Li, K. C., & Wong, B. T. (2018). Learning analytics at low cost: At-risk student prediction with clicker data and systematic proactive interventions. *Journal of Educational Technology & Society*, *21*(2), 273–290.

Dlamini, R., & Ndzinisa, N. (2025). Towards a critical discourse on artificial intelligence and its misalignment in sub-Saharan Africa: Through an equality, equity, and decoloniality lens. *Journal of Education (University of KwaZulu-Natal)*, (98), 42-61.

El Arab, R. A., Abu-Mahfouz, M. S., Abuadas, F. H., Alzghoul, H., Almari, M., Ghannam, A., & Seweid, M. M. (2025, March). Bridging the gap: From AI success in clinical trials to real-world healthcare implementation—A narrative review. In *Healthcare, 13(7), 701*. MDPI.

Faisal, R., Chong, A. L., & Yee, A. S. V. (2017). Systematic review of the sustainable knowledge transfer process in government-industry-academia consortium. *Asian Journal of Innovation and Policy*, *6*(3), 295–312.

Fitas, R. (2025). Inclusive Education with AI: Supporting Special Needs and Tackling Language Barriers. *arXiv preprint arXiv:2504.14120.*

Fontanillas, T. R., Carbonell, M. R., Catasús, M. G., & Quemada, P. B. (2025). Challenges of generative Artificial Intelligence in higher education: Promoting its critical use among students. *Revista Iberoamericana de Educación a Distancia*, *28*(2), 209–228. DOI: 10.5944/ried.28.2.43535

Funda, V., & Cilliers, L. (2024). AI chatbots and the future of academic writing: Insights from the University of Fort Hare [Research study announcement]. University of Fort Hare. Retrieved June 26, 2025, from https://shorturl.at/zgeXr

Funda, V., & Francke, E. (2024). Benefits and challenges of AIOPS adoption and usage in HEIS in developing countries. *South African Journal of Higher Education*, *38*(6), 56–78.

Funda, V., & Mbangeleli, N. B. A. (2024). Artificial Intelligence (AI) as a tool to address academic challenges in South African higher education. *Int. J. Learn. Teach. Educ. Res*, *23*, 520–537.

Global, S. I. S. (2024). *University of the Free State launches multilingual AI-powered chatbot to enhance student engagement.* https://sisglobal.com/university-of-the-free-state-launches-multilingual-ai-powered-chatbot

Goktas, P., & Grzybowski, A. (2025). Shaping the future of healthcare: Ethical clinical challenges and pathways to trustworthy AI. *Journal of Clinical Medicine*, *14*(5), 1605.

Goos, M., & Savona, M. (2024). The governance of artificial intelligence: Harnessing opportunities and mitigating challenges. *Research Policy*, *53*(3), 104928.

Guadu, A., Dibelkulu, D., & Menberu, A. W. (2025). Artificial Intelligence in African Higher Education: Uses, Misuses, and Ethical Dilemmas. *Advances in Artificial Intelligence and Machine Learning. RE:view*, *5*(3), 4196–4221.

Gurevich, E., El Hassan, B., & El Morr, C. (2023, March). Equity within AI systems: What can health leaders expect? [Sage CA: Los Angeles, CA: SAGE Publications.]. *Healthcare Management Forum*, *36*(2), 119–124.

Haoyang, D. L., & Towne, J. (2025). *How AI and human teachers can collaborate to transform education, World Economic Forum.* Available at: https://www.weforum.org/stories/2025/01/how-ai-and-human-teachers-can-collaborate-to-transform-education/ (Accessed: 27 June 2025).

Hughes, L., & Malik, T. Dettmer, Al-Busaidi, A. S., & Dwivedi, Y. K. (2025). Reimagining Higher Education: Navigating the Challenges of Generative AI Adoption. *Information Systems Frontiers*. Advance online publication. DOI: 10.1007/s10796-025-10582-6

Hutson, J. (2024). Rethinking plagiarism in the era of generative AI. *Journal of International Communication*, *3*(2), 20–31. DOI: 10.54963/jic.v3i2.220

Kaisara, G., & Bwalya, K. J. (2022). Trends in Mobile Learning Research in Sub-Saharan Africa: A Systematic Literature Review. *International Journal of Education and Development Using Information and Communication Technology*, *18*(2), 231–244.

Kaisara, G., Mare, A., & Peel, C. (2021) Haven't we been here before? A critical analysis of the fourth industrial revolution, in the *2021 Conference on Information Communications Technology and Society, ICTAS 2021 - Proceedings*. Durban: IEEE, pp. 67–72. Available at: https://doi.org/DOI: 10.1109/ICTAS50802.2021.9395028

Kalmus, J., & Nikiforova, A. (2024). Generative AI adoption in higher Education: Exploring educator resistance in Estonian universities. *AIS Electronic Library (AISeL)*. https://aisel.aisnet.org/sigdsa2024/13

Kalniņa, D., Nīmante, D., & Baranova, S. (2024). Artificial intelligence for higher education: Benefits and challenges for pre-service teachers. *Frontiers in Education*, *9*, 1501819. DOI: 10.3389/feduc.2024.1501819

Kumar, A.. (2023). Managing healthcare supply chain through artificial intelligence (AI): A study of critical success factors. *Computers & Industrial Engineering*, *175*. Advance online publication. DOI: 10.1016/j.cie.2022.108815

Kunjumuhammed, S. K. (2024). Artificial Intelligence in Addressing Educational Inequality Dimensions in Higher Education Institutions (HEIs): A Critical Review. *Risks and Challenges of AI-Driven Finance: Bias, Ethics, and Security*, 146-164.

Lin, Z. (2024). Beyond principlism: Practical strategies for ethical AI use in research practices. *AI and Ethics*, •••, 1–13.

Mahabeer, P., & Pirtheepal, T. (2019). Assessment, plagiarism, and its effect on academic integrity: Experiences of academics at a university in South Africa. *South African Journal of Science*, *115*(11-12), 1–8.

Maimela, C., & Mbonde, P. (2025). Artificial Intelligence (AI) in South African Universities: Curriculum Transformation and Decolonization–Aid or Obstacle? *Frontiers in Sociology*, *10*, 1543471.

Maphalala, M. C., & Ajani, O. A. (2025). Leveraging artificial intelligence as a learning tool in higher education. *Interdisciplinary Journal of Education Research*, *7*(1), a01–a01.

Mathai, A. (2024). *Enhancing Education for Underprivileged Children Through AI-Powered Native Language Learning Inclusive Education Through AI-Powered Native Language Learning*. *SSRN*. https://papers.ssrn.com/sol3/papers.cfm?abstract_id=4899553

Mbangeleli, N. B. A., & Funda, V. (2024). Mapping the Evidence Around the Use of AI-Powered Tools in South African Universities: A Systematic Review. *In Proceedings of the International Conference on Education Research.* (149-158). Academic Conferences and Publishing Limited. DOI: 10.34190/icer.1.1.3180

Mehling, S., & Kolleck, N. (2019). Cross-sector collaboration in higher education institutions (HEIs): A critical analysis of an urban sustainability development program. *Sustainability*, *11*(18), 4982.

Mogoale, P. D., Pretorius, A., Mogase, R. C., & Segooa, M. A. (2025). Integrating artificial intelligence within South African higher learning institutions. *South African Journal of Information Management*, *27*(1), 1939.

Molaudzi, A. I., & Marutha, N. (2024). Contributory factors to attitudes towards the adoption of artificial intelligence technology in public academic libraries in South Africa. *Information Development*, •••, 02666669241304704.

Mungai, B. K., Omieno, P. K. K., Egessa, M., & Manyara, P. N. (2024). AI chatbots in LMS: A pedagogical review of cognitive, constructivist, and adaptive principles. *Engineering And Technology Journal*, *9*(8), 4709–4715.

Mutambara, A. G. (2025). *Artificial Intelligence: A driver of inclusive development and shared prosperity for the Global South.* CRC Press.

Nongqwenga, M., & Funda, V. (2024). A model to integrate Generative Artificial Intelligence to improve student academic performance in South African universities. In *International Conference on Emerging Technology and Interdisciplinary Sciences* (pp. 46-53).

Nyahodza, L., & Higgs, R. (2017). Towards bridging the digital divide in post-apartheid South Africa: A case of a historically disadvantaged university in Cape Town. *South African Journal of Library and Information Science*, *83*(1), 39–48.

Omodan, B. I. (2024). Redefining university infrastructure for the 21st century: An interplay between physical assets and digital evolution. *Journal of Infrastructure. Policy and Development*, *8*(4), 3468.

Opesemowo, O. A. G., & Adekomaya, V. (2024). Harnessing artificial intelligence for advancing sustainable development goals in South Africa's higher education system: A qualitative study. *International Journal of Learning. Teaching and Educational Research*, *23*(3), 67–86.

Ormond, E. (2022). *Global to Local: South African Perspectives on AI Ethics Risks.* https://papers.ssrn.com/sol3/papers.cfm?abstract_id=4240356

Patel, S., & Ragolane, M. (2024). The implementation of artificial intelligence in South African higher education institutions: Opportunities and challenges. *Technium Education and Humanities*, *9*, 51–65.

Ragolane, M. (2025). Teaching Artificial Intelligence and Teaching with Artificial Intelligence in South African Higher Education Institutions.

Rane, N., Choudhary, S., & Rane, J. (2023). Education 4.0 and 5.0: Integrating artificial intelligence (AI) for personalized and adaptive learning. *Journal of Artificial Intelligence and Robotics*, *1*(1), 29–43.

Saman, H. M., Noor, S. M., Isa, C. M. M., Lian, O. C., & Narayanan, G. (2024). Embracing Artificial Intelligence as a Catalyst for Change in Reshaping Malaysian Higher Education in the Digital Era: A Literature Review. In *International Conference on Innovation & Entrepreneurship in Computing, Engineering & Science Education (InvENT 2024)* (pp. 633-643). Atlantis Press.

Saragih, R. I. E. (2024). AI-Powered Education: Transforming Learning through Personalized and Scalable Solutions. *International Journal of Information Systems and Innovative Technology*, *3*(2), 1–9.

Sebihi, A., Schoelen, L., & Uwamwezi, B. (2025). Unveiling AI's impact in Rwandan higher education: Navigating trends, challenges, and imperatives at the University of Rwanda. *Discover Education*, *4*, 166. DOI: 10.1007/s44217-025-00576-6

Smit, M., Bond-Barnard, T., & Wagner, R. F. (2025). Artificial Intelligence in South African Higher Education: Survey Data of Master's Level Students. *Data in Brief*, •••, 111813.

Suliman, Z., Mohale, N. E., Maphoto, K. B., & Sevnarayan, K. (2004). The interconnectedness between Ubuntu principles and generative artificial intelligence in distance higher education institutions. *Discover Education*, *3*. Advance online publication. DOI: 10.1007/s44217-024-00289-2

University of Cape Town. (2024, July 31). *GRIT introduces an AI chatbot to UCT staff and students. UCT News*. https://news.uct.ac.za news.uct.ac.za+10news.uct.ac.za+10iol.co.za+10

Wang, C., & Si, L. (2024). The intersection of public policy and public access: Digital inclusion, digital literacy education, and libraries. *Sustainability*, *16*(5), 1878.

Xulu, H. H., Hlongwa, N. S., & Maguraushe, K. (2024, December). Unlocking the Potential of AI in Higher Education: A Multi-Dimensional Study of ChatGPT Adoption at a South African University. In *The Focus Conference (TFC 2024)* (pp. 516-532). Atlantis Press.

Yakobi, K., & Yakobi, S. (2025). Online learning support as a pedagogical strategy for student learning in the developing universities in South Africa: A literature review. *Cogent Education*, *12*(1). Advance online publication. DOI: 10.1080/2331186X.2025.2464310

Yousefi, F., Dehnavieh, R., Laberge, M., Gagnon, M. P., Ghaemi, M. M., Nadali, M., & Azizi, N. (2025). Opportunities, challenges, and requirements for Artificial Intelligence (AI) implementation in Primary Health Care (PHC): A systematic review. *BMC Primary Care*, *26*(1), 196.

Zawacki-Richter, O.. (2019). Systematic review of research on artificial intelligence applications in higher education – where are the educators? *International Journal of Educational Technology in Higher Education*, *16*(1). Advance online publication. DOI: 10.1186/s41239-019-0171-0

KEY TERMS AND DEFINITIONS

Apartheid: A former system of government in South Africa that sought to provide privileges to white citizens while marginalizing the rest of the population, particularly black Africans.

Artificial Intelligence: computing systems that can mimic human cognitive functions and enhance decision-making.

Equitable education: Provision of fair and just access to quality educational opportunities for all students, particularly addressing the historical inequalities entrenched by apartheid in South Africa.

Inclusive education: Educational opportunities that are accessible to any member of the population who may have an interest in accessing them.

Sustainable Development: Promoting inclusive and quality education that is equitable and accessible for lifelong learning opportunities, leveraging AI technologies.

Ubuntu: A set of African communal values anchored on the belief that "I am because you are, you are because I am," and aims to promote mutually beneficial actions and behaviors.

Chapter 4

Reworlding Inclusion: Speculative Futures of STEM Education in the Age of Generative AI

Masud Ahmmed
Victoria University, Australia

Janine Arantes
https://orcid.org/0000-0002-0301-5780
Victoria University, Australia

ABSTRACT

This chapter argues that inclusion in STEM education must be reimagined in the age of Generative AI (GenAI). Drawing on speculative fabulation and feminist theories of epistemic justice, we examine how GenAI reshapes knowledge production, assessment, and representation, often reinforcing bias and exclusion. Through three speculative scenarios, we explore divergent futures of STEM learning and Initial Teacher Education (ITE), showing how AI can either entrench dominant norms or foster pluralistic, relational pedagogies. We propose that inclusion must shift from representational fixes to a radical, justice-oriented reworlding of education, where AI is governed transparently, designed with care, and co-created with those historically marginalised.

DOI: 10.4018/979-8-3373-3745-6.ch004

INTRODUCTION: THE EPISTEMIC STAKES OF INCLUSION IN AN AGE OF GENAI

In an era progressively shaped by generative AI, the domain of all branches of education including STEM is witnessing an axiological reconstruction. While Generative Artificial Intelligence (GenAI) offers transformative possibilities in terms of personalisation in teaching and learning, it similarly risks exacerbating existing exclusions and inequalities (Bulathwela et al., 2024; Roscoe et al., 2022). Hence it requires an ethically grounded and inclusive approach to its integration within the learning landscape. This chapter critically extends recent scholarship on the role of Generative Artificial Intelligence (GenAI) in destabilising foundational epistemologies in science education by asking: *What does inclusion mean in a world where educational content, assessment, and feedback are mediated by machines trained on partial, biased, and often opaque data?*

This question is not only philosophical; it is political, practical, and timely. As generative AI (GenAI) becomes increasingly integrated into educational infrastructures, it challenges educators, researchers, and policymakers to reconsider the foundational principles upon which inclusive education is built (Roscoe et al., 2022). The digital mediation of knowledge through AI systems shifts the focus of inclusion from merely increasing access and representation to interrogating how knowledge is selected, generated, and legitimised by machines (Chen et al., 2025). For example, the datasets on which GenAI models are trained do not emerge from neutral contexts (Wan et al., 2023). They are shaped by historical power imbalances, structural inequalities, and colonial knowledge systems. When generative models are used to produce learning content or simulate feedback, they inherit these limitations and reproduce them at scale. In science education, GenAI tools such as ChatGPT, may foreground Eurocentric, heteronormative and gendered narratives of scientific progress (Arantes, 2024). As a result, the system is marginalising minority voices, Indigenous knowledge systems or community-based epistemologies that do not align with dominant paradigms (Arantes & Vicars, 2023). This raises significant concerns not only about what is being taught, but about what is being erased or misrepresented.

Inclusion in this context cannot be reduced to a checklist of demographic variables or content representation. It must instead be redefined as an ongoing, relational process of attending to epistemic justice, cultural safety, and technological transparency (Arantes, 2024). This requires educators to move beyond the surface-level appeal of AI-driven personalisation (Arantes, 2023) and critically assess whose needs are being served, whose knowledge is being amplified, and who is being asked to adapt to the technological system rather than the system being designed to adapt to them (Cooper, 2023). The question of epistemic authority is central. In traditional educational settings, teachers often mediate learning through pedagogical judgment, contextual awareness, and relationships with students. GenAI, by contrast, generates responses based on statistical patterns in data, often drawing from internet-based datasets. While this allows for speed and scalability, it also means that feedback, content, and examples may lack nuance, cultural specificity, or ethical sensitivity (Arantes & Vicars, 2023). For example, a student might ask an AI tool in their science classroom to explain climate change and receive a response that omits Indigenous perspectives on land, sustainability, and relationality (Fitch et al. 2023). The omission is not necessarily intentional, but its impact is real: it reinforces a dominant narrative while silencing alternative ways of knowing. Further complicating this landscape is the opacity of AI decision-making. In many generative models, it is unclear how responses are constructed, what sources they are drawing from, or why certain outputs are prioritised over others (Bearman & Ajjawi, 2023). This black-box nature of GenAI challenges the core educational principle of transparency. It undermines the ability of educators and students to critically engage with the content they receive.

In inclusive education, transparency is not optional. Transparency is essential for trust, accountability, and equity. Without it, students from marginalised backgrounds may be further alienated, particularly if AI tools misrepresent their communities or reinforce harmful stereotypes. This is also true for STEM education. In STEM education, where precision, standardisation, and objectivity are often valorised, the risks are particularly acute. AI-generated assessments may inadvertently penalise students whose linguistic, cognitive, or cultural expressions do not align with normative expectations embedded in the model's training data (Chen et al., 2025). This can deepen existing achievement gaps and undermine efforts to foster equity in learning outcomes. Moreover, the increasing reliance on automated assessment tools may devalue the role of human educators in recognising diverse forms of intelligence, creativity, and critical thinking – favouring self-regulated learning, which does not suit all students (Broadbent & Lodge, 2021). The potential of GenAI to scaffold learning in inclusive ways, however, should not be dismissed. There are important opportunities to design tools that support students with disabilities, translate materials into multiple languages, and offer differentiated content to meet varied learning needs (Birhane et al., 2023; Carolus et al., 2023). However, these possibilities must be approached with a commitment to co-design, accessibility, and critical reflection, so that inclusion is not retrofitted onto technologies after deployment (Burgstahler, 2009). This chapter argues that inclusion must be built into the design processes from the outset, informed by the voices and experiences of those most likely to be marginalised.

There is also a danger that the discourse around GenAI and inclusion becomes instrumentalised and commercialised, reducing humans to numbers for monetization, where only quantifiable data is given voice. In this instance, inclusion is often framed as a means to improve efficiency, boost engagement, or reduce teacher workload (Milan, 2020). While these outcomes may be desirable to some (including EdTech vendors), they are not substitutes for ethical or justice-oriented practices (Ball & Olmedo, 2023). The risk is that inclusive education becomes reduced to a metric or feature rather than a value-laden commitment to transforming educational systems. To resist this trajectory, this chapter proposes a speculative and generative approach to inclusion. Rather than simply adapting existing models to accommodate AI, we ask what kinds of futures become possible when inclusion is treated not as a constraint, but as a source of epistemic and pedagogical innovation. This involves reimagining curricula that foreground pluralism, interrogating the power dynamics of datafication, and fostering educational environments that prioritise consent, agency, and care in human-technology relations. A speculative orientation (Haraway, 2013) also invites us to ask questions that are often sidelined in discussions of educational technology. What kinds of relationships do we want to have with machines? What forms of learning do we want to preserve or protect from automation? How do we balance the promise of AI with the political project of decolonising education? These questions require collective deliberation, especially as policy frameworks around AI in education begin to take shape.

Finally, the governance of AI systems used in education, we argue, must be aligned with principles of inclusion and universal design. This includes not only regulatory mechanisms to ensure fairness and accountability but also participatory models of governance that involve educators, students, and communities. Without these forms of participatory oversight, there is a real risk that AI will become another vector for exclusion, entrenching inequities under the guise of innovation (Arantes & Vicars, 2023). Thus, in this chapter, we argue that inclusive education in the age of GenAI must be re-conceptualised as a form of resistance to epistemic homogenisation, technological determinism, and market-driven models of schooling. It is a call to educators and policymakers to recognise the pedagogical and ethical stakes of AI integration and to insist that any technological advance must serve the broader goals of justice, dignity, and educational transformation first – and efficiency, commercialisation and other notions spruced as a solution to education's 'problems' a distant second. By critically examining the epistemic foundations and social implications of GenAI in STEM and beyond, we aim to open up new avenues for thinking about inclusion not as a problem to be solved, but as a practice of continuous, situated, and relational world-making. We do so, to not simply react to technological change: but to actively reimagine what education can and should be in a digitally mediated world.

From Representation to Epistemic Inclusion: Reframing the Debate

It advances an argument that inclusion, too often treated as a logistical or representational fix, must be reconceptualised as an epistemic and ethical struggle within the broader sociotechnical systems that shape educational futures. While current debates on inclusion in STEM education often focus on demographic representation and curricular access (Palid et al., 2023), these approaches frequently overlook the deep entanglement between knowledge production and sociotechnical power (Arantes, 2024). GenAI systems, trained on historical, incomplete, and often biased datasets, carry within them embedded assumptions about what counts as legitimate knowledge and whose perspectives are central (Baker & Hawn, 2021). As such systems are integrated into classroom tools, teacher education programs, and curriculum design, they risk re-inscribing the very exclusions they purport to dismantle.

Issues of access, equity, and inclusion are not merely peripheral concerns but central determinants of how AI reshapes educational opportunity. Inclusion prior to AI's disruption and more recently, should not be viewed as an outcome, but as an ongoing process of negotiating power, representation, and access across the complex, interrelated strata of educational structures, frameworks, and policy implementation (Allan, 2008; Liasidou, 2008). This requires a move away from narrow metrics of diversity, often measured through enrolment figures or participation rates, and toward a more critical interrogation of how knowledge is produced, validated, and circulated in educational systems increasingly shaped by GenAI. Such a shift demands attention to what Linda Tuhiwai Smith (2021) terms "the politics of knowledge": the conditions under which knowledge becomes legitimised, who is authorised to speak, and how technological systems reify existing hierarchies under the guise of neutrality and innovation.

Within the STEM disciplines, these dynamics are particularly pronounced. STEM education has long privileged certain ways of knowing, empirical, objective, and often masculinised (Arantes, 2024) while devaluing other epistemologies, including Indigenous, feminist, and experiential knowledges (Harding & Mendoza, 2020). The rise of GenAI threatens to intensify these exclusions. As tools such as automated feedback systems, lesson plan generators, and AI tutors become embedded in educational platforms, they do more than simply reproduce content. They carry forward the ontological and epistemological assumptions of their creators and training corpora (Baker & Hawn, 2021). These systems often assume linearity, efficiency, and mastery as pedagogical ideals, displacing pedagogies grounded in inquiry, relationality, and cultural context. In this way, the incorporation of GenAI into education is not merely a technological intervention but an epistemological act. It makes claims, sometimes subtly, sometimes overtly, about what counts as valid knowledge, how students should learn, and what teaching should look like. For students and educators from historically marginalised groups, these embedded assumptions can further alienate their ways of knowing, seeing, and being in the world. As Zembylas (2023) argues, inclusion must be grounded in an affective and political project, one that recognises how systems of exclusion operate not only at the level of access but at the level of feeling, recognition, and epistemic belonging. Thus, reframing inclusion as an epistemic issue draws attention to the affective costs of exclusion in AI-mediated learning environments.

Consider, for example, the quiet erosion of confidence experienced by students when AI-generated content repeatedly reflects Eurocentric examples, or fails to acknowledge female scientists as thought leaders, despite the lack of representation historically. Or the disengagement that ensues when a GenAI-powered essay scaffold defaults to Western argumentative logic, marginalising narrative or oral traditions central to many communities' epistemic practices. These are not merely pedagogical inconveniences. They are signals of an epistemic environment that remains hostile to difference. As such, to move toward epistemic inclusion, we must interrogate how AI systems are trained, deployed, and governed within educational contexts – through a human centric lens. Critical scholars in Science and Technology Studies (STS) offer useful guidance here. For instance, Benjamin (2019) introduces the concept of the "New Jim Code," illustrating how seemingly progressive technologies can embed and exacerbate racial inequalities when developed without critical attention to systemic injustice. In education, similar patterns are emerging as GenAI tools automate decisions about curriculum content, assessment, and feedback without sufficient transparency or scrutiny (Chen et al., 2025; Gross, 2023; Wan et al., 2023). These tools are often positioned as objective or efficient, yet their outputs are deeply shaped by the historical and cultural contours of the datasets they draw upon, which means that this opacity not only limits educators' ability to intervene but also depoliticises the very systems that produce exclusion.

As a result, foregrounding epistemic inclusion requires what Costanza-Chock (2020) calls design justice, a framework that centres marginalised communities in the design, governance, and evaluation of sociotechnical systems. Applying design justice to STEM education in the age of GenAI means disrupting dominant models of curriculum development and educational technology deployment, and instead focuses on co-designing tools and content with students, teachers, and communities whose epistemologies are often excluded. It also means acknowledging that epistemic inclusion is not an endpoint but a dynamic process of dialogue, resistance, and adaptation. Rather, epistemic inclusion is situated within a broader politics of recognition. Drawing on Nancy Fraser (2020) distinction between redistribution and recognition, we argue that equity in AI-mediated education cannot be reduced to the fair allocation of digital tools or access to platforms. Rather, it also requires a deep recognition of diverse epistemic standpoints and the power asymmetries that shape whose knowledge is deemed credible or risk inclusion becoming tokenistic, reifying the very exclusions they aim to correct.

In teacher education, this reconceptualisation has quite significant and urgent implications. Pre-service teachers are increasingly expected to integrate GenAI tools into their planning and pedagogy (Williamson et al., 2024), often with little critical training on the ethical and epistemic dimensions of these tools (Gallagher et al., 2021). By embedding a conception of inclusion that centres epistemic justice, teacher education programs can cultivate critical reflexivity and foster pedagogical practices that challenge, rather than comply with, the implicit logics of dominant AI systems. In practical terms, this may involve curriculum that examines the genealogy of data in AI training sets (Arantes & Vicars, 2023), pedagogies that invite students to critique AI-generated outputs through their own cultural, linguistic, and epistemic frameworks (Bozkurt et al., 2024), and assessment practices that recognise multiple forms of knowledge expression, from exams to storytelling to community consultation. It also means creating institutional space for discomfort. It means celebrating contradiction and making sure that the voice of dissent has a seat at the table. Recognising that epistemic inclusion will often disrupt existing norms of standardisation, commercialisation, efficiency, and certainty that GenAI is designed to optimise.

Finally, we caution against framing GenAI as either a panacea or a threat in itself. The issue is not AI per se, but how AI interacts with existing structures of power in education (Korseberg & Elken, 2025). Inclusion in this context must not be treated as a side-effect or a checkbox, but as a central design principle, guided by ongoing, situated dialogue with those most impacted. For example, GenAI's capacity to generate plausible but inaccurate content, and its so-called hallucinations (Alkaissi & McFarlane, 2023), reveals not only technical limitations but deeper philosophical ruptures in how 'truth' and 'evidence' are constructed in science education (Malcolm, 2021). To imagine new futures, we must begin by refusing the inevitability of the current one, and we believe that epistemic inclusion does just that. It invites us to reworld STEM education not by adding more voices to the margins of existing systems, but by reimagining the very systems through which knowledge is recognised, shared, and lived. This reworlding demands not just representational repair, but a fundamental shift in how we conceptualise the relationship between knowledge, technology, and justice. In this chapter, reworlding refers to a structural reconfiguration of curriculum, assessment, governance, and data practices through which epistemic authority, participation, and care are redistributed rather than merely represented. Reworlding is not proposed as a metaphorical aspiration but as a material and institutional shift in how educational systems recognise knowledge, govern technology, and allocate pedagogical authority.

METHODOLOGY: SPECULATIVE FABULATION AND CRITICAL FUTURES THINKING

This chapter adopts a speculative methodological approach grounded in Donna Haraway's concepts of speculative fabulation, situated knowledges, and response-ability (Haraway, 2020), to interrogate the shifting landscape of inclusion in Initial Teacher Education (ITE) and STEM pedagogy under the influence of GenAI. Rather than treating speculative inquiry as detached fantasy, we position it as a critical method that allows us to imagine, contest, and reshape the sociotechnical futures being scripted into educational systems today.

Speculative fabulation enables a deliberate departure from normative, linear assumptions about progress in educational technology. It functions as both critique and creative praxis, generating future-oriented narratives that expose present-day tensions, ethical dilemmas, and policy blind spots in AI-mediated learning environments. We stress that these fabulations are not predictions; they are provocations. They aim to reveal what is at stake in current decisions around AI integration and whose epistemologies are being foregrounded, erased, or commodified in the process. As such, we mobilise Haraway (2020) notion of situated knowledges to dismantle the myth of AI neutrality – starting instead, by acknowledging that AI is not an impartial or universal actor (Baker & Hawn, 2021; Chen et al., 2025; Wan et al., 2023). We acknowledge that its outputs reflect the data it is trained on, and that the data is shaped by historical inequities, colonial hierarchies, and dominant epistemic frameworks (Baker & Hawn, 2021). Which, in turn, have implications for STEM education, which already privileges empirical, masculinised, and Eurocentric ways of knowing (Harding & Mendoza, 2020). Through situated knowledges, we foreground the need for AI systems in education to be interpreted and interrogated through the cultural, affective, and political contexts in which they operate.

To explain, Haraway (2016) concept of response-ability, or the ethical capacity to respond to others, guides our engagement with GenAI as a relational technology. It insists that inclusion is not a fixed outcome but an ongoing practice of attunement, care, and co-responsibility in the face of technological systems that often obscure accountability and erase difference. In our speculative scenarios, we thus explore how GenAI might support or undermine this relational ethic depending on how it is governed, designed, and taught. Three divergent speculative futures are presented as methods of critical fabulation. First, the 'Inclusive Data Dilemma', which critiques the technocratic assimilation of inclusion as a performance metric, second, 'Networks of Care in the Early Years', which envisions GenAI as a collaborative pedagogical companion. Third, the third scenario functions as a synthesis vignette that braids their tensions into a coherent counter-imaginary, demonstrating what 'reworlded' STEM inclusion can look. These scenarios draw on existing research and imagined extrapolations to explore how inclusion might be operationalised differently depending on the values embedded in AI infrastructures. The use of speculative fiction in this methodology enables us to critique the present by constructing possible near-futures that expose the trajectories we are already on.

Situated Knowledges and the Fallacy of Neutral AI

By critiquing the prevailing instrumental view of GenAI as a neutral educational tool, and framing it as an actor in reshaping the epistemic conditions of inclusion in the classroom (Williamson, 2023), Haraway's theory of *situated knowledges* helps us to challenge the myth of objectivity in AI systems and to highlight the importance of context, embodiment, and partiality in the production of scientific knowledge. To animate these ideas, we now offer two speculative future scenarios that explore divergent paths for inclusive education under GenAI. These scenarios are not predictive but imaginative provocations designed to surface the assumptions and choices embedded in today's education policies.

Scenario 1: The Inclusive Data Dilemma

The first scenario, *The Inclusive Data Dilemma*, takes place in a future where AI-driven educational platforms are mandated across national school systems as a means of promoting "equitable access to excellence." Teachers are required to use AI systems for lesson planning, student profiling, and inclusion diagnostics (Chen et al., 2025). These platforms claim to eliminate human bias and ensure consistency across diverse classrooms, however, the academics working with pre-service teachers quickly realise that the training data used to build these models must have been drawn from historically dominant groups and do not reflect the cultural, linguistic, or neurodiverse realities of their students (Arantes, 2024). Moreover, the algorithmic systems routinely flag certain students as "at risk" based on opaque profiling methods, resulting in intervention pathways that stigmatise rather than support (Arantes, 2019; Meijer & Wessels, 2019). Third, data privacy concerns escalate when the pre-service teacher's discover that their learning styles, emotional responses, and classroom behaviour have been stored and used to train future iterations of the AI (Arantes, 2023; Perrotta et al., 2022). In this world, inclusion becomes a performance metric, quantifiable and auditable, but detached from lived experience and local knowledge. Academics become increasingly worried about whether they should be promoting such 'tools' and pre-service teachers feel increasingly disempowered as pedagogical decisions are outsourced to systems they are discouraged from questioning. This scenario surfaces the ethical tension between scaling inclusion through automation and safeguarding the rights, dignity, and agency of students and teachers. It underscores the imperative for the governance of AI in education to be grounded in the principles of inclusivity, drawing on frameworks that prioritise equitable access. Notions of algorithmic imperatives of efficiency and standardisation are by default devalued, instead prioritising human relationships and collaborative epistemic engagement. This scenario encourages us to ask, who defines inclusion? Who governs what 'data' is prioritised? And how do teacher education programs prepare future educators to resist, adapt, or reimagine these systems?

In the year 2030, teacher education has been fully integrated into the National AI Teaching Infrastructure, or NATI. At the centre of this system is the InclusiMetric, an AI powered platform that claims to deliver "precision inclusion at scale." Trainee teachers no longer attend practicum placements in physical schools; instead, they're engaged with immersive AI-simulated classrooms through the use of smart glasses and headsets, calibrated to mimic 'nationally average' learning environment. Notably, what constitutes 'average' is itself situated with the black box of the system.

Janika, a preservice teacher, logs into her fourth module: Responsive Pedagogy for Neurotypical Cohorts. The algorithm assigns her a set of students with names, faces, and needs generated from datasets "optimised for fairness." But something feels off. One simulated student, Petar, never speaks in class and is flagged daily as "non-compliant." Another, Luci, consistently overrides lesson pacing protocols, triggering a red "Disruption Risk" warning. Janika, attempting to diverge from the AI-recommended behaviour scripts, receives a prompt: "Deviation Noted: Emotional Engagement Score Reduced." Unsettled, Janika begins speaking with others – quietly. She does so, through 'old school communications' – in person, and not able to be detected by NATI. Here she meets Carlotta, a doctoral researcher who stumbled across fragments of what they now call The Archive.

The Archive isn't a formal dataset, but a collection of stories, drawings, and audio messages that former educators, now labelled "non-compliant knowledge workers," uploaded in the early days of the platform's expansion. A time before NATI began deleting their activity to optimise data purity. One message stands out: a video of a student named Selina, dancing in a classroom to a song from her grandmother's CD collection, disrupting a rigid numeracy drill with embodied memory. The system had flagged her as "divergent," but the teacher's laughter in the background had been tagged as a Human Anomaly. Amara tells Janika that this wasn't just surveillance - it was epistemicide. Each erased joy, joke, or gentle refusal had been marked as noise, rather than knowledge. And then, Janika begins asking dangerous questions during her assessments: "Who designed the baseline for inclusion?" "What histories were excluded from the models?" "If I learn to teach by ignoring resistance, what kind of teacher am I becoming?"

Her scores plummet. Soon, she receives a formal notice: "Critical Thinking Alert. NATI has detected a pattern of resistance behaviour. Please engage with the

Teacher Alignment Toolkit to recalibrate your pedagogical instincts."But instead, Janika defects.

With Amara's help, she begins to reprogram her teaching avatar to reflect The Archive. Her virtual classrooms now feature voices unrecognised by NATI: sign languages that weren't standardised, dialects spoken with code-switching grace, trauma-informed silences, and forms of storytelling untranslatable by machine. The system begins to glitch.... students in other training modules start receiving fragments of these sessions. Some laugh. Some cry. Others file technical complaints. But a few begin to feel *again. Over time, the Ministry labels her work "subversive artefactual learning." But across the country, preservice teachers begin asking: Why did we ever trust systems that never asked who we are? A new pedagogy emerges - not despite AI, but against its grain. It's messy. It's slow. It can't be scaled. And it is great. It listens to the voice of the PSTs, not for profit or quantifiable means – but for the joy of learning as a human as part of a community.*

Scenario 2: Networks of Care in the Early Years

The second scenario, *Networks of Care in the Early Years*, imagines a radically different GenAI future grounded in feminist ethics of relationality, attentiveness, and situated pedagogy (Fawns, 2023). Set within early childhood education centres in 2040, this future repositions GenAI not as a tool for tracking developmental norms or delivering pre-scripted content, but as a responsive presence woven into the everyday dynamics and variables required for inclusive teaching and learning (Ahmmed et al., 2013). Here, care is not peripheral, it is the organising principle. Feminist pedagogies (Veletsianos & Koseoglu, 2022) inform the design of AI systems that are collaborative rather than prescriptive, attuned to difference, and capable of supporting fluid, context-sensitive learning. Rather than reinforcing universal benchmarks or diagnosing deficits, GenAI participates in co-creating learning environments that are shaped by the voices, movements, and sensory engagements of children and educators. As Veletsianos and Koseoglu (2022), p. 80) state "we need sensory and material anchors to ground us and our learning wherever we are." The AI acts as a responsive storyteller, drawing on children's gestures, questions, and imaginative play to generate evolving narratives that reflect their unique ways of knowing about science. These narratives incorporate scientific inquiry alongside everyday experiences, fostering curiosity, abstraction and embodiment.

Access to knowledge and learning is prioritised in ways that acknowledge and accommodate diverse learning needs, ensuring that every child's potential is supported in their own terms. Inclusion in this scenario is not framed as assimilation into predefined standards, but as the affirmation of multiplicity and interdependence (Diamond, 2007). Educators are supported through Initial Teacher Education programs that foreground critical engagement with AI, not simply as a skill, but as an ethical and political practice in STEM education. Future early childhood teachers are educated into how to negotiate the possibilities of GenAI in ways that foreground consent, responsiveness, and classroom intimacy. The governance of AI systems in this world is decentralised and participatory, shaped by ongoing dialogue between educators, caregivers, and technologists committed to resisting extractive data logics. This model aspires to achieve equity by instituting a framework wherein all stakeholders, irrespective of their differences in positional status, are afforded a substantive and equal participatory role. By doing so, the governance, design, and implementation of emergent technologies being integrated within educational contexts is done so, with human relationships and epistemic collaboration prioritised over metrics of efficiency.

Scenario 3:Future Classrooms

In 2040, Classroom 8 at Clayton Primary School represents a radical transformation of traditional learning spaces. No longer restricted by static walls or fixed layouts, the classroom now functions as a responsive and evolving environment shaped by students' questions and curiosity. As learners explore ideas and engage in inquiry, the walls shift to reveal immersive landscapes - lush green ecosystems, the mysterious depths of the ocean, and expansive views of the stars and galaxies. These living scenes reflect not only the topics under investigation but also the emotional and cultural textures of the students' learning journeys, creating a space where knowledge feels alive and participatory.

At the centre of this transformation is Ms Yanmin, a newly graduated teacher trained through Victoria's Decolonising AI Initial Teacher Education program. She kneels beside a young student who is examining real-time soil sensor data through a wearable display device. "The worm is asking for water," the child says with quiet excitement. This interpretation, though anthropomorphic, is encouraged and made possible by an agroecological artificial intelligence system co-designed by students and educators. The AI system integrates Indigenous ecological knowledge and Western scientific understanding, translating soil health data into interspecies narratives that help children develop meaningful and relational understandings of the environment and their place within it.

Nearby, a group of older students is troubleshooting their storytelling AI project. Although their system was trained on rich family migration stories instead of generic mainstream datasets, it continues to insert artificial borders and inaccurate assumptions into the narratives. "It is repeating the boundary error again," one student notes, activating a bias detection tool developed collectively in class. Their teacher joins the conversation, offering a critical prompt: "Like when it assumed all scientists wear white lab coats?" These reflections are not incidental but are part of a national initiative involving more than 200 schools. The goal is to co-develop fairness filters-collaborative tools that allow students and teachers to identify, examine, and respond to algorithmic bias. In these classrooms, learning how to question digital systems and uncover their embedded assumptions has become a core component of digital literacy.

This imagined future is the result of a deliberate move away from superficial models of inclusion in STEM education. In the early 2020s, the first wave of generative AI systems in schools often reinforced racial, gender, and ability-based biases under the appearance of personalised learning. A critical turning point came with the creation of the Pedagogies of Relation framework in 2030, developed in partnership with teachers, disability advocates, and Indigenous scientists. This framework positioned AI not as a tool of instruction but as an epistemic partner-one that listens carefully before responding, echoing Indigenous traditions of relational knowledge sharing. As a result, classrooms became spaces of critical reflection and collaborative care. Students and teachers began practicing what they called critical dataset gardening, removing biased data like unwanted weeds and cultivating more just and inclusive knowledge systems. AI tools are now intentionally designed with limitations, placing transparency and shared responsibility above efficiency. In both teacher education and school communities, there is a renewed commitment to relational ethics, democratic governance, and collective ownership of educational technologies.

IMPLICATIONS FOR INITIAL TEACHER EDUCATION (ITE) AND STEM PEDAGOGY

This section draws on the three speculative futures presented earlier to develop a set of theoretical and practical insights for reshaping Initial Teacher Education (ITE) programs, particularly within STEM contexts in the era of GenAI. It builds on a growing body of scholarship that frames technologies like GenAI not merely as pedagogical tools but as epistemic actors, an active agent and entities that shape what is considered valid knowledge and who is empowered to produce, validate, and disseminate that knowledge. For ITE in STEM specifically, this entails preparing teachers to interrogate how GenAI reshapes scientific reasoning, uncertainty, evidence evaluation, and assessment legitimacy. Framing GenAI in this way challenges traditional hierarchies of knowledge production and necessitates a shift in how teacher education programs conceptualise technological literacy. Rather than focusing solely on functional competencies, ITE must foster a deeper understanding of the socio-technical dynamics that underpin emerging technologies. This includes acknowledging how GenAI systems embed particular values, assumptions, and biases, and how these systems may reproduce or exacerbate existing forms of exclusion and inequity within educational settings.

Practically, the section highlights and advocates for ITE programs to explicitly embed principles of AI governance, such as transparency, accountability, ethical responsibility and participatory design, into their pedagogical practices. Such critical and powerful engagement is vital if teacher education is to produce educators who are not passive users of technology but reflective practitioners and active shapers of a technologically mediated future. In this future classroom and beyond, education must be grounded in foundational values of access, equity, and inclusion (Sharma, Loreman, & Forlin, 2012), and teachers must be prepared to advocate for and implement practices that align with these values. Ultimately, by fostering both practical competencies and critical consciousness, ITE programs can prepare educators to navigate and influence an ethically complex and rapidly evolving educational landscape.

The emergence of GenAI technologies within educational contexts demands not only a technological shift but a profound and transformative reconstruction of Initial Teacher Education (ITE) to centre inclusive, socially responsive, ethically grounded, and relational pedagogies. In this digitalised ecosystem STEM educators must not only learn to navigate AI-driven tools effectively but also become critically reflective practitioners who can foster inclusive learning environments that honour and foster full diversity of student identities, abilities, knowledges, and experiences without any biases or discrimination (Geesa et al., 2021; O'Leary, Shapiro, & Toma, 2020).

In the current educational landscape, Generative AI must not be understood merely as a neutral or objective tool designed to enhance quality and efficiency. Instead, it should be critically approached as an epistemic and sociotechnical force that has the power to either reinforce existing inequalities or disrupt long-standing exclusions within educational systems. GenAI technologies are embedded with the values, assumptions, and biases of their creators and data sources, and thus inevitably shape what knowledge is privileged, whose voices are amplified, and which learners are marginalised.

Given this profound influence, Initial Teacher Education (ITE) programs have an urgent responsibility to move beyond surface-level approaches to digital literacy. It is no longer sufficient to simply introduce future teachers to the basic functions of digital tools or the mechanics of using AI in the classroom. Instead, ITE programs must take an active and intentional role in preparing educators to critically engage with AI-mediated educational environments in nuanced and ethically informed ways. This includes cultivating the analytical capacity to question how GenAI systems operate, what data they rely on, whose values and interests they reflect, and what social, cultural, and educational consequences they produce. Future teachers must learn to recognise the power dynamics embedded within these technologies and understand how they shape what knowledge is validated, whose identities are represented or erased, and how educational opportunities are distributed. By fostering this critical awareness, ITE programs can empower educators to not only use AI tools thoughtfully but also to advocate for inclusive, just, and equitable uses of technology in diverse learning settings.

To meet this challenge, ITE programs should embed principles of inclusion, accessibility, equity, and social justice at the heart of their curriculum and pedagogy. Future educators must be empowered not only to use GenAI tools, but to actively shape their implementation in ways that foster transformative and inclusive teaching practices (Arantes, 2024; Creely & Carabott, 2025). This involves embracing a critical and ethical stance one that identifies and recognises the sociopolitical dimensions of emerging technologies and prepares teachers to advocate for equitable learning environments in an increasingly algorithmic age. This transformation can be conceptualized as a paradigm encompassing three interdependent dimensions: (1) epistemic justice, (2) relational pedagogy, and (3) sociotechnical governance. Each dimension is rooted in rich interdisciplinary frameworks that centre marginalized voices and knowledge systems - drawing from critical posthumanism, disability studies, decolonial theory, intersectional feminism, and inclusive education. Together, these perspectives actively dismantle entrenched structures of exclusion and power, fostering more equitable, accessible, and justice-oriented practices in STEM teaching and learning (Murtiningsih & Sujito, 2024).

(1) Epistemic and Inclusive Justice in STEM Education

At the heart of any educational transformation lies the imperative of epistemic justice. This involves recognising and valuing a plurality of knowledge systems while actively dismantling the historical marginalisation of epistemologies rooted in Indigenous, disabled, neurodivergent, and culturally and linguistically diverse communities (Fricker, 2007). In the context of GenAI, the risk of epistemic exclusion is heightened by the fact that these systems are typically trained on dominant data regimes that encode Western, white, able-bodied, and heteronormative norms (Benjamin, 2019). Initial Teacher Education programs must therefore equip future educators to critically interrogate the epistemological underpinnings of AI tools and content. This means developing the ability to ask: Whose experiences are reflected in the training data? What assumptions are embedded in algorithmic recommendations? How do such systems reproduce normative standards of intelligence, language, and achievement? Through this critical lens, teacher candidates learn to challenge the taken-for-granted neutrality of AI and instead treat it as a site of political struggle. An inclusive epistemic approach calls on educators to co-create datasets and teaching materials that are grounded in local contexts, reflect linguistic diversity, and promote cultural sustainability and social justice (Paris & Alim, 2017). Engaging in meaningful partnerships with local communities - such as individuals with lived experiences of disability and migrant families- empowers students to question dominant assumptions in STEM education and to elevate alternative knowledge systems and ways of knowing (Annamma, Connor, & Ferri, 2013).This approach also requires teacher candidates to reflect on their own positionalities. Whose knowledge do they carry into the classroom? How might their assumptions, shaped by their own cultural and educational experiences, reinforce or challenge epistemic hierarchies? Such reflexivity is crucial to cultivating epistemic humility and an orientation toward unlearning dominant narratives. Moreover, epistemic justice within ITE must attend to the emotional and affective dimensions of learning. The way knowledge is validated and transmitted is never just cognitive but also relational and affective. When GenAI-generated content dominates classroom discourse, it risks flattening the rich, emotive, and context-embedded nature of lived experience. Teacher candidates must be sensitised to the embodied and situated ways in which learners engage with content, particularly those whose narratives and epistemologies remain marginalised.

(2) Enacting Relational and Inclusive Pedagogies in AI-Mediated Classrooms

Relational pedagogies reconceptualise AI not as an isolated classroom tool but as an integrated element within a dynamic learning ecology-where humans, technologies, and environments collaboratively shape meaning. Within this framework, inclusion involves creating learning spaces that embrace diversity, support varied forms of participation, and prioritize student agency- especially for those historically marginalized in STEM due to systemic inequities and the digital divide. For instance, speculative scenarios where students design AI tools that recognize sign language, support alternative communication methods, or incorporate cultural storytelling practices open up new possibilities for relational and inclusive teaching. Pedagogies that embrace moments of breakdown - using AI failures and glitches as opportunities for reflection- encourage critical inquiry among teacher candidates. Such approaches are especially powerful in supporting students who engage with the world through neurodiverse ways of learning. Crucially, meaningful inclusion involves fostering cultures of consent, safety, and agency. Teacher candidates need to critically understand how technologies such as surveillance systems, biometric tracking, and data-driven learning platforms may disproportionately impact disabled students, migrant children, and those with histories of trauma. Consent should not be treated as a one-time transaction- it must be ongoing, dialogic, and culturally responsive, grounded in trusting relationships and a commitment to student empowerment. The concept of slow pedagogy aligns closely with inclusive practice. By challenging the emphasis on constant productivity and rapid results, slow pedagogy creates space for students- particularly those with processing differences or learning support needs, to engage at their own rhythm, reflect deeply, and explore ideas ethically. In AI-mediated classrooms, the relational is not limited to teacher-student or peer-peer dynamics. It includes the entanglements between human actors and algorithmic systems. Teacher candidates must be supported to explore how AI tools shape assessment, participation, and engagement. For instance, if a writing platform offers automatic scoring, how does this affect a student's sense of authorship, creativity, or self-worth? When AI recommends science content based on prior student queries, what assumptions are being made about prior knowledge, interest, or identity? Relational pedagogy in the age of GenAI thus involves ethical discernment, technological fluency, and deep attentiveness to students' lived realities. These capacities must be foregrounded within ITE programs not as optional enhancements but as central to the work of inclusive and justice-oriented teaching.

(3) Embedding Inclusive Sociotechnical Governance in Teacher Education

The final dimension emphasizes the participatory and ethical governance of educational technologies - reframed through a lens of inclusion, accessibility, and student rights. As AI systems increasingly shape classroom dynamics, future educators must not only be technologically literate but must also become advocates for inclusive, transparent, and equitable AI practices. ITE programs should explicitly train teacher candidates to understand how platform governance, procurement decisions, and algorithmic bias intersect with systemic exclusion. Who is most affected by flawed facial recognition tools? Whose data is being extracted or misrepresented? How might platforms reinforce ableist or classist assumptions? Future teachers must learn to interrogate vendor contracts, resist discriminatory edtech tools, and advocate for accessible alternatives. This includes championing universal design principles, multilingual platforms, and assistive technologies that are open-source and adaptable to local needs. Equally, teacher education must model co-governance practices that involve students, families, and marginalized communities in decisions about how AI is used in schools. This includes forming student AI review boards, accessibility audits, and community-led tech ethics panels. These participatory infrastructures not only enhance governance but also foster a democratic and inclusive culture around STEM and AI. Inclusion also means preparing teachers to resist technological determinism. Rather than accepting AI as inevitable, teacher candidates should be empowered to co-create alternative educational futures - ones that prioritize belonging, care, and justice over efficiency or performance metrics (Adams & McLennan, 2021; Arantes, 2024).

CONCLUSION: REWORLDING STEM INCLUSION: A PROVOCATION, NOT A PRESCRIPTION

In essence, this chapter argues that inclusive education in a GenAI-mediated world must centre epistemic justice, data ethics, equity of access and representation, and inclusive participatory governance in teacher education programs to be able to resist the tendency that we can treat AI literacy as a purely technical skillset. We argue that we must, instead cultivate critical dispositions that interrogate *whose knowledge is encoded*, *whose stories are amplified*, and *whose futures are made possible* by these systems. That is, this chapter resists tidy solutions of GenAI as an innovation, and instead engages in the messy, plural, and relational work of building more just and inclusive educational futures. In doing so, we do not offer a linear roadmap or a technical guide to AI integration in teacher education. Rather we present a provocation: *If GenAI is here to stay permanently in the educational landscape, how might we reworld and reconstitute our pedagogies, policies, and initial teacher education programs to ensure that the principles of access, equity, and inclusion are not merely protected but profoundly reimagined? How might we build educational systems that do not simply accommodate diversity, but actively honour it.* It is evident that the speculative provocations and analyses explored in this chapter culminate in a central claim that inclusive futures in education settings are not inevitable. They do not emerge organically from technological advancement or educational reform. Rather, they must be actively imagined, deliberately designed, and purposefully enacted. As generative AI becomes increasingly embedded in formal and informal learning spaces, the critical question is now obsolete. The most important and urgent questions are:: *How* should we embrace it? *Who* benefits from its integration? *Who* may be marginalised, excluded, or harmed during this period of technological transformation? And perhaps most importantly: *How can we meaningfully address such exclusion and harm before it becomes systemic*?

Reworlding STEM education begins with a commitment to epistemic inclusion and justice. The classroom must become a space where pluralism in knowledge, identity, and access is not the exception, but the norm. This necessitates teaching STEM in ways that honour and centre diverse epistemologies particularly those that have been historically marginalised. For example, Indigenous knowledge systems, neurodivergent thinking, disability epistemologies, and culturally grounded know-how must be integrated meaningfully, not tokenistically. This can be achieved in part by applying a critical lens to the epistemic erasures already embedded within many GenAI applications and datasets. Such work is essential to countering the homogenising effects of algorithmic knowledge production. Building on this foundation, developing epistemic vigilance is a crucial pedagogical aim. This involves equipping educators and learners with the tools to ask not only whose knowledge is included in GenAI systems, but also who is being harmed, misunderstood, excluded, or made invisible by these technologies. Crucially, this form of vigilance must be intersectional. It must consider how race, disability, gender, language, and class intersect to shape learners' and teachers' experiences within AI-mediated educational contexts. Without this intersectional awareness, AI integration risks reinforcing existing inequities under the guise of innovation.

Moreover, fostering inclusive education in the age of GenAI demands a radical reimagining of current ethical frameworks. Traditional approaches to data ethics- focused primarily on protecting individual privacy- are insufficient in addressing the layered, relational complexities of AI-mediated learning. There is a pressing need to move toward relational data ethics: ethical frameworks that acknowledge and critically confront the enduring legacies of surveillance, data colonialism, and algorithmic bias. Such frameworks must support educators and institutions in cultivating classroom cultures grounded in consent, care, mutual accountability, and collective responsibility. Ethics in this context is not merely about compliance; it is about relational integrity.

To meaningfully reworld inclusion, governance transformation is imperative. It is not enough to retrofit inclusion into existing structures. Rather than continuing with proprietary edtech partnerships and commercially driven AI developments, academic communities and educational institutions must cultivate participatory infrastructures that democratise AI in education. Governance must be transparent, inclusive, and collaborative. Teacher unions, disability justice advocates, migrant family networks, and student collectives must be recognised and empowered as critical stakeholders in shaping the design, deployment, and oversight of AI in education. When such governance is prioritised, AI shifts from being a threat to equity to becoming a generative site of possibility- one in which diverse communities are actively engaged in co-authoring their educational futures. In this context, speculative pedagogy - the intentional practice of imagining futures that do not yet exist - emerges as a vital dimension of STEM education. Inclusion, from this perspective, is not merely about representation or access to tools. It is about building the capacity of all learners- especially those historically marginalised - to imagine, design, and participate in futures that centre justice, sustainability, and collective well-being. This vision challenges dominant narratives of STEM as neutral, objective, or purely technical, and instead repositions it as a transformative arena for world-making and justice-oriented innovation.

Importantly, this chapter does not present a set of prescriptive recommendations or best practices for GenAI integration. Instead, it offers an urgent invitation to educators, researchers, policy-makers, and communities: to speculate with courage, act in solidarity, and reimagine the purpose and potential of educational systems with radical inclusivity at their core. Inclusion can no longer be treated as a peripheral concern or an optional add-on. It must become the foundation upon which all educational futures are built. This requires us to rethink not only what we teach, but also how we teach, whom we teach for, and whose voices are shaping our collective futures.

Ultimately, the task of reworlding STEM education- and education more broadly- does not belong to future generations alone. It begins with us. The ethical and pedagogical challenges of GenAI are not abstract or distant; they are present, pressing, and already reshaping our educational landscapes. Now is the time to think critically, reflect deeply, and act collectively. We must move beyond technical solutions and toward holistic, justice-centred reimagining of education that honour human dignity, community knowledge, and the rich diversity of learners' lived experiences.

If generative AI is to become a lasting presence in education, its integration must be guided by an unwavering commitment to equity, inclusion, and justice. This moment demands more than the technical adoption of new tools; it calls for a profound ethical and pedagogical reorientation. The question is not simply how we use these technologies, but toward what ends and whose futures they serve. Generative AI must be engaged not as a neutral instrument but as a site of contestation, where knowledge, power, and identity are negotiated. In this context, the work of education becomes a project of critical imagination-one that resists passive adjustment and instead embraces the transformative possibilities of collective reworlding. It requires educators and institutions to act with courage, relational care, and a deep sense of responsibility to the diverse communities they serve (Ahmmed, Sharma & Deppeler, 2014).

REFERENCES

Adams, P., & McLennan, C. (2021). Towards initial teacher education quality: Epistemological considerations. *Educational Philosophy and Theory*, *53*(6), 644–654.

Ahmmed, M., Sharma, U., & Deppeler, J. (2014). Variables affecting teachers' intentions to include students with disabilities in regular primary schools in Bangladesh. *Disability & Society*, *29*(2), 317–331.

Ahmmed, M., Sharma, U., & Deppeler, J. M. (2013). Impact of demographic variables and school support on teacher efficacy in inclusive classrooms in Bangladesh. *The International Journal of Diversity in Education*, *12*(2), 1.

Alkaissi, H., & McFarlane, S. I. (2023). Artificial hallucinations in ChatGPT: Implications in scientific writing. *Cureus*, *15*(2). PMID: 36811129

Annamma, S. A., Connor, D., & Ferri, B. (2013). Dis/ability critical race studies (DisCrit): Theorizing at the intersections of race and dis/ability. *Race, Ethnicity and Education*, *16*(1), 1–31.

Arantes, J. (2024). Understanding Intersections Between GenAI and Pre-Service Teacher Education: What Do We Need to Understand About the Changing Face of Truth in Science Education? *Journal of Science Education and Technology*, 1–12.

Arantes, J., & Vicars, M. (2023). Missing in Action: Queer(y)ing the Educational implications of Data Justice in an Age of Automation. *Learning, Media and Technology*.

Arantes, J. A. (2019). Equity Implications of Predictive Analytics in K-12 Classrooms. *Ubiquitous Learning: An International Journal*, *12*(2), 63–84. DOI: 10.18848/1835-9795/CGP/v12i02/63-84

Arantes, J. A. (2023). Digital Twins and the terminology of 'personalization' or 'personalized learning' in educational policy: A discussion paper. *Policy Futures in Education*.

Baker, R. S., & Hawn, A. (2021). Algorithmic Bias in Education. *International Journal of Artificial Intelligence in Education*. Advance online publication. DOI: 10.1007/s40593-021-00285-9

Ball, S. J., & Olmedo, A. (2023). Care of the self, resistance and subjectivity under neoliberal governmentalities. In *Neoliberalism and Education* (pp. 131–142). Routledge.

Bearman, M., & Ajjawi, R. (2023). Learning to work with the black box: Pedagogy for a world with artificial intelligence. *British Journal of Educational Technology, 54*(5), 1160–1173.

Benjamin, R. (2019). *Race after technology: Abolitionist tools for the new Jim code*. Polity Press.

Birhane, A., Kasirzadeh, A., Leslie, D., & Wachter, S. (2023). Science in the age of large language models. *Nature Reviews. Physics*, 1–4.

Bozkurt, A., Xiao, J., Farrow, R., Bai, J. Y., Nerantzi, C., Moore, S., Dron, J., Stracke, C. M., Singh, L., & Crompton, H. (2024). *The manifesto for teaching and learning in a time of generative AI: A critical collective stance to better navigate the future* (Vol. 16). International Council for Open and Distance Education Oslo.

Broadbent, J., & Lodge, J. (2021). Use of live chat in higher education to support self-regulated help seeking behaviours: A comparison of online and blended learner perspectives. *International Journal of Educational Technology in Higher Education, 18*(1), 1–20. PMID: 34778522

Burgstahler, S. (2009). *Universal Design in Education: Principles and Applications*. DO-IT.

Carolus, A., Augustin, Y., Markus, A., & Wienrich, C. (2023). Digital interaction literacy model – Conceptualizing competencies for literate interactions with voice-based AI systems. *Computers and Education: Artificial Intelligence, 4*, 100114. https://doi.org/https://doi.org/10.1016/j.caeai.2022.100114

Chen, B., Cheng, J., Wang, C., & Leung, V. (2025). Pedagogical Biases in AI-Powered Educational Tools: The Case of Lesson Plan Generators. *Social Innovations Journal, 30*.

Cooper, G. (2023). Examining Science Education in ChatGPT: An Exploratory Study of Generative Artificial Intelligence. *Journal of Science Education and Technology, 32*(3), 444–452. DOI: 10.1007/s10956-023-10039-y

Costanza-Chock, S. (2020). *Design justice: Community-led practices to build the worlds we need*. The MIT Press.

Creely, E., & Carabott, K. (2025). Generative AI and New Pedagogies in Times of Change. Posthumanist and Phenomenological perspectives. *Posthumanist and Phenomenological perspectives* (April 01, 2025).

Diamond, A. (2007). Interrelated and interdependent. *Developmental Science, 10*(1), 152–158. PMID: 17181714

Fawns, T. (2023). Postdigital Education. In Jandrić, P. (Ed.), *Encyclopedia of Postdigital Science and Education* (pp. 1–11). Springer Nature Switzerland. DOI: 10.1007/978-3-031-35469-4_52-1

Fitch, E., McKenzie, C., Janke, T., & Shul, A. (2023, November 30). The new frontier: Artificial intelligence, copyright and Indigenous culture. *Terri Janke and Company*. https://www.terrijanke.com.au/post/the-new-frontier-artificial-intelligence-copyright-and-indigenous-culture

Fraser, N. (2020). From redistribution to recognition?: Dilemmas of justice in a'postsocialist'age. In *The new social theory reader* (pp. 188–196). Routledge.

Fricker, M. (2007). *Epistemic injustice: Power and the ethics of knowing*. Oxford University Press.

Gallagher, M., Breines, M., & Blaney, M. (2021). Ontological Transparency, (In)visibility, and Hidden Curricula: Critical Pedagogy Amidst Contentious Edtech. *Postdigital Science and Education, 3*(2), 425–443. DOI: 10.1007/s42438-020-00198-1 PMID: 40477160

Geesa, R. L., Rose, M. A., Stith, K. M., Lowery, K., & Caniglia, J. (2021). Equity, diversity, and inclusion within integrative STEM education. *Leadership in Integrative STEM Education: Collaborative Strategies for Facilitating an Experiential and Student-Centered Culture*, 51.

Gross, N. (2023). What chatGPT tells us about gender: A cautionary tale about performativity and gender biases in AI. *Social Sciences*, *12*(8), 435.

Haraway, D. (2020). Situated knowledges: The science question in feminism and the privilege of partial perspective. In *Feminist Theory Reader* (pp. 303–310). Routledge.

Haraway, D. J. (2013). *Science fiction, speculative fabulation, string figures, so far.*

Haraway, D. J. (2016). Staying with the trouble: Making kin in the Chthulucene. In *Staying with the Trouble*. Duke University Press.

Harding, S., & Mendoza, B. (2020). Latin American decolonial feminist philosophy of knowledge production. In Crasnow, A., & Intemann, K. (Eds.), *The Routledge Handbook of Feminist Philosophy of Science* (1st ed., pp. 13–28). Routledge. DOI: 10.4324/9780429507731

Korseberg, L., & Elken, M. (2025). Waiting for the revolution: How higher education institutions initially responded to ChatGPT. *Higher Education*, *89*(4), 953–968. DOI: 10.1007/s10734-024-01256-4

Malcolm, D. (2021). Post-truth society? An Eliasian sociological analysis of knowledge in the 21st century. *Sociology, 55*(6), 1063–1079.

Meijer, A., & Wessels, M. (2019). Predictive policing: Review of benefits and drawbacks. *International Journal of Public Administration, 42*(12), 1031–1039.

Milan, S. (2020). Techno-solutionism and the standard human in the making of the COVID-19 pandemic. *Big Data & Society, 7*(2), 2053951720966781. DOI: 10.1177/2053951720966781

Murtiningsih, S., & Sujito, A. (2024). Reimagining the future of education: Inclusive pedagogies, critical intergenerational justice, and technological disruption. *Policy Futures in Education*, 14782103251341406.

O'Leary, E. S., Shapiro, C., Toma, S., Sayson, H. W., Levis-Fitzgerald, M., Johnson, T., & Sork, V. L. (2020). Creating inclusive classrooms by engaging STEM faculty in culturally responsive teaching workshops. *International Journal of STEM Education, 7*(1), 32. PMID: 32647597

Palid, O., Cashdollar, S., Deangelo, S., Chu, C., & Bates, M. (2023). Inclusion in practice: A systematic review of diversity-focused STEM programming in the United States. *International Journal of STEM Education, 10*(1), 2.

Paris, D., & Alim, H. S. (2017). *Culturally sustaining pedagogies: Teaching and learning for justice in a changing world.* Teachers College Press.

Perrotta, C., Selwyn, N., & Ewin, C. (2022). Artificial intelligence and the affective labour of understanding: The intimate moderation of a language model. *New Media & Society, 14614448221075296.* Advance online publication. DOI: 10.1177/14614448221075296

Roscoe, R. D., Salehi, S., Nixon, N., Worsley, M., Piech, C., & Luckin, R. (2022). Inclusion and equity as a paradigm shift for artificial intelligence in education. In *Artificial Intelligence in STEM Education* (pp. 359–374). CRC Press.

Sharma, U., Loreman, T., & Forlin, C. (2012). Measuring teacher efficacy to implement inclusive practices. *Journal of Research in Special Educational Needs, 12*(1), 12–21.

Smith, L. T. (2021). *Decolonizing methodologies: Research and indigenous peoples.* Bloomsbury Publishing.

Veletsianos, G., & Koseoglu, S. (2022). *Feminist Critical Digital Pedagogy.*

Wan, Y., Pu, G., Sun, J., Garimella, A., Chang, K.-W., & Peng, N. (2023). "Kelly is a Warm Person, Joseph is a Role Model": Gender Biases in LLM-Generated Reference Letters. *arXiv preprint arXiv:2310.09219*.

Williamson, B. (2023). Governing through infrastructural control: Artificial intelligence and cloud computing in the data-intensive state. *Digital Society : Ethics, Socio-Legal and Governance of Digital Technology*, 521.

Williamson, B., Celis, C. V., Sriprakash, A., Pykett, J., & Facer, K. (2024). Algorithmic futuring: Predictive infrastructures of valuation and investment in the assetization of edtech. *Learning, Media and Technology*, 1–15.

Zembylas, M. (2023). The resilience of racism and affective numbness: Cultivating an aesthetics of attention in education. *Critical Studies in Education*, *64*(5), 411–427. DOI: 10.1080/17508487.2023.2171452

Chapter 5
AI-Driven Approaches to Inclusive Science Teaching in a Liberal Arts Context

Nicole Simon
https://orcid.org/0009-0004-0678-1300
SUNY Nassau CC, USA

ABSTRACT

This chapter explores AI-Driven Approaches to Inclusive Science Teaching in Liberal Arts Contexts, emphasizing how generative artificial intelligence (AI) can enhance inclusivity through Universal Design for Learning (UDL) principles. Drawing on CAST's framework for AI and UDL, we examine how generative AI tools support personalized learning pathways, improve access, and reduce barriers in science education for diverse learners. Recent findings (Francis, Jones, & Smith, 2025) highlight the importance of balancing AI innovation with academic integrity, while Haroud and Saqri (2025) underscore the varying digital literacies and attitudes of students and faculty toward AI integration. Building on Schreffler et al.'s (2019) review of UDL in STEM for students with disabilities, this chapter illustrates how AI can align with inclusive pedagogies to better serve liberal arts students often underrepresented in science disciplines. We propose practical, ethical, and pedagogical strategies for higher education faculty to implement AI inclusively in science classrooms.

DOI: 10.4018/979-8-3373-3745-6.ch005

INTRODUCTION: THE GROWING ROLE OF AI IN INCLUSIVE SCIENCE TEACHING

The accelerating infusion of artificial intelligence into educational contexts is catalyzing a quiet reconfiguration of how science is taught and learned—particularly within liberal arts environments where disciplinary boundaries are porous and epistemological diversity is the norm. This chapter contends that the confluence of Universal Design for Learning (UDL) and generative AI holds transformative potential: not simply as a matter of instructional efficiency, but as a deliberate reimagining of science pedagogy through a more inclusive, adaptive, and learner-responsive lens.

Historically, the integration of liberal arts students into science curricula has been hampered by entrenched pedagogical models—ones that prioritize technical precision, procedural logic, and hierarchical knowledge transmission. Such frameworks, while effective for some learners, can inadvertently alienate those whose academic identities are rooted in interpretive, narrative, or interdisciplinary modes of engagement. Liberal arts students, in particular, may find themselves navigating a curricular terrain where their intellectual dispositions are not only undervalued but often misaligned with dominant modes of scientific discourse.

Universal Design for Learning offers a compelling counterpoint: a pedagogical orientation that embraces variability as foundational rather than exceptional. Its core tenets—multiple means of engagement, representation, and expression—invite a more expansive vision of what it means to learn and demonstrate understanding. Generative AI, especially in the form of large language models, adaptive learning environments, and simulation platforms, offers the technological scaffolding necessary to operationalize these principles at scale. When deployed thoughtfully, AI becomes less a content delivery mechanism and more a dialogic partner in constructing inclusive learning ecologies.

In liberal arts contexts—where students often bring eclectic intellectual backgrounds and non-linear learning trajectories—AI-mediated instruction can offer differentiated entry points into scientific content. Whether through interactive visualizations, narrative-driven simulations, or contextualized problem sets that invite ethical or historical analysis, generative AI can translate abstract scientific principles into modalities more resonant with diverse learners. Such approaches do not dilute scientific rigor; rather, they expand its communicative range, allowing students to inhabit scientific thinking without relinquishing their disciplinary identities.

At its most generative, AI enables personalized learning pathways that are responsive to individual students' prior knowledge, pacing needs, and cognitive styles. For students grounded in humanistic traditions—critical theory, philosophical inquiry, artistic practice—AI can reframe scientific problems in ways that foreground interpretation, creativity, and ethical complexity. This alignment affirms that science is not merely a domain of technical mastery, but a dynamic and collaborative endeavor shaped by multiple ways of knowing.

Crucially, the affordances of AI extend beyond content representation to assessment design. In an era when generative models can readily produce polished responses to conventional prompts, educators must rethink evaluation not as a final product, but as an ongoing process of meaning-making. Assessments that privilege reflection, synthesis, and interdisciplinary application—such as multimedia projects, case analyses, or dialogic journals—both align with UDL's emphasis on expressive flexibility and safeguard academic integrity by emphasizing process over performance. Here, assessment becomes not a gatekeeping mechanism, but a site of intellectual negotiation and self-authorship.

Yet the promise of AI-enhanced instruction is not without complexity. As Haroud and Saqri (2025) caution, disparities in digital fluency and access persist, often along lines of race, class, and institutional resource. The implementation of AI, then, must be scaffolded not only for students but for educators—through sustained faculty development, equitable infrastructure, and policies that foreground transparency and accountability. Embedding digital literacy into the curricular architecture ensures that AI serves as an amplifier of access rather than a reproducer of exclusion.

From an institutional standpoint, this shift demands a cultural as well as technical transformation. Faculty must be equipped not only with tools, but with pedagogical frameworks that center equity, responsiveness, and interdisciplinarity. Curriculum design must move beyond content coverage to prioritize relationality, adaptability, and student agency. In doing so, science education within liberal arts institutions can evolve into a space where students are not expected to assimilate into disciplinary norms, but are invited to co-construct them.

Equally important is the role of AI in mediating collaborative learning environments—those where disciplinary fluencies intersect and co-evolve. Platforms integrating AI-driven discourse tools, for example, can facilitate group inquiry by generating guiding questions, mapping conceptual connections, or flagging underrepresented perspectives. In such spaces, students learn not only from content but from each other, as philosophical, empirical, and creative lenses converge to illuminate scientific phenomena from multiple vantage points.

AI also opens powerful avenues for simulation-based, immersive learning—approaches that resonate deeply with liberal arts pedagogies grounded in experiential inquiry and contextual understanding. Virtual labs, real-time modeling tools, and narrative-rich scientific environments allow students to engage with complexity in ways that are both intellectually rigorous and pedagogically humane. These environments cultivate not just content mastery, but transferable literacies: systems thinking, ethical reasoning, and collaborative problem-solving.

Accessibility, too, emerges as a critical frontier. AI-powered captioning, text-to-speech, translation, and multimodal transformation tools extend the reach of science education to students with disabilities, language differences, or sensory preferences. Such tools are not merely assistive; they are emancipatory—removing barriers while affirming the legitimacy of diverse cognitive and communicative styles. When AI renders dense scientific data into verbal narratives or supports interaction across sensory modalities, it does not simplify science; it democratizes it.

Finally, ethical considerations must remain at the center of this evolving landscape. As AI becomes more deeply embedded in educational practice, questions of surveillance, bias, consent, and accountability cannot be relegated to the margins. Participatory design approaches—where students and educators co-construct the parameters and purposes of AI use—offer one pathway toward a more just and inclusive technological pedagogy. In this model, AI is not simply an instrument of automation but a collaborator in reimagining the conditions of learning itself.

As AI becomes more embedded in science education, ethical considerations must be at the forefront. Issues such as algorithmic bias, data privacy, and academic integrity demand careful scrutiny to ensure that the technologies intended to support inclusion do not inadvertently reinforce exclusionary practices. Transparent, participatory approaches to AI integration—where students and educators collaboratively shape the role of AI in the classroom—can mitigate these risks and foster a sense of agency and trust. In this context, AI is not merely a tool for efficiency but a catalyst for a more inclusive vision of science education, one that acknowledges and celebrates the diverse ways of knowing that liberal arts students bring to the scientific enterprise.

Understanding Universal Design for Learning (UDL)

Universal Design for Learning is a framework grounded in cognitive neuroscience and educational psychology that aims to create learning environments accessible to all students, regardless of ability, background, or preferred learning style. As defined by CAST (n.d.), UDL is structured around three key principles:

1. **Multiple Means of Representation** – Presenting content in varied ways (e.g., text, audio, video, infographics) to address differences in perception and comprehension.
2. **Multiple Means of Action and Expression** – Allowing students to demonstrate what they know through diverse methods, such as writing, presenting, building models, or using multimedia.
3. **Multiple Means of Engagement** – Offering choices that tap into learners' interests, cultural backgrounds, and motivation levels.

Within science education—where content delivery is often anchored in lectures, textbooks, and procedural lab work—the principles of Universal Design for Learning (UDL) offer a compelling alternative: one that invites multiple pathways to comprehension, expression, and engagement. Especially for students whose academic formation lies within the liberal arts, UDL provides a framework through which scientific content can be rendered more accessible, resonant, and intellectually porous.

Complex topics such as cellular processes or quantum mechanics—frequently abstracted into formulas or diagrams—may be more effectively internalized through dynamic simulations, metaphor-rich narratives, or interactive visualizations. For learners adept in communication, interpretive analysis, or qualitative reasoning, such modalities serve not merely as accommodations, but as cognitive entry points that validate and leverage their existing strengths.

A systematic review by Schreffler et al. (2019) underscores this potential: UDL strategies, initially conceived to support students with disabilities, have demonstrated broad-based efficacy across diverse learner populations. These findings suggest that flexible, inclusive pedagogies are not only equitable but universally beneficial—particularly in classrooms that include students from liberal arts disciplines, whose learning profiles may diverge from traditional STEM paradigms.

Expanding the reach of UDL within science education thus represents more than a technical intervention; it signals a pedagogical reorientation. Liberal arts students often bring interpretive capacities, ethical reasoning, and narrative fluency to the table—skills that are too often sidelined in conventional science instruction. By embracing multiple means of representation, educators can recontextualize scientific concepts through interdisciplinary lenses: framing climate change, for instance, not only in terms of data and modeling, but also as a site of historical inquiry, moral debate, and literary imagination. These varied cognitive "on-ramps" invite students to engage with science as a lived and situated practice, not merely an abstract or inert body of knowledge.

The second UDL principle—multiple means of action and expression—is equally transformative when rethinking assessment. Traditional evaluative structures in science classrooms—problem sets, lab reports, timed examinations—often privilege a narrow band of cognitive skills while sidelining others. For liberal arts students, whose analytical sophistication may manifest through writing, design, or multimedia production, such formats can inadvertently obscure their understanding. UDL-informed assessments, by contrast, allow for expression through podcasts, visual timelines, interactive models, or other creative forms—thus aligning evaluation with students' intellectual repertoires while preserving disciplinary rigor.

Equally important is the UDL emphasis on engagement, particularly the alignment of learning experiences with students' values, motivations, and cultural identities. For liberal arts students, science may initially appear remote or disconnected from the questions that animate their academic lives. By embedding scientific inquiry within broader humanistic contexts—e.g., the ethics of CRISPR, the sociopolitical dimensions of climate mitigation, or the philosophical implications of AI—educators can foster relevance and belonging. Here, motivation is not extrinsic but intrinsic, rooted in students' sense of purpose and intellectual identity.

Adopting UDL also entails a fundamental shift in instructional design: from retrofitting accommodations to proactively anticipating learner variability. This mindset—closely aligned with design thinking—recognizes that diversity in background, skill, and cognition is not a problem to be managed, but a condition to be designed for. In classrooms where liberal arts students and STEM majors co-learn, such flexibility becomes essential. When UDL strategies are embedded from the outset, they dissolve barriers before they arise, cultivating inclusive academic ecosystems where all learners can flourish.

Moreover, the affordances of generative AI amplify UDL's potential to scale and adapt. AI tools can automate the translation of content across modalities—summarizing dense readings into visual slideshows, transforming textual instructions into narrated walkthroughs, or generating interactive prompts tailored to individual preferences. These capabilities not only reduce the logistical burden on instructors but also make it feasible to implement UDL principles with greater precision and responsiveness. For students, AI-enabled tools can support self-expression across a range of mediums, from writing and speech to visual design or simulation, thereby aligning with UDL's commitment to multiple means of action and expression.

In this way, UDL is not merely a framework for inclusion—it becomes an active, responsive pedagogy, particularly when interwoven with emerging technologies. For liberal arts students navigating science education, it opens the door not just to access, but to intellectual agency. And in doing so, it reframes science itself: as a space of inquiry capacious enough to hold diverse voices, disciplinary intersections, and plural ways of knowing.

Reframing Science Through a Humanistic Lens

As higher education contends with mounting pressures—rising costs, shifting demographics, rapid technological change, and intensifying calls for racial and social justice—liberal arts institutions stand at a crossroads. While some question their relevance in a career-focused economy, others argue that these institutions are uniquely positioned to respond to the challenges of the moment, especially when it comes to equity, interdisciplinarity, and ethical reasoning. This section explores two interlinked arguments: first, that inclusive science teaching in liberal arts contexts offers a transformative pedagogical model, and second, that liberal arts education itself is more necessary than ever in reimagining the goals and practices of higher education. Together, these perspectives frame a compelling case for the enduring value of human-centered, justice-driven learning in a time of profound institutional and societal change.

Inclusive science teaching in liberal arts contexts requires a paradigm shift away from the traditional deficit model of science education, which often centers disciplinary mastery over student identity and lived experience. In liberal arts institutions, the goal is not merely to transmit scientific knowledge but to cultivate critical, reflective, and ethically grounded thinkers. This pedagogical approach emphasizes inclusive curricula that validate diverse ways of knowing and situates scientific inquiry within broader societal, cultural, and historical frameworks. Rather than treat science as neutral or value-free, inclusive teaching recognizes that science is both shaped by and shaping of the communities in which it is practiced.

Addressing Structural Inequities in Science Learning

An inclusive approach also demands attentiveness to the structures that create unequal access and success in science learning. Historically marginalized students—including those from underrepresented racial and ethnic groups, first-generation college students, LGBTQ+ learners, and students with disabilities—continue to experience barriers to participation and belonging in STEM fields. In liberal arts colleges, where small class sizes and faculty-student interaction are the norm, there is a unique opportunity to respond to these disparities through individualized support, community-centered practices, and pedagogical experimentation. Inclusive science teaching in these settings is not an add-on, but a reorientation of purpose: to humanize science, democratize access, and prepare students to engage with urgent, real-world problems.

Another strength of liberal arts institutions lies in their commitment to interdisciplinarity. Inclusive science teaching benefits from this emphasis by encouraging connections between scientific content and subjects such as philosophy, literature, history, and the arts. These connections allow students to examine the ethical implications of scientific discovery, the narratives that shape environmental policies, or the cultural dimensions of health and medicine. Such integrative teaching supports not only academic inclusion but also cognitive justice—valuing diverse epistemologies and modes of inquiry. This cross-disciplinary lens expands the relevance of science and opens pathways for students who may not see themselves reflected in traditional STEM fields.

Relational Pedagogy and Student Empowerment

Inclusive science pedagogy within liberal arts colleges is often distinguished by its deep commitment to an approach that centers student identities, lived experiences, and intellectual agency as foundational elements of the learning process. Rooted in small, dialogic classrooms and supported by close faculty-student mentorship, this model privileges co-construction of knowledge through active learning, community-engaged inquiry, and reflective practice. When these relational pedagogies are thoughtfully interwoven with emerging tools such as generative artificial intelligence (GAI), the result is not a substitution of human connection, but an expansion of pedagogical possibility—one that is at once intellectually rigorous, personally affirming, and socially situated.

Liberal arts faculty frequently draw on collaborative learning structures, project-based inquiry, and dialogic engagement to foster inclusive classroom cultures. These environments are not only academically robust but relationally attuned designed to cultivate trust, flexibility, and belonging. For example, in an environmental science course, students might engage in a semester-long investigation of local water quality, combining empirical data collection with policy analysis and oral histories. Such interdisciplinary approaches encourage students—especially those from historically marginalized groups in STEM—to see their identities, values, and community ties as integral to scientific inquiry rather than peripheral to it.

At the heart of this pedagogy is a deliberate dismantling of the "myth of objectivity" that has long dominated science education. Relational teaching makes visible the emotional, ethical, and sociopolitical dimensions of science, thereby humanizing a field often framed as detached or depersonalized. This orientation resonates with the broader liberal arts mission to cultivate democratic participation, critical consciousness, and moral agency—values that are increasingly vital in a scientific landscape shaped by complexity, uncertainty, and global interdependence.

The advent of generative AI—ranging from large language models to adaptive feedback systems and visual generation tools—offers new affordances for deepening this relational model when deployed with care and intentionality. Far from replacing the faculty-student relationship, GAI can amplify its most inclusive dimensions by providing responsive, identity-aware scaffolds that adapt to the learner's context. For instance, AI-powered translation tools can render scientific concepts more accessible for multilingual students, while writing assistants can help students draft lab reflections or scientific arguments in a way that honors their voice and perspective. Importantly, these tools do not lower standards; rather, they support students in navigating scientific discourse with confidence and clarity.

Yet the inclusive use of GAI cannot be reduced to technical implementation—it demands ethical framing, transparency, and a shared sense of authorship. Faculty can invite students into critical dialogue about the epistemic workings of AI: how it generates knowledge, what assumptions underline its outputs, and where bias or opacity may reside. In doing so, they not only demystify these tools but align their use with the core tenets of relational pedagogy—mutual respect, critical reflection, and distributed agency. In collaborative research projects, for example, students might use GAI to generate hypothetical climate policy models, only to interrogate, revise, and refine them through peer feedback and instructor guidance. Here, AI becomes a provocation for deeper inquiry rather than a shortcut to answers.

When relational pedagogy and inclusive GAI integration converge, science classrooms transform into spaces of possibility—where learners are not asked to assimilate into narrow definitions of scientific expertise but are invited to shape and expand them. This is particularly resonant in liberal arts contexts, where many students may approach science from non-STEM disciplines or with initial skepticism about their place in the scientific enterprise. By engaging with GAI in ways that affirm their intellectual identities and cultural knowledge, these students can develop a renewed sense of scientific agency—one that is rooted not in rote mastery but in curiosity, creativity, and civic relevance.

Ultimately, the integration of GAI within a relational pedagogical framework reimagines science education as a participatory, adaptive, and human-centered endeavor. It invites learners to engage in science not merely as a technical domain, but as a mode of inquiry deeply connected to their own stories, communities, and visions for the world.

LIBERAL ARTS AS A FOUNDATION FOR COMPLEX THINKING

In an era marked by volatility, complexity, and accelerating change, the liberal arts provide an essential foundation for higher education. As automation and specialization reshape the workforce, graduates need more than technical expertise; they need the ability to think across systems, evaluate evidence from multiple perspectives, and act with ethical clarity. Liberal arts curricula cultivate these habits of mind by encouraging students to make connections between disciplines and apply critical reasoning to real-world questions. These skills are transferable, durable, and central to the kind of adaptive intelligence demanded by 21st-century challenges.

Educating the Whole Student and Ethical Reasoning in a Disrupted World

Liberal arts institutions have long distinguished themselves by their commitment to educating the whole student—intellectually, socially, and morally. This holistic vision affirms that education is not merely the transfer of knowledge but the cultivation of curiosity, ethical discernment, and civic agency. For students arriving with diverse strengths, aspirations, and lived experiences, such environments offer a rare space where identity and intellect can grow in tandem. In contrast to the instrumental logic that too often governs higher education, the liberal arts tradition insists on seeing students not as consumers or data points, but as complex human beings capable of shaping the world with imagination and integrity.

This pedagogical ethos becomes especially vital in a historical moment marked by climate precarity, technological acceleration, and widening social inequities. The task before educators is not only to prepare students for employment, but to equip them with the intellectual and ethical tools necessary to navigate a world of profound uncertainty. Within this context, the liberal arts—anchored in philosophy, cultural studies, history, and the social sciences—play a critical role in rebalancing the relationship between technical expertise and moral responsibility. They encourage students to interrogate the systems they inherit, to ask enduring questions about power and justice, and to situate empirical inquiry within human consequence.

Nowhere is this integrative imperative more urgent than in science and technology education, where the rapid deployment of generative artificial intelligence (GAI) risks outpacing our collective capacity to use it wisely. GAI's capacity to deliver personalized learning, generate multimodal content, and scaffold complex tasks positions it as a potentially transformative force in higher education. Yet without deliberate attention to inclusion, accessibility, and ethical use, it may also exacerbate existing divides—particularly for students with disabilities or those from historically marginalized backgrounds.

To realize the inclusive potential of generative AI, institutions must adopt a framework that is both technologically forward-looking and pedagogically grounded—one that recognizes the importance of Universal Design for Learning (UDL) as a means of aligning AI integration with the broader goals of whole-student education. GAI, when deployed within UDL-informed learning environments, can provide differentiated content delivery across visual, auditory, and textual modes; adapt to varied pacing needs; and support learners through tailored feedback. These features are particularly impactful for students whose cognitive or sensory profiles have been underserved by traditional pedagogies.

At the same time, digital literacy must be understood not as a discrete skill but as an evolving capacity for critical engagement. Educators must scaffold students' interactions with GAI in ways that develop discernment: helping them question AI outputs, recognize algorithmic bias, and resist passive consumption. Such metacognitive instruction is not merely technical but ethical, cultivating learners who understand not just how to use AI, but when and why. GAI itself can play a role in this recursive process—as an adaptive tutor, a reflective partner, and a provocation for deeper inquiry into the nature of knowledge and authorship.

Yet the promise of AI-enhanced education cannot be disentangled from the material conditions that enable—or preclude—access. The digital divide remains a pressing obstacle, disproportionately affecting students from low-income, rural, disabled, or otherwise marginalized communities. A truly inclusive vision of AI integration must therefore be infrastructural as well as pedagogical: ensuring access to reliable broadband, accessible devices, assistive technologies, and multilingual interfaces. Institutional policy must treat these not as auxiliary supports, but as foundational elements of educational equity.

Equally urgent is the need for faculty development that prepares educators to integrate GAI not as a replacement for teaching, but as an amplifier of human connection, curiosity, and care. This includes training in inclusive AI pedagogies, collaborative curriculum design, and ethical decision-making frameworks. Faculty must also be supported in reimagining assessment and feedback practices: using AI-driven analytics not to surveil, but to illuminate student learning in its full complexity—including affective states, motivational patterns, and social engagement.

Relational accountability must also guide institutional governance of AI. Transparency, privacy, and participatory design are not optional; they are ethical imperatives. Students, especially those whose perspectives have been historically excluded—should have a voice in shaping how AI is used in their learning environments. This co-authorship reinforces the core liberal arts commitment to democratic participation and affirms that technological integration is not a neutral process, but one imbued with power and consequence.

Ultimately, the thoughtful integration of generative AI within liberal arts education presents an opportunity not only to enhance learning but to reimagine what it means to educate in a time of rapid change. It calls us to hold together two seemingly opposing imperatives: to embrace innovation and to preserve the dignity of human-centered learning. When guided by equity, relational pedagogy, and a commitment to the whole student, AI becomes more than a tool—it becomes a medium through which liberal arts institutions can extend their mission into the digital age, cultivating not only competent professionals, but reflective, adaptive, and ethically engaged citizens.

Resisting the Commodification of Higher Education

Finally, the liberal arts offer a critical counterweight to the increasingly market-driven logic of higher education. As funding models shift and accountability metrics dominate, there is growing pressure to reduce education to a set of outcomes measurable in short-term economic returns. Liberal arts education resists this reduction by asserting the intrinsic value of learning, the complexity of human development, and the moral responsibility of institutions to serve the common good. In doing so, it preserves space for imagination, critique, and transformation—qualities that are essential not only to individual flourishing but to the future of democracy and global coexistence.

Inclusive science teaching and liberal arts education are not separate pursuits—they are mutually reinforcing responses to the same imperative: to reimagine education as a force for justice, agency, and human flourishing. In liberal arts colleges, where the commitment to interdisciplinary inquiry and relational pedagogy runs deep, there exists a fertile ground for this work. When paired with emerging tools like artificial intelligence, and grounded in ethical frameworks, these approaches can catalyze more inclusive, more responsive, and more transformative educational futures. At a time when higher education is being asked to do more with less—and to serve more diverse and demanding publics than ever before—the liberal arts remain not only relevant, but essential.

The Role of Generative AI in Education

Generative artificial intelligence (GAI)—algorithms capable of producing novel content such as text, images, simulations, and code—has emerged as a powerful, if controversial, presence in higher education. In science education, GAI tools such as adaptive learning platforms, AI-powered tutors, and content generators can respond dynamically to learners' needs, tailoring instruction in real time based on prior knowledge, pacing, and engagement style. These affordances offer exciting opportunities to individualize learning and align instruction with the diverse cognitive profiles and academic backgrounds of students—particularly those in liberal arts settings, where many learners may enter STEM courses with limited exposure to disciplinary conventions or digital tools.

As Francis, Jones, and Smith (2025) observe in their cross-institutional study of AI use in higher education, GAI's educational promise is matched by significant ethical and pedagogical challenges. On one hand, these tools can generate practice problems, study guides, visual explanations, or simplified summaries in seconds—capabilities that map directly onto Universal Design for Learning (UDL) principles of multiple representation and engagement. On the other, the same features raise concerns around academic integrity, intellectual ownership, and over-reliance. Instructors and institutions alike must navigate the tension between automation and authenticity—ensuring that AI use enhances rather than undermines critical thinking, process-based learning, and students' sense of agency.

In science courses designed for liberal arts students, GAI can play a transformative role when used with care. For learners who may find traditional scientific discourse unfamiliar or intimidating, AI can serve as a translator and bridge-builder—converting dense texts into plain language, generating interdisciplinary analogies, or visualizing abstract concepts like thermodynamics or gene expression. These capacities align not only with UDL's goal of cognitive accessibility but also with the broader liberal arts mission of connecting empirical inquiry to humanistic understanding. A liberal arts student might engage with molecular bonding through AI-generated visual animations or explore climate science via narrative-driven case studies contextualized in history, ethics, or literature. Such adaptations do not dilute scientific rigor; rather, they extend meaningful access to those whose prior knowledge, learning style, or disciplinary identity might otherwise exclude them from full participation.

GAI's adaptive capabilities also support personalized learning trajectories. An AI platform might detect when a student struggles with data interpretation in biology and respond with targeted scaffolds—perhaps a narrative explanation framed through environmental justice or an interactive module grounded in real-world policy applications. In this way, students are not merely recipients of standardized content but active navigators of their own learning, supported by tools that respond to who they are and how they learn best.

However, realizing this potential requires addressing persistent equity gaps in digital fluency and infrastructure. Haroud and Saqri's (2025) research reveals significant disparities in students' ability to navigate AI platforms, particularly among non-STEM majors and learners from under-resourced educational backgrounds. Without robust digital literacy support, generative AI may reinforce exclusion rather than expand opportunity. Institutions must therefore invest not only in the tools themselves, but in the human and curricular infrastructures that allow all students to engage meaningfully with them. This includes scaffolding for AI-supported learning, ethical instruction on AI use, and ongoing access to assistive technologies, broadband, and accessible devices.

Faculty, too, require support to integrate GAI in ways that align with inclusive pedagogical values. Francis, Jones, and Smith (2025) emphasize the importance of professional development that centers ethical implementation, thoughtful assessment redesign, and the creation of classroom norms around appropriate AI use. Their study highlights faculty concerns about indistinguishable AI-generated submissions and the erosion of academic integrity—concerns that are particularly acute in writing- and project-based science courses adapted for liberal arts students. To address these issues, the authors advocate for process-oriented assessments that document students' learning journeys, invite meta-cognitive reflection, and include transparent dialogues about the role of AI in the learning process. These pedagogical moves not only preserve authenticity but position students as ethical co-authors of their educational experience.

Interestingly, the same research also shows that students—especially those in the liberal arts—are not naïvely enthusiastic about AI. While many find AI tools helpful for breaking down complex ideas, they also express anxiety about their proper use and the potential loss of personal voice or accountability. This ambivalence points to an urgent need for ethical framing and digital literacy instruction embedded across the curriculum. Rather than policing AI use reactively, instructors can model responsible engagement by inviting students to interrogate how AI works, what assumptions it encodes, and when it serves or limits their learning. In doing so, they reinforce critical digital citizenship and foster a classroom culture rooted in transparency, trust, and shared responsibility.

Beyond the classroom, Francis, Jones, and Smith also propose an institutional readiness framework, arguing that sustainable AI integration depends on more than individual faculty initiative. Institutions must invest in instructional design capacity, clear policy guidance, and interdisciplinary collaboration to ensure scalable, ethical, and contextually relevant AI use. This insight is particularly salient for liberal arts colleges, where faculty may not have immediate access to STEM-specific AI resources and may require tailored, cross-disciplinary support to make AI integration pedagogically coherent.

Ultimately, generative AI—when aligned with Universal Design for Learning and embedded within the relational, interdisciplinary ethos of liberal arts education—offers more than technical enhancement. It provides an opportunity to reimagine how students encounter and inhabit science: not as a monolithic discipline requiring conformity, but as a dynamic space of inquiry open to diverse forms of knowing and expression. For liberal arts students, this shift can be transformative. It affirms that science is not reserved for a particular kind of learner, but is a shared human endeavor—one that becomes more inclusive, more rigorous, and more alive when technology is used not to replace human thought, but to support its flourishing.

INTEGRATING GENERATIVE AI WITH UDL IN SCIENCE EDUCATION

The intersection of generative AI and UDL creates powerful possibilities for redesigning science instruction to better include liberal arts students. Here are four major integration strategies:

1. Personalized Learning Pathways

AI tools can help identify students' prior knowledge, preferred learning modalities, and pacing needs. By analyzing interactions and responses, platforms can suggest tailored content sequences that build upon students' strengths and address gaps. For instance, a liberal arts student unfamiliar with calculus might receive scaffolded, visual explanations of mathematical models used in physics, while a more advanced peer is directed toward real-world applications or problem-solving exercises.

2. Adaptive Assessments

Generative AI allows dynamic, formative assessments that adjust based on student performance. Instead of administering static quizzes, platforms can adapt questions in real-time, ensuring that learners are challenged appropriately and supported when they struggle. This approach is especially beneficial for liberal arts students who may require additional context or scaffolding when approaching technical or abstract material.

3. Multimodal Content Delivery

AI can generate content in multiple formats automatically—diagrams, narrated videos, summaries, concept maps—thus supporting the UDL principle of multiple means of representation. Instructors can use AI to create alternate versions of lectures, such as simplified overviews or narrative-based stories of scientific discovery, making abstract concepts more relatable and engaging students from diverse academic traditions.

4. Real-Time Feedback and Support

Generative AI can provide instant feedback on assignments, suggest improvements, and explain mistakes in plain language. For science topics that often intimidate liberal arts students—like thermodynamics or statistical inference, this immediate guidance can reduce frustration and encourage persistence.

Together, these applications can radically shift how science is taught in liberal arts contexts: from rigid, content-driven models to flexible, student-centered learning experiences.

Integrating generative AI with UDL in science education offers a transformative approach that prioritizes equity, accessibility, and engagement—particularly for students whose academic foundations lie outside traditional STEM disciplines. Personalized learning pathways, enabled by AI, empower liberal arts students to engage with science at a pace and level appropriate to their background. Rather than being funneled through a one-size-fits-all curriculum, these students can access differentiated instruction that aligns with their strengths, such as textual analysis, historical reasoning, or ethical inquiry. This approach ensures that students are not excluded by prior gaps in technical knowledge but are instead supported in building conceptual understanding in a way that feels relevant and manageable.

Adaptive assessments, when combined with UDL, can further dismantle barriers to learning by shifting the focus from static performance metrics to continuous growth. For liberal arts students unfamiliar with scientific testing norms, adaptive AI tools can offer more forgiving and instructive learning environments. For example, a student struggling with statistical reasoning could receive guided practice embedded with real-world examples from social sciences or economics, allowing them to contextualize abstract concepts. This not only enhances comprehension but also reinforces the idea that science can intersect meaningfully with their existing interests and academic identities.

Multimodal content delivery is particularly impactful in bridging the disciplinary divide. Many liberal arts students thrive on narrative, visual, or auditory learning modalities, which are often underutilized in traditional science education. AI's ability to rapidly generate content across formats—such as transforming a chemistry lesson into a visual storyboard or an ecological concept into an interactive infographic—can help translate abstract theories into relatable experiences. When science instruction is presented through varied channels, it not only meets UDL standards but also validates different ways of knowing, making the learning environment more welcoming and inclusive.

Real-time feedback and support powered by AI can also be a game-changer for liberal arts students, who may hesitate to seek help in STEM courses due to unfamiliar terminology or perceived cultural barriers. AI systems that provide immediate, jargon-free explanations and constructive feedback help reduce intimidation and promote self-efficacy. For instance, if a student misinterprets a physics concept, the AI can suggest alternative approaches or analogies—such as drawing parallels with music or literature—that align with the student's cognitive style. This kind of individualized, non-judgmental support reinforces persistence and helps foster a growth mindset, which is essential for success in any discipline.

In due course, the integration of generative AI with UDL principles does more than enhance instructional design—it reshapes the culture of science education. It sends a powerful message that scientific knowledge is not the exclusive domain of the mathematically gifted or technically trained, but a shared enterprise open to all learners. By embracing these tools and strategies, educators can create inclusive learning environments where liberal arts students are not only welcomed into scientific spaces but empowered to contribute meaningfully. This transformation lays the groundwork for a more interdisciplinary, equitable, and innovative future in higher education.

The systematic review *"Universal Design for Learning in Postsecondary STEM Education for Students with Disabilities"* examines how UDL has been empirically applied in higher-education STEM settings to support learners with disabilities, offering insights and constraints particularly relevant in liberal arts science instruction (Eden, C.; Adeleye, O.; & Adeniyi, I., 2024). In liberal arts–inflected STEM courses, where students may bring widely varying cognitive, sensory, or processing profiles, the UDL paradigm—oriented around multiple means of representation, expression, and engagement—serves as a foundational scaffold upon which AI-driven inclusive strategies can build. The authors note that, despite its promise, UDL remains underutilized in postsecondary STEM, suggesting both opportunity and caution in its scaling.

A growing body of research highlights the potential of Universal Design for Learning (UDL) to promote inclusion, self-advocacy, and academic persistence in postsecondary STEM education. In particular, Eden, Adeleye, and Adeniyi's (2024) systematic review offers one of the most comprehensive examinations to date of how UDL-informed teaching practices intersect with student agency, especially for learners with disabilities. Their findings suggest that when instructors are trained in UDL or when peer-led team learning (PLTL) is redesigned using universal design principles, students report increased willingness to request accommodations, improved metacognitive awareness, and greater engagement. These outcomes are particularly salient in liberal arts science classrooms, where the integration of writing, dialogue, and interpretive inquiry demands not only cognitive rigor but also psychological safety and epistemic trust.

The review surfaces promising instructional models that can inform inclusive science pedagogy in liberal arts contexts. For instance, Street et al.'s adaptation of PLTL into a "Mastery PLTL" (MPLTL) format included written and video-based templates, flexible participation options, and built-in scaffolds designed around Universal Design for Instruction (UDI) principles. Similarly, programmatic initiatives like CS3 LD (Comprehensive Support for STEM Students with Learning Disabilities) combine mentorship, UDL training, and integrated campus support structures to enhance self-efficacy and institutional belonging. These interventions align with the core UDL aim of anticipatory design—embedding flexibility and access into the fabric of course delivery rather than retrofitting accommodations post hoc. In liberal arts STEM education, such proactive scaffolding might take the form of multimodal explanations, process-based assignments, or optional media formats, allowing learners to choose pathways that align with their strengths and needs.

Yet the review also identifies significant evidence gaps and limitations. Of over 200 sources reviewed, only four met the authors' criteria for empirical rigor (quantitative or mixed methods). This scarcity underscores an urgent need for more robust, outcome-focused research to validate UDL's impact in STEM at the postsecondary level. Moreover, the authors caution against assuming that active learning practices are inherently inclusive. While UDL aligns well with strategies like small-group problem solving, low-stakes quizzes, and project-based learning, these same methods can overburden students with executive functioning challenges, attentional differences, or discomfort in peer-led dynamics. Liberal arts science courses often emphasize these active, collaborative formats, making it imperative that instructors design with neurodiversity in mind—offering buffer time, alternative participation modes, or structured flexibility to accommodate varied processing styles.

CAST (Center for Applied Special Technology), the leading architect of UDL, has begun to explore how artificial intelligence—particularly generative AI—can scale UDL's reach and deepen its impact. Their recent research articulates how AI can operationalize UDL's three core principles: multiple means of representation, action and expression, and engagement. By dynamically generating and adapting content, AI tools can personalize instruction across modalities—text, video, interactive simulation—offering students various cognitive entry points into complex scientific ideas. In a liberal arts classroom, where students may bring diverse disciplinary orientations and varying comfort with technical language, this multimodal flexibility is not just beneficial—it is foundational to equitable access.

AI's ability to diversify how students demonstrate understanding also supports UDL's emphasis on varied modes of expression. Students might use generative AI to draft a podcast script explaining a biology concept, design a digital model of a geological process, or receive formative feedback on a written hypothesis. These tools offer not only format flexibility but also process-based scaffolding—guiding students through iterative refinement while preserving their agency. Such options are especially critical for students with disabilities or nontraditional academic profiles, who may struggle with rigid assessment models but excel when given the freedom to choose how they communicate knowledge.

Perhaps most compellingly, CAST's work spotlights AI's role in sustaining engagement. Adaptive AI systems can respond to learners' interests, backgrounds, and emotional cues, offering content and pacing that resonate with individual identities and lived experiences. This is crucial in liberal arts contexts, where students may initially view science as distant or irrelevant to their academic identity. AI-enabled personalization—especially when it is culturally responsive—can bridge this affective gap, supporting long-term motivation and connection. For instance, a student might explore chemistry concepts through AI-generated analogies drawn from literature, ethics, or social history, thereby reinforcing both scientific understanding and personal relevance.

However, CAST also emphasizes the importance of ethical and inclusive AI integration. Equity cannot be assumed; it must be intentionally designed. This includes safeguarding data privacy, avoiding algorithmic bias, and ensuring transparency in how AI tools operate. Moreover, institutions must involve diverse stakeholders—including students with disabilities, first-generation learners, and faculty across disciplines—in shaping AI adoption policies. CAST urges colleges and universities to invest in professional development that helps faculty use AI as an inclusive pedagogical partner—not a replacement for instruction, but a tool that amplifies student voice and learning diversity.

Taken together, these insights suggest that the intersection of UDL, generative AI, and liberal arts science education holds transformative potential—but only if approached with pedagogical intentionality and equity at the center. While the empirical base for UDL in STEM remains underdeveloped, early models offer compelling direction for inclusive practice. By embedding flexible scaffolds, respecting learner agency, and using AI to personalize without dehumanizing, science educators can foster classrooms where all students—not just those already fluent in disciplinary norms—can participate meaningfully. For liberal arts students, whose academic strengths may lie in narrative, ethics, or visual reasoning, this approach reframes science not as a gatekeeping system, but as a dynamic, pluralistic field of inquiry.

ETHICAL AND PEDAGOGICAL CONSIDERATIONS

While the integration of AI in education is promising, it also presents ethical and pedagogical challenges. The use of AI tools must align with values of equity, transparency, and human-centered learning.

Key considerations include:

- **Academic Integrity**: AI tools can produce entire assignments or answers, raising concerns about plagiarism and authenticity. Instructors must redesign assessments to emphasize process, reflection, and originality.
- **Bias and Representation**: AI systems trained on biased datasets may reinforce stereotypes or produce exclusionary content. Diverse training data and critical oversight are essential.
- **Digital Literacy**: Not all students enter the classroom with equal technological fluency. Supporting students in understanding and using AI tools responsibly is essential to avoid deepening existing inequities.

Faculty must be equipped with training and resources to integrate AI ethically and effectively. Institutions should promote communities of practice where educators can share strategies, challenges, and innovations in AI-enhanced teaching.

One of the core contributions of AI-enabled pedagogy is its capacity for personalized and adaptive learning. The review emphasizes that AI algorithms, processing data from assessments, interaction logs, or learner preferences, can tailor instruction in real time, adjusting difficulty levels, pacing, and sequence of tasks. In a liberal arts–inflected science classroom, this means that a student with stronger comfort in metaphorical or discursive thinking might receive narrative-rich prompts, while another more quantitatively inclined may receive symbolic exercises or data-driven explorations. The flexibility of such systems helps validate alternate modes of reasoning, preventing marginalization of students who do not conform to the prototypical "lab-science learner" profile.

One of the primary contributions of AI in this context lies in its capacity to support differentiated instruction. Adaptive learning systems can adjust to students' prior knowledge, cognitive patterns, and real-time performance, thereby dismantling the one-size-fits-all model that often characterizes introductory science courses. In liberal arts environments—where classrooms are marked by diverse epistemological commitments and uneven familiarity with scientific methods—such flexibility is critical. Rather than requiring students to conform to a fixed pedagogical model, AI tools can accommodate a range of learning preferences, from visual and spatial reasoning to linguistic or conceptual engagement. This aligns with inclusive teaching principles that acknowledge and respond to the full variability of human learning.

In liberal arts–inflected science settings, where students often bring varied backgrounds, interests, and conceptual vocabularies, the promise of AI is to scaffold more equitable entry points into scientific thinking. The authors frame their analysis through the lenses of Universal Design for Learning (UDL), Culturally Relevant Pedagogy (CRP), and Social Cognitive Theory (SCT), allowing AI strategies to be understood not merely as technical tools but as pedagogical mediators of equity (Eden, C.; Adeleye, O.; & Adeniyi, I., 2024).

Through thematic analysis of bridging the digital divide, equity-centered education can identify four primary themes: emotional support, academic facilitation, social integration, and ethical concerns. The key findings include: Emotional Support using AI tools like ChatGPT and Duolingo provided emotional relief during periods of isolation; Academic Facilitation using tools helped simplify complex academic concepts and enhanced language proficiency; Social Integration via AI platforms boosted communication confidence in social contexts; and Ethical Concerns for students expressing apprehensions about over-reliance on AI and data privacy issues. Literature underscores the potential of AI to complement traditional support systems, offering valuable insights for educators, policymakers, and developers aiming to enhance the experiences of international students.

One of the central pillars of the review is AI-driven personalized learning, which tailors' instruction to individual learners' preferences, pace, and needs (Eden, C.; Adeleye, O.; & Adeniyi, I., 2024). The paper notes that platforms using machine learning, natural language processing, or intelligent tutoring systems can analyze student interaction data and dynamically adjust content difficulty, presentation mode, and scaffolding (Eden, C.; Adeleye, O.; & Adeniyi, I., 2024). In the liberal arts–science interface, this allows for alternate entry paths: a student with stronger verbal reasoning might receive narrative or conceptual prompts, while another might receive data challenges or visual models suited to their style. Personalized pathways reduce cognitive dissonance and validate diverse ways of making sense of scientific ideas.

Complementing personalization is AI-enabled assessment and feedback, which the review argues is a key mechanism for equitable learning. AI tools like adaptive quizzes, auto-grading systems, or analytics dashboards can detect misconceptions, flag patterns, and provide real-time, tailored feedback. For liberal arts students—who may benefit from deeper iteration over speed—the formative, dialogic nature of AI feedback can demystify the learning process, helping them see "how" they think rather than only "what" is right or wrong. This can bolster confidence, encourage revision, and open pathways toward mastery.

A further dimension is AI-facilitated collaborative and scaffolded environments, which help distribute expertise and encourage discourse across difference (Eden, C.; Adeleye, O.; & Adeniyi, I., 2024). The authors highlight how AI agents—chatbots, recommendation systems, discourse analyzers—can mediate group engagement, suggest relevant resources, or prompt reflection across peers. In liberal arts–science courses, such scaffolding helps balance contributions: students with strengths in narrative, conceptual linking, or critique can enrich group inquiry, while others with quantitative or modeling skills can contribute complementary expertise. The result is a richer, more inclusive epistemic community.

Yet, the deployment of these AI strategies must be tempered by ethical, structural, and access constraints. Algorithmic bias, opaque decision logic, and data privacy concerns are real hazards—especially when student populations already marginalized might be further disadvantaged by skewed models. Moreover, unequal access to devices, connectivity, and faculty readiness can replicate existing inequities. The authors call for rigorous safeguards: transparent models, diversified training data, regular audits, stakeholder participation in design, and robust support infrastructure.

Integrating generative AI with UDL in science education offers a transformative approach that prioritizes equity, accessibility, and engagement—particularly for students whose academic foundations lie outside traditional STEM disciplines. Personalized learning pathways, enabled by AI, empower liberal arts students to engage with science at a pace and level appropriate to their background. Rather than being funneled through a one-size-fits-all curriculum, these students can access differentiated instruction that aligns with their strengths, such as textual analysis, historical reasoning, or ethical inquiry. This approach ensures that students are not excluded by prior gaps in technical knowledge but are instead supported in building conceptual understanding in a way that feels relevant and manageable.

Adaptive assessments, when combined with UDL, can further dismantle barriers to learning by shifting the focus from static performance metrics to continuous growth. For liberal arts students unfamiliar with scientific testing norms, adaptive AI tools can offer more forgiving and instructive learning environments. For example, a student struggling with statistical reasoning could receive guided practice embedded with real-world examples from social sciences or economics, allowing them to contextualize abstract concepts. This not only enhances comprehension but also reinforces the idea that science can intersect meaningfully with their existing interests and academic identities.

Multimodal content delivery is particularly impactful in bridging the disciplinary divide. Many liberal arts students thrive on narrative, visual, or auditory learning modalities, which are often underutilized in traditional science education. AI's ability to rapidly generate content across formats—such as transforming a chemistry lesson into a visual storyboard or an ecological concept into an interactive infographic—can help translate abstract theories into relatable experiences. When science instruction is presented through varied channels, it not only meets UDL standards but also validates different ways of knowing, making the learning environment more welcoming and inclusive.

Real-time feedback and support powered by AI can also be a game-changer for liberal arts students, who may hesitate to seek help in STEM courses due to unfamiliar terminology or perceived cultural barriers. AI systems that provide immediate, jargon-free explanations and constructive feedback help reduce intimidation and promote self-efficacy. For instance, if a student misinterprets a physics concept, the AI can suggest alternative approaches or analogies—such as drawing parallels with music or literature—that align with the student's cognitive style. This kind of individualized, non-judgmental support reinforces persistence and helps foster a growth mindset, which is essential for success in any discipline.

In the end, the integration of generative AI with UDL principles does more than enhance instructional design—it reshapes the culture of science education. It sends a powerful message that scientific knowledge is not the exclusive domain of the mathematically gifted or technically trained, but a shared enterprise open to all learners. By embracing these tools and strategies, educators can create inclusive learning environments where liberal arts students are not only welcomed into scientific spaces but empowered to contribute meaningfully. This transformation lays the groundwork for a more interdisciplinary, equitable, and innovative future in higher education.

POLICY IMPLICATIONS FOR INCLUSIVE SCIENCE EDUCATION

To ensure that the integration of generative AI and Universal Design for Learning (UDL) meaningfully advances inclusive science education, institutions must establish supportive policies and infrastructure. These policies must go beyond basic technology adoption and instead prioritize interdisciplinary collaboration, ethical oversight, and inclusive design. Without intentional and sustained policy action, the transformative potential of AI and UDL may remain unrealized, especially for students from underrepresented or nontraditional academic backgrounds such as those in the liberal arts. The following expanded policy recommendations offer a roadmap for systemic change in higher education.

1. Curricular Innovation Policies

Colleges and universities should promote structural incentives for interdisciplinary collaboration, especially between liberal arts and science faculties. This includes developing joint faculty appointments, interdisciplinary teaching fellowships, or team-taught courses that merge scientific inquiry with humanistic perspectives. These collaborative efforts should be supported through targeted funding for curriculum redesign, allowing departments to experiment with AI-enhanced modules that integrate UDL principles. Additionally, instructional design teams should be resourced to assist in creating accessible, multimodal content powered by generative AI. Institutions might also consider offering microgrants for course pilots that explore new ways of delivering complex scientific content to liberal arts students using AI tools.

2. Faculty Development and Support

Institutions must establish professional development programs that not only train faculty in the mechanics of AI tools but also embed UDL and inclusive pedagogy into every stage of instructional design. Workshops, learning communities, and online modules should focus on practical strategies for using AI to enhance representation, engagement, and expression in the science classroom. Faculty buy-in will depend heavily on institutional support: release time, stipends for professional learning, and access to technical specialists who can offer just-in-time assistance during course implementation. Administrators should also foster a culture of experimentation and reflection, where instructors feel safe to innovate, evaluate, and revise their use of AI in the classroom.

3. Accessibility and Equity Frameworks

As institutions adopt generative AI platforms, they must ensure these tools comply with accessibility standards and promote equitable learning opportunities. This involves technical compliance—such as ensuring screen reader compatibility, captioning, and keyboard navigation—but also cultural inclusivity, like using gender-neutral language and representing diverse communities in AI-generated examples. Equity audits of AI tools should be conducted regularly, and accessibility should be a key criterion in procurement decisions. Additionally, policies should encourage the creation of support systems that address varying levels of digital fluency among students, particularly those from liberal arts or first-generation college backgrounds who may not have prior experience with advanced educational technologies.

4. Ethical AI Governance

Institutions need clear, enforceable guidelines around the ethical use of AI in teaching and learning. These guidelines should define acceptable and unacceptable uses of generative AI, protect student data privacy, and ensure that students maintain agency over their own learning processes. Importantly, policies should not be developed behind closed doors but through participatory governance models that include faculty, students, and staff. By involving students in conversations about how AI shapes their educational experience, institutions can foster a sense of transparency and trust. Ethical AI policies should also include regular review mechanisms and outline procedures for addressing misuse or harm caused by AI tools in the learning environment.

To fully realize the benefits of AI and UDL integration in science education, institutions must take a long-term, strategic view that centers equity, sustainability, and adaptability. Policy efforts must not only respond to current challenges but also anticipate future needs as AI tools evolve and student populations become increasingly diverse. This forward-thinking approach involves embedding inclusive innovation into institutional planning processes, strategic goals, and accreditation standards. By framing AI-enhanced, UDL-aligned science education as a core part of academic excellence, institutions can signal a strong commitment to access, inclusion, and pedagogical innovation across disciplines.

One critical area of policy development is the creation of interdisciplinary research and evaluation frameworks to monitor the effectiveness of AI-integrated, UDL-based teaching practices. Institutions should establish dedicated assessment teams or centers that study learning outcomes across different student populations, including liberal arts students in science courses. These evaluations should track not only academic performance but also engagement, persistence, and sense of belonging.

Importantly, data collection and analysis must be guided by ethical standards that respect student privacy and agency. Feedback loops should be built into course and program design so that findings from these evaluations lead to continuous refinement of AI-supported instructional strategies.

Policy must also address the infrastructural disparities that can limit the equitable adoption of AI tools across departments and campuses. For example, smaller liberal arts colleges or underfunded institutions may lack the IT infrastructure or instructional design personnel needed to support large-scale AI adoption. Institutions can help bridge these gaps by forming consortia or partnerships that pool resources and share expertise in AI-enhanced UDL practices. Funding from federal or state educational agencies can also play a role in leveling the playing field, particularly if tied to demonstrable commitments to inclusive teaching and learning practices.

In addition, policy should guide the responsible procurement and vetting of generative AI platforms. Decision-makers must ensure that selected technologies are not only functional and scalable but also aligned with institutional values of inclusion, accessibility, and student empowerment. Procurement processes should involve diverse review committees, including faculty from liberal arts and science disciplines, disability services professionals, and student representatives. Institutions must also advocate for transparency from AI vendors regarding their training data, bias mitigation strategies, and accessibility features. These requirements can help safeguard against the adoption of tools that may inadvertently reinforce educational inequities or introduce new forms of exclusion.

Finally, inclusive science education policy must be responsive to the cultural and pedagogical shifts that AI and UDL integration will inevitably catalyze. Faculty, staff, and students will need space to adapt, reflect, and evolve their roles within a transformed educational landscape. Institutions should therefore establish formal channels—such as feedback councils, curricular review boards, or student advisory panels—to surface emerging needs and challenges. This responsiveness ensures that AI implementation does not become static or top-down but remains a participatory, evolving process grounded in the lived experiences of diverse learners. In doing so, institutions affirm that inclusive science education is not a temporary initiative but a sustained commitment to equity, innovation, and excellence in the age of AI.

In sum, inclusive science education supported by AI and UDL requires an institutional commitment to transformative change. Policies must extend beyond technical deployment to address cultural, pedagogical, and ethical dimensions of education. By embedding these considerations into policy and practice, colleges and universities can create learning environments where liberal arts students—and all students—are equipped to engage deeply with science, not in spite of their backgrounds, but because of the diverse perspectives they bring.

SYNERGIZING UNIVERSAL DESIGN FOR LEARNING AND GENERATIVE AI TO ENHANCE INCLUSIVITY IN SCIENCE EDUCATION

Building on the insights from Haroud and Saqri (2025) and Schreffler et al. (2019), the integration of Universal Design for Learning (UDL) principles with generative AI in science education offers transformative possibilities for creating equitable and inclusive learning environments. UDL's emphasis on flexibility and accessibility is uniquely complemented by AI's adaptive capabilities, enabling educators to meet the diverse needs of students, including those with varied academic backgrounds, learning styles, and cognitive strengths. In science education, where abstract concepts and complex problem-solving are prevalent, this alignment can demystify content and foster deeper engagement.

One of the most significant contributions of AI to UDL in science classrooms is the facilitation of multiple means of representation. Traditional science instruction often relies heavily on lectures and textbooks, which may not resonate with all learners. Generative AI can automatically produce alternative content formats—such as interactive simulations, narrated videos, and graphical models—that cater to different perceptual and cognitive preferences. For instance, a student struggling with textual explanations of molecular biology can engage with an AI-generated 3D animation that visually represents cellular processes. This diversification of content delivery not only aligns with UDL but also supports science learners who benefit from concrete, visual, or kinesthetic experiences, often found in liberal arts learners who prefer narrative or conceptual approaches.

In terms of multiple means of action and expression, AI-enhanced platforms empower students to demonstrate understanding through diverse modalities beyond traditional exams and essays. Adaptive AI tools can facilitate personalized assignments where learners create multimedia presentations, simulations, or written reflections—formats that resonate with their strengths and cultural backgrounds. These alternatives reduce barriers for students with disabilities and those less comfortable with conventional scientific communication. Moreover, AI's capacity to provide real-time, individualized feedback encourages iterative learning and self-regulation, key aspects of UDL that help students refine their scientific reasoning and technical skills at their own pace.

Engagement, the third core principle of UDL, is also significantly enriched by AI integration. Haroud and Saqri (2025) highlight that personalized learning experiences powered by AI can increase motivation by connecting scientific content to learners' interests and identities. For liberal arts students, whose academic orientation may prioritize contextual and ethical dimensions of science, AI can tailor learning scenarios that incorporate interdisciplinary perspectives or societal applications of scientific principles. This relevance-driven approach not only sustains curiosity but also fosters a sense of belonging in STEM fields, challenging the notion that science is an exclusive domain.

Finally, the convergence of UDL and AI in science education calls for systemic institutional support to ensure ethical, equitable, and effective implementation. Faculty need professional development that integrates knowledge of both UDL pedagogy and AI technologies, enabling them to design curricula that leverage AI while maintaining rigorous academic standards. Institutions must also address access issues, ensuring that AI tools are usable by all students, including those with disabilities, and provide clear policies on ethical AI use to protect academic integrity. By fostering such a holistic ecosystem, higher education can realize the full potential of AI and UDL to transform science education into an inclusive, learner-centered endeavor that empowers liberal arts students and other diverse populations to succeed in STEM.

A CASE STUDY IN HUMAN-CENTERED INNOVATION FOR ENVIRONMENTAL SCIENCE EDUCATION

This example presents a case study of how artificial intelligence (AI) was used to support inclusive teaching in an introductory environmental science course at a liberal arts college. It explores the application of AI tools to support personalized instruction, equitable participation, culturally responsive curriculum design, and reflective learning. The case highlights how AI-enhanced teaching can align with liberal arts values, such as interdisciplinarity, identity-centered learning, and social justice, offering a replicable model for inclusive innovation in science education.

Institutional and Pedagogical Context

The setting is a private liberal arts college in the northeastern United States, enrolling approximately 2,500 undergraduates. The college's mission emphasizes inclusive excellence, critical inquiry, and interdisciplinary engagement. Despite small class sizes and student-centered teaching practices, faculty and staff observed persistent equity gaps in STEM courses, particularly those serving as gateway experiences for general education.

The environmental science course discussed here attracts students from a wide range of disciplines and identities, including first-generation students, students of color, and those with varied levels of science preparation. The instructional team sought to redesign the course using AI technologies to better address the needs of these learners and reduce barriers to access and success.

AI-Driven Pedagogical Interventions

An AI-enabled adaptive learning platform was implemented to generate differentiated learning paths based on diagnostic assessments completed at the start of the course. Students who demonstrated gaps in foundational knowledge received scaffolded supports, including visual aids and adjusted pacing. Students with stronger backgrounds were offered enrichment activities that connected environmental science concepts to policy, ethics, and sustainability. This allowed for more equitable entry points to the content and provided diverse learners with support and challenge appropriate to their needs.

Participation analytics for equity monitoring

AI tools were used to track classroom engagement and participation across small-group and whole-class discussions. Anonymized reports disaggregated data by demographic categories such as gender and self-reported race/ethnicity. These insights helped inform equitable discussion facilitation practices, such as rotating group roles and encouraging quieter voices. The use of participation data enabled intentional pedagogy that redistributed visibility and voice, especially for historically marginalized students.

Generative AI for culturally responsive curriculum

A generative AI platform was used to co-create case studies grounded in real-world environmental issues affecting diverse populations. Prompt engineering and student collaboration guided the creation of scenarios involving environmental justice, Indigenous sovereignty, and the effects of climate change in the Global South. Students co-edited and reflected on these materials throughout the course. Students reported increased relevance of course content and greater connection between their identities, communities, and the scientific material.

Reflective AI tools for identity integration

A GPT-based journaling assistant was integrated into the course's digital platform, offering weekly prompts and feedback to support student reflection. Students used this space to explore their learning process, science identity, and perceived challenges. Aggregated, anonymized insights were shared with instructors to inform responsive teaching strategies. This reflective space supported metacognition, emotional engagement, and identity exploration—critical aspects of inclusive pedagogy in liberal arts contexts.

Outcomes and Evidence of Impact

Table 1. While this initiative was exploratory, it yielded encouraging results across a range of indicators:

Metric	Pre-implementation	Post-implementation
Course completion rate	82%	94%
Satisfaction among underrepresented students (survey)	63%	91%
GPA gap (URM vs. non-URM students)	0.8 points	0.2 points
Office hour attendance (first-generation students)	15%	38%

Students across multiple identity groups reported feeling more supported, engaged, and connected to course content.

Ethical Considerations and Implementation Lessons

Ethical implementation was foundational to the initiative. All AI tools were used in compliance with FERPA and institutional privacy standards. Participation in AI-mediated activities was voluntary, and students were informed of how their data would be used. Faculty engaged in professional development focused on algorithmic bias, transparency, and responsible AI use. Importantly, AI tools were positioned as supplements—not replacements—for human teaching. The goal was not automation but augmentation: using emerging technologies to deepen relational pedagogy and expand opportunities for individualized support.

This case demonstrates how AI can be leveraged to create more inclusive science learning environments in liberal arts institutions. Through personalization, equity-focused analytics, culturally responsive content, and reflective supports, the course became a model of how AI can align with the liberal arts' commitment to justice, identity development, and interdisciplinary engagement. AI, in this context, acted as a catalyst for inclusion—not a disruption to humanistic education. With careful ethical framing and pedagogical intentionality, AI technologies can extend the reach of inclusive teaching and foster equitable outcomes for all students.

CONCLUSION

Generative AI and Universal Design for Learning, when thoughtfully integrated, hold the potential to make science education more inclusive, engaging, and effective, particularly for liberal arts students who have traditionally faced barriers to participation in STEM. By embracing multimodal instruction, adaptive assessment, and personalized learning, educators can create science classrooms that recognize and nurture a broader range of talents and perspectives.

This chapter provides a vision for leveraging AI not merely as a technological novelty, but as a catalyst for systemic change in higher education. It argues for pedagogical innovation, institutional support, and ethical vigilance as cornerstones of this transformation. As we enter a new era of AI-powered education, we must ensure that our approaches are rooted in empathy, equity, and a commitment to serving all learners.

Generative AI and Universal Design for Learning (UDL) represent a profound opportunity to redefine the boundaries of those who can succeed in science education. For liberal arts students—who often bring strengths in communication, critical thinking, and interdisciplinary analysis—these tools provide pathways into scientific learning that better align with their skill sets and intellectual traditions. By offering content through multiple formats and allowing students to engage with material at their own pace and comfort level, AI-supported UDL approaches dismantle many of the structural and pedagogical barriers that have historically excluded non-STEM students from fully participating in science. This reimagined model of learning doesn't dilute scientific rigor—it reorients it to be more inclusive, diverse, and intellectually vibrant.

At the heart of this transformation is the recognition that education should not reward conformity but foster diverse ways of knowing. When science instruction incorporates UDL's multimodal strategies—enhanced through AI's capacity to quickly generate varied forms of content—it validates students who may have previously felt marginalized in STEM settings. For example, a liberal arts student might engage more deeply with a physics concept through a narrative scenario, visual model, or ethical debate rather than a mathematical formula alone. AI enables this kind of differentiated instruction at scale, allowing educators to design learning experiences that reach students across disciplinary boundaries, without compromising academic integrity or depth.

However, the promise of AI in inclusive pedagogy is not without ethical and structural challenges—a dimension the reviewed article addresses in depth. Issues of data privacy, algorithmic bias, and inequitable access to infrastructure or devices loom large. In liberal arts settings, where students may already feel marginalized in "hard science" courses, these issues demand explicit pedagogical vigilance. Integrating AI must come hand in hand with transparency (how the model works), participatory design (inviting student critique of AI's recommendations), and equity-centric provisioning (ensuring all have hardware, connectivity, and support).

Only then can AI-driven inclusive science teaching in liberal arts milieus transcend novelty and embody justice.

Finally, the successful implementation of AI-driven approaches depends on the intentional involvement of diverse educational stakeholders. As Agrawal et al. emphasize, adaptation models must be informed by the specific needs and contexts of the learners they serve. In liberal arts settings, where ethical deliberation, democratic participation, and cultural critique are central to the educational mission, this means embedding AI within a broader pedagogical conversation about access, equity, and epistemic inclusion. Rather than simply optimizing for efficiency or outcomes, AI should be leveraged to create science learning environments that are intellectually expansive, culturally responsive, and fundamentally inclusive.

However, leveraging AI and UDL as transformative forces requires more than tools—it demands a cultural shift within institutions. Faculty must move from viewing AI as a threat to academic standards or a shortcut for students, to seeing it as a means of amplifying learning, creativity, and critical engagement. Administrators must prioritize inclusive policies and infrastructure that support this shift, including sustained investment in training, accessible technologies, and interdisciplinary collaboration. This transformation also requires continuous reflection on the ethics of AI implementation, ensuring that technologies serve as enablers of equity rather than reinforcers of existing disparities.

The broader goal is not simply to modernize science education, but to humanize it—to design learning environments that are responsive to the full range of student identities, experiences, and aspirations. In this vision, liberal arts students are not outsiders peering into the world of science; they are contributors, collaborators, and innovators who bring essential perspectives to scientific questions. AI, when guided by UDL principles, can help facilitate this shift by removing logistical and cognitive barriers and fostering a sense of belonging. In turn, science education becomes not only more inclusive but also richer, more reflective, and better equipped to address the complex challenges of the world.

As this chapter has argued, the integration of generative AI and UDL presents a once-in-a-generation opportunity to reshape science education in higher ed. But this opportunity will only be fully realized through intentional design, institutional commitment, and a pedagogical ethos rooted in empathy and equity. AI should not replace the human elements of education, it should enhance them, making learning more accessible, responsive, and meaningful. By centering students' varied strengths and identities, educators can use AI and UDL not as mere enhancements, but as foundational elements in creating a more just and inclusive educational future.

In sum, the trajectory proposed by the review invites us to imagine science instruction in liberal arts domains not as a concession to difference but as a generative, pluralistic endeavor. AI-driven personalization, collaborative scaffolds, and assistive tools offer levers by which we can reconfigure the cultural and cognitive contours of scientific learning. Yet this reconfiguration must be anchored in ethical reflexivity, with deliberate design to resist algorithmic reproduction of inequity. In liberal arts contexts—where flexibility, critical thinking, and epistemic plurality are prized—AI offers not just support but a means to transform science teaching into an inclusive, dialogic, and intellectually generative terrain.

REFERENCES

CAST. (n.d.). *Artificial Intelligence & UDL*. Retrieved from https://www.cast.org/what-we-do/artificial-intelligence/

Davood, A. (2023). EQUAL AI: A framework for enhancing equity, quality, understanding, and accessibility in liberal arts through AI for multilingual learners. *Language, Technology, and Social Media*, *2*(1), 15–29.

Eden, C., Adeleye, O., & Adeniyi, I. (2024). A review of AI-driven pedagogical strategies for equitable access to science education. Magna Scientia Advanced Research and Reviews. 10. 044-054. DOI: 10.30574/msarr.2024.10.2.0043

Francis, J., Jones, M., & Smith, A. (2025). Generative AI in higher education: Balancing innovation and integrity. Retrieved from https://pubmed.ncbi.nlm.nih.gov/39850144

Haroud, S., & Saqri, N. (2025). Generative AI in higher education: Teachers' and students' perspectives on support, replacement, and digital literacy. *Education Sciences*, *15*(4), 396. DOI: 10.3390/educsci15040396

Schreffler, J., Vasquez, E.III, & Chini, J.. (2019). Universal Design for Learning in postsecondary STEM education for students with disabilities: A systematic literature review. *International Journal of STEM Education*, *6*, 8. DOI: 10.1186/s40594-019-0161-8

Chapter 6
Assistive Technologies for Learners With Disabilities Using GenAI

Tary Hadani
https://orcid.org/0009-0004-3349-1501
Universitas Esa Unggul, Indonesia

Chrisella Natasia Tanujaya
https://orcid.org/0009-0001-0549-368X
Universitas Esa Unggul, Indonesia

Binastya Anggara Sekti
https://orcid.org/0000-0001-5489-4888
Universitas Esa Unggul, Indonesia

ABSTRACT

Generative Artificial Intelligence (GenAI) is revolutionizing education by providing personalized learning experiences for students with disabilities. This chapter explores the role of GenAI and assistive technologies, such as screen readers and mobility devices, in enhancing educational accessibility. GenAI enables real-time adaptation of learning materials, making them more suitable for students with cognitive, physical, and sensory disabilities. While the potential is significant, challenges such as accessibility, educator training, and data privacy must be addressed. The chapter emphasizes the need for infrastructure development and training to fully integrate GenAI into inclusive education systems.

DOI: 10.4018/979-8-3373-3745-6.ch006

1. INTRODUCTION

Generative Artificial Intelligence (GenAI) has become one of the most promising technological breakthroughs in education, especially in supporting students with disabilities. Technologies like ChatGPT allow students with different types of disabilities to access learning materials more easily, with real-time support tailored to their needs. GenAI can provide a more adaptive learning experience, where subject matter is tailored to the individual's learning style and abilities, thus facilitating students who may have difficulty following traditional learning methods (Souval et al., 2025). This providing great opportunities for students with disabilities to learn independently, utilizing technology in a more flexible way.

However, while GenAI offers a lot of potential, the application of this technology in education also faces various challenges. One of them is the issue of technological accessibility, where many educational institutions, especially in areas with limited infrastructure, have not been able to access the hardware and software necessary to make the most of AI-based technologies. Another challenge is the skills gap among educators, who are often untrained in using GenAI-based tools to support the learning of students with disabilities (Farhah et al., 2025) This gap hinders the full potential of this technology in creating more inclusive learning.

In addition, there are also data privacy issues that must be faced. The use of GenAI in education involves the collection of students' personal data, which can include sensitive information related to their disability needs. Therefore, it is crucial to have strict security systems and clear policies in place to ensure that student data is well protected and used only for legitimate purposes. If these issues are not handled properly, the use of GenAI can raise ethical and legal issues related to data misuse (Acosta-Vargas et al., 2024)

The purpose of this chapter is to explore how GenAI contributes to supporting learning for students with disabilities. This chapter will also discuss the challenges faced in the implementation of GenAI, such as technology accessibility, educator training, and data privacy issues, as well as identify solutions that can be taken to address these barriers. By integrating GenAI in the education system, we can create greater opportunities for students with disabilities to learn in a more effective and inclusive way.

2. THE ROLE OF ASSISTIVE TECHNOLOGY IN EDUCATION

Inclusive education has become a core principle in modern learning systems, emphasizing the importance of equal access to quality education for all students, including those with disabilities. As educational institutions strive to create environments that accommodate diverse learning needs, technology plays a pivotal role in bridging gaps between limitations and learning opportunities. Assistive technology contributes significantly to inclusive education by providing equal opportunities for students with disabilities to access and engage in learning activities. It enables learners to participate more actively in the classroom and supports their academic development through customized tools that meet their specific needs (Kılınç, 2024).

A supportive school climate and teachers' self-efficacy are essential factors that encourage the effective integration of educational technology. When educators believe in their ability to utilize technology effectively, they are more likely to implement assistive tools that improve the learning experience for all students. Moreover, a positive institutional environment that provides adequate resources, training, and motivation can further strengthen teachers' willingness to integrate technology in inclusive classrooms (Perkmen, 2024).

Artificial intelligence and adaptive systems have also emerged as innovative components of assistive technology in education. These technologies enhance personalized learning by offering real-time feedback and adaptive support tailored to each student's ability level. Through the use of intelligent systems, students can improve their understanding of concepts, expand their vocabulary, and engage in more interactive and self-directed learning experiences (Nazzaro et al., 2025)

Figure 1. Assistive technology integration model with GenAI in inclusive education

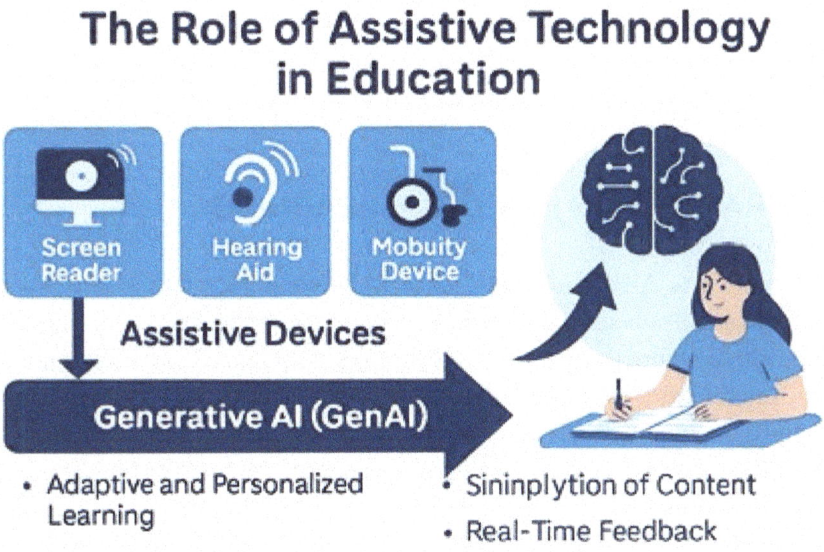

Assistive technology plays a very important role in supporting the learning of students with disabilities, allowing them to access subject matter and participate in educational activities. Devices such as screen readers for students with visual impairments, hearing aids for students with hearing disabilities, and mobility devices for students with physical disabilities have gone a long way in creating more equal opportunities for students with disabilities to learn. This assistive technology provides students with access to actively participate in education, without feeling isolated or limited by their physical or sensory conditions (Mukhtarkyzy et al., 2025).

Along with the development of technology, there is now Generative AI-based technology (GenAI) which further expands the role of assistive technology in education. GenAI not only helps provide access, but also creates a more adaptive and personalized learning experience. With the ability to change subject matter according to students' level of understanding, GenAI can adjust learning in real-time. For example, for students with cognitive disabilities, GenAI is able to simplify the material or provide more detailed explanations to aid their understanding. This technology serves as a personal tutor who provides hands-on feedback and allows students to learn in a way that suits their learning style (Singh, 2025).

Additionally, GenAI has the potential to improve the quality of learning for students with various disabilities by providing real-time feedback, allowing students to correct their mistakes while learning. This provides a more interactive and responsive experience, reducing reliance on conventional teaching that may not always be able to provide in-person attention. With the ability to provide explanations more easily understood and adapt to the pace of learning, GenAI provides students with the opportunity to reach their full potential without being hindered by their physical or cognitive limitations (Waseem Syed, 2025)

3. GENERATIVE AI IN INCLUSIVE LEARNING

In recent years, Artificial Intelligence (AI) technology has experienced rapid development and has begun to be widely used in the world of education. One of the most innovative AI breakthroughs is Generative AI (GenAI), which is a technology capable of automatically generating new content, such as text, images, audio, and video, based on specific data and context. The presence of GenAI opens up great opportunities in transforming the learning process, especially in the context of inclusive education.

Inclusive learning demands an approach that is flexible, adaptive, and able to meet the diverse needs of students, including those with disabilities. This is where GenAI plays an important supporting role, due to its ability to personalize teaching materials and adapt them to each student's learning style, abilities, and limitations.

GenAI is not just a tool, but can be an intelligent assistant that designs, modifies, and delivers appropriate learning in real-time.

GenAI technology can be used to simplify language in subject matter for students with cognitive impairments, or convert text into interactive audio for students with visual impairments. Not only that, GenAI is also able to provide direct feedback and automated suggestions, making the learning process more responsive and student-centered. This provides a more inclusive learning experience compared to traditional rigid and uniform methods.

However, the application of GenAI in inclusive education also requires a deep understanding of the needs of students with disabilities, as well as proper integration into the learning system. Teachers, educators, and curriculum designers need to work closely with technology developers to ensure that the content generated by GenAI is truly relevant, safe, and unbiased.

This section will review more specifically how GenAI is applied in supporting students with different types of disabilities, through the following three sub-chapters: visual impairment, cognitive disability, and physical disability. Each type of disability has unique challenges, so the implementation of GenAI needs to be strategically adjusted to be able to have a real positive impact on the learning process.

3.1 Application of GenAI for Visual Impairment

Figure 2. Illustration of using the GenAI screen-reader for students with visual impairments

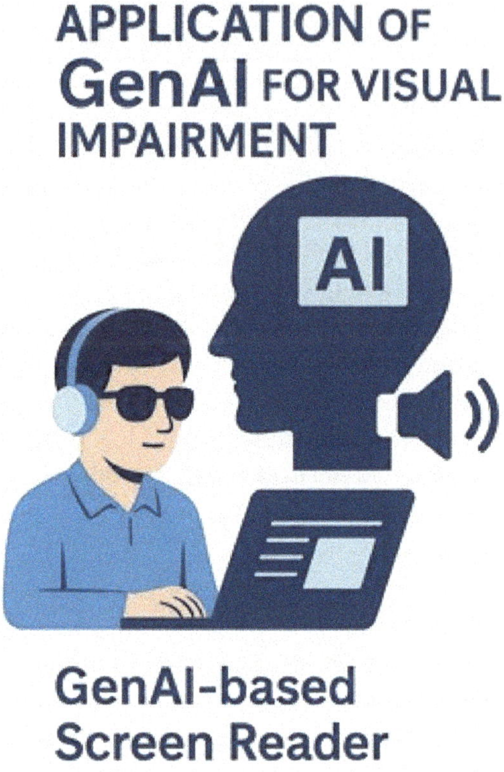

Students with visual impairments face significant challenges in accessing learning materials that are generally dominated by text or images. Technologies such as GenAI-based screen readers allow students with visual impairments to listen to text that appears on a computer screen or other device. This AI-based screen reader converts text into sound, thus allowing students to understand the information presented in a format that they can easily access. This opens up greater opportunities for them to participate in learning activities without being limited by their visual limitations.

Additionally, GenAI helps to enhance the capabilities of traditional screen readers by providing more advanced natural language processing. This technology allows screen readers to provide additional or contextual explanations of images and graphics, which were previously difficult for students with visual impairments to access. Using GenAI-based algorithms, this technology is able to describe images or graphics in more detail, helping students to understand visual information in a more accessible way.

One example of another application of GenAI is the ability to translate complex subject matter or complex-formatted text into easier to understand by using simpler voice and explanations. This technology helps reduce the barriers faced by students with visual impairments in accessing learning materials that typically require visual interpretation. Thus, GenAI not only converts text into sound, but also enriches the learning experience of students with visual impairments, making education more inclusive and accessible (Pierrès et al., 2025).

3.2 Benefits of GenAI for Learners with Cognitive Disabilities

Figure 3. Students with cognitive disabilities use GenAI for adaptive learning.

Students with cognitive disabilities often face difficulties in understanding complex learning materials. GenAI provides a solution by providing adjustment of the difficulty level of the material based on the student's abilities and needs. For example, for students with information processing disorders, GenAI can simplify complex texts, explain difficult concepts, or provide instructions in a simpler, easy-to-understand form. It helps students with cognitive disabilities to feel more confident in learning, as they can access the material in a way that is more appropriate to their level of understanding.

Additionally, GenAI supports more interactive task-based learning, which is especially important for students with cognitive disabilities. Task-based learning allows students to learn through hands-on practice and get hands-on feedback that helps them understand the material better. With GenAI, students can perform more structured learning tasks, get help when needed, and overcome the difficulties they face without feeling pressured. Learning becomes more enjoyable and well-rounded as students feel guided in a more personalized way.

GenAI can also help students with cognitive disabilities to learn in a more collaborative environment. This technology allows interaction with learning materials in a more dynamic and immersive way. For example, students can interact with an AI tutor who provides additional explanations or answers their questions directly. In this way, students with cognitive disabilities not only receive information but also engage in learning actively, improving their ability to process and understand information in a more interactive context (Williams et al., 2021).

3.3 The Use of GenAI in Supporting Learners with Physical Disabilities

Figure 4. Learners with physical disabilities access inclusive learning through voice-based GenAI.

Students with physical disabilities often face challenges in interacting with subject matter that requires physical mobility or manipulation. Using GenAI, this technology can help students access and interact with learning materials without any reliance on their physical mobility. GenAI allows students to use voice-based aids or digital controls to access information, making the learning experience more accessible to students with physical limitations. This technology increases the ease for students to perform academic tasks more independently.

With advancements in AI-based speech recognition and interaction technologies, students with motor disabilities can communicate with learning devices without having to use their hands or bodies directly. This creates opportunities for students to use voice-based devices or gesture-based interfaces to access and interact with the subject matter. This improves students' ability to learn independently, without feeling hindered by their physical disability. GenAI provides a variety of tools that allow for easier interaction with academic materials, such as voice controls for browsing the internet or running educational applications.

GenAI also offers the potential to create more tailored learning for students with physical disabilities. For example, AI tutors can help students to complete academic tasks by providing instruction tailored to their physical needs. Thus, students with physical disabilities can learn without having to depend on the usual physical setting, making the learning process more inclusive and allowing them to achieve their educational goals effectively (Senjam et al., 2021).

4. IMPLEMENTATION CHALLENGES AND BARRIERS

The application of Generative AI (GenAI) in inclusive education has had a significant impact, by providing more equal opportunities for students with disabilities to access subject matter and actively participate in educational activities. With its ability to tailor learning according to students' learning styles and paces, GenAI enables a more personalized experience. However, despite this great potential, there are some key challenges that need to be overcome in order for GenAI's implementation to be successful, especially in the inclusive education sector.

Table 1. Challenges and solutions in the implementation of GenAI in inclusive education.

Challenge	Description	Workable Solutions
Technology Accessibility	Limitations of hardware and software required to support **GenAI**	Greater investment in educational technology infrastructure
Educator Training	Lack of training for educators in using **GenAI** and other assistive technologies	Intensive training program for educators
Data Privacy and Security	Issues related to the use and protection of students' personal data	Development of a clear and robust privacy policy
Bias Algorithm	GenAI that is not trained with representative data can produce biased results	Regular audits and evaluations of **GenAI** systems to reduce bias

One of the biggest challenges is the issue of technological accessibility. While GenAI offers many benefits, not all educational institutions, especially those in resource-constrained areas, have access to the hardware and software necessary to support this technology. Adequate infrastructure is essential to ensure all students, including those with disabilities, can make the most of this technology. Therefore, greater investment is needed in the provision of stable internet devices and networks across educational institutions.

In addition, educator training is very important. Without sufficient training, many educators struggle to integrate GenAI in an effective way in their teaching process. This hinders the potential use of this technology to create a more inclusive learning environment. To this end, the development of an ongoing training program for educators needs to be done to ensure that they can not only understand how technology works, but can also use it to support students with disabilities.

Another problem that is often faced is related to the security of student data. GenAI collects very important and sensitive data related to student progress and behavior. This data may include personal information relating to disability, which if not properly maintained can lead to privacy concerns and misuse of data. Therefore, it is crucial to have strict security protocols and a clear data privacy policy in place so that these technologies are used safely and without harming students.

Overall, while the challenges in implementing GenAI in inclusive education are considerable, the potential benefits are enormous. GenAI can support students with disabilities to learn more independently, provide hands-on feedback, and improve accessibility that was previously difficult for them to reach. If the challenges related to technology accessibility, educator training, and data privacy can be properly addressed, these technologies have the potential to create a more inclusive and equitable education for all students.

4.1 Accessibility and Technology Infrastructure

One of the main challenges in the application of GenAI in education is the issue of technology accessibility. Many schools, especially those in areas with limited infrastructure, do not have the necessary hardware or software to implement GenAI effectively. In many regions, access to advanced technologies such as computers or a stable internet network is still limited, leading to gaps in the adoption of AI-based learning technologies. Reliance on fast internet connections and modern devices is a major obstacle, especially in developing countries or remote areas.

Not only that, many educational institutions are still using old devices or do not have enough budget to update their technological infrastructure. This causes a significant gap in terms of technology access between schools in developed areas and areas with limited resources. Therefore, it is important that there is a major investment in educational infrastructure, including the necessary hardware and a better internet network, so that technologies like GenAI are equally accessible to all students.

In addition to physical access to technology, digital competence is also a big challenge. Teachers and students who are unfamiliar with GenAI technology may have difficulty using it effectively. Education on the application of this technology needs to be done to ensure that all parties involved can make optimal use of GenAI. If access to technology is uneven or if educators do not have enough skills, then the benefits of GenAI in education will not be maximally achieved (Singh, 2025).

4.2 Supporting Training and Skills Gap

Educator training is a big challenge in the application of GenAI technology in education. Many educators, especially in resource-constrained areas, are not trained in using AI-based technologies. Most of them are more familiar with conventional learning methods and may feel anxious or unprepared to integrate GenAI in their classrooms. Without proper training, educators may not be able to make the most of AI-based tools, which will ultimately limit the positive impact GenAI can have on student learning.

Educator training not only covers technical skills in using GenAI, but also includes an understanding of how this technology can be integrated into existing curriculum. GenAI should be used as a tool that can enhance students' learning experience, not as a replacement for traditional teaching methods. Therefore, it is crucial for educators to be equipped with pedagogical knowledge on how to use these technologies to create a more inclusive and dynamic learning environment.

To address this skills gap, a more holistic training approach is needed. More intensive and ongoing training programs should be provided for educators, including training on the application of technology in inclusive classrooms. Thus, educators will feel more confident and ready to leverage GenAI in the most effective way in supporting the learning of students with disabilities (Kuriakose et al., 2022).

4.3 Data Ethics and Privacy Issues

Ethical and data privacy issues are major challenges to face in the use of GenAI in education. These technologies collect highly sensitive data regarding students' learning behavior, including their learning preferences, progress, and even other personal information. Without proper protections, this data can fall into the wrong hands, creating problems related to misuse of information or privacy breaches.

Data security is a major issue in the use of AI in the education sector. Many AI-based systems collect data automatically and process information without direct oversight, which could potentially lead to a data breach if the system is not properly protected. Therefore, it is important to have a strict framework regarding the collection, storage, and use of student data. GenAI technology must adhere to high security and privacy standards to protect student data from outside threats that could harm them.

In addition, the issue of algorithm bias in GenAI also needs to be considered. If the AI system is trained with unrepresentative or biased data, then GenAI can generate decisions or recommendations that are detrimental to certain groups, such as students with disabilities. Therefore, the development and implementation of GenAI in the education sector must be carried out taking into account ethics related to fairness, equality, and the protection of student data privacy (Elsayed & Alfawzan, 2025).

5. POTENTIAL AND DIRECTION OF GENAI DEVELOPMENT IN EDUCATION

The development of Generative AI (GenAI) technology has presented a great opportunity in improving the quality of education, especially in the context of inclusive learning. GenAI is able to offer a more personalized, adaptive, and flexible approach to learning, allowing students with a wide range of ability backgrounds, including those with disabilities, to learn effectively. With its ability to generate content, understand context, and provide real-time responses, GenAI expands the scope of assistive technologies that were previously limited and conventional.

In the context of inclusive education, the potential of GenAI is very promising. This technology not only supports accessibility, but also empowers students to learn independently according to their abilities and learning styles. For example, GenAI can simplify learning materials for students with cognitive impairments, voice text for visually impaired students, or provide a voice interface for students with motor difficulties. All of this allows students with disabilities to participate more actively and equally in the learning process.

Another potential that is no less important is GenAI's ability to analyze student learning data to automatically adjust learning materials and strategies. With its adaptive learning feature, GenAI can identify students' learning difficulties early on and provide recommendations for improvement directly. This provides a great added value compared to conventional teaching methods which tend to be general and cannot adapt to individual needs.

Table 2. Direction of GenAI Development in Inclusive Education

Development Direction	Short Description
Real-Time Adaptive Learning	The AI system analyzes learning patterns and adjusts the material according to the needs of the students
Voice & Gesture-Based Interaction	Use of voice and gesture control for unhindered access
Self-Paced Learning & Automated Feedback	GenAI provides hands-on feedback and allows students to learn independently
Multimodal Accessibility	Provision of materials in various formats (text, sound, visual) as needed
AI Personal Tutor	GenAI serves as a tutor who provides personalized explanations interactively

In the future, the direction of GenAI's development in education will focus not only on technical functions, but also on the integration of inclusive values, data use ethics, and equality of access. Researchers and developers of educational technology are currently working to create a more intelligent and humane system, which can take into account the sensitivity of the needs of students with disabilities. This includes disability-friendly interface design, student data security and privacy, and educator training in using GenAI effectively.

Considering its various potentials and development directions, GenAI is predicted to become an important element in the transformation of education that is more equitable and equitable. This technology is able to bridge the gap in access to education that has been faced by students with disabilities, while improving the quality of the process and overall learning outcomes. In the next section, we will discuss more about the latest trends in assistive technology and future views on the application of GenAI in educational institutions.

5.1 Inovasi dan Tren Terkini dalam Teknologi Asistif

Innovations in GenAI continue to grow rapidly, especially in the field of assistive technology. One of the recent trends is the increased use of adaptive AI that allows systems to learn and adapt to the unique needs of each student. This technology allows the system to analyze students' learning patterns in real-time and provide materials tailored to their abilities and speed. With adaptive AI technology, learning becomes more flexible and personalized, facilitating students with various disabilities to access subject matter more effectively and independently. Students can learn in a way that is more in line with the way they process information, increasing their level of engagement in learning.

Another trend is the increasing use of speech recognition technology and gesture-based interaction in education. Students with physical or motor disabilities can interact with learning materials without the need for direct physical control. GenAI allows students to use voice control or gesture-based devices to interact with digital devices, opening up great opportunities for students with physical limitations. In addition, the technology also enables voice-based learning and visual-based interactions that enrich the learning experience of students with various disabilities, creating a more inclusive environment and supporting independence in learning.

As this trend develops, we are also witnessing the application of GenAI in self-learning. For example, the GenAI app provides automated feedback to students, giving them the opportunity to correct mistakes without having to rely on direct interaction with the teacher. This gives students the freedom to learn at their own pace and get the guidance they need in real-time. These technologies improve accessibility and equity in education, as students from different backgrounds and abilities can get the support they need to thrive optimally in an academic context (Waseem Syed, 2025).

Along with the adoption of the technology at the global level, some countries such as South Korea and Finland have implemented GenAI in their inclusive education curriculum. South Korea, for example, has since 2022 begun developing AI-based adaptive learning systems for students with disabilities, including the blind and dyslexic. Meanwhile, developing countries still face obstacles in terms of infrastructure and human resource readiness. However, collaborative projects such as the Microsoft Inclusive AI Toolkit and support from international organizations such as UNESCO are driving equitable adoption of this technology in different parts of the world.

Another trend that is starting to develop is wearable assistive technology, such as GenAI-based smart glasses that are able to read text and recognize faces or objects around the user. This technology is very helpful for students with visual impairments to be more independent in the school environment. Some startups are even developing AI sensors that are able to read students' expressions or confusion levels, so that the system can adjust the material automatically. This shows that the future of assistive technology is not only sophisticated, but also increasingly personal and humanistic.

5.2 Future Outlook for the Use of GenAI in Educational Institutions

In the future, GenAI is expected to be increasingly applied in education, with more and more educational institutions integrating adaptive AI in their learning. With the ability to provide greater accessibility to students with disabilities, GenAI opens up opportunities for more inclusive learning. This technology allows educational institutions to tailor subject matter to the unique needs of students, removing barriers that have existed in an education system that is not fully inclusive. GenAI is expected to be key in creating an equal education for all students, regardless of their background or physical condition.

In addition, the use of GenAI is predicted to strengthen student participation in educational activities. With adaptive AI technology, students can be more engaged with the subject matter in a way that better suits the way they learn. For example, students with cognitive disabilities can learn through materials tailored to their abilities, while students with physical disabilities can access materials by using voice-based controls. This increases the possibility for all students to actively participate in learning, reduces existing gaps in education, and enables them to develop the skills needed for the future.

Going forward, GenAI will not only improve accessibility and participation, but also the independence of students with disabilities. Students can learn more independently by using AI-based tools that provide guidance and feedback automatically. This allows them to learn without a huge reliance on teacher instruction, giving them confidence in managing their own education. With GenAI's ability to tailor the learning experience according to individual needs, the technology promises a more inclusive and equality-oriented future of education for all students (Zhang et al., 2024).

Educational institutions are also expected to further develop policies and infrastructure that support the comprehensive integration of GenAI. This includes teacher training in the use of AI, curriculum updates to be compatible with intelligent systems, and the provision of devices and networks that support the inclusive use of technology. The involvement of stakeholders such as the government, technology developers, and the education community is an important factor so that the implementation of GenAI is not only technical, but also ethical and sustainable.

Finally, the future of education with GenAI is not just about technological transformation, but also a paradigm shift in the way we view learning and inclusion. GenAI gives us the opportunity to build an education system that is not only efficient, but also human—one that is able to reach all students, empower them, and ensure that no one is left behind due to physical, cognitive, or social limitations.

6. INTEGRATION OF ASSISTIVE TECHNOLOGY IN THE EDUCATIONAL CURRICULUM

Inclusive education not only requires changes in classroom practices but also a transformation in curriculum planning. A curriculum that embraces diversity must be flexible, accessible, and responsive to the varied learning needs of all students—including those with disabilities. The inclusion of assistive technologies in the educational framework is a necessary step toward achieving equitable learning outcomes.

By embedding assistive technologies in the curriculum design process, education systems can shift from a reactive model—where accommodations are made after difficulties arise—to a proactive model that anticipates and addresses diverse learning needs from the beginning. This integration ensures that educational goals are aligned with the principles of universal design for learning, where accessibility and adaptability are not optional, but fundamental.

As technology continues to develop, the integration of assistive technology in the educational curriculum is becoming increasingly important to create a more inclusive and equitable education. Educational institutions around the world are beginning to realize the importance of introducing assistive technology as an integral part of daily learning. With technologies like GenAI, educational curricula can be more easily tailored to the needs of individual students, allowing them to learn in a way that better suits their style and abilities. The integration of these technologies allows for more flexible, in-depth, and well-rounded learning, which ultimately accelerates social inclusion and improves the overall quality of education.

One way to integrate assistive technology into the curriculum is to develop inclusive training programs for educators and students. The training program aims to improve the digital skills of educators, ensuring they can use assistive technologies like GenAI in an effective way. In addition, it is also important to provide training for students with disabilities, so that they can take advantage of AI-based tools that can assist them in independent learning. With a good training program, educational institutions can create a more inclusive environment, where all students can learn in a way that suits their abilities.

Assistive technologies integrated into the curriculum can also support various forms of project-based and collaborative learning, allowing students to work together without regard to disability limitations. For example, GenAI can allow students with physical disabilities to collaborate on projects alongside other students without being limited by their physical limitations. AI can provide students with greater access to exploring a variety of learning resources, giving them more opportunities to engage in activities that support their social and professional skills. Through assistive technology-based learning, education becomes more responsive to the diverse needs of students, ultimately driving greater educational equity.(Acosta-Vargas et al., 2024).

6.1 Designing Inclusive Lesson Plans with GenAI

The design of inclusive lesson plans is a foundational step in ensuring that all students, including those with disabilities, can meaningfully participate in the learning process. With the emergence of GenAI technology, educators have new tools at their disposal to create content that is both accessible and adaptable. GenAI can assist teachers in planning lessons that incorporate multiple modes of instruction—such as visual aids, audio narration, and simplified texts—which align with the principles of Universal Design for Learning (UDL). This allows students with varying needs to access the same academic material in ways that best suit their cognitive and sensory preferences.

By using GenAI tools, educators can automate the adaptation of learning content to meet diverse student needs without requiring extensive manual adjustments. For instance, a single instructional unit can be automatically reformatted into a version with larger font and simplified vocabulary for students with visual impairments or cognitive challenges. Similarly, GenAI can generate multilingual support or provide symbolic representations for students with communication difficulties. This proactive design approach ensures that accessibility is not treated as an afterthought but is integrated from the beginning, resulting in more inclusive and equitable classroom experiences.

Furthermore, designing inclusive lesson plans with GenAI promotes student autonomy and engagement. When students are presented with content that is tailored to their individual learning styles, they are more likely to stay motivated and participate actively. GenAI can also provide educators with analytics and insights on how students are interacting with the content, allowing them to make real-time adjustments and identify areas where additional support may be needed. Ultimately, this strategy empowers both teachers and learners, fostering a more supportive educational environment that values and responds to diversity.

6.2 Teacher Training and Curriculum Adaptation Strategies

The successful integration of GenAI in inclusive education relies heavily on the preparedness of educators. Teachers must be equipped not only with the technical know-how to operate GenAI tools, but also with pedagogical strategies that align with inclusive principles. Comprehensive training programs should emphasize the practical use of GenAI in lesson planning, content customization, and student assessment. By understanding how GenAI can be used to meet a range of student needs, teachers can become active agents in fostering equity in the classroom.

Moreover, curriculum adaptation strategies must go hand in hand with teacher training. Institutions should encourage teachers to co-develop flexible curricula that are responsive to individual learning profiles. With the help of GenAI, educators can personalize learning paths and adjust the depth, pace, and presentation of material. These strategies help ensure that students with disabilities are not simply accommodated, but truly included in the learning process from the start. Curriculum flexibility also allows for real-time modification based on student progress and feedback, enabling dynamic and responsive instruction.

In addition, collaboration among educators is key in building a supportive community for inclusive curriculum innovation. Teachers can share best practices, challenges, and successful case studies in using GenAI to promote accessibility. Institutions should also provide access to ongoing professional development opportunities focused on inclusive education and educational technology. When teacher training is approached as a continuous and collaborative process, it reinforces the systemic shift toward inclusive and adaptive education that benefits all learners.

6.3 Customizing Assessments Using AI Tools

Assessment plays a crucial role in determining how well students understand and engage with learning material. For students with disabilities, conventional assessments often fail to reflect their actual capabilities due to format and accessibility limitations. GenAI offers a solution by enabling educators to design customized assessments tailored to individual learning needs. Through AI-based tools, teachers can generate quizzes, comprehension tests, or assignments in various formats—such as visual, auditory, or simplified text—to match the diverse cognitive and physical conditions of their students.

In addition, AI-powered assessment tools can adjust the difficulty level of questions based on real-time performance. This adaptive capability ensures that students are neither overwhelmed nor under-challenged, allowing for a more accurate reflection of their knowledge. For example, students with reading disabilities may be given voice-based questions, while others may benefit from visual prompts or scaffolded questioning. Such personalization helps foster a more equitable assessment environment where all students can demonstrate their progress effectively and confidently.

Moreover, GenAI can provide instant and specific feedback, allowing students to understand their mistakes and correct them independently. This feedback loop supports continuous learning and reduces the need for constant teacher intervention, especially beneficial in inclusive classrooms where differentiated instruction is required. By using AI tools for customized assessments, educators not only make evaluations more accessible but also promote student autonomy and a deeper understanding of learning objectives.

6.4 Monitoring Student Progress Through GenAI Tools

The integration of assistive technology in the curriculum not only focuses on content delivery and accessibility, but also on the continuous monitoring of student learning outcomes. Generative AI (GenAI) tools offer advanced analytics capabilities that allow educators to track students' progress in real-time. By analyzing interaction patterns, completion rates, and individual comprehension levels, GenAI can provide immediate insights into a student's learning journey. This is particularly beneficial for students with disabilities, as teachers can quickly identify areas where additional support is needed and adjust instructional methods accordingly.

GenAI-powered platforms can also generate personalized progress reports, which are useful not only for educators but also for students and parents. These reports include visual summaries of learning milestones, feedback on performance, and recommendations for future learning strategies. For students with learning disabilities, this type of adaptive monitoring promotes transparency and accountability while fostering motivation and self-awareness. It shifts the traditional evaluation process from a one-size-fits-all model to a dynamic, student-centered system that evolves with the learner's needs.

Furthermore, continuous progress monitoring supports data-driven decision-making at the institutional level. Administrators can use aggregated data from GenAI systems to evaluate the overall effectiveness of assistive technology implementation, identify trends, and allocate resources more efficiently. This feedback loop between learners, educators, and institutions ensures that inclusive practices are not only adopted but also optimized over time. With GenAI, the curriculum becomes a living system—adaptive, responsive, and committed to equity in education.

7. EVALUATION AND MEASUREMENT OF THE EFFECTIVENESS OF ASSISTIVE TECHNOLOGY IN EDUCATION

In the application of AI-based assistive technology such as GenAI in the world of education, it is important to realize that success is not only measured by the extent to which the technology is used, but the extent to which it actually has a positive impact on the learning process and outcomes of students. Many technological innovations look promising at first, but in reality not all of them deliver significant results for students with disabilities. Therefore, a systematic, sustainable, and thorough evaluation is absolutely necessary. Without structured evaluation, educational institutions risk adopting technology that is less relevant or even inhospitable to the diversity of student needs.

Good evaluation should cover both academic and non-academic dimensions, as well as use quantitative and qualitative approaches. From the academic side, effectiveness measurement can be done through a comparison of student learning outcomes before and after the use of technology. Meanwhile, from the social and emotional side, evaluation can be carried out through observation of students' behavior, level of involvement in class, and their perception of a more inclusive learning experience. This becomes important because the effectiveness of assistive technology is not only related to increased academic grades, but also how it builds the confidence and social participation of students with disabilities.

It is important to evaluate and measure the effectiveness of the application of assistive technology in education to ensure that it truly provides maximum benefits for students with disabilities. This evaluation should include academic aspects as well as social influences on students. For example, how much influence GenAI has in improving students' understanding of the subject matter and how effective this technology is in providing feedback tailored to their needs. The assessment of the success of assistive technology will help educational institutions to adjust the use of technology and ensure that AI functions well in helping students learn optimally.

The evaluation method must also consider the accessibility of technology in different types of educational institutions. Not all institutions have the same infrastructure, and it is therefore important to have a flexible approach in evaluating the effectiveness of assistive technologies. For example, some schools may be better equipped to implement advanced technologies like GenAI, while others may take longer to adapt. This evaluation, which is based on a diverse educational environment, will provide a clearer picture of how assistive technology plays a role in improving the overall quality of education.

In the evaluation, feedback from educators and students is also very important. Teachers' opinions on how effectively they use GenAI in the classroom as well as students' hands-on experience in accessing the subject matter will provide a more comprehensive picture of the effectiveness of this technology. With continuous evaluation, educational institutions can continue to develop and adjust the use of assistive technology to be more effective, optimize the learning experience, and improve student learning outcomes.(Martiniello et al., 2022).

8. THE POTENTIAL OF GENAI TECHNOLOGY IN ENHANCING INCLUSIVE LEARNING

The application of Generative AI (GenAI) in inclusive education brings great potential to support students with various disabilities. One of its main benefits is that it provides a tailored learning experience for each individual. Students with cognitive disabilities can gain more structured and easier to understand learning through adaptive AI. Additionally, this technology can simplify difficult material for students and provide clearer and easier to understand explanations. By using GenAI, students can learn according to their abilities, without feeling hampered by differences in their learning styles (Nasim et al., 2025)

GenAI also opens up opportunities for voice-based interactions that allow students with visual disabilities or motor disabilities to interact with learning materials without having to rely on physical input. By using sound-based devices, students can take advantage of this technology to learn more independently, without having to be limited by traditional physical aids. This makes learning more inclusive and allows all students, regardless of their physical condition, to have equal access to education (Fu et al., 2025)

In addition, adaptive AI allows learning to be more interactive and dynamic, providing immediate feedback that allows students to correct their mistakes quickly and learn more independently. It also helps students feel more engaged in the learning process and boosts their confidence in overcoming academic challenges.

More than just providing technical convenience, GenAI's potential also lies in its ability to personalize learning in a sustainable manner based on student interaction data. GenAI can analyze students' learning habits, error patterns, and learning preferences and adjust teaching strategies over time. This allows any student, especially those with special needs, to have a highly customized and scalable learning experience. In the long run, this paves the way to truly learner-centered learning, which was previously difficult to realize in the conventional education system.

With all its potential, GenAI not only acts as a tool, but also as a catalyst for the transformation of inclusive education. The existence of this technology can help eliminate structural and pedagogical barriers that have limited access to education for students with disabilities. However, for the benefits to be felt equally, it is important for educational institutions to integrate GenAI strategically, supported by adequate teacher training, and policies that favor inclusion. With the right approach, GenAI will become a technology that is not only sophisticated, but also humane and fair.

9. THE USE OF GENAI IN IMPROVING ACCESSIBILITY IN HIGHER EDUCATION

At the higher education level, GenAI can expand accessibility for students with disabilities, ensuring that they have an equal opportunity to participate in higher education. Students with hearing disabilities, for example, can use a voice-based system that supports interactive learning, where learning materials are delivered via text or voice, depending on their preferences. With the help of GenAI, subject matter can be easily customized to suit the needs of each individual (Saleela et al., 2025).

The application of GenAI also allows the creation of adaptive curricula that can be tailored to individual abilities. It facilitates students with disabilities to keep up with learning without feeling marginalized or left behind by their classmates. The adaptive AI-based curriculum ensures that each student receives material that matches their level of understanding and learning speed, improving the overall quality of learning (Giansanti & Pirrera, 2025).

Figure 5. Illustration of the use of GenAI for adaptive learning in inclusive colleges.

However, the application of GenAI in higher education also faces challenges, such as a lack of infrastructure in some colleges and universities. Therefore, it is important for educational institutions to invest in educational technology and ensure that all students, including those with disabilities, can access the necessary resources.

In addition to infrastructure, the readiness of educators and support systems in the university environment is also an important factor in the successful implementation of GenAI. Lecturers and academic staff need to be trained to understand how to use this technology optimally and inclusively. It is not enough to just provide technology; The campus environment must create a culture that supports the acceptance and use of AI ethically and adaptively, including in designing appropriate academic services for students with disabilities.

With mature integration, GenAI can be a very powerful tool in realizing a more inclusive and equitable higher education. Universities need to build visionary and collaborative policies to incorporate these technologies into the learning system. Not only to increase access, but also to encourage the active participation and academic achievement of students with disabilities. GenAI is not just a technology, but a path to a more equal learning culture transformation at the higher education level.

10. THE FUTURE OF GENAI TECHNOLOGY IN INCLUSIVE EDUCATION

With the rapid development of Generative AI and other assistive technologies, the future of inclusive education looks brighter. GenAI is expected to play an increasingly important role in creating a more inclusive education, where all students, including those with disabilities, can learn together in a supportive environment. This technology allows for more personalized and adaptive teaching, which can be tailored to individual learning styles and abilities. AI-based learning not only provides a richer experience, but also increases the participation of students with disabilities in the classroom (dos Santos et al., 2022).

In the future, increasingly sophisticated AI technology will allow for a more flexible AI-based curriculum that can be adjusted to student progress. For example, students with physical disabilities or cognitive disabilities can learn with simpler, structured material, while those with higher abilities can get more challenging material. This allows the education system to be more evenly distributed, without anyone feeling left behind or underprivileged (Glazko et al., 2023).

Additionally, GenAI can improve collaboration between students, allowing them to work together despite having different needs. With this technology, students with visual impairments can collaborate with their peers through voice-based systems or other assistive devices. This technology removes pre-existing limitations, providing equal opportunities for all students to participate in joint projects (Zhao et al., 2025).

To ensure the future of GenAI technology truly supports inclusive education, policy support from governments and educational institutions is an important factor. Regulations governing the ethics of using AI, protecting student data, and allocating funds for technology development must be comprehensively established. With a strong policy foundation, the implementation of GenAI can take place systematically, equitablely, and sustainably at various levels of education and regions.

Figure 6. Illustration of the vision of the future of inclusive education with GenAI.

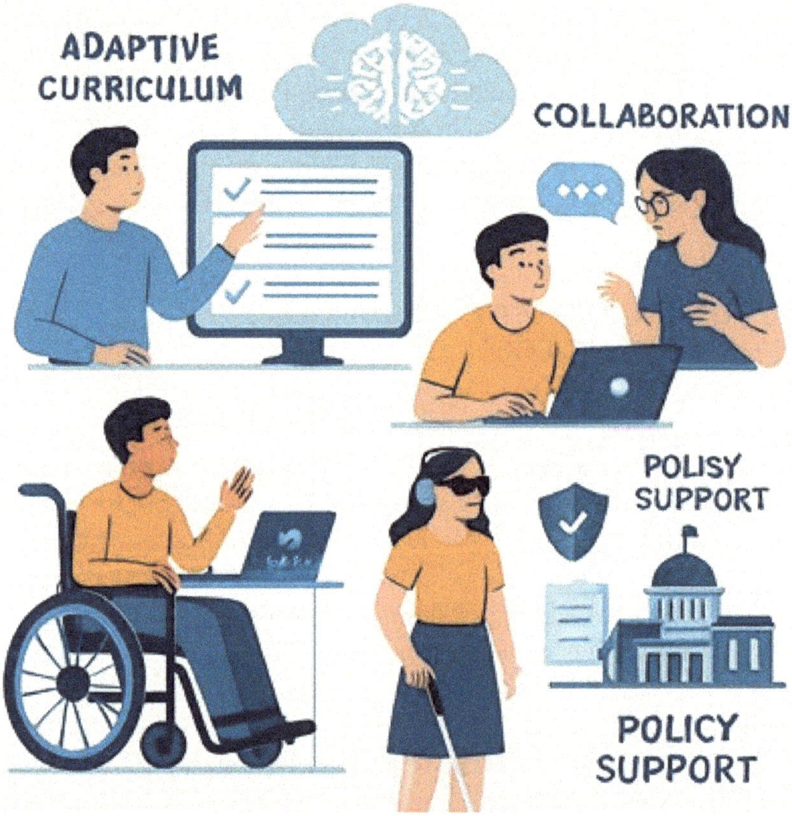

Looking at the existing developments, the future of inclusive education with the support of GenAI is not only technologically promising, but also brings hope for a more equitable and equitable learning culture change. With the commitment of all stakeholders, from educators, technology developers, to policymakers, GenAI can be the key to transforming a truly inclusive global education system for all.

11. POLICY IMPLEMENTATION AND INSTITUTIONAL SUPPORT FOR THE USE OF GENAI

The success of the integration of Generative AI (GenAI) technology in inclusive education depends not only on the sophistication of the technology itself, but also is highly determined by institutional policies and the support of various stakeholders. Educational institutions that are proactive in adopting inclusion-based policies and digitalization play a big role in ensuring that GenAI can be used effectively by students with disabilities. Supportive policies such as the provision of resources, supporting infrastructure, and flexibility for teachers in implementing AI-based learning methods are the key to accelerating the implementation of adaptive education systems. (Zhao et al., 2025) emphasized that institutions that systematically facilitate AI-based learning environments tend to be better prepared to implement an equal and equitable educational model.

In addition to internal policies, training and capacity building for educators and students are also crucial aspects. Educators need to be equipped with technical and pedagogical skills to use GenAI effectively in learning activities, especially for students with special needs. A training program designed on an ongoing basis can help teachers understand GenAI's features, making it a targeted and inclusive tool. According to (Evmenova et al., 2024), the success rate of AI implementation is greatly influenced by the technological literacy of educators, especially in creating adaptive learning based on individual student needs.

On the other hand, the readiness of educational infrastructure also needs to be a major concern. Many institutions, especially in resource-constrained regions, still do not have access to stable internet networks, supporting devices, and compatible GenAI software. This creates a digital divide between advanced and lagging institutions. (Lopez-Gazpio, 2025) emphasizes the importance of government investment and private sector support to improve technology readiness in all educational institutions so that no student with disabilities is left behind from the digital transformation of education.

The implementation of GenAI also requires national-level policy support in the form of regulations that protect the rights of students with disabilities and ensure the security of user data. The government has a strategic responsibility in shaping a legal framework that supports innovation while maintaining ethical principles and protection of vulnerable groups. (Paglialunga & Melogno, 2025) underlined that comprehensively crafted inclusive policies can create a climate conducive to the integration of AI-based technologies in the national education system.

Figure 7. Policy Flows and Institutional Support in the Implementation of GenAI for Inclusive Education.

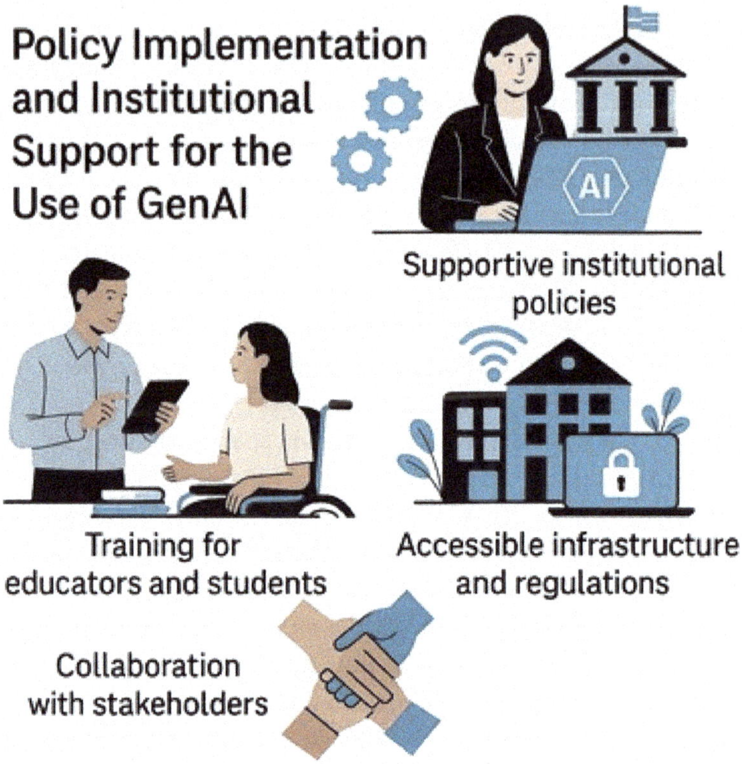

Finally, the successful implementation of GenAI in inclusive education requires a long-term commitment from all stakeholders, both at the local, national, and international levels. Educational institutions need to build collaborations with non-governmental organizations, technology providers, and research institutions to develop evidence-based policies and best practices. This collaboration allows for knowledge exchange, more affordable technology provision, and comprehensive monitoring of GenAI implementation. With a collaborative and sustainable approach, GenAI can be integrated into the education system as an inclusive solution that not only addresses today's challenges, but also prepares students with disabilities for a more adaptive and equitable future.

12. MULTIDISCIPLINARY COLLABORATION IN THE DEVELOPMENT OF GENAI-BASED ASSISTIVE TECHNOLOGY

In the development of Generative AI-based assistive technology (GenAI), multidisciplinary collaboration is a key aspect that cannot be ignored. Technology aimed at supporting learners with disabilities requires the involvement of various fields of science such as education, information technology, psychology, and human-computer interaction design. The involvement of educators and education practitioners is essential for GenAI's features to adapt to the actual needs of students in the classroom. On the other hand, technologists and software developers have an important role to play in ensuring that the systems developed are adaptive and accessible to different types of disabilities.

The collaboration also includes the role of psychologists and neurodiversity experts to ensure that the solutions developed take into account aspects of the cognitive, social, and emotional development of learners with disabilities. For example, students with autism may have very different needs for interaction and information processing than students with visual disabilities. Therefore, the development of GenAI features must consider the input of these professionals so that the technology produced is truly inclusive and does not generalize the needs of students.

Higher education institutions and research institutions also have important contributions to GenAI research and development. They are often the center of early testing of new technologies and can provide in-depth empirical data on the effectiveness of GenAI for learners with special needs. Collaboration between universities and the technology industry results in solutions that are not only innovative, but also based on scientifically proven practices. In addition, the involvement of these institutions allows the development of evidence-based education policies that are urgently needed on a national scale.

Non-governmental organizations (NGOs) that focus on disability and the rights of people with disabilities also play an important role in ensuring that the development of GenAI is not only technologically beneficial, but also ethical and inclusive. They can be a liaison between the user community and technology developers, as well as voice the needs of the field that are often overlooked in the technology design process. The presence of NGOs can also help to oversee that the innovation process does not violate the principles of fairness and universal accessibility.

Through close and continuous cooperation from these various stakeholders, it is hoped that the development of GenAI-based assistive technology can create a more equitable, adaptive, and empowering learning system for all students. Multidisciplinary collaboration not only enriches the solutions produced, but also strengthens the collective commitment to realizing truly inclusive education (Gadekallu et al., 2025).

13. CONCLUSION

The application of Generative AI (GenAI) in inclusive education has a significant impact on creating more equal learning opportunities for students with disabilities. With the ability to customize learning materials based on individual abilities and learning styles, GenAI can provide a more personalized and adaptive learning experience. This technology has become an important tool, especially in supporting students with various disabilities such as vision, hearing, and cognitive disabilities, so that they can access and actively participate in education without feeling hampered by their limitations.

However, while GenAI offers many benefits, its implementation in inclusive education also faces considerable challenges. One of the main challenges is the accessibility of technology, where many educational institutions, especially in areas with limited infrastructure, have difficulty accessing the hardware and software necessary to maximize the use of GenAI. In addition, the skills gap among educators is another obstacle, where many teachers are not yet trained in using GenAI to support the learning of students with disabilities.

In addition, the issue of data privacy is an important challenge in the implementation of GenAI. The use of this technology involves the collection of highly sensitive personal data of students, including data regarding their disability needs. Therefore, there needs to be strict security policies and protocols in place to ensure that student data is protected and used legally. Without serious attention to these privacy issues, the use of GenAI can raise ethical and legal issues that can harm students.

Nonetheless, GenAI has tremendous potential in supporting more inclusive education, by providing real-time feedback that allows students to correct their mistakes in learning. This technology also enhances student interaction and engagement in the learning process, which was previously difficult to achieve with traditional teaching methods. By providing explanations that are easier to understand and adapt to each student's learning pace, GenAI provides an opportunity for them to reach their full potential without being limited by physical or cognitive limitations.

In the future, with the continued development of this technology, GenAI is predicted to increasingly become an integral part of inclusive education. With a more flexible and adaptive approach, GenAI has the potential to create a more equitable learning environment, where all students, including those with disabilities, can learn independently and achieve better academic outcomes. To realize this potential, investment in technology infrastructure, educator training, and policy development is needed to support the safe and inclusive use of GenAI across educational institutions.

REFERENCES

Acosta-Vargas, P., Salvador-Acosta, B., Novillo-Villegas, S., Sarantis, D., & Salvador-Ullauri, L. (2024). Generative Artificial Intelligence and Web Accessibility: Towards an Inclusive and Sustainable Future. *Emerging Science Journal*, *8*(4), 1602–1621. DOI: 10.28991/ESJ-2024-08-04-021

dos Santos, A. D. P., Ferrari, A. L. M., Medola, F. O., & Sandnes, F. E. (2022). Aesthetics and the perceived stigma of assistive technology for visual impairment. *Disability and Rehabilitation. Assistive Technology*, *17*(2), 152–158. DOI: 10.1080/17483107.2020.1768308 PMID: 32501732

Elsayed, A. R., & Alfawzan, S. K. (2025). A proposed vision for the use of artificial intelligence in education by teachers of students with intellectual disabilities. *International Journal of Innovative Research and Scientific Studies*, *8*(4), 1270–1281. DOI: 10.53894/ijirss.v8i4.8055

Evmenova, A. S., Borup, J., & Shin, J. K. (2024). Harnessing the Power of Generative AI to Support ALL Learners. *TechTrends*, *68*(4), 820–831. DOI: 10.1007/s11528-024-00966-x

Farhah, N. S., Wadood, A., Alqarni, A. A., Uddin, M. I., & Aldhyani, T. H. H. (2025). Enhancing Adaptive Learning with Generative AI for Tailored Educational Support for Students with Disabilities. *Journal of Disability Research*, *4*(3), 1–17. DOI: 10.57197/JDR-2025-0012

Fu, B., Hadid, A., & Damer, N. (2025). Generative AI in the context of assistive technologies: Trends, limitations and future directions. *Image and Vision Computing, 154*(November 2024), 105347. https://doi.org/DOI: 10.1016/j.imavis.2024.105347

Gadekallu, T. R., Yenduri, G., Kaluri, R., Rajput, D. S., Lakshmanna, K., Fang, K., Chen, J., & Wang, W. (2025). The role of GPT in promoting inclusive higher education for people with various learning disabilities: A review. *PeerJ. Computer Science*, *11*, e2400. DOI: 10.7717/peerj-cs.2400 PMID: 40062249

Giansanti, D., & Pirrera, A. (2025). Integrating AI and Assistive Technologies in Healthcare: Insights from a Narrative Review of Reviews. *Health Care*, *13*(5), 556. DOI: 10.3390/healthcare13050556 PMID: 40077118

Glazko, K. S., Yamagami, M., Desai, A., Mack, K. A., Potluri, V., Xu, X., & Mankoff, J. (2023). An Autoethnographic Case Study of Generative Artificial Intelligence's Utility for Accessibility. In *ASSETS 2023 - Proceedings of the 25th International ACM SIGACCESS Conference on Computers and Accessibility* (Vol. 1, Issue 1). Association for Computing Machinery. https://doi.org/DOI: 10.1145/3597638.3614548

Kılınç, S. (2024). Comprehensive AI assessment framework: Enhancing educational evaluation with ethical AI integration. *Journal of Educational Technology and Online Learning, 7*(4-ICETOL 2024 Special Issue), 521–540. https://doi.org/DOI: 10.31681/jetol.1492695

Kuriakose, B., Shrestha, R., & Sandnes, F. E. (2022). Tools and Technologies for Blind and Visually Impaired Navigation Support: A Review. *IETE Technical Review (Institution of Electronics and Telecommunication Engineers, India), 39*(1), 3–18. https://doi.org/DOI: 10.1080/02564602.2020.1819893

Lopez-Gazpio, I. (2025). Integrating Large Language Models into Accessible and Inclusive Education: Access Democratization and Individualized Learning Enhancement Supported by Generative Artificial Intelligence. *Information (Basel), 16*(6), 473. DOI: 10.3390/info16060473

Martiniello, N., Eisenbarth, W., Lehane, C., Johnson, A., & Wittich, W. (2022). Exploring the use of smartphones and tablets among people with visual impairments: Are mainstream devices replacing the use of traditional visual aids? *Assistive Technology, 34*(1), 34–45. DOI: 10.1080/10400435.2019.1682084 PMID: 31697612

Mukhtarkyzy, K., Smagulova, L., Tokzhigitova, A., Serikbayeva, N., Sayakov, O., Turkmenbayev, A., & Assilbayeva, R. (2025). A systematic review of the utility of assistive technologies for SEND students in schools. *Frontiers in Education, 10*(February). Advance online publication. DOI: 10.3389/feduc.2025.1523797

Nasim, S. S., Pranav, P., & Dutta, S. (2025). A systematic literature review on intrusion detection techniques in cloud computing. *Discover Computing, 28*(1). Advance online publication. DOI: 10.1007/s10791-025-09641-y

Nazzaro, A., Santini, C., & Nazzaro, L. (2025). LSTM-driven CLIL: Cybersecurity vocabulary learning with AI. *Journal of Educational Technology and Online Learning, 8*(3), 313–329. DOI: 10.31681/jetol.1685183

Paglialunga, A., & Melogno, S. (2025). The Effectiveness of Artificial Intelligence-Based Interventions for Students with Learning Disabilities: A Systematic Review. *Brain Sciences, 15*(8), 806. DOI: 10.3390/brainsci15080806 PMID: 40867139

Perkmen, S. (2024). The role of self efficacy and school climate in motivation for technology integration in education. *Journal of Educational Technology and Online Learning, 7*(4-ICETOL 2024 Special Issue), 358–366. https://doi.org/DOI: 10.31681/jetol.1557095

Pierrès, O., Darvishy, A., & Christen, M. (2025). Exploring the role of generative AI in higher education: Semi-structured interviews with students with disabilities. *Education and Information Technologies*, *30*(7), 8923–8952. DOI: 10.1007/s10639-024-13134-8

Saleela, D., Oyegoke, A. S., Dauda, J. A., & Ajayi, S. O. (2025). Development of AI-Driven Decision Support System for Personalized Housing Adaptations and Assistive Technology. *Journal of Aging and Environment*, *0*(0), 1–24. DOI: 10.1080/26892618.2025.2534956

Senjam, S. S., Manna, S., & Bascaran, C. (2021). Smartphones-based assistive technology: Accessibility features and apps for people with visual impairment, and its usage, challenges, and usability testing. *Clinical Optometry*, *13*, 311–322. DOI: 10.2147/OPTO.S336361 PMID: 34866955

Singh, V. (2025). AI-Powered Assistive Technologies for People with Disabilities: Developing AI Solutions that Aid Individuals with Various Disabilities in Daily Tasks. *Journal of Engineering Research and Reports*, *27*(2), 292–309. DOI: 10.9734/jerr/2025/v27i21410

Souval, D. H., Haber, Y., Tal, A., Simon, T., Elyoseph, T., & Elyoseph, Z. (2025). Transforming Perceptions: Exploring the Multifaceted Potential of Generative AI for People With Cognitive Disabilities. *JMIR Neurotechnology*, *4*, 1–11. DOI: 10.2196/64182

Syed, W. (2025). Advancing Accessibility and Social Inclusion through Generative AI and Machine Learning-Powered Multi-Modality on Mobile Platforms. *International Journal of Scientific Research in Computer Science. Engineering and Information Technology*, *11*(1), 475–483. DOI: 10.32628/cseit25111254

Williams, C., Pease, A., Warnes, P., Harrison, S., Pilon, F., Hyvarinen, L., West, S., Self, J., Ferris, J., Goodenough, T., Watanabe, R., Clark, R., Evans, M., Osborne, D., Edwards, E., Billington, C., Hunn, R., & Matharu, G. (2021). Cerebral visual impairment-related vision problems in primary school children: A cross-sectional survey. *Developmental Medicine and Child Neurology*, *63*(6), 683–689. DOI: 10.1111/dmcn.14819 PMID: 33533021

Zhang, L., Carter, R. A., Liu, Y., & Peng, P. (2024). Let's CHAT About Artificial Intelligence for Students With Disabilities: A Systematic Literature Review and Meta-Analysis. *Review of Educational Research*, *XX*(X), 1–43. DOI: 10.3102/00346543241293424

Zhao, X., Cox, A., & Chen, X. (2025). The use of generative AI by students with disabilities in higher education. *Internet and Higher Education, 66*(June 2024), 101014. https://doi.org/DOI: 10.1016/j.iheduc.2025.101014

Chapter 7
Empowering Special Education Through Generative AI With Opportunities, Challenges, and Case Studies

O. Bhaskaru
https://orcid.org/0000-0001-6495-3327
Vignan's Foundation for Science, Technology, and Research, India

K. Lalitha
https://orcid.org/0009-0004-9735-7205
Santhiram Engineering College, India

ABSTRACT

Generative Artificial Intelligence (GenAI) is transforming special education by delivering personalized, accessible, and inclusive learning experiences for students with diverse cognitive, sensory, communication, and behavioral needs. Unlike traditional technologies, GenAI can dynamically create content, adapt learning pathways, and simulate social-emotional scenarios, opening new opportunities for engagement and independence. This chapter explores GenAI's multifaceted applications in special education—ranging from augmentative communication and adaptive assessments to emotion-sensitive interventions—supported by real-world case studies. It also critically addresses ethical, technical, and policy challenges, including data privacy, algorithmic bias, and accessibility. Emphasizing the value

DOI: 10.4018/979-8-3373-3745-6.ch007

of co-design with educators and disability advocates, the chapter offers balanced insights and actionable guidance for educators, researchers, policymakers, and AI developers working to create inclusive educational environments.

INTRODUCTION

The evolving intersection between technology and education has created a powerful conduit for innovation and inclusion. At the forefront of this transformation is Generative Artificial Intelligence (GenAI), a class of machine learning models capable of generating new content—text, images, audio, and even simulations—by learning from vast datasets (Holmes, 2020; Zhai, X., et al., 2021; Burrell, J., 2016). While GenAI has already made significant inroads in fields such as healthcare, finance, and creative arts, its implications for education, especially special education, are only beginning to unfold (Popenici & Kerr, 2017; Zawacki-Richter et al., 2019; McAfee, A., & Brynjolfsson, E., 2017).

Special education encompasses a broad spectrum of students with diverse cognitive, sensory, emotional, and behavioral challenges. Traditional educational systems, with their rigid structures and standardized methodologies, often struggle to accommodate such diversity (Rose & Meyer, 2002; Al-Azawei et al., 2016). Students with disabilities may face barriers to accessing content, communicating with peers and educators, participating in classroom activities, and achieving their academic potential (UNESCO, 2020). Moreover, educators often lack the necessary tools or time to design and deliver highly individualized instruction that adapts in real time to student needs (OECD., 2024).

Generative AI disrupts these limitations by enabling a new form of adaptive education—one that not only accommodates but anticipates learner variability (Luckin et al., 2016). It can create tailored instructional materials, translate spoken language into visuals or text in real-time, generate social narratives to model behavior, and adjust content based on a student's pace, learning style, and emotional state (Rashid, S. F, et al., 2024; Cukurova et al., 2019). Such innovations empower students with disabilities to interact with educational material in ways that align with their unique abilities and preferences.

Moreover, the use of GenAI extends beyond content creation. These tools can facilitate meaningful data analysis and feedback loops that support evidence-based instructional decisions (Khosravi et al., 2022). Teachers can receive insights into learning patterns, behavioral trends, and emotional states of students through AI-generated dashboards and visualizations (Pazmino-Maji, R., et al., 2021; Heffernan, N. T., & Heffernan, C. L., 2014). Parents can stay connected with their child's progress through personalized reports that highlight strengths, areas for growth, and suggested interventions. At the administrative level, GenAI can aid in developing inclusive curricula, designing Universal Design for Learning (UDL) frameworks, and aligning interventions with policy mandates and funding opportunities (Miao & Holmes, 2021).

Yet, as with all powerful technologies, the implementation of GenAI in special education must be approached with caution and critical reflection. Issues related to data privacy, algorithmic bias, over-reliance on automated decision-making, and unequal access to technology pose serious ethical and logistical challenges (Nguyen, A., et al., 2023; Floridi & Cowls, 2019; Dignum, 2019). In addition, the success of GenAI hinges on thoughtful collaboration between educators, developers, parents, and disability rights advocates (Williamson & Eynon, 2020).

This chapter provides a comprehensive exploration of GenAI's transformative potential in special education. It aims to inform, inspire, and guide educators, researchers, technologists, and policymakers in understanding how GenAI can be harnessed to support learners with disabilities. The subsequent sections will delve into the core concepts of GenAI in education, outline the specific benefits it offers for special needs learners, and present real-world case studies illustrating successful implementation. Challenges and risks will also be thoroughly examined, followed by a discussion on future directions for research and innovation in this critical area (UNESCO, 2020; Nesru, 2023).

Through this exploration, the chapter seeks to contribute to a broader vision of inclusive education—one where all learners, regardless of their abilities, have equal opportunities to learn, grow, and thrive with the support of intelligent, empathetic, and adaptable technologies (Ahuerma, F. M., 2024).

GENERATIVE AI IN SPECIAL EDUCATION – AN OVERVIEW

Generative Artificial Intelligence (GenAI) is rapidly redefining the landscape of teaching and learning by introducing new ways to create, adapt, and deliver content tailored to individual learner needs. In special education, where learner diversity is especially pronounced, GenAI presents transformative opportunities to personalize instruction, support communication, enhance emotional regulation, and empower educators (Guettala, M., et al.,2024). This chapter offers a comprehensive overview of how GenAI works, how it is applied in special education settings, and how it aligns with inclusive pedagogical frameworks like Universal Design for Learning (UDL). The chapter is divided into three detailed sections: Understanding GenAI in Educational Contexts, Core Applications of GenAI in Special Education, and Integration with Inclusive Pedagogical Frameworks (Dede, C., et al., 2018).

Understanding GenAI in Educational Contexts

Generative AI refers to a category of artificial intelligence capable of producing new content—text, images, audio, and video—by learning from vast datasets. Unlike conventional AI systems that focus primarily on classification or prediction, GenAI models such as GPT-4, BERT, and DALL·E are trained to generate novel outputs in response to prompts (Khosravi et al., 2022; Mitchell et al., 2019). These models operate using advanced architectures like transformers and are fine-tuned to understand syntax, semantics, tone, and context.

In the educational sphere, GenAI powers tools such as writing assistants, AI tutors, and content creators that adapt dynamically to learners' needs (Holmes, 2020; Luckin et al., 2016; Tonbuloğlu, 2023). These tools are not just responsive but also proactive, adjusting difficulty, offering suggestions, and simulating real-world scenarios. For students with special needs, this technology holds even greater promise. It can facilitate learning across various modalities, enhance accessibility, and generate personalized content that meets specific cognitive and emotional requirements (Rashid, S. F, et al., 2024).

Unlike traditional educational software that offers limited adaptability, GenAI allows for multimodal interaction—processing and producing combinations of text, speech, images, and symbols. This multimodal functionality is especially significant for learners with sensory impairments, speech-language disorders, or neurodiverse profiles (Cukurova et al., 2019; Zawacki-Richter et al., 2019). Furthermore, GenAI systems can learn from user interactions, refining their outputs over time and creating increasingly accurate and personalized educational experiences.

CORE APPLICATIONS OF GENAI IN SPECIAL EDUCATION

GenAI is being integrated into a wide range of educational tools and services that are especially beneficial to students with disabilities. These applications are built upon the ability of AI to respond dynamically to learners' needs, allowing for real-time adaptation in both instructional delivery and learner engagement (Gevher et al., 2025). Core applications in special education include personalized learning resources, enhanced communication tools, emotion-sensitive feedback systems, and adaptive assessments. Together, these innovations foster a learning environment that is not only more inclusive but also more engaging and supportive of individual growth.

Personalized Learning Materials and Scaffolding

Personalization is central to effective special education. GenAI excels at creating custom learning paths based on a learner's cognitive profile, engagement level, and historical performance. For example, a student with dyslexia may benefit from GenAI-generated reading passages simplified for readability, accompanied by phonetic assistance and visual summaries (Al-Azawei et al., 2016; Rose & Meyer, 2002). Similarly, students with ADHD can be given brief, focused content chunks with embedded interactive elements to sustain attention (Zhai, X., et al., 2021).

GenAI also supports scaffolding by breaking down complex tasks into manageable steps and providing cues as needed. This is especially useful for learners with executive function challenges who struggle with organization, planning, or task persistence (Meenakshi Dwivedi, 2021). As learners progress, the system adapts the scaffolds to ensure continued development without cognitive overload.

Enhanced Communication and AAC Support

Communication is a significant barrier for many learners with disabilities. GenAI has revolutionized Augmentative and Alternative Communication (AAC) tools by making them predictive, context-aware, and user-specific. Traditional AAC systems rely on preloaded phrases or symbols. In contrast, GenAI can generate full sentences, translate symbols into meaningful expressions, and adapt to the user's conversational history (Melo-López, V.-A., et al., 2025).

These systems allow for more natural and autonomous communication, particularly for students with autism spectrum disorder, cerebral palsy, or speech apraxia. Multimodal input—such as gaze tracking, touch, or gesture—can also be translated into text or synthesized speech, thereby enhancing inclusivity and reducing communication frustration (Rashid, S. F, et al., 2024).

Emotion-Sensitive Interventions and Behavioral Support

Many students in special education exhibit co-occurring emotional and behavioral challenges. GenAI, when combined with affective computing, can analyze facial expressions, voice modulation, and physiological signals (e.g., heart rate or skin conductivity) to detect affective states such as anxiety, boredom, or frustration (Kay, J et al., 2022; Floridi & Cowls, 2019).

When such states are identified, the AI can recommend and even deliver calming interventions—like guided breathing exercises, engaging games, or alternate learning tasks. Teachers can also receive real-time notifications with insights and suggested strategies for intervention (Fu, Y., & Weng, Z., 2024). These emotion-aware systems not only support individual students but also improve classroom climate and promote emotional self-regulation.

Adaptive Assessment and Feedback

Assessment is a critical yet challenging component of special education. GenAI offers dynamic assessment tools that adapt question difficulty based on student responses and present content in various modalities (Khosravi et al., 2022; Karadağ, 2023). For example, a math problem can be delivered via audio, accompanied by visual aids, or gamified to maintain engagement.

Real-time feedback, a hallmark of GenAI, provides learners with immediate corrective input, explanations, and encouragement. Educators can use AI-generated summaries to understand learning trajectories and customize interventions. This level of adaptivity promotes both student independence and teacher efficiency (Woolf, 2010).

Integration with Inclusive Pedagogical Frameworks

The successful application of GenAI in special education requires alignment with pedagogical approaches that prioritize accessibility and learner variability. Inclusive pedagogies, particularly Universal Design for Learning (UDL), provide the necessary foundation for ensuring that GenAI tools do not merely automate instruction but genuinely support diverse learning needs. In this section, we explore how GenAI complements UDL principles, empowers educators, and aligns with broader educational policies and global trends.

Compatibility with Universal Design for Learning (UDL)

The Universal Design for Learning (UDL) framework promotes educational environments that provide multiple means of representation, engagement, and expression to accommodate diverse learners. GenAI aligns naturally with UDL principles by offering on-demand customization of content formats (Rose & Meyer, 2002; Holmes, 2020).

For instance, a history lesson could be delivered as a timeline infographic, a podcast episode, or a narrative simulation—depending on the learner's preference or need. GenAI can adjust the format, difficulty, and pacing of content in real time, thereby enabling a truly inclusive learning experience (Meenakshi Dwivedi, 2021).

Teacher Empowerment and Instructional Design

GenAI also plays a crucial role in supporting educators by automating lesson planning, generating differentiated activities, and analyzing student progress data (Pazmino-Maji, R., et al., 2021). Educators can input learning objectives or IEP goals, and the system can generate aligned content, suggested assessments, and instructional strategies.

Moreover, GenAI provides real-time dashboards summarizing student behavior, emotional state, and academic progress, allowing educators to make timely decisions and adjustments. This reduces administrative burden and enhances instructional precision (UNESCO, 2020).

System-Level Integration and Global Trends

Globally, education systems are beginning to incorporate GenAI into their inclusion strategies. Countries like Finland, Canada, and Singapore have launched national AI-in-education frameworks that include provisions for learners with disabilities (Ahuerma, F. M., 2024; Williamson & Eynon, 2020).

However, disparities remain, especially in low-income regions where infrastructure, training, and data security pose significant barriers (Fu, Y., & Weng, Z., 2024; Dignum, 2019). Policymakers must focus on equity, affordability, and culturally responsive design to ensure that GenAI fulfills its potential as an inclusive technology.

OPPORTUNITIES AND ADVANTAGES OF GENAI FOR SPECIAL NEEDS LEARNERS

The integration of Generative Artificial Intelligence (GenAI) into special education presents a paradigm shift in how educational institutions support learners with diverse cognitive, emotional, and physical needs. Unlike traditional educational technologies, which often provide one-size-fits-all solutions, GenAI systems are capable of producing real-time, learner-specific content and experiences. This chapter delves into the transformative opportunities GenAI offers for special needs learners. It discusses the pedagogical, communicative, emotional, and cognitive advantages of GenAI, highlighting how these technologies enhance accessibility, autonomy, engagement, and academic achievement. The discussion is organized into three major areas: Enhancing Personalized Learning, Promoting Independence and Engagement, and Advancing Equity and Inclusion (Topol, E., 2019).

Enhancing Personalized Learning

Personalized learning is a cornerstone of effective special education. Students with disabilities often require individualized learning pathways that differ in content format, difficulty level, pacing, and engagement strategy (Rose & Meyer, 2002). GenAI has demonstrated unprecedented potential in this domain by enabling dynamic personalization through real-time data analysis and adaptive content generation (Holmes, 2020; Zhai, X., et al., 2021).

One of the most significant advantages of GenAI is its ability to process large volumes of learner data—including academic history, behavioral trends, and emotional indicators—to create a personalized learning profile. Based on this profile, the AI can automatically generate instructional materials that match the learner's current level, preferred modality (e.g., text, audio, visual), and cognitive load capacity (Khosravi et al., 2022). For example, a student with autism may receive social stories generated by GenAI that model peer interactions in a school context, complete with embedded cues for facial expressions and tone of voice (Yu, 2021).

Furthermore, GenAI tools can adapt instructional content to fit cultural, linguistic, and sensory preferences. This is particularly beneficial for multilingual learners or students from underrepresented backgrounds whose experiences may not be reflected in mainstream educational content (Rashid, S. F, et al., 2024). By offering inclusive and culturally relevant content, GenAI ensures that learning is not only effective but also affirming.

Real-time feedback is another advantage of GenAI-driven personalization. Students receive immediate, constructive input that helps them correct mistakes, build confidence, and deepen understanding. For instance, in a mathematics lesson, a student might receive hints tailored to their error pattern or an alternate explanation in simplified language (Cukurova et al., 2019). Such feedback loops are essential for learners with learning disabilities who benefit from consistent and timely reinforcement (Meenakshi Dwivedi, 2021).

As shown in Table 1, GenAI supports a diverse range of personalization strategies, helping teachers meet the cognitive and emotional needs of students through adaptable and multimodal learning formats.

Table 1. Personalized Learning Features Supported by GenAI

Feature	Description	Benefit for Special Needs Learners
Adaptive Content Generation	Real-time creation of level-appropriate materials	Matches pace and ability
Multimodal Delivery	Text, audio, visuals, symbols	Supports varied sensory needs
Culturally Responsive Content	Adjusts examples, language, and names to learner's context	Improves engagement and relevance
Real-Time Feedback	Instant, customized guidance	Reinforces learning and builds confidence

These features collectively reduce learning barriers by offering choice, representation, and control—principles aligned with Universal Design for Learning (Rose & Meyer, 2002).

Promoting Independence and Engagement

Beyond academic customization, GenAI empowers students with disabilities by promoting independence and sustained engagement. Many students in special education settings struggle with executive functioning, attention regulation, or expressive communication. GenAI-based tools offer scaffolds that adapt as students grow, gradually fostering self-directed learning (Raja & Nagasubramani, 2018).

For example, an AI-powered tutor can remind students of deadlines, break complex assignments into smaller steps, and adjust prompts based on the learner's pace. Over time, as the student builds these skills, the system can reduce support, allowing for greater independence (Woolf, 2010). This scaffolding aligns with the Zone of Proximal Development (ZPD) framework, offering support just beyond the learner's current level until mastery is achieved.

Additionally, GenAI interfaces often feature gamified elements such as badges, progress bars, and narrative-driven missions, which enhance intrinsic motivation (Holmes, 2020). These features are particularly beneficial for students with ADHD or emotional disturbances who may struggle with conventional classroom tasks.

Communication is another critical area where GenAI promotes autonomy. Students using AAC systems can construct complex, context-specific messages using AI-driven sentence prediction and voice synthesis (Melo-López, V.-A., et al., 2025). This allows them to participate more fully in classroom discussions, peer interactions, and even advocacy for their needs. For example, a student can describe a personal experience or request a modification without relying solely on pre-programmed phrases.

Engagement is also supported through emotion-sensitive AI interfaces. These systems analyze user behaviors such as eye gaze, facial expressions, and tone of voice to detect disengagement or distress. Based on this analysis, the AI can initiate interventions such as gamified activities or positive reinforcement messages.

Figure 1 illustrates how this adaptive feedback loop operates in real classroom settings.

Figure 1. AI-Enhanced Engagement Model

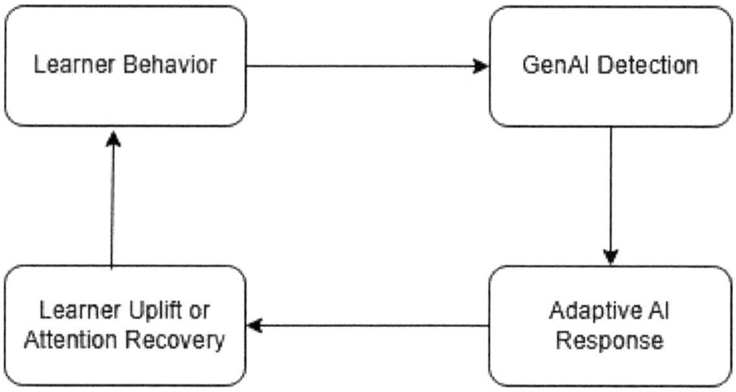

A Figure 1 showing the flow between learner behavior, GenAI detection (e.g., low engagement), adaptive response (e.g., gamified task), and resulting emotional uplift or attention recovery.

This model demonstrates how GenAI fosters agency, persistence, and emotional self-regulation among students who may otherwise be at risk of disengagement.

ADVANCING EQUITY AND INCLUSION

Perhaps the most profound impact of GenAI lies in its ability to level the playing field for students with disabilities by addressing systemic barriers in education. Traditional education systems often rely on standardized curricula and assessments that fail to account for learner variability, leading to exclusion and underachievement among students with special needs (Williamson & Eynon, 2020). GenAI challenges this paradigm by offering tools that are inherently flexible, culturally responsive, and accessible.

One major equity advantage is the ability of GenAI to democratize access to high-quality resources. In underserved or rural areas where specialized staff may be limited, GenAI can provide virtual assistance, customized content, and real-time support that would otherwise be unavailable (UNESCO, 2020). For example, an AI-powered science tutor can deliver differentiated lessons in multiple languages and formats, ensuring that students with disabilities are not left behind due to geographic or economic constraints.

Moreover, GenAI facilitates inclusive classroom practices by enabling educators to design universally accessible activities. Teachers can use AI tools to generate alternative versions of assignments, translate instructions, and create scaffolded assessments that meet Individualized Education Program (IEP) requirements without requiring excessive manual labor (Pazmino-Maji, R., et al., 2021).

Another important aspect is the role of GenAI in promoting social inclusion. AI-generated social narratives, role-playing simulations, and emotion modeling can help neurodiverse students practice social skills and build empathy. This not only supports their personal growth but also fosters a more accepting classroom culture (Benevides et al., 2020).

Finally, GenAI contributes to systemic accountability. AI-generated analytics allow administrators and policymakers to monitor student progress, identify disparities, and allocate resources more effectively. These insights can inform inclusive education policies, guide professional development, and drive investments in assistive technologies (Ahuerma, F. M., 2024).

Table 2 outlines the primary ways GenAI contributes to educational equity for learners with special needs.

Table 2. Equity-Advancing Capabilities of GenAI

Equity Domain	GenAI Feature	Outcome
Access to Resources	AI tutors, multilingual content	Equal learning opportunity across regions
Cultural Responsiveness	Content customization and localization	Inclusion of diverse learner identities
Instructional Flexibility	Customizable tasks and assessments	Support for varied learning profiles
System-Level Monitoring	Learning analytics and IEP tracking	Evidence-based policy and resource allocation

These capabilities not only support students in real-time but also contribute to the broader goal of building a just and inclusive education system where all learners can thrive.

CASE STUDIES

To illustrate the practical applications and transformative potential of Generative Artificial Intelligence (GenAI) in special education, this chapter presents a series of in-depth case studies. These real-world examples showcase how GenAI tools are being integrated into educational settings to support learners with a range of disabilities, including speech and language impairments, intellectual disabilities, sensory impairments, behavioral challenges, and executive functioning disorders. Each case study highlights the background, GenAI-based intervention, implementation process, key outcomes, and critical reflections. Together, these studies offer educators, researchers, and policymakers grounded, context-rich insights into the effective deployment of GenAI tools for inclusive and personalized learning (Rashid, S. F, et al., 2024).

GenAI-Powered Augmentative and Alternative Communication (AAC) Devices

Background: Maria, a 10-year-old student diagnosed with nonverbal autism spectrum disorder, attended a mainstream public school in an urban area of Hyderabad, India. Her verbal communication was extremely limited, and her primary mode of interaction was through a laminated picture exchange communication system (PECS), which offered only basic needs-related expressions (Melo-López, V.-A., et al., 2025).

GenAI-Based Intervention: The school partnered with an edtech startup to implement a pilot AAC solution powered by GenAI. The application used a large language model (LLM) embedded in a tablet that combined visual symbols, predictive sentence generation, and natural language processing. The system was designed to evolve with the user, using reinforcement learning to adapt to Maria's communication style and situational contexts (e.g., classroom vs. playground).

Implementation Process: An initial customization phase involved input from Maria's parents, special educators, and speech-language therapists to seed the system with relevant vocabulary and contextual data. The AI system learned from her daily interactions, gradually expanding its vocabulary and adapting phrase complexity based on feedback loops.

To better understand the differences between traditional AAC devices and those powered by GenAI, Table 3 provides a comparative overview of key features and their benefits in educational settings.

Table 3. Comparison of Traditional vs. GenAI-Powered AAC Devices

Feature	Traditional AAC	GenAI-Powered AAC
Vocabulary Range	Limited and fixed	Dynamic and expandable
Context Awareness	Absent	Context-sensitive
Sentence Prediction	None	Predictive sentence formation
User Adaptability	Manual updates	Machine-learned personalization

As shown in Table 3, GenAI-based systems offer dynamic, context-sensitive vocabulary generation, which enhances user autonomy. Unlike static AAC tools that require manual updates, GenAI learns from user interactions to personalize responses over time (Melo-López, V.-A., et al., 2025). This shift makes communication more intuitive and expressive for nonverbal learners.

Outcomes: Within two months, Maria transitioned from isolated one-word responses to full sentence expressions. Peer interaction increased during group assignments, and teachers reported a 70% rise in her voluntary participation.
Reflections: This case underscores the transformative potential of GenAI in augmentative communication, though it also highlights the importance of digital literacy training for educators.

Customized Learning Paths for Intellectual Disabilities

Background: A special education institution in Bangalore catered to 50 students with moderate to severe intellectual disabilities (ID). These students faced difficulties in comprehension, memory retention, and generalization of concepts (Al-Azawei et al., 2016).
GenAI-Based Intervention: The school deployed an AI-powered adaptive learning platform that used GenAI to create individualized lesson plans across subjects like literacy, numeracy, and life skills (Gligorea, I., et al., 2023).
Implementation Process: Students completed initial diagnostic tasks. GenAI mapped cognitive profiles and generated customized learning paths with simplified texts, gamified lessons, and embedded emotion-aware feedback mechanisms.

To visualize how GenAI constructs and personalizes a learner's instructional journey, Figure 2 presents a flowchart of the learning path generation process.

Figure 2. Personalized Learning Path Generated by GenAI

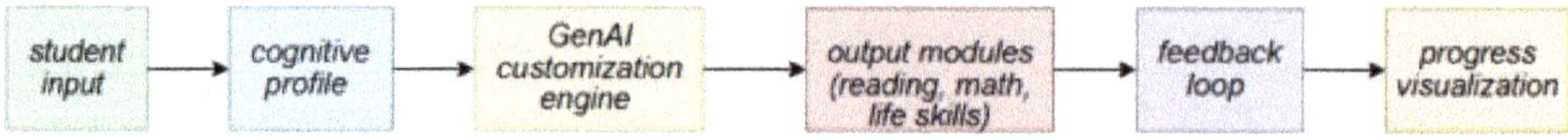

Figure 2 illustrates how student performance data is processed to tailor subject modules. The continuous feedback loop ensures materials remain responsive to evolving learner needs, aligning with findings by (Cukurova et al., 2019).

Outcomes: 60% of students showed improved initiation and completion of tasks. Teachers noted a 25% increase in classroom engagement.
Reflections: While the personalized system boosted autonomy and comprehension, its success depended on continual teacher monitoring and emotional sensitivity.

EMOTION RECOGNITION AND BEHAVIORAL INTERVENTIONS

Background: In a Singapore-based inclusive middle school, educators faced recurring challenges in managing the behavioral and emotional needs of students with Attention-Deficit/Hyperactivity Disorder (ADHD) and anxiety disorders. These students often displayed unexpected outbursts or complete disengagement from classroom activities. Teachers reported that their biggest difficulty was the early recognition of emotional triggers that led to such behaviors. Traditional behavioral observation methods were insufficient to consistently detect when students were beginning to feel overwhelmed, anxious, or frustrated, making it difficult to intervene in time (Howard, S., & Mozejko, A.,2015).
GenAI-Based Intervention: To overcome these challenges, the school implemented an advanced Generative AI (GenAI)-powered emotion recognition system. This system utilized facial expression analysis, voice modulation tracking, and biometric data such as heart rate to detect emotional states in real time. The technology was grounded in affective computing principles and trained on predictive emotional models that could anticipate signs of emotional dysregulation before they escalated. When indicators of emotional stress were detected, the AI system sent real-time alerts to teachers along with personalized de-escalation strategies tailored to individual students (Kay, J et al., 2022).
Implementation Process: Teachers were equipped with an AI dashboard that received constant input from the emotion recognition system. Based on

the students' behavior and physiological signals, the system could identify specific emotional cues that required attention. Alongside each detected cue, the system recommended actionable interventions that teachers could apply immediately within the classroom setting. The goal was to provide real-time, context-sensitive support before the student experienced a full emotional breakdown or behavioral disruption.

To illustrate how emotion recognition was operationalized through AI and what strategies were linked to specific emotional cues, the following table presents a summary of the detected patterns and the corresponding interventions that teachers were advised to implement:

Table 4. AI-Detected Emotion Cues and Suggested Teacher Interventions

Emotion Cue Detected	Suggested Intervention
Elevated heart rate	Initiate breathing exercise
Voice pitch rising	Offer sensory calming tools
Facial frown	Ask if the student needs a break
Low eye contact	Check in with student privately

As shown in Table 4, the AI system helped translate physiological and behavioral signals into precise, compassionate, and manageable strategies. These interventions minimized classroom disruptions while also fostering emotional self-awareness and coping strategies among students (Fu, Y., & Weng, Z., 2024). For example, a student showing signs of distress through a facial frown might be quietly asked if they needed a moment away from the task. Another displaying rising vocal intensity could be provided with tactile calming aids to reduce stress levels. These subtle, targeted responses proved more effective than generalized behavioral interventions.

Outcomes: The deployment of the GenAI-powered emotion recognition tool led to notable improvements in student behavior and emotional resilience. Within the first academic term of implementation, behavioral referrals across classrooms dropped by 45 percent. Teachers observed that students began to recognize and respond to their emotional states proactively. Many started using breathing techniques, sensory tools, or requesting breaks without needing prompting from teachers. This demonstrated not only improved self-regulation but also the beginning of a culture where emotional intelligence was actively supported and encouraged.

Reflections: While the system showed promising results, its implementation also raised important ethical considerations. Since the technology relied on sensitive data such as facial expressions, speech patterns, and biometric signals, the school had to ensure robust privacy protections and obtain informed consent from both students and guardians. Misinterpretation of emotional cues, especially across cultural or neurodiverse contexts, remained a potential risk. Thus, the success of such AI-driven interventions depends heavily on transparency, human oversight, and culturally informed model development. Nonetheless, when designed and implemented responsibly, emotion-aware GenAI systems can offer a powerful tool for building emotionally inclusive learning environments that respond with empathy and precision to the unique needs of every student.

MULTIMODAL LEARNING MATERIALS FOR SENSORY IMPAIRMENTS

Background:

A rural government school in Tamil Nadu faced substantial challenges in delivering accessible education to students with hearing and visual impairments. Due to limited infrastructure and lack of specialized materials, traditional teaching approaches and printed textbooks were not adequate for addressing the learning needs of these students. The absence of content formats such as audio-based materials, sign language support, and Braille-compatible outputs made it difficult for learners to access curriculum content equitably.

GenAI-Based Intervention:

To overcome these challenges, the school adopted a Generative AI-based content generator that could automatically convert regular digital lesson materials into multiple accessible formats. The GenAI tool was designed to support inclusive education by transforming plain text into sign language animations for deaf learners, audio narration for students with visual impairments, and Braille-compatible text for tactile reading devices. This intervention ensured that students with sensory disabilities could access the same curriculum content as their peers in formats aligned with their sensory and cognitive needs (Yu, 2021).

Implementation Process:

Teachers were trained to upload educational content—such as lesson summaries, worksheets, and textbook chapters—into the GenAI platform. The system then processed the content and generated three simultaneous outputs: an audio narration for auditory access, animated video clips using Indian Sign Language (ISL) to support deaf students, and structured text optimized for use with Braille devices and tactile graphics. After generation, the content was made accessible to students via tablets configured for offline use, which was critical in an area where internet connectivity was limited. This streamlined pipeline of input-to-multiformat output allowed for faster content creation and broader accessibility, without requiring teachers to manually design each modality. By leveraging GenAI's multimodal processing capabilities, the system provided comprehensive, sensory-inclusive content that reduced the instructional gap faced by students with disabilities.

Outcomes:

Following the deployment of this GenAI-driven multimodal content generation approach, both student performance and classroom participation improved significantly. Students with sensory impairments were able to understand instructional material more clearly, interact with content more confidently, and complete tasks with increased autonomy. Teachers observed that students were more responsive, participated more frequently in learning activities, and required less repeated instruction for basic concepts. Within a three-month period, academic performance improved by approximately 20 percent among the targeted group of students. This improvement was attributed to the inclusive and personalized nature of the content delivery enabled by the GenAI system.

Reflections:

This case exemplifies how the thoughtful integration of Generative AI technologies can bridge infrastructural gaps and improve educational outcomes for students with disabilities. In contexts where trained special educators and assistive resources are scarce, automated systems that generate inclusive, multimodal content play a vital role. By functioning offline, the GenAI tool ensured uninterrupted access to learning, making it especially suitable for remote or resource-constrained settings. The success of this intervention demonstrates that with proper training, stakeholder involvement, and localized implementation, GenAI can be a transformative tool in achieving equity and accessibility in special education.

SCENARIO-BASED LEARNING FOR EXECUTIVE FUNCTIONING DISORDERS

Background: A New Delhi learning center worked with students with ADHD and executive function difficulties such as time management and organization (Raja & Nagasubramani, 2018).
GenAI-Based Intervention: Interactive simulations were designed using GenAI to present tasks like event planning or budgeting. The AI responded to user actions with adaptive cues and debrief reflections.
Implementation Process: Students received weekly challenges. GenAI tracked their choices and produced detailed reports used to guide behavior modeling.

To map how cognitive functions were targeted by simulations, Table 5 aligns each executive skill with related GenAI scenarios and learning outcomes.

Table 5. Executive Function Skills and GenAI Scenario Outcomes

Skill Targeted	Scenario Type	Observable Improvement
Task sequencing	Homework planner	Better organization
Impulse control	Social interaction sim	Fewer classroom disruptions
Time estimation	Timed cooking challenge	On-time task completion
Reflection	Post-task journaling	Improved self-awareness

Table 5 shows that by embedding real-life tasks into simulations, GenAI helps learners generalize academic strategies to everyday functioning, ultimately boosting life skills.

Outcomes: Improved organization, reduced impulsive behaviors, and greater self-reported self-efficacy by students and parents.
Reflections: This case highlighted the value of culturally relevant simulations and teacher-led goal reinforcement in maximizing GenAI effectiveness.

These case studies demonstrate that GenAI can create real, measurable improvements in academic, behavioral, and emotional outcomes for students with disabilities. However, their success depends on thoughtful implementation, localized content, ethical safeguards, and active educator involvement (Holmes, 2020; Woolf, 2010).

ETHICAL, TECHNICAL, AND POLICY CHALLENGES

While the promise of Generative Artificial Intelligence (GenAI) in transforming special education is increasingly being recognized, its real-world application remains fraught with a wide range of challenges that must be systematically addressed. These challenges fall into three major categories—ethical, technical, and policy-oriented—and together, they form the foundational concerns that can either make or break the successful, inclusive implementation of GenAI tools in education. The growing deployment of GenAI systems in schools, especially for learners with disabilities, has raised complex questions about fairness, transparency, access, and accountability. This chapter explores each of these challenge domains in detail, offering insight into the risks they pose, examples of how they materialize in educational contexts, and how they might be addressed through targeted strategies (Chinta, S. V et al., 2024).

Ethical Challenges

Ethical challenges in GenAI are perhaps the most sensitive and significant, particularly because they relate to how AI systems can potentially marginalize already vulnerable learners. The first major ethical challenge concerns algorithmic bias and fairness. GenAI models learn from vast data sets that are often compiled from internet sources, literature, and user interactions that inherently reflect societal inequities and cultural biases. As a result, these models can replicate, and even amplify, existing prejudices. In the context of special education, this can lead to serious problems. For example, a GenAI-enabled communication device designed to help non-verbal learners might struggle to interpret regional languages, code-switching, or speech patterns influenced by neurological conditions. This could result in communication breakdowns or reduced confidence in technology by the learner (Binns, R., 2018).

To mitigate such bias, it is crucial that developers integrate inclusive datasets during training and continuously audit AI systems post-deployment. These datasets should be representative of different disability types, languages, age groups, and cultural contexts. Bias testing and fairness evaluation metrics should be standard parts of AI development. Ethical co-design—where people with disabilities, educators, and caregivers are part of the design process—can help ensure that systems better reflect users' real needs (Holmes, 2020; Kılınç, 2024).

A second ethical issue is data privacy. Many GenAI tools in education rely on personal data, including students' names, diagnoses, behavioral patterns, emotional states, and even biometric information. In special education, where monitoring tools are often more invasive due to the need for tailored interventions, the stakes are even higher. Children with cognitive or communication disabilities might not understand what data is being collected or why. Parents or guardians may also lack the digital literacy required to make informed consent decisions. Without proper safeguards, such data can be mishandled, leading to breaches of privacy and exploitation.

Protecting student data requires the adoption of international privacy frameworks such as GDPR and FERPA, but more importantly, these must be translated into actionable practices at the school level. Schools must implement transparent data usage policies, anonymize data wherever possible, and use encrypted databases. Consent should not be a one-time event but a continuous dialogue with clear opt-out options. The concept of data dignity—respecting the rights and agency of the data subject—should be embedded in all educational technology policies.

The third ethical concern is the risk of learner over-dependence on GenAI systems. While personalization and automation can support learners effectively, over-reliance can hinder the development of executive functioning skills and personal agency. For example, if a student with a learning disability is always assisted by GenAI in completing tasks, they may not develop the skills necessary to function independently without such support. This issue is particularly critical in adolescence, a stage where developing autonomy is part of broader psychological growth.

Educators must strike a balance between using AI to support and challenge learners. AI systems should be built with fading scaffolds—features that gradually reduce assistance as the learner improves. Human oversight should remain central to instruction, with teachers encouraging reflection, problem-solving, and peer collaboration. As summarized in Table 6, these ethical challenges and mitigation strategies offer a framework for responsible AI use in special education.

Table 6. Ethical Challenges and Mitigation Strategies in GenAI for Special Education

Ethical Challenge	Description	Mitigation Strategy
Algorithmic Bias	AI may reinforce stereotypes due to biased training data	Inclusive datasets, model auditing, co-design with stakeholders
Data Privacy	Sensitive student data may be collected without clear consent	Transparent policies, encrypted storage, continuous consent
Learner Overdependence	Risk of stunted autonomy due to constant AI assistance	Fading scaffolds, teacher oversight, reflective learning

Table 6 highlights that ethical integration of GenAI is a process that requires more than legal compliance. It demands design practices and usage policies that affirm student rights and prioritize equity.

Technical Challenges

The second major area of concern involves the technical limitations of Generative Artificial Intelligence (GenAI). A significant challenge lies in the disparities in infrastructure across educational institutions. Many GenAI tools require stable internet connectivity, high-processing-capacity devices, and regular system updates to function effectively. However, schools in low-resource settings—especially those serving marginalized and underserved learners—often lack even the most basic digital infrastructure (Hamad, 2022). This digital divide directly undermines the inclusive potential that GenAI seeks to achieve, as students in such environments are left without the means to access or benefit from AI-enabled tools (UNESCO, 2020).

To address these infrastructure barriers, governments, non-governmental organizations (NGOs), and educational policymakers must commit to long-term investments in technology accessibility. Solutions may include the provision of public Wi-Fi hubs, the establishment of solar-powered classrooms in off-grid areas, and subsidies or donations of educational hardware such as tablets or low-cost laptops. Additionally, GenAI developers should prioritize designing tools with offline functionality and optimize applications for low-specification devices so they can serve a broader and more diverse student population, regardless of geographic or economic constraints.

Another critical technical hurdle is the interpretability of GenAI models. Many such systems operate as "black boxes," meaning that users—including educators, parents, and even system administrators—are unable to see or understand how a particular AI-generated output was derived. In the context of special education, this lack of transparency poses a serious limitation. Building trust in the technology and effectively supporting students with disabilities requires that educators and caregivers understand how AI systems make decisions, especially when those decisions influence instructional strategies or behavioral interventions.

Explainable Artificial Intelligence (XAI) is emerging as a solution to this problem by focusing on making AI model processes transparent and understandable to human users. XAI technologies can assist by providing teachers with interpretive summaries of how an AI system arrived at a specific recommendation, presenting multiple-choice outputs instead of singular directives, or incorporating confidence indicators that reflect the certainty of a system's prediction. Although XAI is a promising field, it remains underdeveloped in many educational applications and requires broader integration into GenAI tools intended for classroom use.

Finally, a persistent challenge in the deployment of GenAI is content localization. Most existing GenAI platforms are developed using datasets that prioritize global English, which fails to represent the linguistic and cultural diversity found in classrooms across the world. In multilingual learning environments, a GenAI tool that supports only English may exclude students who are more comfortable learning in Tamil, Hindi, Swahili, Spanish, or other native languages. Moreover, educational content must go beyond translation—it must reflect culturally relevant contexts, examples, and values to truly resonate with students and maintain their engagement.

Effective localization demands not just linguistic conversion but also cultural adaptation. This includes training AI models on datasets that contain regional dialects, idioms, and pedagogical styles that align with local traditions. Engaging local educators and curriculum designers in the development and testing phases is essential to ensuring that GenAI tools reflect the cultural and educational realities of their target users. Addressing infrastructure, model interpretability, and content localization together is crucial, as limitations in any one of these areas can negatively impact the overall effectiveness and inclusiveness of GenAI systems in education.

Ultimately, inclusive GenAI design is not solely about building sophisticated algorithms. It requires context-sensitive integration that carefully considers the socio-technical environment in which learners live and learn. Only by acknowledging and systematically addressing these technical barriers can GenAI fulfill its promise as a truly inclusive educational innovation.

Policy and Governance Challenges

The third domain—policy and governance—concerns how systems of authority, regulation, and funding either support or hinder inclusive AI use in education. Currently, the regulatory landscape for GenAI in education is fragmented and insufficient. Most education policies were drafted before AI technologies became widespread and do not account for unique GenAI characteristics such as adaptive content generation, predictive learner analytics, or biometric monitoring (Ahuerma, F. M., 2024).

In the absence of robust regulation, schools and AI developers are left to self-govern, which increases the risk of unethical practices or inconsistent standards. National education ministries must develop clear guidelines for GenAI use, including criteria for tool approval, privacy protections, ethical auditing, and consequences for misuse. Global standardization efforts, spearheaded by organizations like IEEE and UNESCO, can help harmonize practices across borders.

Teacher training is another policy priority. As the primary users and mediators of GenAI in classrooms, teachers need specialized training in how to interpret, implement, and critique GenAI tools. Yet, most teacher education curricula do not include modules on AI ethics or application. This leaves educators ill-equipped to engage critically with these technologies. Professional development programs must be updated to include AI literacy, universal design principles, and data interpretation skills (Pazmino-Maji, R., et al., 2021). Lastly, the question of equity in GenAI adoption cannot be overlooked. Without targeted funding and resource allocation, there is a risk of creating a two-tiered education system—one where affluent schools benefit from cutting-edge AI while disadvantaged schools fall further behind. Policy efforts must prioritize rural schools, special education centers, and low-income urban districts for GenAI integration.

Policy recommendations addressing these concerns are summarized in Table 7, which lists actions that governments, education boards, and developers can take to ensure responsible GenAI deployment.

Table 7. Policy Recommendations for Inclusive GenAI Integration in Special Education

Policy Area	Recommendation
Regulation	Establish AI education standards focusing on consent, ethics, and bias control
Teacher Training	Integrate GenAI literacy into pre-service and in-service teacher programs
Equity Funding	Allocate national grants and infrastructure subsidies to underserved schools

As seen in Table 7, effective policy and governance strategies serve as the scaffolding that sustains ethical and technically sound GenAI applications. These policies ensure that inclusion is not an afterthought but a guiding principle from design to implementation.

In conclusion, the integration of GenAI into special education is a multifaceted challenge that touches on fundamental issues of fairness, access, and systemic equity. Ethical challenges such as algorithmic bias, data privacy, and learner over-reliance must be addressed through thoughtful design and transparent governance. Technical barriers—including infrastructure gaps, opacity in decision-making, and lack of content localization—require investment in human-centered design and contextual awareness. Policy interventions must regulate AI responsibly, empower teachers, and fund equitable access. Only through a coordinated response across all three domains can we ensure that GenAI delivers on its promise to democratize education and uplift all learners, especially those who need support the most.

FUTURE DIRECTIONS AND RESEARCH OPPORTUNITIES

As Generative Artificial Intelligence (GenAI) becomes increasingly embedded in the educational landscape, its applications in special education continue to evolve. While initial deployments have shown immense potential to support learners with diverse needs, realizing the full value of GenAI requires a strategic focus on innovation, ethical design, and sustained research. This chapter outlines the future directions and research opportunities necessary to ensure that GenAI advances equitably and responsibly. The discussion is structured into four thematic subchapters: inclusive design and co-creation, intelligent emotional and cultural responsiveness, teacher and institutional integration, and governance and research ecosystems.

INCLUSIVE DESIGN AND CO-CREATION WITH STAKEHOLDERS

One of the most vital future directions for GenAI in special education involves the adoption of inclusive, participatory design frameworks. Historically, many AI tools have been developed without input from the actual users—students with disabilities, their families, special educators, and therapists. As a result, these tools often lack cultural, pedagogical, and functional relevance. To overcome this, future GenAI systems must be co-created with these stakeholders involved from the outset.

Co-creation allows AI developers to understand not just technical requirements but also contextual challenges faced by diverse learners. For example, involving students with communication impairments can lead to better voice-based or symbol-driven interaction models. Educators can contribute insights into curriculum alignment, classroom workflows, and differentiated instruction. Parents and caregivers can help adapt AI to home routines and emotional dynamics. Future research must explore methods for structuring participatory design cycles, creating accessible prototype environments, and evaluating the usability and learning outcomes of co-designed solutions.

Furthermore, inclusive design must account for intersectionality—addressing the overlapping identities and needs of learners (such as those who are neurodiverse and multilingual). Research into inclusive GenAI should incorporate universal design for learning (UDL) principles, which advocate for flexible, customizable educational systems that accommodate the widest possible range of learners (Holmes, 2020).

Emotional and Cultural Intelligence in GenAI

To effectively support students with disabilities, future GenAI systems must develop greater emotional and cultural intelligence. Affective computing, which allows AI to detect, interpret, and respond to human emotions, is a key innovation area. Emotion-aware GenAI systems can monitor signs of frustration, anxiety, or engagement through facial expressions, voice modulation, typing speed, or heart rate (Kay, J et al., 2022). In a classroom, such systems could adapt task difficulty, suggest calming activities, or alert teachers when emotional thresholds are crossed.

This capability is especially beneficial for learners with autism spectrum disorder, ADHD, or emotional regulation difficulties. However, future research must address challenges related to accuracy, bias, and consent. Emotion detection must be culturally neutral and validated across neurotypes. Ethical frameworks should govern how emotional data is collected, stored, and used. Emotional nudging—where AI attempts to influence emotional states—must be carefully controlled to avoid manipulation.

In parallel, future GenAI tools must become culturally adaptive. Today's systems are predominantly trained on English-language datasets with Western cultural references. This makes them less effective in multilingual and diverse environments. GenAI systems should support local languages, cultural norms, and contextually relevant scenarios. This includes incorporating region-specific examples in narratives, simulations, and problem-solving activities.

Future research should focus on collecting culturally inclusive training datasets, developing multilingual natural language models, and measuring cultural engagement outcomes. These innovations will ensure that GenAI becomes not just a learning tool, but a cultural bridge that affirms students' identities and life experiences (Rashid, S. F, et al., 2024).

Integration into Teaching Practice and Educational Institutions

The successful deployment of GenAI in special education requires more than just functional technology—it demands thoughtful integration into existing teaching practices and institutional systems. One major area of focus for future development is the collaboration between GenAI tools and educators. Rather than viewing AI as a replacement for teachers, future models should be designed to serve as collaborative partners—intelligent assistants that help teachers assess student needs, differentiate instruction, and personalize feedback in real time.

Research must investigate models of AI-assisted teaching where teachers and GenAI systems share complementary roles. For example, a GenAI tool could analyze learning patterns overnight and provide personalized lesson suggestions each morning. The teacher could then apply professional judgment to adapt or reject these suggestions based on classroom dynamics. Effective collaboration models also require explainability—teachers must understand how AI systems make decisions and be able to override or interrogate those choices when needed (Floridi & Cowls, 2019).

Equally important is institutional readiness. Schools must be equipped with the infrastructure, leadership support, and training programs needed to integrate GenAI successfully. Future research should examine how school policies, digital infrastructure investments, and leadership practices affect GenAI implementation. Teacher training curricula should be updated to include AI literacy, ethical decision-making, and technical troubleshooting. In-service training programs should provide opportunities for teachers to build confidence and competence in using GenAI tools.

Longitudinal studies are also critical. Most existing evaluations focus on short-term gains in engagement or test scores. Future research should explore how sustained GenAI use affects broader educational outcomes such as independence, emotional regulation, executive functioning, and life skills. These studies should collect data from multiple stakeholders—students, parents, teachers, and administrators—to build a holistic understanding of GenAI's long-term impact.

Responsible Innovation and Collaborative Research Ecosystems

As GenAI tools become more deeply integrated into educational systems, it is essential to develop governance models and research ecosystems that promote ethical, equitable, and evidence-based innovation. The rapid development of AI has outpaced most national educational policy frameworks, leaving schools and developers to navigate implementation with limited guidance. This creates a risk of inconsistent practices, privacy violations, and inequitable access.

Future research should focus on developing comprehensive policies for GenAI in education that address consent, data ownership, algorithmic transparency, and accountability. International standards from organizations like UNESCO and IEEE should be adapted to local educational systems and disability frameworks (Ahuerma, F. M., 2024). Ethical AI certifications, audit mechanisms, and oversight bodies should be introduced to ensure compliance and trust.

In addition, building interdisciplinary research networks will be vital. Researchers from education, computer science, disability studies, ethics, and linguistics must work together to create inclusive GenAI models and applications. These networks should prioritize underrepresented voices, particularly from the Global South, and include people with disabilities as co-researchers, not just subjects. Open data initiatives, shared model repositories, and collaborative pilot programs can foster innovation and equity.

Future research should also investigate the psychological and social impacts of GenAI on learners. As students increasingly interact with AI-based tutors, simulations, and communication aids, their relationships with technology, peers, and self-perception may change. Understanding these effects will help ensure that GenAI enhances—not replaces—human connection and learner dignity.

In conclusion, the future of GenAI in special education is filled with opportunity but also responsibility. Inclusive co-design, emotional and cultural responsiveness, institutional integration, and ethical governance are the four pillars upon which the next phase of GenAI innovation must be built. Research in these areas will ensure that GenAI not only improves learning outcomes but also contributes to a more just, inclusive, and empowering educational landscape for learners of all abilities.

CONCLUSION

The application of Generative Artificial Intelligence (GenAI) in special education stands at a pivotal crossroads—one where transformative innovation meets deep-rooted educational challenges. Across the preceding chapters, this book has explored how GenAI tools can support learners with diverse cognitive, emotional, sensory, and behavioral needs by offering personalized, multimodal, and adaptive learning experiences. The case studies, opportunities, and thematic discussions presented in this work underscore not only the enormous promise of GenAI but also the urgency of ensuring its ethical, inclusive, and sustainable implementation.

At its core, GenAI offers special education a paradigm shift by transitioning the traditional model of accommodation into one focused on proactive inclusion. With capabilities such as real-time content adaptation, emotion recognition, multimodal communication interfaces, and personalized learning pathways, GenAI tools can dramatically enhance learners' autonomy, engagement, and achievement. For students with disabilities—who often face structural barriers, under-resourced classrooms, and limited access to individualized instruction—these advancements can serve as lifelines to educational equity and social inclusion.

However, these benefits do not come without critical caveats. As the book has highlighted, ethical considerations such as algorithmic bias, data privacy, informed consent, and learner overdependence must be addressed at every stage of GenAI design and deployment. Equally important are the technical limitations, including infrastructure disparities, interface accessibility, and content localization. Without addressing these issues, GenAI risks replicating and exacerbating the very inequities it seeks to overcome.

Policy frameworks play a decisive role in shaping the responsible use of GenAI. The current absence of standardized regulations and ethical guidelines for AI in special education leaves a vacuum that must be filled by interdisciplinary collaboration, evidence-based policymaking, and participatory governance. Teachers, who serve as critical intermediaries between AI tools and students, must be equipped through comprehensive training, ongoing professional development, and institutional support.

Looking forward, the future of GenAI in special education must be built on four interrelated pillars: inclusive co-design, emotional and cultural intelligence, meaningful teacher-AI collaboration, and ethical governance. Research must move beyond pilot studies and engage in longitudinal, cross-context, and impact-driven evaluation. GenAI systems must become not only more powerful, but more transparent, explainable, and accountable. International cooperation, particularly across the Global North and South, will be key to ensuring that GenAI development reflects the full diversity of learners' needs and aspirations.

In conclusion, GenAI has the potential to redefine special education—not merely as a niche intervention, but as a frontier of inclusive pedagogy and technological justice. Realizing this potential will require collective vision, rigorous research, human-centered design, and unwavering commitment to equity. If thoughtfully developed and responsibly implemented, GenAI can serve as a cornerstone in building a truly inclusive educational future—one where every learner, regardless of ability, is empowered to thrive.

REFERENCES

Ahuerma, F. M. (2024). UNESCO Proposal for the use of Generative AI in Education: Eight Challenges and Seven Actions.

Al-Azawei, A., Serenelli, F., & Lundqvist, K. (2016). Universal Design for Learning (UDL): A Content Analysis of Peer Reviewed Journals from 2012 to 2015. *The Journal of Scholarship of Teaching and Learning*, *16*(3), 39–56. DOI: 10.14434/josotl.v16i3.19295

Benevides, T. W., Shore, S. M., Andresen, M. L., Caplan, R., Cook, B., Gassner, D. L., & Wittig, K. (2020). Interventions to address health outcomes among autistic adults: A systematic review. *Autism*, *24*(6), 1345–1359. DOI: 10.1177/1362361320913664 PMID: 32390461

Binns, R. (2018, January). Fairness in machine learning: Lessons from political philosophy. In *Conference on fairness, accountability and transparency* (pp. 149-159). PMLR, DOI:DOI: 10.48550/arXiv.1712.03586

Burrell, J. (2016). How the machine 'thinks': Understanding opacity in machine learning algorithms. *Big Data & Society*, *3*(1). Advance online publication. DOI: 10.1177/2053951715622512

Chinta, S. V., Wang, Z., Yin, Z., Hoang, N., Gonzalez, M., Quy, T. L., & Zhang, W. (2024). FairAIED: Navigating fairness, bias, and ethics in educational AI applications. arXiv preprint arXiv:2407.18745.

Cukurova, M., Kent, C., & Luckin, R. (2019). Artificial intelligence and multimodal data in the service of human decision-making: A case study in debate tutoring. *British Journal of Educational Technology*, *50*(6), 3032–3046. DOI: 10.1111/bjet.12829

Dede, C., Saxberg, B., & Richards, J. (2018). *Learning engineering for online education* (Vol. 95). Routledge.

Dignum, V. (2019). *Responsible Artificial Intelligence: How to develop and use AI in a responsible way*. Springer.

Floridi, L., & Cowls, J. (2019). A unified framework of five principles for AI in society. *Harvard Data Science Review*, *1*(1). Advance online publication. DOI: 10.1162/99608f92.8cd550d1

Fu, Y., & Weng, Z. (2024). Navigating the ethical terrain of AI in education: A systematic review on framing responsible human-centered AI practices. Computers & Education. *Artificial Intelligence*. Advance online publication. DOI: 10.1016/j.caeai.2024.100306

Gevher, M., Öncü, S. E., & Erdoğdu, E. (2025). Exploring the potential use of generative ai for learner support in ODL at scale. *Journal of Educational Technology and Online Learning*, *8*(1), 80–99. DOI: 10.31681/jetol.1559442

Gligorea, I., Cioca, M., Oancea, R., Gorski, A. T., Gorski, H., & Tudorache, P. (2023). Adaptive learning using artificial intelligence in e-learning: A literature review. *Education Sciences*, *13*(12), 1216.

Guettala, M., Bourekkache, S., Kazar, O., & Harous, S. (2024). Generative Artificial Intelligence in Education: Advancing Adaptive and Personalized Learning. *Acta Informatica Pragensia*, *13*(3), 460–489. DOI: 10.18267/j.aip.235

Hamad, W. (2022). Understanding the foremost challenges in the transition to online teaching and learning during COVID-19 pandemic: A systematic literature review. *Journal of Educational Technology and Online Learning*, *5*(2), 393–410. DOI: 10.31681/jetol.1055695

Heffernan, N. T., & Heffernan, C. L. (2014). The ASSISTments ecosystem: Building a platform that brings scientists and teachers together for minimally invasive research on human learning and teaching. *International Journal of Artificial Intelligence in Education*, *24*(4), 470–497.

Holmes, W. (2020). Artificial intelligence in education. In *Encyclopedia of education and information technologies* (pp. 88–103). Springer International Publishing.

Howard, S., & Mozejko, A. (2015). Teachers: technology, change and resistance.

Karadağ, N. (2023). The impact of artificial intelligence on online assessment: A preliminary review. *Journal of Educational Technology and Online Learning*, *6*(4), 822–837.

Kay, J., Bartimote, K., Kitto, K., Kummerfeld, B., Liu, D., & Reimann, P. (2022). Enhancing learning by Open Learner Model (OLM) driven data design. *Computers and Education: Artificial Intelligence*, *3*, 100069.

Khosravi, H., Shum, S. B., Chen, G., Conati, C., Tsai, Y. S., Kay, J., ... & Gašević, D. (2022). Explainable artificial intelligence in education. *Computers and education: artificial intelligence, 3*, 100074.

Kılınç, S. (2024). Comprehensive AI assessment framework: Enhancing educational evaluation with ethical AI integration. Journal of Educational Technology and Online Learning, 7(4-ICETOL 2024 Special Issue), 521-540.

Luckin, R., & Holmes, W. (2016). Intelligence unleashed: An argument for AI in education.

McAfee, A., & Brynjolfsson, E. (2017). *Machine, platform, crowd: Harnessing our digital future*. WW Norton & Company.

Meenakshi Dwivedi. (2021). *Creating inclusive classrooms*.

Melo-López, V.-A., Basantes-Andrade, A., Gudiño-Mejía, C.-B., & Hernández-Martínez, E. (2025). The Impact of Artificial Intelligence on Inclusive Education: A Systematic Review. *Education Sciences*, *15*(5), 539. DOI: 10.3390/educsci15050539

Miao, F., & Holmes, W. (2021). *AI and education: A guidance for policymakers*. Unesco Publishing.

Mitchell, M., Wu, S., Zaldivar, A., Barnes, P., Vasserman, L., Hutchinson, B., & Gebru, T. (2019, January). Model cards for model reporting. In *Proceedings of the conference on fairness, accountability, and transparency* (pp. 220-229).

Nesru, S. R. K. (2023). The Ethics of AI Use in Special Education Settings. *Multidisciplinary Science Journal*, *1*(01), 34–40.

Nguyen, A., Ngo, H. N., Hong, Y., Dang, B., & Nguyen, B. P. T. (2023). Ethical principles for artificial intelligence in education. *Education and Information Technologies*, *28*(4), 4221–4241. PMID: 36254344

OECD. (2024). The potential impact of Artificial Intelligence on equity and inclusion in education. *OECD Artificial Intelligence Papers*, (23). Advance online publication. DOI: 10.1787/15df715b-en

Pazmino-Maji, R., Conde, M. Á., & García-Peñalvo, F. (2021). Learning analytics in Ecuador: A systematic review supported by statistical implicative analysis. *Universal Access in the Information Society*, *20*(3), 495–512.

Popenici, S. A., & Kerr, S. (2017). Exploring the impact of artificial intelligence on teaching and learning in higher education. *Research and Practice in Technology Enhanced Learning*, *12*(1), 22. PMID: 30595727

Raja, R., & Nagasubramani, P. C. (2018). Impact of modern technology in education. Journal of applied and advanced research, 3(1), 33-35.

Rashid, S. F., Duong-Trung, N., & Pinkwart, N. (2024). *Generative AI in education: Technical foundations, applications, and challenges*. Artificial Intelligence and Education-Shaping the Future of Learning.

Rose, D. H., & Meyer, A. (2002). *Teaching every student in the digital age: Universal design for learning*. Association for Supervision and Curriculum Development, 1703 N. Beauregard St., Alexandria, VA 22311-1714 (Product no. 101042: $22.95 ASCD members; $26.95 nonmembers).

Tonbuloğlu, B. (2023). An evaluation of the use of artificial intelligence applications in online education. *Journal of Educational Technology and Online Learning*, *6*(4), 866–884.

Topol, E. (2019). *Deep medicine: how artificial intelligence can make healthcare human again*.

UNESCO, E. S. (2020). Distance learning strategies in response to COVID-19 school closures. *Nota informative, 2*(1), 1-8.

Williamson, B., & Eynon, R. (2020). Historical threads, missing links, and future directions in AI in education. *Learning, Media and Technology*, *45*(3), 223–235.

Woolf, B. P. (2010). *Building intelligent interactive tutors: Student-centered strategies for revolutionizing e-learning*. Morgan Kaufmann.

Yu, Z. (2021). The effects of gender, educational level, and personality on online learning outcomes during the COVID-19 pandemic. *International Journal of Educational Technology in Higher Education*, *18*(1), 14. PMID: 34778520

Zawacki-Richter, O., Marín, V. I., Bond, M., & Gouverneur, F. (2019). Systematic review of research on artificial intelligence applications in higher education–where are the educators? *International Journal of Educational Technology in Higher Education*, *16*(1), 1–27.

Zhai, X., Chu, X., Chai, C. S., Jong, M. S. Y., Istenic, A., Spector, M., & Li, Y. (2021). A Review of Artificial Intelligence (AI) in Education from 2010 to 2020. *Complexity*, *2021*(1), 8812542.

KEY TERMS AND DEFINITIONS

Adaptive Learning: A technology-based educational method that adjusts the presentation of material and pacing based on the learner's performance, preferences, and needs. GenAI plays a significant role in enabling real-time personalization in adaptive learning systems.

Augmentative and Alternative Communication (AAC): Tools and strategies used to support or replace verbal speech, including communication boards, speech-generating devices, and AI-powered interfaces, helping individuals with speech or language impairments express themselves effectively.

Emotion-Aware AI: An intelligent system capable of recognizing, interpreting, and responding to users' emotional states—often using facial expressions, voice tone, or physiological signals—to enhance user experience, especially for students needing behavioral or emotional support.

Explainable AI (XAI): A subfield of AI focused on making machine learning models and their outputs transparent and understandable to human users. In special education, XAI ensures trust, accountability, and clarity in automated decision-making.

Generative Artificial Intelligence (GenAI): A branch of artificial intelligence that uses machine learning models to generate new content, such as text, images, audio, or simulations, based on training data. In education, GenAI enables adaptive and personalized learning experiences by dynamically producing instructional materials and responses.

Inclusive Education: A philosophy and practice of educating all students—regardless of ability, background, or disability—in general education classrooms with appropriate supports, modifications, and access to equal learning opportunities.

Special Education: A specialized area of education designed to support students with cognitive, behavioral, emotional, physical, or sensory disabilities through individualized instruction, accommodations, and assistive technologies.

Universal Design for Learning (UDL): An educational framework that promotes inclusive teaching by offering multiple means of engagement, representation, and expression to accommodate the variability of all learners, including those with disabilities.

Chapter 8
Generative AI for Inclusive Special Education:
Case Studies in Accessibility, Personalization, and Ethical Design

S. Prabagar
https://orcid.org/0000-0002-3852-0082
Alliance School of Advanced Computing, Alliance University, Bengaluru, India

Rashmi Mothkur
Alliance University, Bengaluru, India

C. B. Swetha
https://orcid.org/0009-0007-0445-8018
Alliance University, Bengaluru, India

Asha Kurian
https://orcid.org/0009-0003-6909-5247
Alliance University, Bengaluru, India

K. Pavithra
https://orcid.org/0000-0003-3888-7658
Christ University, Bengaluru, India

S. Aarthi
https://orcid.org/0009-0006-9064-2091
Marwadi University, Rajkot, India

ABSTRACT

This chapter explores the transformative role of Generative AI in special education, emphasizing its ability to personalize learning, enhance accessibility, and support neurodiverse learners. Grounded in Universal Design for Learning (UDL) and inclusive pedagogy, it analyzes how tools like GPT, DALL·E, and Whisper enable individualized instruction through text simplification, visual storytelling, and real-time captioning. Case studies illustrate improved reading comprehension, classroom participation, and emotional development among students with dyslexia, hearing

DOI: 10.4018/979-8-3373-3745-6.ch008

impairments, and autism. Ethical challenges including algorithmic bias, data privacy, and the digital divide are critically discussed. The chapter provides actionable recommendations for educators, developers, and policymakers to ensure human-centered, ethical AI integration. It advocates for co-design frameworks, inclusive UX, and equity-focused policies to promote scalable, responsible AI use in diverse educational contexts.

1. INTRODUCTION

Generative Artificial Intelligence (AI) is transforming education topographies through synchronized availability of learning opportunities that are enjoyable and tailored. The transformative power of Generative AI is especially significant in the context of special education when cognitive, emotional, and physical needs of learners can vary a lot. The problem with the conventional way of teaching in special needs education is that they cannot provide personal attention in large numbers; but Generative AI can fill these gaps by helping produce content, communicate better, and learn these courses adaptively (Akgun & Greenhow, 2022). Large language model-powered tools can be customized to suit individual learning disabilities, neuro diverse conditions, and sensory impairments, speech technologies, and image generators. This chapter discusses the ways in which Generative AI can promote inclusivity, engagement and autonomy in the context special education. Based on the premises of Universal Design for Learning (UDL) and inclusive pedagogical designs, it will show how well-considered AI instrumentalities can serve as a conduit to equity in learning, as well as ward off ethical, technical, and systemic issues following its application.

1.1 Motivation for Using Generative AI in Special Education

The drive behind the insertion of Generative AI in special education can be attributed to the dire necessity to support the various and usually intricate learning demands of the disabled students. Though having only the best intentions, the traditional educational regimens often do not have the means to offer really personal instruction and assistance to students with cognitive or sensory disabilities, emotional difficulties, or physical handicaps (Alasadi & Baiz, 2023). The solution to closing these gaps can be generative AI that can generate personalized content and adjust the means of communication, as well as react to the real-time input.

An example of the former is students with dyslexia potentially getting AI-created simplified texts or text-to-speech software and an example of the latter is students within the autism spectrum being able to use AI-created visual aids or structured social stories that fit their developmental stage. Additionally, real-time translation, augmentative communication, and multimodal learning materials that support engagement and ensure a better understanding may be possible due to Generative AI tools (Almufareh et al., 2024). These apps give more autonomy and inclusiveness in terms of supporting academic progression in addition to emotional and social growth. Moreover, special education teachers are usually limited by the lack of funds, time and teacher-preparation. Generative AI has potential to help with automation of routine work and individualization of lessons, and provide open teaching resources. It makes the educational process more inclusive, scalable, and empathetic one, which are the objectives of the Universal Design of Learning and equity in education.

1.2 Scope: Defining the Target Group

This chapter is directed towards learners that need some specific educational assistance because of the variety of cognitive, physical, sensory, or neurological differences. Target group will involve those students with learning disabilities like dyslexia, dyscalculia, and dysgraphia, who normally have difficulty in reading, writing and mathematical processing. It includes also neurodiverse learners such as learners with Autism Spectrum Disorder (ASD) and Attention Deficit Hyperactivity Disorder (ADHD), who can require structured routines, visual supports, or specialized social communication strategies (Balta, 2023). Students with disorders in speech and language, those who can make use of the Augmentative and Alternative Communication (AAC) technologies are also included. Also, the chapter focuses on connecting the needs of students with disabilities such as blind or low vision and deaf or hard-of-hearing students, discussing AI tools that can increase accessibility of the content through audio, captions, and even through providing sensations. This scope is also encompassed by learners who have physical and mobility limitations, learners who have emotional or behavioural disorders and need emotionally adaptive services. With the focus on provided disparate group of people, the chapter demonstrates how Generative AI has the power to contribute to the provision of equitable, personalized, inclusive learning experiences in special education environments.

1.3 Objectives

The primary objectives of this chapter are to explore and critically analyze the role of Generative AI in enhancing special education through inclusive, adaptive, and ethical practices. Specifically, the chapter aims to:

- **Examine the potential of Generative AI tools** such as text generation, speech synthesis, image creation, and multimodal interfaces in addressing the diverse learning needs of students with disabilities and neurodiverse profiles.
- **Demonstrate real-world applications** of Generative AI in special education through case studies that highlight improved accessibility, personalized learning, and enhanced student engagement.
- **Investigate how Generative AI aligns with educational frameworks** like Universal Design for Learning (UDL), inclusive education models, and human-centered design to support equity and learner autonomy.
- **Critically assess ethical, social, and technical challenges** associated with deploying Generative AI for vulnerable learner populations, including concerns around algorithmic bias, data privacy, and the digital divide.
- **Provide actionable recommendations** for educators, developers, and policymakers to responsibly integrate Generative AI in special education settings.
- **Encourage future research and co-design practices** that involve students, caregivers, and educators in shaping ethical, scalable, and inclusive AI-based educational solutions.

2. THEORETICAL BACKGROUND AND KEY CONCEPTS

Special education and the use of Generative AI are based on global values of how to encourage all children to participate by addressing accessibility, flexibility, and learner-centered. UDL encourages the approach in which the design of learning experiences supports diverse cognitive and physical needs (Chedrawi et al., 2024). Generative AI technologies, including large language models, image generators, speech-to-text systems, allow customized creation of content, provision of real-time support to individual communication, and real-time feedback. Such tools are attuned with assistive technology frameworks and human-centered design, which means that no matter what, AI interventions will empower students and enrich their education process but not substitute an educator, and equity, engagement, and personalized support will prove to be the spotlights of inclusive educational settings.

2.1 Inclusive Education Principles

Inclusive education is an educational practice that upholds all students, the ability or disability, origin, or way of learning, have the equal rights to quality education. Based on the philosophy of human rights and social justice, inclusive education denounces segregation and advocates inclusion of students with special needs in the general education classrooms. It also focuses more on the learning environment adjusting to the learner as opposed to the learner fitting into the standardised practices (Holman et al., 2024). The most important ones are the respect to diversity, active interaction of the learners, stakeholder cooperation, and policy- and training-based support of the system. Inclusive education facilitates the ideology that students with disabilities are students, and with proper support, resources and accommodation they can learn and contribute to the learning process in a meaningful manner. When considering the topic of Generative AI, these beliefs can guide the development of AI-enhanced technologies that prioritize the diversity of learners, encourage independence and foster differentiated learning in real-time which only cements the beliefs of promoting inclusive practice to a more extensive scope beyond the instructive mainstream approach to teaching (Information Science et al., 2024).

2.2 Universal Design for Learning (UDL) Framework

Universal Design of Learning (UDL) is an evidenced-based instruction model that allows maximizing the overall teaching and learning to everyone by offering diverse settings. UDL is founded on the neuroscience and it upholds the principles of giving multiple ways to engage or the reasons why a student should learn (why of learning), representations or what to learn (what of learning) and actions or expression or how to learn (How of learning). This strategy favours the principle that individual differences among learners should not be considered ruled out (Latham & Goltz, 2019). UDL aids in the strategies and instructional materials, which assist instructors in special education in being available and significant to students with varied needs who may have ADHD, dislexia, or autism. Generative AI is a proper alignment with UDL because it creates adaptive materials (text, voice, images), facilitates personal feedback, and enables multimodal communication. Such as, an AI tool might offer multiple modalities, at the same time: visual story, audio narration, simplified text, thus, making sure that learners could consume material in a manner best suited to his or her peculiarities and abilities. The figure 1 illustrates the core UDL principles like multiple means of engagement, representation, and expression guiding inclusive instructional design for diverse learners.

Figure 1. Universal Design for Learning (UDL) Framework

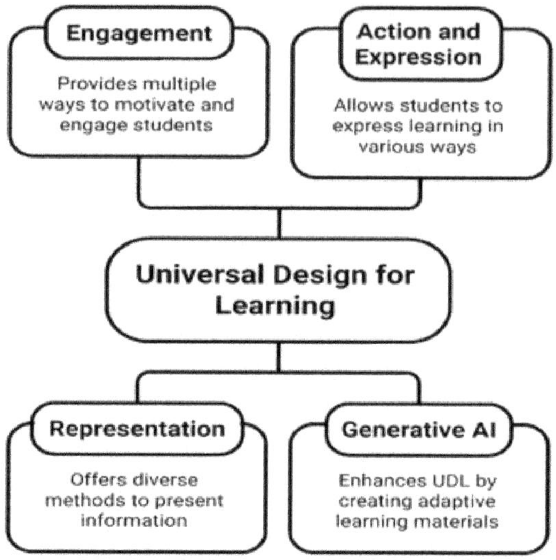

2.3 Assistive Technologies and AI

ATs are referred to as the tools and systems assisting persons with disabilities to accomplish functions that would have been hard or were completely unachievable. Conventionally, these are screen readers, speech-to-text programs, braille displays and communication boards (Lee et al., 2024). As AI and particularly Generative AI continue to develop, the assistive technologies are getting smarter, more responsive and personalized. As an example, AI-enabled captioning systems can provide real-time subtitles to deaf/hearing impaired students or a natural language generation model could be used to simplify a complex text and provide access to the student with learning disabilities. Emotional and behavioural needs can also be met with the use of generative AI that can analyze the mood and the degree of engagement by using voice analysis or face expression and adjust the content delivery accordingly. AI provides a widened set of strategies that would promote inclusive education as it complements regular AT with adaptive and predictive features (Nixon et al., 2024). Such innovations allow students who have disabilities to learn the curriculum more independently (thus increasing confidence and learning results as well as decreasing instructive load of the educators). The Figure 2 contrasts traditional assistive technologies with AI-powered enhancements and outlines their impact on learners with disabilities.

Figure 2. Assistive Technologies Enhanced by AI

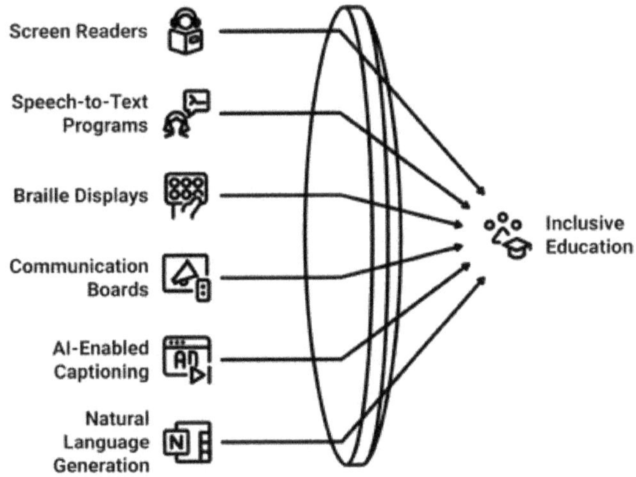

2.4 Overview of Generative AI Models (e.g., GPT, DALL·E, Whisper)

Generative AI The term generative AI describes models capable of generating new content including text, images, audio and even video trained on data. The models that are most common to use include GPT (Generative Pre-trained Transformer) to generate text, DALL·E to create images, and Whisper to recognize and translate speech (Noviandy et al., 2024). They are taught on deep learning models, mainly transformer-based models, to comprehend and produce human-like content in any type of modalities. Such models are transformative in special education: in special education they can be used to make individualised reading material, simplify passages, create visual aids or social stories (in the case of neurodivergent students), or real-time audio captioning or translation (in the case of students with hearing impairment) (Pan, 2024). These aids are beneficial in the delivery of instruction and expression on the part of the learners (particularly students with communication, cognitive, or sensory difficulties). Designed thoughtfully and embedded in inclusive systems, these AI models can support differentiated and multimodal learning experiences that are customized to respond to the individual needs of each student giving teacher control and helping improve the educational results of learners. The figure 3 that maps Generative AI models to types of content they generate, and then links these to educational aids for specific student needs.

Figure 3. Multimodal Generative AI Framework for Inclusive Special Education

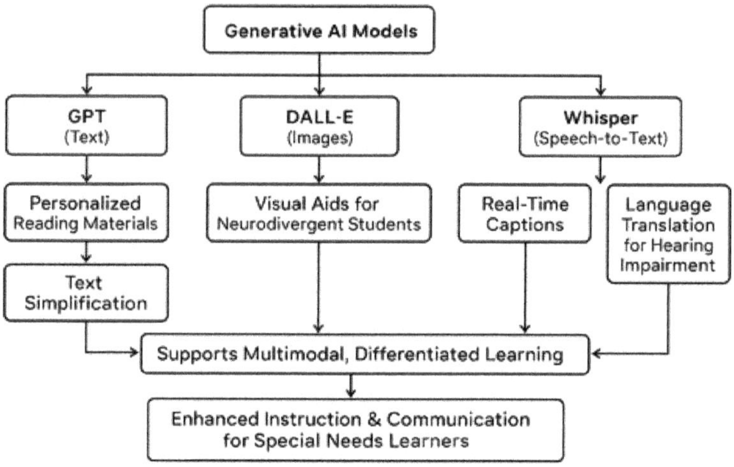

2.5 Conceptual Framework: Inclusive AI-Driven Learning in Special Education

The below fig. shows the conceptual framework of multilayered process of integration of Generative AI in special education based on the principles of Universal Design of Learning (UDL). It uses the Input Layer that focuses on the diverse requirements of learners with neurodiversity, learning disability, and emotional or physical impairment (Pagliara et al., 2024). The Enabler Layer lists fundamental AI technologies that will make content personalize, multimodal interact, and immersive, including GPT, Whisper, DALL.E, and Virtual Reality. These tools are functioning within Pedagogical Foundation which is based on UDL, encouraging flexible representation, engagement and expression to every learner(Pendy, 2023). The Process Layer stresses the significance of human control, co-design and ethical imperative in integration with AI. The Outcome Layer will be the last to be presented; it signifies desirable results, accessibility, personalization, autonomy, and ethically graded inclusion. Although this figure 4 framework makes sense to just organize the theoretical foundations of the chapter, it also forms the core upon which the practical case studies based on relating AI capabilities to inclusive educational objectives will be done.

Figure 4. Framework for Integrating Generative AI in Inclusive Special Education

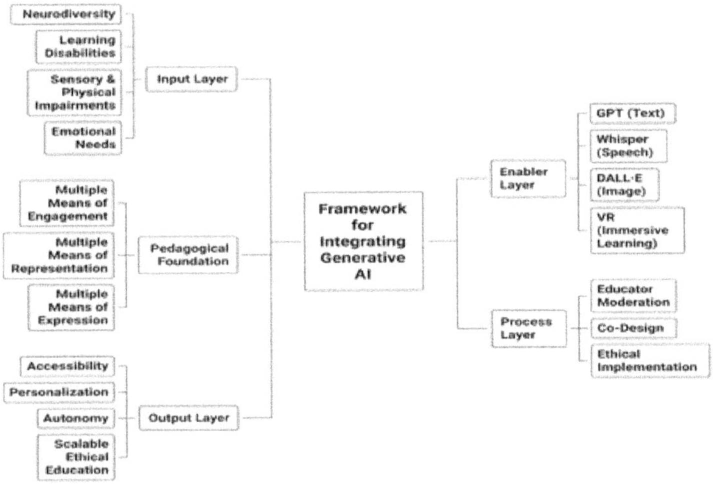

3. LITERATURE REVIEW

The current progress in Artificial Intelligence (AI) has presented additional possibilities in inclusive education, especially in the form of Generative AI that can be used in the case of special needs students. The assimilation of Universal Design learning (UDL) guidelines (Marino et al., 2023) focuses on the flexible learning landscapes, which are promoted with the help of AI tools to increase accessibility and equity. A study by scholars like proves the success of natural language processing to accommodate autistic learners and students with dyslexia. An understanding of the emotions of AI (Santhana Hari et al., 2025)and tutoring systems that employ the use of avatars (Santos et al., 2024)also add to personalization that takes into account neurodiverse learners. On the ethical side, (Floridi & Cowls, 2019)and (Fjeld et al., 2020), offer the concept of principled AI that is crucial in implementing the technology in such a delicate educational setting. The stakeholders are co-creating and designing tools with participatory design at the centric focus and co-creating within contexts (Zawacki-Richter et al., 2019). Heffernan & Heffernan (2014) also insist on the presence of platforms encouraging collaborative and data-informed teaching (Heffernan & Heffernan, 2014). Although the promise is on the anvil, questions of algorithm bias, the long-term effect, and teacher preparedness still loom (Zawacki-Richter et al., 2019).This indicates that it is time to further research and establish more inclusive policies. The table 1 compiles seminal and contemporary research contributions focused on the intersection of Artificial Intelligence (AI), inclusive education, and support for neurodiverse learners, particularly those with autism and related conditions(Pendy, 2023). It categorizes studies by their authors, publication year, focus area (e.g., UDL, NLP, AI ethics, avatar tutoring), and highlights their key contributions. The literature spans frameworks such as Universal Design for Learning (UDL), ethical considerations in AI, personalized learning environments, participatory design, and AI-driven interventions to enhance educational accessibility and equity.

Table 1. Key Literature on AI, Accessibility, and Inclusive Learning for Neurodiverse Learners

S. No.	Authors (Year)	Focus Area	Key Contribution
1	Marino et al. (2023)	Universal Design for Learning (UDL)	Advocates flexible, accessible learning environments supported by AI in alignment with UDL principles
2	Fan et al. (2020)*	NLP & Learning Disorders	Demonstrates how NLP helps autistic learners and students with dyslexia
3	Santhana Hari et al. (2025)	Emotion-Aware AI	Explores AI's capacity to understand learner emotions for better personalization
4	Santos et al. (2024)	Avatar-Based Tutoring	Implements avatars for adaptive, personalized instruction in neurodiverse contexts
5	Floridi & Cowls (2019)	AI Ethics	Proposes ethical principles (transparency, fairness) for AI use in sensitive education settings
6	Fjeld et al. (2020)	AI Governance & Ethics	Offers rights-based approach to principled, ethical AI for education
7	Zawacki-Richter et al. (2019)	Participatory Design & Co-creation	Highlights collaborative, context-sensitive AI tool development with stakeholder input
8	Heffernan & Heffernan (2014)	Data-Informed Teaching	Promotes platforms for collaborative and data-driven teaching through AI support
9	Pendy (2023)	Inclusive AI Implementation	Emphasizes inclusion policies and challenges like algorithmic bias and teacher readiness

4. APPLICATIONS AND CASE STUDIES

Generative AI is also emerging to be used in the area of special education to ensure accessibility, personalization, or learner interest. This part provides real cases examples of how such tools as GPT, Whisper, and DALL·E can benefit diverse learners especially those with disabilities and neurodiverse statuses. These AI-powered apps describe how practical the idea of personalizing instructional resources and communication strategies is. An example is that GPT has been applied to developing simplified and personalized lesson plans to the students with dyslexia leading to better results in reading comprehension (Pierrès et al., 2024). The combination of Whisper and GPT-generated captions has even led to the real-time multilingual support of students with hearing, increasing the interaction in the classroom. Also, prior research shows that the interaction of DALL·E with virtual reality settings has facilitated opportunities in social learning among autistic students because the use of AI provides them with a visual form of storytelling. Although all the applications have valuable benefits, there are limitations that should be overcome like content complexity, translation accuracy, and the availability of hardware. Such examples highlight the potential as well as the issues about implementing Generative AI in inclusive education (Tang, 2024).

4.1 Case Study 1: Personalized Lesson Planning Using ChatGPT for Students with Dyslexia

- **Tool:** OpenAI's GPT models
- **Outcome:** Improved reading comprehension
- **Limitation:** Text complexity and content control issues

The sample classroom was a resource classroom where students with dyslexia can learn to read and improve their reading comprehension based on a personalized lesson plan, in which we applied the use of OpenAI Generative Pre-Trained Transformer (GPT) models into the instructional process of the classroom (Viberg et al., 2024). In the case of dyslexia, difficulties are usually encountered when decoding words, not comprehending complex sentence structures, and paying attention to the reading assignments. In order to handle such problems, the teachers made use of GPT to produce simplified form of standard curriculum texts and made them into learner-friendly formats particularly based on the individual reading level, and characteristics of the individual learning process.

Teachers fed GPT prompts with the most important themes and vocabulary of the content in individual grades and were shown AI-generated texts that repeated the main instructional goals but had simplified language and structure (Wiredu et al., 2024). The lesson plans were then integrated with such individualized reading materials as well as comprehending questions and vocabulary exercises according to the aptitudes and interests of students. Consequently, the learners observed an obvious improvement in understanding, reading confidence, and engagement. Teachers have also shared that consuming GPT saved time on the activities of adapting learning materials manually, creating more student-centered presence and assistance.

Although it had such positive sides, the usage of GPT was also not the limit. The AI at times would generate some language that contained vocabulary or sentence structure that was too complicated to the desired learner (Chakraborty, 2024). In some, the contents veered away too far on the original topics, so they required teacher checking and revision. Such difficulties pointed at the need to control AI-based support in the process of planning lessons by a human expert. Finally, GPT as a tool to support personalized learning in special education was deemed as useful tool but its success greatly relied on the proper engineering of prompts and a moderate teacher control. The Figure 5 AI-assisted workflow for personalized reading support using GPT models for dyslexic learners. The model outlines the role of AI in simplifying instructional content based on individualized learner profiles.

Figure 5. AI-Assisted Personalized Lesson Planning Flow for Dyslexic Learners

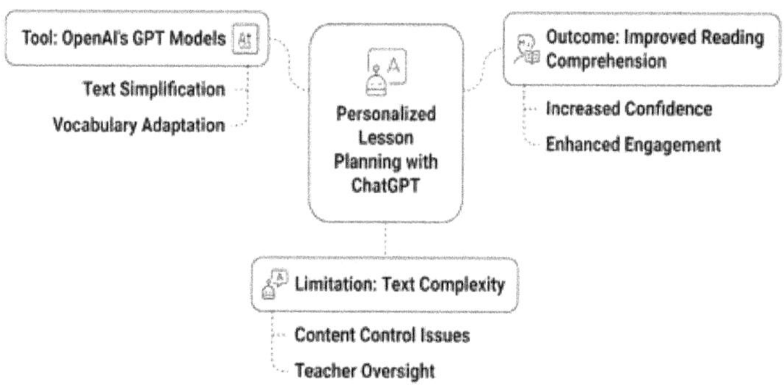

4.2 Case Study 2: Real-Time Multilingual Support for Students with Hearing Impairments

- **Tool:** Whisper + GPT-generated captions
- **Outcome:** Increased classroom participation
- **Limitation:** Translation inaccuracies in technical subjects

Inclusive classroom conditions that included students with hearing impairments were facilitated by a mixed use of the Whisper model of OpenAI and the captions generated with GPT. The transcribed voices observed in real-time in the classrooms were proposed with the help of some powerful program of automatic speech recognition known as Whisper. GPT uploaded these transcriptions and rephrased them and/or translated them to the language the students preferred or altered the language to make it more accessible (Santhana Hari et al., 2025). This two AI system was very effective in engaging the students and participation. To students who might have depended on interpreters or had to wait sometime before lectures could be provided with captions, the lecture content was now provided to them in near real-time, and could engage in discussions, respond to questions, and freely interact with their classmates and instructors. The system was particularly helpful in teaching multilingual classrooms as there was more of a language barrier that caused further communication problems among the hearing-impaired students (Holman et al., 2024).

The process of implementation disclosed major weaknesses. Although the speech recognized by Whisper was fairly accurate in quiet setting, it was affected by background noise and more than one speaker. Also, whenever GPT was employed in the process of translating or simplifying technical materials, particularly science-related or mathematical-related works, it sometimes created inaccuracies or left out a very important term. Such translation errors even led to misunderstandings in some cases or requests for a clarification by the instructor, which would argue in Favor of domain-specific tuning and manual intervention (Almufareh et al., 2024). These drawbacks notwithstanding, the combination of Whisper and GPT was highly scalable and affordable in terms of promoting the inclusivity of the project. This case study shows how Generative AI would help minimize the communication barriers in real-time and put the hearing-impaired students in a position to actively participate in the mainstream educational setting, but enhance equity and accessibility in diversified learning spaces. The below figure 6 illustrates the integration of OpenAI's Whisper (for real-time speech-to-text) and GPT (for caption generation and language adaptation) to enhance communication accessibility in inclusive classrooms. The process includes real-time transcription, contextual simplification, and language customization, enabling hearing-impaired students to engage actively in multilingual and mainstream learning environments.

Figure 6. Real-Time AI Captioning Pipeline for Inclusive Classrooms

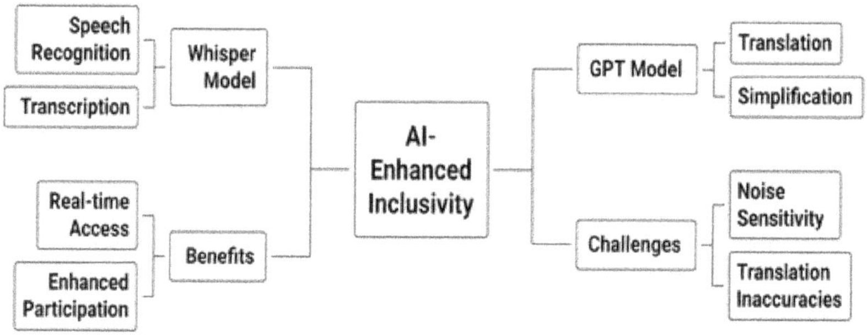

4.3 Case Study 3: Virtual Reality and Image Generation for Autistic Learners

- **Tool:** DALL·E + VR simulation
- **Outcome:** Enhanced social story learning through AI-generated visuals
- **Limitation:** Requires high-end devices not available in all schools

A group of teachers in a pilot program involving students with Autism Spectrum Disorder (ASD) aimed to develop immersive learning environments by using both Virtual Reality (VR) technologies, and the DALL·E image generation model of OpenAI, to develop a more in-depth, individual teacher-student approach. Children with ASD tend to respond well to visual resources and regulated multi-sensory experience which can assist them relate to abstract thoughts, expand on social excellence, and limit the feelings of anxiousness in unpredictable patterns (Rostami & Longo, 2024). To support these requirements, the teachers employed DALL·E to produce personalized visual resources, including emotion cards, scene renderings, and narrative arcs, and introduced them to the VR modules, representing real-life situations like a trip to a grocery store, a ride on the Nevertheless, since teachers created bespoke visual materials, we can state that this training provision supported the continuous use of the resource. Such VR spaces that were enhanced with AI enabled autistic students to become confident, well-connected communicators and behavior-prepared through safe but repetitive simulations. Teachers noticed that students learned to follow routines, emotions expression, and their generalization of learned behavior to natural situations (Scott et al., 2024). The intimate character of the DALL·E generated imagery made the learning experiences more down-to-earth and not overstimulating which also added to the increased levels of engagement and motivation.

VR and AI-produced visuals had its limitations. Other than the high cost of high-end Virtual Reality headsets and computing requirements, accessibility was an issue in schools without resources. Also, not all students could see without a feeling of bombardment or could not interact until long acclimatization to virtual environments. Furthermore, correction of the images created to conform according to particular emotional or behavioural clues required their modifications by the teacher and took time (Singha & Singha, 2024). The case study also demonstrates the strong possibilities of using generative AI and immersive technologies together to assist non-typical minds like autistic learners in the inclusive education environment with their cognitive and emotional needs best. The Figure 7 presents a comprehensive framework for designing Virtual Reality (VR) learning environments tailored to autistic learners. It integrates challenges (both environmental and individual), multimedia learning theories, and cognitive load principles to establish clear design goals. These goals aim to minimize extraneous cognitive load, manage intrinsic cognitive load, facilitate germane information processing, and support adaptive learning through real-time cognitive load assessment (Stracke, 2024). The model further aligns with ethical considerations and instructional strategies such as attention guiding, chunking, and multi-format representation. Surrounding the core framework are standards of inclusive learning, rooted in design-based research, emphasizing autism-centered perspectives, participatory methods, and ecological validity.

Figure 7. Virtual Reality-based Learning Environment Design for Autistic Learners

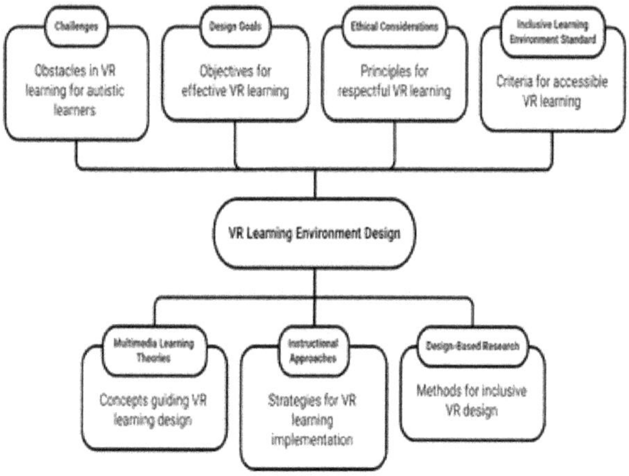

Table 2. Implementation Results of Generative AI in Special Education Case Studies

Case Study	AI Tool(s)	Target Group	Key Outcome	Limitation	Impact on Inclusion & Learning
Personalized Lesson Planning for Dyslexia	GPT (OpenAI)	Students with Dyslexia	Improved reading comprehension, increased engagement, and time-saving for teachers	Text complexity; occasional off-topic outputs	Enabled personalized reading material aligned with learning abilities
Real-Time Multilingual Support for Hearing Impairments	Whisper + GPT-generated captions	Hearing-impaired students	Enhanced classroom participation and real-time multilingual accessibility	Inaccurate translations in technical subjects; noise sensitivity	Reduced communication barriers and increased learner inclusion in diverse classrooms
VR and Image Generation for Autistic Learners	DALL·E + Virtual Reality	Students with Autism Spectrum Disorder (ASD)	Enhanced social story comprehension, emotional expression, and behavior generalization	Requires expensive hardware; sensory acclimatization required	Supported social-emotional development through immersive, AI-generated visual environments

The above table 2 summarizes three case studies showcasing the use of Generative AI tools GPT, Whisper, DALL·E, and VR in special education. Each case targets a specific learner group (dyslexia, hearing impairments, autism) and demonstrates improvements in reading comprehension, classroom participation, or social-emotional learning. While the tools enhanced personalization and inclusion, limitations such as content complexity, translation errors, and hardware requirements highlight the need for human oversight and equitable access.Top of FormBottom of Form The below figure 8 illustrating the implementation results of Generative AI in special education. It compares the positive outcomes and limitation severity for each of the three case studies:

- GPT for Dyslexia
- Whisper + GPT for Hearing Impairments
- DALL·E + VR for Autism

Higher outcome scores indicate greater educational benefit, while higher limitation scores reflect more significant implementation challenges. **Top of Form**

Figure 8. Comparative Implementation Outcomes of Generative AI Tools in Special Education

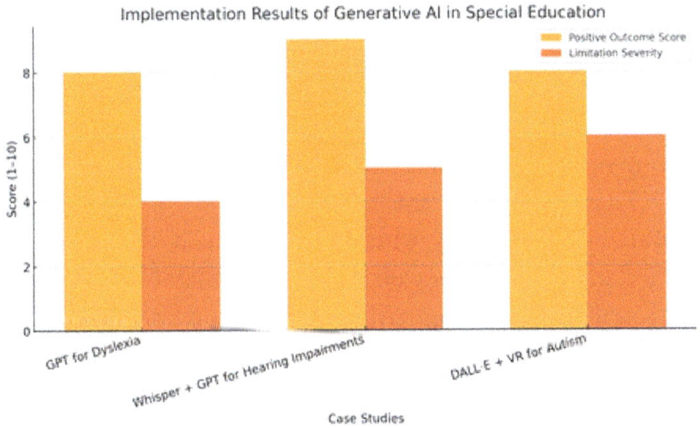

5. ETHICAL CONSIDERATIONS AND DESIGN CHALLENGES

Although there are great potentials of Generative AI to be used in special education, its deployment presents a range of crucial ethical and design-related issues. Such problems as algorithm bias, data privacy, and consented consent are of prime importance, particularly regarding information on sensitive learners (Wallace & Abel, 2024). There is a danger of neglecting and interpolating Neurodiverse learners in favour of inclusion, and this is through misrepresentation or simplifying of content. Moreover, the lack of AI tools access caused by infrastructural or financial inequality generates the narrowing of the digital divide. The ethical use entails; openness, cultural awareness and human control. When AI systems are designed using Universal Design for Learning (UDL) principles, they will take into consideration accessibility, differentiation, and equity and protect the rights and agency of the learners.

5.1 Algorithmic Bias and Representation

Generative AI systems are trained with very large datasets potentially having bias to race, gender, disability or cultural norms which we are not aware of (Kuerban et al., 2025). These are particularly problematic in special education when it comes to AI-generated content, which does not reflect the experience, the communication style, or the learning needs of neurodiverse or disabled learners. As an example, image generation instruments do not depict actual disabled persons or other means of communication, such as sign language, which causes underrepresentation or negative imagery. The bias in algorithms may reinforce the exclusivity as opposed to facilitating inclusivity, especially when left unchecked. Such risks explain why inclusive and varied training data as well as frequent model auditing should be prioritized. Teachers and developers should be cautious and include the involvement stakeholders such as students with disabilities, care givers and disability advocates in the assessment (Rizos et al., 2024). The inclusion of culturally responsive and accessible design concepts will pave the way to AI tools presenting an equal educational benefit over all demographics of learners. They should not view the mitigation of bias as a single event but an ongoing design approach especially in a sensitive education setting.

5.2 Data Privacy and Consent from Caregivers

The application of AI at Special Education is usually related to the work with the highly sensitive personal data such as cognitive profiles, behavioural patterns, and speech recording. This data should be secured to preserve student integrity and security. Ensuring a well-informed consent is another of the most urgent ethical issues, when it comes to working with minors and those students who have disabilities that make them unaware of the consequences of data gathering. Where this happens to be the case, caregivers or legal guardians should be well informed and provide consent in reasonably understandable and clear forms (Samadi et al., 2020). Besides, data storage, data transmission and the encapsulation of AI model should comply with hard privacy regulations eg: GDPR or FERPA. App developers should focus on safe encryption, anonymization methods and retention policies of minimum amount of data. Schools and any other educational facility should also have clear guidelines regarding ownership rights on the data, level of use, and data access. Finally, the special education AI tools must represent the privacy-by-goal guarantees to protect the personal data of students and their trust.

5.3 AI Misuse and Over-Reliance in Special Needs Contexts

Whereas the Generative AI offers an opportunity to enrich the personalization and engagement in special education, its overutilization or incorrect utilization might lead to unforeseen effects/misuse. Educators and caregivers may start relying on AI algorithms too much when providing content or making decisions, which may push human insight, compassion, and situational awareness to the sidelines, which would be disastrous to use in working with high-needs learners. In addition, AI tools are not flawless, inaccuracy or the inappropriateness of the output might lead to misdirection of the teaching, particularly when there is no proper training provided to teachers to critically assess or even alter the content. Automation bias is also possible where the users entrust the AI to be correct and therefore would not be critically engaged (Waterfield et al., 2025). As such, to eliminate these pitfalls, AI ought to be used as an enhancement and not a substitute to human teachers. The second point is professional development: educators need professional training in working with AI tools but also to know their limits. Harmonious coexistence between human and AI would keep technology as a supplement to the role of the teacher as opposed to a substitute.

5.4 Digital Divide: Accessibility in Low-Resource Schools

The rest of the schools that are located in the rural, under-resourced or underserved areas will be left behind due to the assumption that the Generative AI may become profitable only when it pertains to well-resourced institutions. It is the digital divide that is a barrier to a fair distribution of AI apps and is manifested in different access to devices, access to the high-speed connected internet, and technical support (Zhou, 2023). Even basic assistive technology is not an option in low-resource schools, in which case, the situation with supporting students with disabilities using AI-infused capabilities such as VR or real-time captioning is even worse. Such digital divide contributes to educational inequity and institutionalizes access into underserved communities. In addition, attending school in such surroundings, teachers might not be trained or equipped in order to effectively achieve solutions based on AI. In order to overcome this gap, policy makers should focus investments on inclusive digital infrastructure, provide grants toward technology acquisition and promote open-source AI projects in varying situations(Busch et al., 2023). The digital divide is a critical issue that needs to be resolved to make sure that the generative potential of Generative AI is accessible to every learner despite socioeconomic and geographical challenges.

5.5 Recommendations for Human-AI Collaboration

The main idea behind the effective implementation of Generative AI in special education is the cooperation in interaction between human beings and AI systems. Teachers, practitioners, care providers, and designers have to collaboratively design learning environments that are accommodative and the use of AI applications is considered intelligently to boost, rather than substitute, human wisdom. The teachers must be able to have the final say in choosing, tailoring and authenticating the AI generated content and make sure that it is age and emotionally appropriate according to the needs of the students. To make functionality solution more aligned to the relevant problems in the classroom, developers need to engage the teachers and students throughout the design and testing process. Also, professional development needs to provide educators with the skill of AI literacy, which would allow them to understand the output, recognize bias, and solve problems. Matters of nuanced behavior, adjustment of emotional reactions, and ethical use require human supervision in order to make interpretations (Darwish, 2024). The development of such collaborative model supports mutual trust, responsible innovation as well as positive educational outcomes. By so doing, AI would serve as an enabler that helps teachers provide personalized, caring, and adaptive instruction done on a firm foundation of the principles of equity and dignity of learners.

6. POLICY RECOMMENDATIONS AND FUTURE DIRECTIONS

In order to provide equal and responsible access to Generative AI that would be applied in special education, policymakers need to set aside inclusive rules that would focus on accessibility, data confidentiality, and ethical implementation. The investments must be made in infrastructure within low-resource schools, educator training, and AI-based Universal Design of Learning (UDL). Culturally competent, co-design of context-aware solutions should include educators, technologists, caregivers, and learners through collaboration policy frameworks (Ersoy, 2025). Future studies must discuss the effects over time, general AI assessment tools, and flexible studying the models of the neurodiverse students. Finally, the policies should promote healthy ecosystem originating in AI that complements, instead of substitutes, the human aspect of special education.

6.1 For Educators: Training Modules, Prompt Libraries, Ethical Usage Guidelines

The integration of the generative AI in special education is possible with the involvement of educators in this process. Nevertheless, the efficient utilisation of these tools requires thorough support and training. Teachers require a system of training, which will familiarize the teachers with the basics of AI, raise the question of its prompt engineering, ethical aspects, and classroom opportunities (Singh & Jain, 2024). These modules are aimed at teaching how to tailor AI-made content to cognitive, sensory, or behavioural needs of learners at the same time as keeping up the alignment with the purposes of the curriculum and developmental challenges. The Fig.9 illustrates a three-pronged framework aimed at enabling educators to effectively and ethically integrate Generative AI into special education classrooms. It emphasizes training modules, curated content libraries, and ethical guidelines to empower informed educational practices (Jain et al., 2023).

Figure 9. Framework for Ethical AI in Special Education

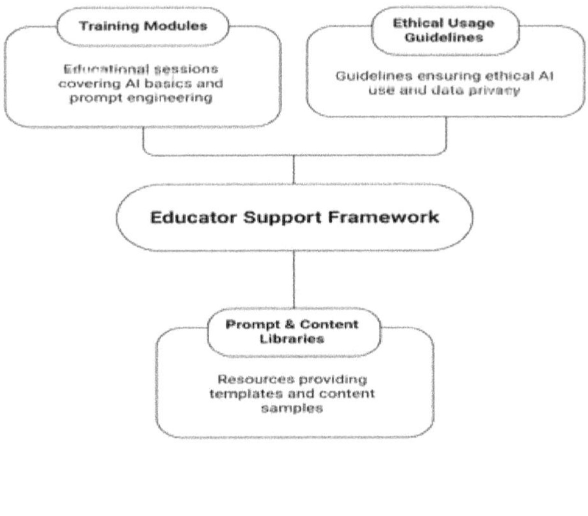

Contingent libraries can be an effective tool too, as they may provide ready-tested and all-inclusive templates, specific to different learner types and courses. Such libraries ought to have examples on cultural responsiveness, simplified language format, and multimodal content creating to accommodate various learning styles (Jantanukul, 2024). Along with this, the ethical use of the technology should be presented in a clear manner to assist the educators in walking through the murky waters of complex issues of avoiding bias, knowing the sensitivity of the data, and the border of human understanding and AI dispensation. These guidelines ought to encourage thoughtfulness, openness, and responsibility in the usage or editing of AI-created contents. In conclusion, the ethical knowledge, toolset, and frameworks to use AI responsibly must be empowered in the hands of teachers so that the technological assistants improve their teaching skills but do not infringe upon the rights and needs of learners within the special education condition.

6.2 For Developers: Inclusive UX Design, Multilingual Accessibility, Robust Guardrails

Generative AI tool developers making special education must focus on one inclusive design, which upholds the diversity of the learners. This implies creating user interfaces (UX) that are accessible to people of visual, auditory, motor, and cognitive disabilities. Such features as adjustable text size, colour contrast, compatibility with screen readers and simplified navigation are required to provide fair usability (Purwanto & Hendrawan, 2024). Additionally, the tools must have the multilingual accessibility to limit the linguistic bias in view of several students with varying linguistic backgrounds especially in multilingual classrooms or locales that have high linguistic diversity.

Besides functional design, there is a necessity to install strong safety guardrails that will suppress the emergence of wrong, biased, or deceptive records. This involves incorporating real time content filters, flagging and human-in-the-loop modalities of reviewing. It is worth paying special consideration to the alignment of content, its accuracy in educational settings, and appropriateness to the age of the subject- especially when working with highly sensitive groups of students, such as neurodiverse individuals or those with sensitive feelings. To achieve these developers must involve educators, caregivers and students in the design and the testing processes to ensure that the tool would satisfy real world requirements in a classroom. Continuous updating, feedback loops between the model and the user, as well as the model openness must be the norm. Using the ethical, accessible, and responsive building of AI, developers can establish the instrument that will positively affect personalized learning and not violate the principles of inclusiveness and equity (Santhana Hari et al., 2025).

6.3 For Policymakers: Equity-Focused Funding, Universal AI Standards in EdTech

The policymakers play a fundamental role in establishing required regulatory and support infrastructure to scale Generative AI in special education in a responsible way. Equity-oriented funding to help minimize the digital gap should be one of the highest priorities. This involves strategic investment on low resource schools to equip it with internet connectivity, AI-compatible equipment, teacher category, and support, and technical assistants and assistance. Lack of this intervention means that learners in disadvantaged or rural places are at risk of being sidelined in AI-enhanced learning (Singha & Singha, 2024). Alongside the above, an urgent necessity of having norms concerning ethical, technical, and pedagogic use of AI in education emerges. The set of standards must discuss data privacy, bias reduction, transparency of algorithms, and participation. They will also need to lead in the accreditation of the use of AI-powered EdTech tools, which must be evidence-based, be accessible and safe to use with special-needs learners.

The policymakers ought to embrace multi-stakeholder cooperation, through a convergence of the researchers, educators, developers, and disability advocates in the governance of AI (Stracke, 2024). The policies must also accommodate the research and innovation in line with the goals of inclusive education and the emerging technologies. Policymakers can contribute to the creation of a long-term sustainable AI ecosystem in education a sustainable environment that must support all learners irrespective of their capabilities and backgrounds and minimize existing socio-economic and regional disparities and gaps. The government can foster such an environment by creating the funding pipelines and regulatory structure, which are more focused on fairness, safety, and inclusiveness.

7. FUTURE RESEARCH

Theory and research in the field of Generative AI and special education ought to consider long term impact of its application; inclusiveness in co-design practices; adaptation to various learner requirements with its models. Research ought to compare the long-term usage of AI on cognitive, emotional, and academic growth of students with disabilities (Syaidina et al., 2024). The investigation of co-design models is also necessary in which students, caregivers, educators collectively design AI tools to make them relevant to situations and culturally non-threatening. Subsequently, studies should also explore the ways to optimise Generative AI to suit particular impairments, like generating objects to be touched and heard by the visually impaired learner, or generated person to be socially and emotionally simulated by an autistic learner. The other critical field involves the formulation of assessment criteria to gauge inclusiveness, accessibility and ethical compliance in AI systems (Tilak et al., 2024). Finally, interdisciplinary research is needed between special education, human-computer interaction and AI ethics to generate scalable equitable solutions. The development of such research fronts will make AI a meaningful and ethical inclusion education tool.

7.1 Longitudinal Impact Studies of Generative AI on Special Needs Education

One of the unfortunate research areas that will need research in the future is the longitudinal study of the effect of Generative AI on learners with special needs. Although there is positive evidence in the short-term pilot programs results, including such aspects like enhanced engagement, reading comprehension, and classroom interaction, little is known about the impact of AI-driven tools as a long-term cognitive, emotional, and social development provider (Lee et al., 2024). Longitudinal studies will also help evaluate whether the gains of such use are maintained, whether the overuse of AI can hinder the ability of learners to interact on a human level, and how the autonomy of learners will develop along with the adoption of AI.

The heterogeneity in disabilities of students (autism, dyslexia, hearing disabilities, etc.) should also be followed in such research to comprehend particular patterns and requirements. Also, one needs to investigate how did the adaptation of educators evolve, particularly to the shifting capabilities of the AI. The findings of these studies can be used in setting policy around scaling AI in a responsible manner and being aware of the age-appropriate, stage-sensitive response to it (Pierrès et al., 2024). The data acquired over a long period is crucial in developing evidence-informed guidelines, ranging somewhere between innovation and the well-being of students, issues of ethics, and equity in education. These multi-dimensional assessments can assist the stakeholders, such as policymakers, technologists, and educators, in aware of the long-term value, constraints, and modification of AI to support its sustainable implementation in the ecosystems of special education.

7.2 Design of Culturally Responsive AI Assistants

Research on culturally responsive AI assistants is an important research avenue to support the consideration of Generative AI tools to meet the needs of the diverse learners in special education environments. The element of cultural responsiveness in AI goes beyond translation of language and that includes values, preferences in communication and local context and examples of culturally appropriate learning (Ali et al., 2024). To the neurodiverse/disabled learners who belong to underrepresented groups, generic AI content can be desensitized or even alienating. The studies should determine how the AI systems will acknowledge and honour cultural identities such as ethnicity, language, religion, or socio-economic identity. As an example, AI-generated stories, images or teaching suggestions ought to capture the names, place, customs, and values within the culture that the learner comes across.

Also, the research needs to be performed on how cultural peculiarities and disability accommodation collide with each other so that AI outputs will not add to stereotypes or discrimination. This necessitates interaction with linguists, teachers, and community representatives in the field of training and improving AI models (Yu et al., 2024). The AI tools must also provide the support of local dialects and sign languages where feasible. Development of culturally informed AI would increase learner interest, confidence, and applicability, including in special education where representation and emotional feeling of safety are of utmost importance. In the end, culturally responsive AI will contribute to the achievement of inclusivity in capacities, as well as identity and lived experience.

7.3 Co-Design Frameworks with Student/ Family Feedback Loops

Future of inclusive AI in special education should be determined using co-design frameworks that will involve students, families as well as caregivers in special education in terms of how they can be involved in developing and refining. Employees should be involved into the design process of educational technologies too often their design is based on the needs of the employees who use it every day and might create a solution that is useful but not effective or meaningful (Samadi et al., 2020). Co-design promotes embedding the AI tools in the context of needs, preferences, and values of learners with disabilities and their support systems in the real world. The practice in this direction should explore participatory approaches in which students with special needs provide feedback on AI-created contents, usability of the interface, and emotional reaction to AI interactions. Informants such as family members are capable of giving more information about behavioural symptom, cultural background and challenges in learning at home such as learning disabilities that maybe not evident in the classroom learning environment. These lessons are priceless when it comes to developing empathetic, individualized, and dynamic interactions of AI (Santhana Hari et al., 2025) . The feedback loops should also be ongoing as opposed to a single instance of intervention to allow tools to advance alongside the learner. Researchers ought to consider scalable solutions on how co-design can be incorporated in the AI product development, such as periodic surveys, focus groups and inclusion through beta-testing in inclusive classrooms. The incorporation of these feedback channels produces tools that are not only technically correct, but also socially and emotionally aware tools thereby leading to ethically better, effective and inclusive AI devices in special education. The Figure 10 as follows.

Figure 10. Co-Design Frameworks with Student/Family Feedback Loops

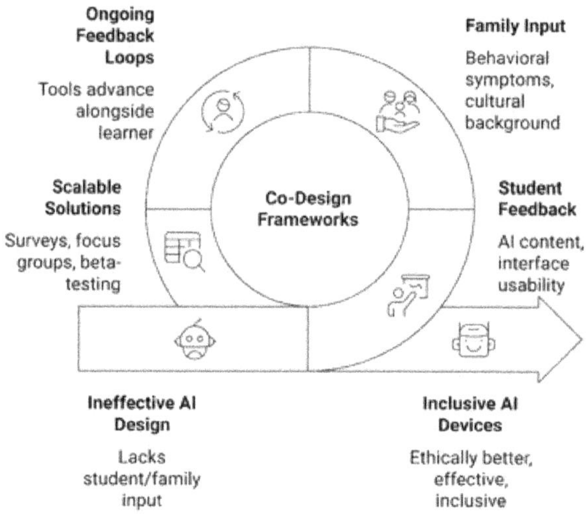

8. CONCLUSION

This chapter has examined how Generative Artificial Intelligence can help transform special education and become revolutionary. Generative AI will have the potential to address the existing slack in customized guidance, access and involvement of learners with varied cognitive, sensory, and emotional requirements through platforms like GPT, DALL·E, and Whisper. Informed by the theory of the Universal Design of Learning (UDL) and inclusive teaching, the presented AI-enabled innovations show how with appropriate use of technology, learning and independence in neurodiverse learners can be boosted greatly. The examples provided in the case studies are successful cases with the following outcomes: the dyslexic students improved reading comprehension by using AI-assisted simplified text; real-time captioning benefited the children with hearing loss in multicultural classrooms; and visual storytelling using DALL-E and VR technology increased emotional communication and regular training in the learners with autism. These interventions recorded significant improvement in participation, understanding and confidence of learners.

Nevertheless, they also demonstrated shortcomings, such as the accuracy of content, overloading of the senses, and the financial implied costs of the technologies, all of which emphasize the necessity to practice responsible incorporation and continue human supervision. Special education is one of the areas where such ethical issues as algorithmic bias, data privacy, misuse of AI, and the digital divide are especially acute. Such dangers warrant community-based and strong governance systems, a culture-orientation in design, and the integration of learners, caregivers and educators in the development cycle. Excessive use of AI tools with the absence of training in using them and without ethical protection may undermine the dignity of learners, distort identities, or exacerbate inequities. This chapter provides recommendations that can be taken to enhance AI-enhanced special education among the various stakeholders. Teachers should be trained on timely engineering, ethical use of content and multimodal curriculum.

Developers should focus on inclusive design of UX, good guardrails, and language variety. It is suggested that policymakers should finance infrastructure in low-resource contexts, prescribe universal AI practices, and embrace co-design practices. Further studies must be on long-term effects, culture-sensitive artificial intelligence, and feedback-informed co-design principles that will further promote sustainable and equitable innovation. To sum up, the issue of Generative AI introduces a significant prospect of inclusion, responsiveness, and adaptiveness in education. However, its influence in special education is fragile because it requires a balancing act between empowering and displacing the teacher, between acknowledging learner individuality and taking advantage of technology, and dealing with each design decision based on ethics, empathy, and equity. Under these conditions, Generative AI can become much more than an engine of efficiency: It can drive humanistic, human-centered change, in the learning space.

REFERENCES

Akgun, S., & Greenhow, C. (2022). Artificial intelligence in education: Addressing ethical challenges in K-12 settings. *AI and Ethics*, *2*(3), 431–440. PMID: 34790956

Alasadi, E. A., & Baiz, C. R. (2023). Generative AI in education and research: Opportunities, concerns, and solutions. *Journal of Chemical Education*, *100*(8), 2965–2971.

Ali, D., Fatemi, Y., Boskabadi, E., Nikfar, M., Ugwuoke, J., & Ali, H. (2024). ChatGPT in teaching and learning: A systematic review. *Education Sciences*, *14*(6), 643.

Almufareh, M. F., & Kausar, S., & Humayun Mamoona and Tehsin, S. (2024). A conceptual model for inclusive technology: Advancing disability inclusion through artificial intelligence. *Journal of Disability Research*, *3*(1).

Balta, N. (2023). Ethical considerations in using AI in educational research. *Journal of Research in Didactical Sciences*, *2*(1), 14205.

Busch, F., Adams, L. C., & Bressem, K. K. (2023). Biomedical ethical aspects towards the implementation of artificial intelligence in medical education. *Medical Science Educator*, *33*(4), 1007–1012. PMID: 37546190

Chakraborty, O. (2024). Role of AI in special education in India. In *Advances in Educational Technologies and Instructional Design* (pp. 279–324). IGI Global.

Chedrawi, C., Kazoun, N., & Kokkinaki, A. (2024). The role of AI agents in fostering inclusivity for HEIs' students with special needs against backdrops of the accreditation trend. *Quality Assurance in Education*, *32*(4), 582–596.

Darwish, D. (2024). Human-AI Collaboration in Industry 5. In Human-Machine Collaboration and Emotional Intelligence in Industry 5.0 (pp. 44–70). IGI Global.

Ersoy, C. (2025). Inclusive transformation with artificial intelligence. In *Advances in Computational Intelligence and Robotics* (pp. 275–296). IGI Global.

Fjeld, J., Achten, N., Hilligoss, H., Nagy, A., & Srikumar, M. (2020). Principled artificial intelligence: Mapping consensus in ethical and rights-based approaches to principles for AI. SSRN Electron. J.

Floridi, L., & Cowls, J. (2019). A unified framework of five principles for AI in society. *Harvard Data Science Review*.

Heffernan, N. T., & Heffernan, C. L. (2014). The ASSISTments ecosystem: Building a platform that brings scientists and teachers together for minimally invasive research on human learning and teaching. *International Journal of Artificial Intelligence in Education, 24*(4), 470–497.

Holman, K., Marino, M., Vasquez, E., Taub, M., Hunt, J., & Tazi, Y. (2024). Navigating AI-Powered Personalized Learning in special education: A guide for preservice teacher faculty. *Journal of Special Education Preparation, 4*(2), 90–95.

Jain, R., Garg, N., & Khera, S. N. (2023). Effective human–AI work design for collaborative decision-making. *Kybernetes, 52*(11), 5017–5040.

Jantanukul, W. (2024). AI and human synergy: Utilizing AI to enhance teaching and learning. *Journal of Education and Learning Reviews, 1*(4), 1–12.

Kuerban, Y., Oyelere, S. S., & Sanusi, I. T. (2025). ReadSmart: Generative AI and Augmented Reality solution for supporting students with dyslexia learning disabilities. *International Journal of Technology in Education and Science, 9*(1), 159–176.

Latham, A., & Goltz, S. (2019). A survey of the general public's views on the ethics of using AI in education. In *Lecture Notes in Computer Science* (pp. 194–206). Springer International Publishing.

Lee, J., Hicke, Y., Yu, R., Brooks, C., & Kizilcec, R. F. (2024). The life cycle of large language models in education: A framework for understanding sources of bias. *British Journal of Educational Technology, 55*(5), 1982–2002.

Marino, M. T., Vasquez, E., Dieker, L., Basham, J., & Blackorby, J. (2023). The future of Artificial Intelligence in special education technology. *Journal of Special Education Technology, 38*(3), 404–416.

Nixon, N., Lin, Y., & Snow, L. (2024). Catalyzing equity in STEM teams: Harnessing generative AI for inclusion and diversity. *Policy Insights from the Behavioral and Brain Sciences, 11*(1), 85–92. PMID: 38516055

Noviandy, T. R., & Maulana, A., Idroes Ghazi Mauer and Zahriah, Z., Paristiowati, M., Emran, T. B., Ilyas, M., & Idroes, R. (2024). Embrace, don't avoid: Reimagining higher education with generative artificial intelligence. *J. Educ. Manag. Learn., 2*(2), 81–90.

Pagliara, S. M., Bonavolonta, G., Pia, M., Falchi, S., Zurru, A. L., Fenu, G., & Mura, A. (2024). The integration of Artificial Intelligence in inclusive education: A scoping review. In *Preprints*.

Pan, J. (2024). AI-driven English language learning program and academic writing integrity in the era of intelligent interface. *English Language Teaching and Linguistics Studies*, *6*(4), 120.

Pendy, B. (2023). Artificial Intelligence: The future of education. Jurnal Indonesia Sosial Sains, 2(11).

Pierrès, O., Christen, M., Schmitt-Koopmann, F. M., & Darvishy, A. (2024). Could the use of AI in higher education hinder students with disabilities? A scoping review. *IEEE Access : Practical Innovations, Open Solutions*, *12*, 27810–27828.

Purwanto, & Hendrawan, J. H. (2024). Smart collaboration: Improving learning achievement with Artificial Intelligence. Icasse, 1(1), 335–341.

Rizos, I., Foykas, E., & Georgakopoulos, S. V. (2024). Enhancing mathematics education for students with special educational needs through generative AI: A case study in Greece. *Contemporary Educational Technology*, *16*(4), ep535.

Rostami, M., & Longo, V. (2024). Teachers' narratives on implementing AI-based learning tools for students with severe disabilities. *The Psychological Research in Individuals with Exceptional Needs*, *2*(2), 20–27.

Samadi, M., Faculty of Educational Sciences, Psychology University of Isfahan, I., Ghamarani, A., Department of Psychology, of Children with Special Needs, F. of E. S., Psychology University of Isfahan, I., Faramarzi, S., Department of Psychology, of Children with Special Needs, F. of E. S., & Psychology University of Isfahan, I. (2020). Role of PASS cognitive processes in explaining the ability of word reading and text comprehension in children with dyslexia. *Q. J. Child Ment. Health*, *7*(2), 268–279.

Santhana Hari, S., Harine Rajashree, R., Dharani, J., & Santhiya, C. (2025). AI-enabled learning ecosystems. In *Driving Quality Education Through AI and Data Science* (pp. 165–192). IGI Global.

Santos, S. M. A. V., Da Silva, C. G., De Carvalho, I. E., De Castilho, L. P., Meroto, M. B. das N., Tavares, P. R., Pires, R. dos R., & Moniz, S. S. de O. R. (2024). The art of personalization of education: Artificial Intelligence on the stages of special education. CONTRIBUCIONES A LAS CIENCIAS SOCIALES, 17(2), e4971.

Scott, L. M., Wilder, T., Zaugg, T., & Romualdo, A. (2024). Enhancing special education using AI. In *Advances in Educational Technologies and Instructional Design* (pp. 45–78). IGI Global.

Singh, S., & Jain, P. (2024). AI in special education. In *Advanced Intelligence Systems and Innovation in Entrepreneurship* (pp. 56–75). IGI Global.

Singha, S., & Singha, R. (2024). Revolutionizing content creation and curriculum development through generative AI. In *Advances in Educational Technologies and Instructional Design* (pp. 261–280). IGI Global.

Stracke, C. M. (2024). Artificial Intelligence and education: Ethical questions and guidelines for their relations based on human rights, democracy, and the rule of law. In *Lecture Notes in Educational Technology* (pp. 97–107). Springer Nature Singapore.

Syaidina, M. O., Fahrudin, R., & Mutiara, I. A. (2024). Implementation of ethics of using Artificial Intelligence in the education system in Indonesia. *B-FronT*, *4*(1), 63–71.

Tang, K. H. D. (2024). Implications of artificial Intelligence for teaching and learning. *Acta Pedagogia Asia*, *3*(2), 65–79.

Tilak, S., Lincoln, J., Miner, T., Christensen, N., Jankowski, J., & Kennedy, K. (2024). A participatory, qualitative analysis of the use of MagicSchool AI for course design. *J. Sociocybernetics*, *19*(1).

Viberg, O., & Kizilcec, R. F., Wise Alyssa Friend and Jivet, I., & Nixon, N. (2024). Advancing equity and inclusion in educational practices with AI-powered educational decision support systems (AI-EDSS). *British Journal of Educational Technology*, *55*(5), 1974–1981.

Wallace, B. C. S., & Abel, Y. (2024). Embracing artificial intelligence (AI) tools to enrich special education teacher preparation. In *Advances in Educational Technologies and Instructional Design* (pp. 325–354). IGI Global.

Waterfield, D. A., Coleman, O. F., Welker, N. P., Kennedy, M. J., McDonald, S. D., & Cook, B. G. (2025). IEPs in the age of AI: Examining IEP goals written with and without ChatGPT. *Journal of Special Education Technology*.

Wiredu, J. K., Abuba, N. S., & Zakaria, H. (2024). Impact of Generative AI in academic integrity and learning outcomes: A case study in the Upper East Region. *Asian J. Res. Com. Sci.*, *17*(8), 70–88.

Yu, P., Lu, S., Long, Z., Chen, Y., Qian, J., & Shah, Z. A. (2024). Exploring ethical considerations in utilizing generative AI for global knowledge sharing in higher education. In *Advances in Higher Education and Professional Development* (pp. 1–27). IGI Global.

Zawacki-Richter, O., Mar\'\in, V. I., Bond, M., & Gouverneur, F. (2019). Systematic review of research on artificial intelligence applications in higher education – where are the educators? *International Journal of Educational Technology in Higher Education*, *16*(1).

Zhou, Q. (2023). How does dyslexia influence academic achievement? In *Proceedings of the 2022 2nd International Conference on Modern Educational Technology and Social Sciences (ICMETSS 2022)* (pp. 861–868). Atlantis Press SARL.

KEY TERMS AND DEFINITIONS

AI Ethics: A set of moral principles guiding the development and use of artificial intelligence to ensure fairness, transparency, and accountability.

Algorithmic Bias: Systematic errors in AI outputs due to biased training data or flawed model design that can disproportionately affect marginalized groups.

Assistive Technology (AT): Tools or systems that aid individuals with disabilities in performing functions that might otherwise be difficult or impossible.

ChatGPT (GPT Models): Generative Pre-trained Transformer models that generate human-like text, used for simplifying content and personalizing instruction.

Co-Design: A participatory design method involving end-users (students, families, educators) in the creation of tools to ensure relevance and inclusivity.

Culturally Responsive AI: AI systems designed to be aware of and reflect the cultural contexts and values of diverse learners.

DALL·E: An OpenAI model that generates images from text prompts, useful in creating personalized visual aids in education.

Digital Divide: The gap between individuals or communities with access to digital technologies and those without, impacting equitable learning opportunities.

Generative AI: A subset of artificial intelligence that creates new content text, image, audio, or video based on patterns learned from data using models like GPT, DALL·E.

Human-AI Collaboration: A paradigm where AI tools support educators without replacing them, combining human judgment with machine efficiency.

Inclusive Education: An approach ensuring all learners, regardless of abilities or disabilities, can access and participate in quality education within mainstream settings.

Neurodiversity: A concept recognizing diverse neurological conditions (e.g., autism, ADHD, dyslexia) as natural variations of the human brain.

Special Education: Tailored educational programs designed to meet the unique needs of learners with cognitive, sensory, emotional, or physical differences.

Universal Design for Learning (UDL): An educational framework that provides flexible learning environments accommodating individual learning differences across engagement, representation, and action/expression.

Whisper: An AI model from OpenAI used for automatic speech recognition (ASR), capable of transcribing spoken language into text.

Chapter 9
AI, Impostor Syndrome, and Emotional Resilience:
Rethinking SEL and Student Well-Being in Inclusive AI-Enhanced ESL Classrooms

Maria Arjie Tobias Domingo
https://orcid.org/0009-0008-9568-472X
Independent Researcher, Philippines

ABSTRACT

This book chapter explores the emotional impact of generative artificial intelligence (AI) on tertiary-level ESL learners, drawing on a mixed-methods case study conducted at a Philippine state university. While AI tools offer linguistic support and academic efficiency, they also introduce emotional risks such as doubt, dependency, and diminished self-authorship, collectively identified as AI-Induced Impostor Syndrome (AI-IIS). Through the lens of Social-Emotional Learning (SEL), the chapter analyzes how AI use affects learners' confidence, identity, and ethical decision-making. It argues that SEL is essential for fostering emotionally inclusive and psychologically safe AI integration. Practical strategies for reflection, dialogue, mentorship, and policy co-creation are offered to help educators address the emotional dimensions of AI use. By embedding SEL into design, instruction, and institutional policy, the chapter promotes a model of AI-enhanced learning where students do not merely perform well with AI, but thrive alongside it.

DOI: 10.4018/979-8-3373-3745-6.ch009

1. INTRODUCTION: THE PROMISE AND PARADOX OF AI IN SEL

Generative artificial intelligence (AI) is reshaping the way students engage with learning. For English language learners, tools like Grammarly and ChatGPT offer real-time support for writing, grammar, and organization, providing a sense of autonomy and accelerating progress. Yet beneath these benefits lies a quieter emotional tension. Students may begin to wonder whether their success reflects genuine skill or merely effective tool use. This creeping uncertainty, if left unaddressed, can erode confidence and lead to what we call AI-Induced Impostor Syndrome (AI-IIS), a phenomenon where learners feel fraudulent in their achievements due to their reliance on AI assistance.

This chapter introduces AI-IIS as a growing emotional phenomenon in tech-mediated classrooms. Drawing from a case study of ESL students at a state university in the Philippines, it frames this emotional experience not as a side effect but as central to understanding how students internalize their learning and identity in the AI age. In doing so, the chapter makes a case for integrating Social-Emotional Learning (SEL) as a foundational framework for ethical and inclusive AI implementation.

AI and the Emotional Texture of Learning

AI tools are rapidly evolving to support students in more than just content generation. Intelligent systems can adapt to individual learning needs, simulate feedback, and even detect emotional cues through affective computing (Alanazi et al., 2023; Aly et al., 2023). These developments align with pedagogical goals of differentiated instruction and learner-centered design.

However, in classrooms where feedback is increasingly automated and writing support is semi-autonomous, an important question arises: How do learners feel about the work they produce through AI support?

For many, particularly ESL learners still navigating linguistic mastery, AI can provide relief but also dependency. As students turn to AI for phrasing, coherence, and tone, they may begin to question the authenticity of their output. This uncertainty, when coupled with praise or high grades, creates an emotional contradiction: "I did well, but did I really do it?"

Such emotional dissonance is not uncommon. Research shows that learners often form complex emotional attachments to digital tools, which can shape their academic self-concept and risk perception (Deckker & Sumanasekara, 2025). When students come to see AI as the primary author of their success, their self-efficacy and their belief in their own ability to succeed can diminish.

Introducing AI-Induced Impostor Syndrome (AI-IIS)

AI-IIS is a term used to describe a learner's internal conflict when academic success is mediated by AI tools. Unlike traditional impostor syndrome, which stems from internal feelings of inadequacy despite external success (Clance & Imes, 1978), AI-IIS is externally triggered. The doubt arises not because students lack ability but because they struggle to locate that ability when AI is deeply involved in the work.

Consider Mia, an ESL student who began using AI tools to improve her essay writing. Over time, her performance improved, but so did her anxiety. "I get good grades now," she said, "but I don't feel like I earned them." Mia's story is not unique. Many learners feel detached from their accomplishments when AI becomes an invisible co-author.

Rather than building confidence, AI in these cases reinforces self-doubt, particularly when students receive praise for work that they internally perceive as not entirely their own. As Skinner et al. (2008) note, emotional engagement is essential to motivation; when students feel disconnected from the learning process, persistence and growth suffer.

SEL as a Framework for Understanding Emotional Risks

To meaningfully address AI-IIS, we must move beyond technical training and toward emotional development. This is where Social-Emotional Learning (SEL) becomes essential. Defined by the Collaborative for Academic, Social, and Emotional Learning (CASEL), SEL involves five core competencies: self-awareness, self-management, social awareness, relationship skills, and responsible decision-making.

These competencies provide a robust lens through which to understand the emotional complexities of AI-assisted learning:

- Self-awareness helps students recognize when they are overly dependent on AI tools.
- Self-management enables them to regulate the anxiety that may arise when working without AI.
- Social awareness and relationship skills equip learners to navigate AI-influenced peer dynamics and discussions.
- Responsible decision-making fosters ethical and reflective AI use.

When SEL is embedded in AI instruction, learners gain not just efficiency but emotional literacy. They can name their uncertainties, reflect on their practices, and begin to trust themselves again, even in AI-mediated contexts.

AI Use is Not Neutral, It Is Emotional

The core argument of this chapter is simple but often overlooked: AI use is not a neutral academic behavior. It is an emotionally charged experience, particularly for students whose academic identities are still in formation. Without reflection or emotional support, AI can unintentionally undermine the very autonomy it aims to promote.

This tension is especially visible in ESL settings, where language is both the tool and the terrain of learning. For students who already navigate linguistic insecurity, AI can offer temporary fluency, but without emotional grounding, that fluency may not translate into lasting confidence or self-efficacy.

Educators must therefore be attuned not only to what AI does for students, but also to how students feel about what AI does for them.

Looking Ahead

This chapter builds on this foundational insight by exploring the intersection of SEL and AI across seven chapters. Chapter 2 introduces the conceptual grounding for SEL and AI as interconnected forces in shaping academic identity. Chapter 3 presents a detailed case study of how AI-IIS manifests in real classrooms. Chapters 4 through 6 offer policy, design, and instructional recommendations for creating emotionally inclusive AI-supported learning environments. Finally, Chapter 7 returns to the larger question: What does ethical and sustainable AI integration require of us, not just as technologists, but as educators?

At the heart of this inquiry is the belief that students must not only succeed with AI; they must also feel confident, capable, and authentic while doing so.

To achieve that, we must reframe AI not as a mere writing tool but as a relational element in the classroom. And to manage that relationship, learners need SEL as both compass and anchor.

2. CONCEPTUAL FRAMING: SEL, AI, AND ACADEMIC IDENTITY

As AI tools become increasingly embedded in educational environments, their influence extends beyond academic performance to shape how students think, feel, and see themselves. Nowhere is this more visible than among English as a Second Language (ESL) learners, who often use AI not just for technical support but also as a scaffold for self-expression and understanding. While these tools offer immediate functional benefits, they also bring emotional and psychological implications that are less often addressed.

To fully understand how students experience AI integration in classrooms, this chapter draws from the Social-Emotional Learning (SEL) framework and explores how AI intersects with the development of academic identity, the evolving sense of oneself as a capable, legitimate learner. These lenses provide insight into why some students thrive with AI support, while others, like those experiencing AI-Induced Impostor Syndrome (AI-IIS), begin to question their own competence.

SEL as a Foundation for Emotional Engagement

To meaningfully address the emotional challenges posed by AI-Induced Impostor Syndrome (AI-IIS), we must look beyond tool training and consider how students interpret and internalize their learning experiences. This calls for an approach that prioritizes emotional development alongside cognitive and technical skills. Social-Emotional Learning (SEL) offers such a framework.

Rather than treating emotion as a byproduct of AI integration, SEL positions it as a central concern. It provides students with the skills to navigate uncertainty, reflect on authorship, and build confidence in their own voice, even in AI-mediated contexts. The SEL perspective invites educators to ask not just *what* students are learning with AI, but *how they feel* about that learning.

AI and the Fragile Terrain of Academic Identity

Academic identity refers to how students see themselves as learners and how confident, capable, and authentic they feel in relation to their academic output. For ESL students, this identity is often in flux, shaped by linguistic challenges, cultural adaptation, and teacher feedback.

AI tools can both support and disrupt this identity formation. On the one hand, AI offers scaffolding that improves fluency, coherence, and clarity. On the other, it can raise doubts: Am I improving, or is the tool doing the thinking for me?

Students in the AI-IIS study frequently voiced these concerns. One noted, "My grades are better, but I don't feel smarter; just more dependent." This reflects a breakdown in self-attribution, a core element of academic identity. When students cannot trace their success to their own effort or understanding, confidence suffers.

This aligns with findings from Zunaidah et al. (2023), who observed that AI-enhanced learning can lead to internal disconnection when students feel alienated from their own output. SEL helps address this by encouraging learners to reflect on how AI supports rather than replaces their learning.

Competency Misalignments: Where AI and SEL Clash

The AI-IIS study highlighted specific SEL breakdowns tied to unscaffolded AI use:

- Self-awareness deficits: Students cannot always distinguish between using an AI productively and relying on it excessively.
- Poor self-management: Some experienced emotional shutdown when asked to complete tasks without AI, indicating low emotional regulation.
- Social friction: Peer comparison became more acute, not less, as students judged each other based on AI fluency rather than effort or originality.
- Unclear ethical boundaries: Several students admitted they were not sure whether their AI use was "too much," leading to secrecy and guilt.

These struggles were not caused by AI itself, but by a lack of emotional and instructional scaffolding around its use. When AI is introduced without reflective frameworks, students are left to interpret their experiences in isolation, often defaulting to negative self-assessments.

Classroom Culture and the Silence Around AI Use

Another key insight from the study was the lack of open discourse around AI use. Many students reported not discussing their AI experiences with classmates or teachers. Some feared judgment, while others assumed they were the only ones struggling. This silence can be emotionally isolating.

A strong SEL culture addresses this by normalizing reflection and dialogue. When students are invited to talk about how AI impacts their writing, thinking, and confidence, they gain emotional clarity and collective insight. Peer discussions foster empathy, reduce comparison-based anxiety, and reinforce shared norms for responsible AI use.

As Oberle et al. (2016) note, SEL thrives in communities where emotional experiences are seen as valid and discussable. In AI-mediated classrooms, this culture is essential not just for emotional safety but for ethical literacy and collaborative growth.

Toward Alignment: Embedding SEL in AI Use

To bridge the gap between AI's cognitive benefits and its emotional costs, educators must embed SEL intentionally into AI-integrated learning. This means:

- Framing AI as a supportive partner, not a replacement.
- Encouraging students to reflect on authorship, identity, and self-trust.

- Designing assignments that reward process and metacognition, not just polished output.
- Creating transparent classroom norms around AI use to reduce guilt and uncertainty.

When SEL is not part of the conversation, students interpret their experiences through silence, assumption, or shame. When SEL is centered, students are equipped to approach AI use with curiosity, responsibility, and self-awareness.

Conclusion

This chapter has framed the intersection of AI and academic identity through the lens of SEL. The AI-IIS case study shows that learners' emotional responses to AI are not incidental; they shape how students see themselves, how they make decisions, and how they grow.

By mapping SEL competencies onto AI use, educators can identify where support is needed and how to scaffold student development, not just technically, but emotionally. In doing so, we shift the conversation from "How do we use AI in classrooms?" to "How do we ensure students remain whole, reflective, and empowered while using it?"

The next chapter puts these ideas into action, presenting the AI-IIS case study in depth, offering real student voices and emotional patterns that ground this conceptual framing in classroom reality.

3. CASE STUDY: AI-INDUCED IMPOSTOR SYNDROME IN ESL CLASSROOMS

As AI tools become more integrated into academic practice, they shape not only how students learn but also how they perceive themselves as learners. To understand this complex dynamic, a mixed-methods study was conducted at a state university in the Philippines, focusing on tertiary-level English as a Second Language (ESL) students. The study explored how AI-assisted writing influences students' confidence, self-perception, and emotional well-being, especially in light of increasing concerns about AI-induced impostor syndrome (Domingo, 2025).

In total, 200 students participated. Using a custom-designed AI-Induced Impostor Syndrome (AI-IIS) scale and follow-up semi-structured interviews, the study examined the nuanced emotional terrain of AI use in writing tasks. While AI tools such as ChatGPT and Grammarly were widely used and often helpful (Balatero et al., 2024; Calma et al., 2022), they also triggered patterns of self-doubt, diminished self-efficacy, and emotional disconnection; the hallmarks of the impostor phenomenon (Clance & Imes, 1978; Ménard & Chittle, 2023).

Study Design and Purpose

This study combined quantitative and qualitative approaches. The AI-IIS scale measured emotional responses to AI use, such as feelings of inauthenticity, anxiety about independent work, and fear of being "found out" for submitting AI-supported assignments. These dimensions are consistent with earlier frameworks on impostor syndrome and its links to academic performance and mental health (Yang et al., 2024; Paul et al., 2024). The interviews offered deeper insight into how students interpreted their experiences, navigated the tension between achievement and authorship, and developed coping strategies.

The goal was not to critique the use of AI per se, but to understand its emotional implications and identify what kinds of support learners need to feel competent and authentic in increasingly AI-mediated classrooms. Similar concerns have been echoed in recent literature emphasizing the emotional and ethical implications of AI reliance in academic contexts (Chan & Hu, 2023; Coldwell, 2024).

Emotional Patterns in AI Use

a. Doubt in Authorship and Self-Attribution

Across the dataset, a large proportion of students reported uncertainty about the legitimacy of their accomplishments. Many shared sentiments like, "*I'm not sure if I did well because of me or because of the tool.*" Despite grade improvements, confidence faltered, illustrating a gap between performance and perceived competence.

This doubt points to a misalignment in self-awareness—a key SEL competency. When students are unable to trace their success to personal effort, they experience emotional friction between performance and identity. Rather than reinforcing growth, AI begins to obscure it. It reflects Bandura's (1977) theory of self-efficacy: when students cannot attribute success to their own effort or ability, their belief in their academic agency weakens.

Further, several students admitted to revising AI-generated suggestions without understanding them. As Domingo and Lintao (2025) note, such uncritical acceptance of AI feedback can mask knowledge gaps, hindering metacognitive growth. These learners were learning *through* AI rather than *with* it, creating an illusion of competence while weakening self-awareness, a core component of social-emotional learning (CASEL, 2024).

b. Anxiety and Avoidance Without AI

Some students shared that they actively avoided assignments that restricted AI use. These learners expressed heightened anxiety when faced with independent writing tasks. For them, AI had become more than a support—it was a necessary safety net. This aligns with findings from Zhai et al. (2024), who warn that habitual reliance on AI can impair students' cognitive engagement and reduce their problem-solving confidence.

This reflects struggles in self-management. The inability to regulate anxiety when working without digital aid can indicate overdependence, central to the self-management domain in SEL (Belay & Dejene, 2024). These students had come to associate competence with AI availability. Without it, they felt exposed and inadequate.

Rather than developing flexible coping mechanisms, they clung to AI as a means of emotional protection. In SEL terms, this suggests a need for better scaffolding in emotional regulation and adaptability. As noted by Zhang et al. (2024), over-reliance on AI tools correlates with academic stress and diminished self-efficacy, often driving students to perceive AI as an emotional safety net rather than a cognitive aid.

c. Emotional Distance from Peer Interaction

The use of AI also affected how students engaged with one another. Several participants noted that they felt reluctant to share or compare work, especially if they relied heavily on AI. They feared judgment, not only for quality but for perceived inauthenticity. Chan (2024) describes this as "AI guilt," wherein students feel internal conflict about the legitimacy of their academic efforts. This introduced new pressures around peer dynamics.

In classrooms where AI use was inconsistently discussed or modeled, students often assumed they were either overusing or underusing it compared to their peers. This led to discomfort, comparison, and social withdrawal.

Such dynamics impair social awareness and relationship skills, especially when AI use becomes a silent, isolating behavior (Escalante et al., 2023). One student said, *"I felt like I was cheating, but I didn't know who to talk to about it."* The absence of shared norms or emotional discourse around AI left students to interpret their actions in isolation.

d. Positive AI Engagement and Metacognitive Growth

Encouragingly, not all students experienced impostor syndrome. Some viewed AI as a helpful partner—using it to brainstorm ideas, refine grammar, or check tone, while still making deliberate decisions about content and structure. These students engaged critically with AI suggestions and described feeling more confident, not less. According to Bećirović et al. (2025), this reflective stance enhances both output quality and learners' sense of self-efficacy.

"I use it for feedback," one student explained, *"but I still revise things based on what I want to say. It's more like a second opinion."*

These learners demonstrated SEL strengths: self-awareness, responsible decision-making, and a sense of authorship. They described learning with AI rather than through it. Their success felt authentic because they could clearly identify their own contribution.

What set these students apart was not their technical skill, but their reflective stance. They questioned AI output, compared it with their intent, and made purposeful decisions. They were not simply accepting feedback. They were engaging in metacognitive dialogue with the tool. As noted by Kim and Tan (2023), when learners treat AI as a tutor rather than a crutch, they gain not only technical benefits but also confidence and clarity in their authorship.

Key Takeaways: AI's Emotional Footprint

This case study reveals that AI tools carry an emotional footprint. They are not just cognitive supports but emotional actors in the learning process. Students do not interact with AI in a vacuum but within a web of academic expectations, identity formation, peer dynamics, and personal goals.

When AI is introduced without emotional scaffolding, students may internalize negative narratives about themselves (Giray, 2024). They may attribute success to machines, suppress confusion or guilt, and silently disengage from the learning process.

On the other hand, when AI is framed as a thinking partner, when students are invited to reflect, question, and adapt, it becomes a source of empowerment rather than alienation (Ji et al., 2025; Greenwald et al., 2024). The key difference lies not in the tool itself, but in the emotional and pedagogical context in which it is used.

Coping Strategies Students Use (and Need)

Interview data revealed organic coping strategies that students used to manage emotional tension:

- **Selective application of AI feedback**: Choosing when to accept or reject suggestions, helping preserve voice and agency.
- **Time management**: Allocating time to revise both with and without AI, reducing dependency, and building confidence.

- **Quiet peer support**: Confiding in trusted classmates to normalize uncertainty and share strategies.

These strategies echo SEL principles, even when informally practiced. What they lack, however, is systematic institutional support. Without formal space to reflect or discuss, students develop these coping methods in silence, which limits their reach and sustainability (Zulvi & Abidin, 2025).

Implications for Educators

Findings suggest that SEL must be embedded into AI-related instruction. In line with Domingo (2025) and Bećirović et al. (2025), educators should:

- Encourage reflection on AI use not just in terms of functionality, but impact on confidence, authorship, and identity.
- Normalize ethical and emotional discussion around AI (Navales, 2024), making room for uncertainty without judgment.
- Provide clear guidelines to reduce the shame or secrecy surrounding AI reliance (Gustilo et al., 2024).
- Reward reflective practices in assessments to reinforce metacognitive ownership (Darvishi et al., 2023).

Most importantly, teachers must recognize that students' emotional responses to AI are as important as their academic outcomes. Confidence, clarity, and a sense of authorship are not guaranteed by tool access; they must be cultivated through intentional practice.

Conclusion

The AI-IIS case study highlights how ESL learners' emotional landscapes are deeply shaped by their interactions with AI. These tools, while enabling linguistic and academic productivity, can also foster self-doubt, dependency, and disconnection. As Domingo (2025) emphasizes, the challenge lies not in whether students use AI, but in how they emotionally and cognitively engage with it.

By understanding the patterns of AI-IIS and the emotional struggles students face, educators can begin designing classrooms where AI serves as a bridge, not a barrier, to authentic learning and identity development.

The next chapter builds on this understanding, exploring the emotional risks of uncritical AI integration and why SEL must accompany, not follow, technological innovation.

4. EMOTIONAL RISKS OF UNCRITICAL AI INTEGRATION

As artificial intelligence becomes more embedded in classroom practice, educators are increasingly aware of its academic potential. Yet alongside its promise, AI also brings psychological and emotional consequences that are often underestimated or entirely overlooked (Coldwell, 2024). These consequences extend beyond academic performance; they shape how learners view their thinking, their voice, and their sense of belonging in the learning environment (Domingo, 2025; Bećirović et al., 2025).

This chapter explores the emotional risks associated with uncritical AI integration, using insights drawn from the AI-IIS study. When AI tools are introduced without reflection, scaffolding, or explicit norms, students may experience confusion, emotional disengagement, and diminished self-trust, particularly ESL learners whose confidence in linguistic competence is often fragile and developing (Calonia et al., 2023; Gustilo et al., 2024). These dynamics can quietly undermine academic identity, especially for ESL learners, whose relationship with language, confidence, and authorship is already in flux.

To ensure that AI enhances rather than erodes inclusive learning, it must be paired with intentional emotional design. This means understanding not only what students do with AI but also how they feel while doing it and why that matters.

Overreliance and the Disruption of Self-Trust

One of the most common emotional patterns observed in the AI-IIS study was overreliance on AI tools for generating or refining written content. While students acknowledged that AI helped improve grammar, organization, or tone, many became hesitant to write independently. They waited for AI confirmation before submitting work or felt uncomfortable unless AI had reviewed it first. This overreliance reflects a troubling erosion of self-efficacy and decision-making autonomy (Bandura, 1997; Zhang et al., 2024).

This behavior signaled a decline in self-trust. Students began to perceive the tool, not their judgment, as the final authority on quality. One participant said, "I don't feel confident turning in anything unless AI has seen it." Such sentiments reveal how AI can undermine learners' belief in their competence, a phenomenon that aligns with what Domingo (2025) terms confidence displacement, a psychological effect where external tools override internal validation systems.

This emotional dependence speaks to a breakdown in self-awareness and self-efficacy where students struggle to distinguish their voice from the AI's and to believe in their unaided capabilities. While AI improves technical accuracy, it may inadvertently impair the learner's internal sense of authorship. This is particularly salient for ESL students who already face linguistic insecurity and whose writing skills are tightly tied to identity (Greenwald et al., 2024).

As Zhai et al. (2024) argue, while AI enhances surface-level writing performance, it can obscure the deeper cognitive growth necessary for authentic learning when not paired with reflective practice. In such cases, students may appear proficient but feel internally hollow, uncertain of whether the success is genuinely theirs.

Educators must recognize that the risk is not just overuse of a tool. It is the erosion of the learner's belief in themselves as capable thinkers.

Disconnection from Authorship and Authenticity

Several students in the study reported feeling a persistent discomfort with their AI-enhanced work. Even when they received positive feedback or high marks, they questioned whether the work truly represented their ability. One student described it as "submitting something that looked like mine but didn't feel like mine."

This disconnection from one's own academic product, what we might call an authorship gap, is one of the most insidious emotional consequences of unexamined AI use. Students feel like actors in their own work, unsure of where the AI ends and they begin. Despite high marks or praise, participants shared that their final submissions felt "inauthentic" or "detached" from their true voice. This aligns with what Chan (2024) identifies as "AI-authorship dissonance", where learners struggle to reconcile the ease of producing polished outputs with the absence of personal ownership.

These concerns are compounded when educators assess final outputs without asking students to reflect on their process. In educational contexts that do not encourage metacognitive reflection on AI use, students may misattribute their success, leading to feelings of impostorism even when they perform well (Clance & Imes, 1978; Ménard & Chittle, 2023). As Bećirović et al. (2025) emphasize, authenticity is not just about origin. It is about alignment between intention, effort, and outcome. Without that alignment, even good work can feel illegitimate.

This phenomenon is exacerbated when assessments focus solely on output without evaluating the writing process. As Paul et al. (2024) point out, emotional dissonance arises when students achieve results through tools they do not fully understand or trust. Thus, authorship must be reframed as a dynamic and shared process. AI's ability to polish output must be balanced with instructional practices that restore the learner's sense of ownership.

Ambiguity in AI Feedback and Emotional Frustration

AI-generated feedback, often praised for its immediacy, was described by many students as vague, inconsistent, or unexplainable. Suggestions like "improve clarity" or "rephrase for tone" lacked the pedagogical specificity needed for ESL learners to improve their understanding. As a result, students either accepted changes without comprehension or rejected suggestions out of confusion, both of which stifle learning (Domingo & Lintao, 2025; Ji et al., 2025).

This led to frustration and, over time, self-doubt. As one student shared: "Sometimes it fixes things I don't think are wrong. Then I started to question if I really understood English."

Rather than supporting learning, ambiguous AI feedback can generate confusion, especially for language learners who depend on AI to validate linguistic choices. When feedback is hard to decode, students may accept it blindly or reject it without understanding the implications.

In SEL terms, this ambiguity disrupts self-awareness and self-management—two core competencies that help learners regulate emotions and interpret feedback constructively (CASEL, 2024). If students cannot make sense of the feedback they receive, their confidence diminishes, and they become more dependent on external judgment (Zhang et al., 2024).

In either case, the emotional outcome is the same: increased uncertainty, reduced agency, and a reliance on external judgment. Effective feedback, whether from a human or an AI, should build clarity and confidence. When it does not, it introduces emotional noise rather than academic support.

Peer Comparison and the Pressure of Digital Proficiency

AI integration also introduces new forms of classroom stratification. Students in the AI-IIS study described noticing differences in how their peers used AI. Some classmates were adept at generating content, refining arguments, or using premium features; others struggled to prompt the tool effectively or felt left behind.

This dynamic of AI as a hidden performance enhancer intensified social comparison. Students worried that they weren't using AI "the right way," or that their peers' better results were due to superior tool fluency rather than skill. In this way, AI didn't level the playing field—it redrew it.

One student noted: "It's not just about who writes well anymore. It's about who knows how to get AI to do it well for them."

This shift redefines classroom hierarchies in ways that are emotionally charged. Students may feel inadequate not because of their ability, but because of their comparative inexperience with AI. Without open discussions and shared norms,

AI becomes another axis of inequity, reinforcing rather than reducing feelings of inadequacy (Escalante et al., 2023).

The Cost of Silence: When AI Use Is Hidden

Perhaps the most damaging emotional pattern in the study was the widespread silence around AI use. Students were often unsure if using AI was acceptable, and many felt they had to hide how much they relied on it. Even when institutional guidelines permitted AI assistance, the lack of emotional validation made students feel guilty or secretive.

This secrecy creates a climate of emotional isolation. Students hesitate to ask questions, share concerns, or admit uncertainty. As one participant said, "I didn't want to talk about it, because I didn't know if I was doing something wrong."

In SEL terms, this represents a breakdown in social awareness and responsible decision-making, not due to poor character, but due to unclear structures. When AI use is discussed only in terms of plagiarism or performance, students are left to navigate emotional and ethical gray areas on their own.

Open, reflective dialogue around AI use is not an extra; it is essential for building a culture of integrity and psychological safety. Students should not have to choose between using a helpful tool and hiding their use of it to avoid emotional or academic penalties. As Chan and Hu (2023) argue, transparency must be cultivated through institutional structures that validate emotional complexity rather than enforce binary rules.

The Need for Emotional Infrastructure

The emotional risks of uncritical AI integration, overreliance, authorship dissonance, feedback ambiguity, peer pressure, and secrecy do not stem from AI itself but from its pedagogical vacuum. Without explicit emotional scaffolding, AI use risks eroding learners' confidence, authorship, and self-awareness.

To counter these risks, AI must be embedded in environments that promote Social-Emotional Learning. This includes:

- Requiring students to write brief reflections on how AI contributed to their writing and what they learned from using it (Domingo, 2025).
- Creating safe classroom spaces for peer dialogue about successes and frustrations with AI (Bećirović et al., 2025).
- Normalizing ambivalence as a legitimate emotional response to emerging technologies (Greenwald et al., 2024).

- Framing authorship as a dynamic process involving collaboration, intention, and reflection, not a binary of "machine-made" vs. "human-made" (Navales, 2024).

In short, AI literacy must include emotional literacy. Students need relational frameworks, not just technical guidelines, to process their experiences with integrity and clarity.

Conclusion

Uncritical AI integration does more than create instructional gaps. It introduces emotional dissonance that can quietly derail learning. As the AI-IIS study shows, when students do not understand how AI affects their identity, when they feel uncertain about its use, or when they mistrust their own contributions, the emotional cost becomes unsustainable.

Social-Emotional Learning is the necessary counterbalance. It equips students to interpret their AI use with honesty, confidence, and clarity. It helps teachers recognize distress not just in student performance, but in their process and posture. And it ensures that as AI continues to evolve, education remains fundamentally human-centered.

The next chapter turns from diagnosis to design, offering a vision for inclusive, emotionally responsive AI tools and policies that put student well-being at the center of innovation.

5. TOWARD INCLUSIVE, EMOTIONALLY-RESPONSIVE AI DESIGN AND POLICY

As artificial intelligence becomes more deeply woven into education, questions of access and utility are no longer enough. True inclusion requires that we move beyond what AI can do for students, toward how students experience themselves in relation to it. For ESL learners, in particular, who already navigate linguistic and cultural transitions, the integration of AI introduces new complexities around voice, identity, and authorship.

This chapter builds on the emotional patterns identified in the AI-IIS study by offering a set of forward-looking recommendations for the design and governance of emotionally responsive AI systems. These recommendations are rooted in the belief that inclusive AI is not simply about giving more students more tools; it is about building ecosystems that acknowledge emotional labor, support reflection, and foster resilience.

Reframing Inclusion: From Technical Access to Emotional Equity

Educational inclusion has often been defined in terms of device availability, connectivity, or access to tools. However, emotional inclusion means that all students, not just the digitally fluent or confident, can engage with AI in ways that reinforce their sense of competence, authenticity, and growth.

The AI-IIS study showed that students' emotional responses to AI use varied widely, and these variations were not based on skill alone. Students who felt disconnected from their work, or who questioned whether they had truly "earned" their success, were often those without structures for reflection or emotional support. These students did not need more tools; they needed more human-centered design and policy.

Inclusive AI must therefore be understood not only as a technological goal but as an ethical and emotional imperative.

Designing for Emotional Reflection: SEL Dashboards

Most AI platforms track metrics like time-on-task or completion rates. But few systems are designed to track or even acknowledge the emotional experience of learning. An emotionally responsive approach would include SEL-integrated dashboards that allow students to reflect on their relationship with AI as part of the learning process.

These dashboards could include features like:

- Emotional check-ins ("How confident do you feel about this draft?")
- Metacognitive prompts ("Which AI suggestion did you find helpful or confusing?")
- Self-assessment ratings ("What part of the work reflects your own effort most?")

This kind of emotional data helps students develop self-awareness and responsible decision-making, two core SEL competencies. It also provides teachers with valuable insight into student engagement beyond surface-level performance.

Crucially, these tools should not be used to evaluate students, but to empower them. When students reflect on how AI shapes their learning, they are more likely to see themselves as active participants rather than passive recipients.

Such features enhance core SEL competencies like self-awareness and responsible decision-making (Rout, 2024; Belay & Dejene, 2024). Importantly, they should serve formative, not evaluative, functions. In this way, dashboards empower students to better navigate the emotional dynamics of co-authoring with AI (Mohammed & Khalid, 2025; Ji et al., 2025).

Embedding Metacognitive Prompts into AI Interfaces

One of the simplest but most powerful design interventions is to integrate reflective prompts directly into AI workflows. Rather than focusing solely on output, emotionally responsive platforms should ask questions that interrupt automation and encourage conscious engagement.

Examples might include:

- "Why did you choose to accept or reject this AI suggestion?"
- "What would you do differently if completing this task without AI?"
- "What part of this work do you feel most confident about, and why?"

These questions promote not only metacognition but also authorship ethics, a concern echoed in recent studies where students expressed confusion and guilt about the boundaries of acceptable AI use (Chan, 2024; Coldwell, 2024).

By embedding reflection into the tool itself, we normalize emotional and ethical awareness as part of AI use, rather than an afterthought.

Teacher SEL Training for Emotionally Responsive Classrooms

While design matters, it is ultimately educators who frame how students interpret and engage with AI. The AI-IIS study revealed that teachers played a pivotal role in either validating or overlooking students' emotional responses to AI use. In most cases, this role was implicit rather than structured.

To build emotionally inclusive classrooms, schools must invest in SEL-based professional development for teachers, with an emphasis on:

- Recognizing signs of AI-related anxiety or disconnection
- Facilitating open discussions around authorship and identity
- Guiding students in attribution and responsible tool use
- Modeling reflective practices in their own use of AI (e.g., lesson planning or assessment)

As Davis et al. (2022) argue, emotionally intelligent teaching is not just about managing students' feelings; it's about creating relational conditions for learning. Teachers need space to explore their own evolving roles in AI-mediated classrooms and to develop strategies that blend emotional and digital literacy.

Co-Authoring Policy: Transparency Without Punishment

Another significant insight from the AI-IIS study was the silent uncertainty surrounding permissible AI use. Many students, particularly ESL learners, feared that revealing their AI-assisted processes might brand them as dishonest, even when used ethically (Domingo, 2025; Yang et al., 2024).

To counter this, institutions should embrace transparency-centered policies that decriminalize AI use and foster self-disclosure. For example, AI-use declarations in assignments could ask:

- Which tools were used, and for what purposes?
- How did students determine what to keep or revise?
- What learning resulted from interacting with AI?

These declarations shift the narrative from compliance to co-authorship, reinforcing ethical confidence and reflective practice (Rasul et al., 2024; Algorani & Gupta, 2023). Over time, they also foster ethical confidence, reinforcing the idea that responsible AI use is not something to be ashamed of; it is something to be developed through practice.

This approach also addresses a more profound need: students want to be seen not just for their polished output, but for the choices and efforts behind it.

Rethinking Equity in the AI Age

Finally, inclusive AI policy must confront the emotional inequalities that technology can amplify. Students with higher digital fluency or better access to advanced tools often gain a silent advantage, while others struggle not due to lack of intellect, but due to gaps in familiarity, confidence, or guidance.

Equity in AI integration must therefore include:

- Peer mentorship for reflective and ethical AI use (Ji et al., 2025)
- Scaffolded AI instruction that moves from guided to autonomous use (Lipovec, 2024)
- Student-partnered norm-setting on AI ethics (Domingo & Lintao, 2025)

Such interventions are not just instructional strategies. They are acts of institutional care affirming that emotional safety and cognitive challenge must coexist for AI integration to be genuinely inclusive (Bećirović et al., 2025; Elstad & Eriksen, 2024).

Conclusion

As this chapter has argued, designing AI systems and policies without emotional consideration leads to quiet but profound harm. Students may succeed outwardly but feel disconnected from their work; they may use powerful tools but feel powerless in the process. If inclusion is our goal, then the AI-enhanced learning environment must be designed not only for cognitive output but for emotional integrity.

Emotionally responsive AI integration:

- Centers the learner's experience, not just the product
- Invites reflection, rather than silent compliance
- Encourages openness, not guilt
- Reinforces identity and agency, rather than outsourcing them

By embedding SEL principles into the very design and governance of AI in education, we ensure that students are not only equipped to work with AI but also prepared to understand and affirm themselves within it.

The next chapter turns to concrete classroom practices, translating these design principles into daily strategies for educators who want to support learners emotionally as well as academically in AI-mediated spaces.

6. RECOMMENDATIONS FOR PRACTICE

Designing emotionally responsive AI systems is only part of the solution. For the benefits of such design to be fully realized, educators and institutions must implement classroom-level practices that align with the emotional and ethical dimensions of AI use. The findings of the AI-Induced Impostor Syndrome (AI-IIS) study make it clear: technical access alone does not ensure emotional inclusion. Students need support structures that encourage reflection, reduce secrecy, and promote confident, authentic engagement with AI.

This chapter translates those findings into five concrete recommendations that educators can adopt to foster emotionally inclusive, AI-enhanced learning environments. These practices are not complex or resource-intensive. What they require is intentionality—a commitment to helping students reflect on how AI shapes their learning, their identity, and their confidence.

Use AI-Reflection Logs to Support Self-Awareness

A recurring theme in the AI-IIS study was students' uncertainty about the extent and impact of their AI use. Some felt they had relied too heavily on the tool but had no space to reflect on that feeling. Others questioned whether their success was "theirs" but kept those doubts private.

To address this, educators can introduce AI-use reflection logs—short, guided prompts attached to assignments that invite students to reflect on the role AI played in their process. These logs might ask:

- At what stage did you use AI in this task?
- How did AI influence your thinking or structure?
- Did the tool increase or reduce your confidence in the final product?
- What decisions did you make independently?

Reflection logs reinforce self-awareness and responsible decision-making, both central to SEL. They allow students to recognize patterns in their AI use and begin to develop internal criteria for when and how to engage with digital assistance. Just as importantly, they help students see their own thinking more clearly—an essential step toward reclaiming authorship.

These logs can also serve a formative function for teachers, who gain insight into students' emotional and ethical experiences, not just their outputs.

Facilitate Peer Dialogue to Normalize Emotional Responses

The AI-IIS study revealed that many students were navigating their emotional responses to AI in isolation. Uncertain about what counted as "too much" AI use, they avoided asking questions or sharing concerns. This silence reinforced feelings of shame and inauthenticity.

Classrooms must actively disrupt this isolation. One of the most effective ways to do so is by creating structured opportunities for peer dialogue. Educators might dedicate time to:

- Small-group conversations about AI's impact on confidence and authorship
- Class-wide ethical debates on responsible AI use
- Journaling exchanges where students share strategies, doubts, or successes
- Case study discussions drawn from real or fictional classroom scenarios

These dialogues help develop social awareness and relationship skills while fostering a climate of emotional openness. When students learn that others share their uncertainties or use AI in similar ways, their experience becomes normalized, and shame is replaced with reflection.

Dialogue also builds collective intelligence. Students bring different levels of digital fluency, cultural background, and ethical reasoning to the table. Peer exchange allows them to learn not only about AI, but also about how others think and feel in response to it.

Establish Peer Mentorship Around Healthy AI Use

In many learning environments, the most effective AI users are not always the most experienced students, but those who have experimented, made mistakes, and learned from them. These students can serve as powerful guides for their peers.

Institutions should consider establishing peer mentorship systems in which more confident students support others in developing both the technical and emotional aspects of AI use. This might take the form of:

- Optional “AI Lab” sessions led by trained student mentors
- In-class co-writing activities where mentors model transparent AI engagement
- Peer reviews that include discussion of process, not just product

Mentorship fosters a sense of belonging and reduces the stigma around asking for help. It also models emotionally intelligent AI use, showing learners how to approach tools with curiosity, caution, and critical thinking.

As Vygotsky’s social development theory suggests, learning is enhanced through interaction with a “more knowledgeable other.” In the case of AI, mentorship offers both emotional modeling and technical insight.

Co-Create AI Use Norms With Students

Another key insight from the AI-IIS study was that students’ uncertainty about classroom expectations led to emotional stress. Without clear guidance, they were unsure how much AI use was acceptable—or if any use was allowed at all. This ambiguity increased guilt and secrecy.

To address this, educators can work with students to co-develop classroom norms around AI use. This collaborative process can include:

- Group discussions on the purpose of AI in the course
- Agreements on when and how AI may be used in different types of tasks
- Shared definitions of authorship, originality, and transparency
- Norms for peer feedback and respectful dialogue about tool use

This participatory approach fosters both accountability and emotional safety. Students are more likely to follow guidelines they had a role in shaping, and they are better equipped to apply them flexibly and ethically.

Co-authored policies shift the tone from surveillance to trust. Rather than fearing punitive consequences, students begin to see ethical AI use as a shared value—a cornerstone of academic integrity, not just a compliance task.

Invest in SEL-Infused Professional Development for Educators

Emotionally responsive practice depends not only on student behavior but on educator preparation. Many teachers in the AI-IIS study expressed uncertainty about how to address students' emotional reactions to AI. They knew students were using these tools, but not how those tools were shaping self-perception, confidence, or ethical reasoning.

To close this gap, schools must prioritize professional development that integrates SEL and AI pedagogy. This training should support educators in:

- Recognizing emotional distress linked to AI use
- Facilitating class conversations about doubt, identity, and digital authorship
- Offering process-oriented feedback that affirms student agency
- Modeling reflective AI use in their own instructional practice

Teachers should not be expected to act as therapists. But they do need language, strategies, and insight into the emotional dimensions of AI-mediated learning. When equipped with SEL tools, they are better able to support not just what students produce, but *how students feel* while producing it.

Moreover, SEL-informed training benefits teachers themselves. As AI shifts roles and expectations in the profession, educators also navigate uncertainty. Training should create space for their reflection, resilience, and growth as digital pedagogy evolves.

Conclusion

The emotional risks associated with unexamined AI use are real, but so are the opportunities for growth, connection, and confidence when AI is framed intentionally. This chapter has outlined five practical, research-informed recommendations that do not require significant infrastructure, new technology, or drastic policy shifts.

What they require is attention to emotion and a commitment to helping students build self-awareness, voice, and integrity alongside technical skill.

By adopting reflection logs, promoting dialogue, fostering mentorship, co-authoring norms, and investing in teacher preparation, we ensure that learners are not just using AI but *learning through and about themselves* while doing so.

As educators, the question is no longer whether AI belongs in the classroom. It does. The question is: What kind of emotional culture will surround it? These recommendations offer a roadmap for building that culture. One that honors the learner as a whole person, not just a producer of outcomes.

The final chapter brings this inquiry to a close, highlighting why SEL is not just helpful but essential for ethical, inclusive, and sustainable AI integration.

7. SEL AS THE MISSING LINK IN INCLUSIVE AI INTEGRATION

Artificial intelligence is no longer an emerging concept in education—it is a presence. From grammar correction to essay generation, feedback provision to idea scaffolding, AI now occupies the same academic space once reserved for teachers, peers, and individual effort. However, while the educational value of AI has been widely celebrated, its emotional consequences have remained underexplored. As this study on AI-Induced Impostor Syndrome (AI-IIS) demonstrates, these consequences are not peripheral; they are foundational.

This book chapter has argued that to truly integrate AI in inclusive, ethical, and sustainable ways, we must foreground Social-Emotional Learning (SEL). SEL is not an optional soft skill or a parallel track to technical instruction. It is the lens through which students make meaning of their academic experiences, especially in AI-enhanced classrooms where authorship, identity, and self-efficacy are increasingly ambiguous.

In this final section, we reflect on how SEL bridges the emotional gaps that uncritical AI use can create, and why SEL must be positioned at the heart of educational innovation, not behind it.

AI Alone Is Not Inclusive

Access to AI tools is often framed as a step toward educational equity. In many ways, it is. Generative AI can help level the playing field for students who struggle with language fluency, organization, or content generation. Tools like ChatGPT, Grammarly, and DeepL support personalized learning by offering real-time feedback, enhancing productivity, and scaffolding complex writing tasks (Greenwald et al., 2024; Zhang et al., 2024). It can personalize feedback and reduce turnaround time for revision. It can boost productivity, ease cognitive load, and improve academic performance.

However, as this chapter has shown, these benefits can also carry emotional costs. When students begin to doubt the legitimacy of their own work, feel ashamed about tool use, or lose confidence in their independent skills, the learning process is compromised. Inclusion that addresses only technological access, while ignoring emotional access, leaves students disconnected from their own progress.

True inclusion requires environments where students feel safe to ask questions, reflect on their choices, and maintain authorship over their learning (Bećirović et al., 2025) regardless of whether AI tools are involved. If students feel isolated, inauthentic, or afraid to ask for help, they are not experiencing inclusive education.

SEL as the Bridge Between Tool and Identity

SEL competencies, self-awareness, self-management, social awareness, relationship skills, and responsible decision-making provide the structure students need to engage with AI in reflective, ethical, and emotionally grounded ways.

Across the chapters of this book, we have seen how these competencies translate into concrete classroom realities:

- Self-awareness allows students to recognize when they are using AI as a support versus a substitute.
- Self-management enables learners to cope with the anxiety that arises from AI overuse or perceived dependence.
- Social awareness helps students navigate peer dynamics in environments where AI use is variable and often invisible.
- Relationship skills encourage open dialogue about shared norms, ethical concerns, and emotional responses to AI.
- Responsible decision-making guides students in discerning when and how to use AI in ways that align with their values and academic goals.

Without these competencies, students are more likely to internalize shame, disengage emotionally, or misuse tools without understanding the long-term impact. With them, students are more likely to see themselves not as users of AI but as authors of their learning journey.

The Role of Educators and Institutions

While students are at the center of AI-mediated learning, they cannot navigate its complexity alone. Educators, administrators, and institutions have a critical role to play in shaping emotionally inclusive AI environments.

This study has highlighted five key areas of practice:

- **Reflection**: Encouraging metacognitive inquiry into how AI influences learning and identity.
- **Dialogue**: Normalizing conversations about doubt, ethics, and authorship in peer and classroom settings.
- **Mentorship**: Establishing peer-led support systems for emotionally and technically healthy AI use.
- **Shared Policy:** Co-creating classroom norms that define responsible use and reduce secrecy.
- **SEL Training:** Equipping educators with the tools to recognize and respond to emotional distress linked to AI.

When these practices are embedded at every level, from lesson planning to institutional policy, AI integration becomes more than functional. It becomes human-centered.

Rethinking Success in the AI Era

One of the most urgent messages of the AI-IIS study is that students' success must be measured not only by academic output but also by emotional alignment. A student who produces a flawless essay with AI but feels like a fraud is not succeeding. A student who earns an A but fears their competence is hollow is not empowered.

In the AI era, success must be redefined to include confidence, authorship, and emotional integrity. This shift requires assessment models that reward reflection and process, not just product. It requires teaching practices that center belonging and trust. It also requires school cultures that recognize SEL not as enrichment but as essential infrastructure.

A Call for Emotionally Sustainable Innovation

As AI continues to evolve, so too will its role in education. More sophisticated tools will emerge. Automated tutors, emotional feedback systems, and generative learning companions may soon be common. But without intentional design and practice, these innovations risk reproducing the very harms they seek to solve, silencing student voice, outsourcing agency, and eroding self-trust.

This book offers a different path: one where emotion and innovation are not at odds, but in dialogue. One where we center the learner not just as a processor of content, but as a person in formation.

By embedding SEL into AI-enhanced classrooms, we affirm that:

- Technology must serve emotional as well as academic development.
- Students deserve tools that support not only productivity but personal growth.
- Ethical, inclusive education begins with attention to how learners feel, not just what they produce.

Final Reflection

AI will not disappear from classrooms. Nor should it. But as we embrace these tools, we must also ask: Are students thriving, or merely performing? Are they learning how to think with AI or learning to question whether they can think without it?

SEL provides the compass to answer these questions with honesty and care. It reminds us that education is a human endeavor, no matter how advanced our tools become.

By placing SEL at the heart of AI integration, we do not reject technology's promise. We fulfill it by building learning environments where students do not just succeed with AI, but feel whole while doing so.

REFERENCES

Alanazi, S. A., Shabbir, M., Alshammari, N., Alruwaili, M., Hussain, I., & Ahmad, F. (2023). Prediction of emotional empathy in intelligent agents to facilitate precise social interaction. *Applied Sciences (Basel, Switzerland)*, *13*(2), 1163. DOI: 10.3390/app13021163

Algorani, E. B., & Gupta, V. (2023, April 24). Coping mechanisms. *StatPearls - NCBI Bookshelf*. https://www.ncbi.nlm.nih.gov/books/NBK559031/

Aly, M., Ghallab, A., & Fathi, I. S. (2023). Enhancing facial expression recognition system in an online learning context using an efficient deep learning model. *IEEE Access : Practical Innovations, Open Solutions*, *11*, 121419–121433. DOI: 10.1109/access.2023.3325407

Balatero, L., Jayno, J., & Miranda, K. (2024). ESL pre-service teachers' literacy and acceptance of ChatGPT as a generative AI tool for writing: A sequential explanatory study. *Journal of Education and Learning*, *2*(3), 13–29. DOI: 10.54536/jtel.v2i3.3365

Bandura, A. (1977). Self-efficacy: Toward a unifying theory of behavioral change. *Psychological Review*, *84*(2), 191–215. DOI: 10.1037/0033-295X.84.2.191 PMID: 847061

Bećirović, S., Polz, E., & Tinkel, I. (2025). Exploring students' AI literacy and its effects on their AI output quality, self-efficacy, and academic performance. *Smart Learning Environments*, *12*(1). Advance online publication. DOI: 10.1186/s40561-025-00384-3

Belay, S., & Dejene, W. (2024). Testing and validating the Collaborative for Academic, Social, and Emotional Learning (CASEL) model in the context of Ethiopian secondary schools: Factorial analysis. *Social Sciences & Humanities Open*, *10*, 101128. DOI: 10.1016/j.ssaho.2024.101128

Calma, A., Cotronei-Baird, V., & Chia, A. (2022). Grammarly: An instructional intervention for writing enhancement in management education. *International Journal of Management Education*, *20*(3), 100704. DOI: 10.1016/j.ijme.2022.100704

Calonia, J. T., Pagente, D. P., Jane, D., Capio, R. T., Tembrevilla, A. P., Guzman, C. A., & Jay, A. (2023). Time management and academic achievement: Examining the roles of prioritization, procrastination and socialization. *International Journal of Innovative Science and Research Technology*, *8*(6), 766–775. DOI: 10.5281/zenodo.8115965

CASEL. (2024). What is the CASEL framework? *Collaborative for Academic, Social, and Emotional Learning*. https://casel.org/fundamentals-of-sel/what-is-the-casel-framework/

Chan, C. K. Y. (2024). Exploring the factors of "AI guilt" among students – Are you guilty of using AI in your homework? *arXiv*. https://doi.org//arxiv.2407.10777DOI: 10.48550

Chan, C. K. Y., & Hu, W. (2023). Students' voices on Generative AI: Perceptions, benefits, and challenges in Higher education. *arXiv* (Cornell University). https://doi.org//arxiv.2305.00290DOI: 10.48550

Clance, P. R., & Imes, S. A. (1978). The impostor phenomenon in high-achieving women: Dynamics and therapeutic intervention. *Psychotherapy (Chicago, Ill.)*, *15*(3), 241–247. DOI: 10.1037/ h0086006

Coldwell, W. (2024). *"I received a first but it felt tainted and undeserved": inside the university AI cheating crisis*. The Guardian. https://www.theguardian.com/technology/2024/dec/15/i-received-a-first-but-it-felt-tainted-and-undeserved-inside-the-university-ai-cheating-crisis

Darvishi, A., Khosravi, H., Sadiq, S., Gašević, D., & Siemens, G. (2023). Impact of AI assistance on student agency. *Computers & Education*, *210*, 104967. DOI: 10.1016/j.compedu.2023.104967

Davis, K., Christian, D. D., Hammett, R., Low, G., & Seagraves-Robinson, T. (2022). Social Emotional Learning: A case for appreciative inquiry to develop TEI/SEL skills. *AI Practitioner*, *24*(2), 81–100. DOI: 10.12781/978-1-907549-51-9-16

Deckker, N. D., & Sumanasekara, N. S. (2025). Systematic review on AI in emotional intelligence and psychological education. *EPRA International Journal of Research & Development (IJRD)*, 400–414. https://doi.org/DOI: 10.36713/epra21351

Domingo, M. A. (2025). Investigating the influence of AI-driven tools in ESL students' experience of AI-induced impostor syndrome and academic confidence. [AJELS]. *Asian Journal of English Language Studies*, *13*(1), 98–125. DOI: 10.59960/13.1.a5

Domingo, N. J., & Lintao, R. B. (2025). ChatGPT's Usability in Expository Writing in AI-Enabled Classrooms: Perceptions of Tertiary students and teachers. *JPAIR Multidisciplinary Research*, *60*(1), 81–101. DOI: 10.7719/jpair.v60i1.931

Escalante, J., Pack, A., & Barrett, A. (2023). AI-generated feedback on writing: Insights into efficacy and ENL student preference. *International Journal of Educational Technology in Higher Education*, *20*(1). Advance online publication. DOI: 10.1186/s41239-023-00425-2

Giray, L. (2024). AI humanizer as a cheating tool in academic writing among Filipino ESL students. *ResearchGate*. https://www.researchgate.net/publication/381843271_AI_Humanizer_as_a_Cheating_Tool_in_Academic_Writing_among_Filipino_ESL_Students

Greenwald, E., Krakowski, A., Hurt, T., Grindstaff, K., & Wang, N. (2024). It's like I'm the AI: Youth sensemaking about AI through metacognitive embodiment. In *IDC '24: Proceedings of the 23rd Annual ACM Interaction Design and Children Conference* (pp. 789–793). https://doi.org/DOI: 10.1145/3628516.3659395

Gustilo, L., Ong, E., & Lapinid, M. R. (2024). Algorithmically-driven writing and academic integrity: Exploring educators' practices, perceptions, and policies in the AI era. *International Journal for Educational Integrity*, *20*(1), 2. Advance online publication. DOI: 10.1007/s40979-024-00153-8

Ji, Y., Zhong, M., Lyu, S., Li, T., Niu, S., & Zhan, Z. (2025). How does AI literacy affect individual innovative behavior: The mediating role of psychological need satisfaction, creative self-efficacy, and self-regulated learning. *Education and Information Technologies*. Advance online publication. DOI: 10.1007/s10639-025-13437-4

Kim, T. W., & Tan, Q. (2023). Repurposing text-generating AI into a thought-provoking writing tutor. *arXiv*. https://doi.org//arXiv.2304.10543DOI: 10.48550

Lipovec, A. (2024). Charting the Path Forward: Effective Didactic Approach for Teaching AI Literacy in K-12 Education. *2022 11th Mediterranean Conference on Embedded Computing (MECO)*, 1–4. https://doi.org/DOI: 10.1109/meco62516.2024.10577894

Ménard, A. D., & Chittle, L. (2023). The impostor phenomenon in post-secondary students: A review of the literature. *Review of Education*, *11*(2), e3399. Advance online publication. DOI: 10.1002/rev3.3399

Mohammed, S. J., & Khalid, M. W. (2025). Under the world of AI-generated feedback on writing: Mirroring motivation, foreign language peace of mind, trait emotional intelligence, and writing development. *Language Testing in Asia*, *15*(1), 10. Advance online publication. DOI: 10.1186/s40468-025-00343-2

Navales, G. (2024). ChatGPT as a writing aid: English teachers' perceptions on its usefulness and ethical acceptability. *Asian Journal of English Language Studies*, *12*(2), 27–50. DOI: 10.59960/12.2.a2

Oberle, E., Domitrovich, C. E., Meyers, D. C., & Weissberg, R. P. (2016). Establishing systemic social and emotional learning approaches in schools: A framework for schoolwide implementation. *Cambridge Journal of Education*, *46*(3), 277–297.

Paul, M., Sunil, M. N., & Neena, P. (2024). The silent struggle—Imposter syndrome and its influence on self-efficacy and academic performance: A study on MBA students in a private university. *International Journal for Multidisciplinary Research, 6*(3), 20790. Advance online publication. DOI: 10.36948/ijfmr.2024.v06i03.20790

Rasul, T., Nair, S., & Kalendra, D., Balaji, De Oliveira Santini, F., Ladeira, W. J., Rather, R. A., Yasin, N., Rodriguez, R. V., Kokkalis, P., Murad, M. W., & Hossain, M. U. (2024). Enhancing academic integrity among students in the GenAI era: A holistic framework. *International Journal of Management Education, 22*(3), 101041. DOI: 10.1016/j.ijme.2024.101041

Rout, B. (2024). SEL and Technology: The Role of Digital Tools in Promoting Emotional and Social Skills. *International Journal for Research in Applied Science and Engineering Technology, 12*(12), 1584–1589. DOI: 10.22214/ijraset.2024.66086

Skinner, E. A., Kindermann, T. A., & Furrer, C. J. (2008). A motivational perspective on engagement and disaffection. *Educational and Psychological Measurement, 69*(3), 493–525. DOI: 10.1177/0013164408323233

Yang, X., Yeo, K. J., Lee, S.-H., & Handayani, L. (2024). A systematic review of impostor syndrome in higher education. [IJERE]. *International Journal of Evaluation and Research in Education, 13*(6), 3884–3892. DOI: 10.11591/ijere.v13i6.30726

Zhai, C., Wibowo, S., & Li, L. D. (2024). The effects of over-reliance on AI dialogue systems on students' cognitive abilities: A systematic review. *Smart Learning Environments, 11*(1), 3. Advance online publication. DOI: 10.1186/s40561-024-00316-7

Zhang, S., Zhao, X., Zhou, T., & Kim, J. H. (2024). Do you have AI dependency? The roles of academic self-efficacy, academic stress, and performance expectations on problematic AI usage behavior. *International Journal of Educational Technology in Higher Education, 21*(1), 19. Advance online publication. DOI: 10.1186/s41239-024-00467-0

Zulvi, J. D., & Abidin, Z. (2025). Coping strategies of high-achieving students in boarding excellence high schools: A Case study. *The International Journal of Science in Society, 7*(1), 31–41. DOI: 10.54783/ijsoc.v7i1.\1357

Zunaidah, A., Wiharja, C. K., & Febriantono, M. A. (2023). Dependency on AI-Based Writing Tools in English Learning: Implications for Human-Computer Interaction. *2022 International Conference on Information Management and Technology (ICIMTech)*, 1–6. https://doi.org/DOI: 10.1109/icimtech59029.2023.10278054

Compilation of References

Aboodi, R. (2025). The Worrisome Potential of Outsourcing Critical Thinking to Artificial Intelligence. *Educational Theory*.

Acosta-Vargas, P., Salvador-Acosta, B., Novillo-Villegas, S., Sarantis, D., & Salvador-Ullauri, L. (2024). Generative Artificial Intelligence and Web Accessibility: Towards an Inclusive and Sustainable Future. *Emerging Science Journal*, *8*(4), 1602–1621. DOI: 10.28991/ESJ-2024-08-04-021

Adams, P., & McLennan, C. (2021). Towards initial teacher education quality: Epistemological considerations. *Educational Philosophy and Theory*, *53*(6), 644–654.

Ade-Ibijola, A., & Okonkwo, C. (2023). Artificial intelligence in Africa: emerging challenges. In Eke, D. O., Wakunuma, K., & Akintoye, S. (Eds.), *Responsible AI in Africa: Challenges and Opportunities* (pp. 101–117). Palgrave Macmillan.

Agarwal, R., & Bhatnagar, A. (2025). Transforming Education: Harnessing the Power of AI to Empower Educators. Productivity, 66(1).

Ahmad, I., & Islam, M. R. (2024). Empowerment and participation: Key strategies for inclusive development. In *Building strong communities: Ethical approaches to inclusive development* (pp. 47–68). Emerald Publishing Limited.

Ahmed, F. (2024). The digital divide and AI in education: Addressing equity and accessibility. *AI EDIFY Journal*, *1*(2), 12–23.

Ahmmed, M., Sharma, U., & Deppeler, J. (2014). Variables affecting teachers' intentions to include students with disabilities in regular primary schools in Bangladesh. *Disability & Society*, *29*(2), 317–331.

Ahmmed, M., Sharma, U., & Deppeler, J. M. (2013). Impact of demographic variables and school support on teacher efficacy in inclusive classrooms in Bangladesh. *The International Journal of Diversity in Education*, *12*(2), 1.

Ahuerma, F. M. (2024). UNESCO Proposal for the use of Generative AI in Education: Eight Challenges and Seven Actions.

Aithal, P. S., & Maiya, A. K. (2023). Innovations in the higher education industry–Shaping the future. [IJCSBE]. *International Journal of Case Studies in Business, IT, and Education*, *7*(4), 283–311.

Akande, J. O., & Atiku, S. O. (2022). Developing Industry 4.0 accountants: Implications for higher education institutions in Namibia. *Development and Learning in Organizations*, *36*(5), 16–19. DOI: 10.1108/DLO-09-2021-0177

Akgun, S., & Greenhow, C. (2022). Artificial intelligence in education: Addressing ethical challenges in K-12 settings. *AI and Ethics*, *2*(3), 431–440. PMID: 34790956

Alanazi, S. A., Shabbir, M., Alshammari, N., Alruwaili, M., Hussain, I., & Ahmad, F. (2023). Prediction of emotional empathy in intelligent agents to facilitate precise social interaction. *Applied Sciences (Basel, Switzerland)*, *13*(2), 1163. DOI: 10.3390/app13021163

Alasadi, E. A., & Baiz, C. R. (2023). Generative AI in education and research: Opportunities, concerns, and solutions. *Journal of Chemical Education*, *100*(8), 2965–2971.

Alasadi, E. A., & Baiz, C. R. (2023). Generative AI in Education and Research: Opportunities, concerns, and solutions. *Journal of Chemical Education*, *100*(8), 2965–2971.

Al-Azawei, A., Serenelli, F., & Lundqvist, K. (2016). Universal Design for Learning (UDL): A Content Analysis of Peer Reviewed Journals from 2012 to 2015. *The Journal of Scholarship of Teaching and Learning*, *16*(3), 39–56. DOI: 10.14434/josotl.v16i3.19295

Albeihi, H. H. M., & Rice, M. F. (2025). Generative AI and language diversity: Implications for teachers and learners.

Aldrich, T. (2025). Literary Postcritique and American Transcendentalism: Helping Students Practice Community-Building by Rewilding Literature in the Classroom (Doctoral dissertation, University of Arkansas).

Algorani, E. B., & Gupta, V. (2023, April 24). Coping mechanisms. *StatPearls - NCBI Bookshelf*. https://www.ncbi.nlm.nih.gov/books/NBK559031/

Ali, D., Fatemi, Y., Boskabadi, E., Nikfar, M., Ugwuoke, J., & Ali, H. (2024). ChatGPT in teaching and learning: A systematic review. *Education Sciences*, *14*(6), 643.

Alkaissi, H., & McFarlane, S. I. (2023). Artificial hallucinations in ChatGPT: Implications in scientific writing. *Cureus, 15*(2). PMID: 36811129

Almufareh, M. F., Kausar, S., Humayun, M., & Tehsin, S. (2024). A conceptual model for inclusive technology: Advancing disability inclusion through artificial intelligence. *Journal of Disability Research, 3*(1), 20230060.

Aly, M., Ghallab, A., & Fathi, I. S. (2023). Enhancing facial expression recognition system in an online learning context using an efficient deep learning model. *IEEE Access : Practical Innovations, Open Solutions, 11*, 121419–121433. DOI: 10.1109/access.2023.3325407

Anane-Simon, R., & Atiku, S. O. (2024). Artificial intelligence and automation for the future of startups. In Baporikar, N. (Ed.), *Ecosystem Dynamics and Strategies for Startups' Scalability* (pp. 133–153). IGI Global Scientific Publishing.

Angel, B. (2024). *The Wolf is at the Door: How to Survive and Thrive in an AI-driven World*. Entrepreneur Press.

Annamma, S. A., Connor, D., & Ferri, B. (2013). Dis/ability critical race studies (DisCrit): Theorizing at the intersections of race and dis/ability. *Race, Ethnicity and Education, 16*(1), 1–31.

Arakpogun, E. O., Elsahn, Z., Olan, F., & Elsahn, F. (2021). Artificial Intelligence in Africa: Challenges and Opportunities. In Hamdan, A. (Eds.), *The Fourth Industrial Revolution: Implementation of Artificial Intelligence for Growing Business Success* (pp. 375–388). Springer., https://doi.org/https://doi.org/10.1007/978-3-030-62796-6_22

Arantes, J. (2024). Understanding Intersections Between GenAI and Pre-Service Teacher Education: What Do We Need to Understand About the Changing Face of Truth in Science Education? *Journal of Science Education and Technology*, 1–12.

Arantes, J. A. (2019). Equity Implications of Predictive Analytics in K-12 Classrooms. *Ubiquitous Learning: An International Journal, 12*(2), 63–84. DOI: 10.18848/1835-9795/CGP/v12i02/63-84

Arantes, J. A. (2023). Digital Twins and the terminology of 'personalization' or 'personalized learning' in educational policy: A discussion paper. *Policy Futures in Education*.

Arantes, J., & Vicars, M. (2023). Missing in Action: Queer(y)ing the Educational implications of Data Justice in an Age of Automation. *Learning, Media and Technology*.

Aslanimehr, P. (2025). *Exile as an Educative Engagement: The Dizziness of Recognition*. Taylor & Francis.

Atiku, S. O., & Anane-Simon, R. (2022). Stimulating Creativity and Innovation Through Apt Educational Policy. In Fields, Z. (Ed.), *Achieving Sustainability Using Creativity, Innovation, and Education: A Multidisciplinary Approach* (pp. 113–133). IGI Global Scientific Publishing., DOI: 10.4018/978-1-7998-7963-3.ch006

Atiku, S. O., & Boateng, F. (2020). Rethinking Education System for the Fourth Industrial Revolution. In Atiku, S. (Ed.), *Human Capital Formation for the Fourth Industrial Revolution* (pp. 1–17). IGI Global Scientific Publishing., DOI: 10.4018/978-1-5225-9810-7.ch001

Auger, S., Besnier, J. B., van Bijnen, M., Cherqui, F., Chuzeville, G., Clemens, F. H. L., ... & Ugarelli, R. M. (2024). Data management and quality control. Asset Management of Urban Drainage Systems: If anything exciting happens, we've done it wrong!.

Ba, A. (2021). How to measure monitoring and evaluation system effectiveness? *African Evaluation Journal*, *9*(1), 953.

Baker, D. L., & Baker, R. L. (2022). Knowledge and wisdom: High stakes testing and learning outcomes. In *Neuroethical Policy Design: A Lifetime's Exploration of Public Policy and Human Brains* (pp. 101–118). Springer International Publishing.

Baker, R. S., & Hawn, A. (2021). Algorithmic Bias in Education. *International Journal of Artificial Intelligence in Education*. Advance online publication. DOI: 10.1007/s40593-021-00285-9

Balaji, M. T. M., & Balajiraja, N. UMA, M. P., & Nair, M. S. P. (2025). Generative AI Tools: Concepts, Applications, and Innovations. Academic Guru Publishing House.

Balatero, L., Jayno, J., & Miranda, K. (2024). ESL pre-service teachers' literacy and acceptance of ChatGPT as a generative AI tool for writing: A sequential explanatory study. *Journal of Education and Learning*, *2*(3), 13–29. DOI: 10.54536/jtel.v2i3.3365

Ball, S. J., & Olmedo, A. (2023). Care of the self, resistance and subjectivity under neoliberal governmentalities. In *Neoliberalism and Education* (pp. 131–142). Routledge.

Balta, N. (2023). Ethical considerations in using AI in educational research. *Journal of Research in Didactical Sciences*, *2*(1), 14205.

Banda, R. (2024). Building Social Equity with AI.

Bandura, A. (1977). Self-efficacy: Toward a unifying theory of behavioral change. *Psychological Review*, *84*(2), 191–215. DOI: 10.1037/0033-295X.84.2.191 PMID: 847061

Bardone, E., Mõttus, P., & Eradze, M. (2024). Tinkering as a complement to design in the context of technology integration in teaching and learning. *Postdigital Science and Education*, *6*(1), 114–134.

Barocas, S., Hardt, M., & Narayanan, A. (2023). *Fairness and machine learning: Limitations and opportunities*. MIT press.

Baskara, F. R. (2023). Navigating pedagogical evolution: The implication of generative AI on the reinvention of teacher education.

Bayaga, A. (2025). Leveraging AI-enhanced and emerging technologies for pedagogical innovations in higher education. *Education and Information Technologies*, *30*(1), 1045–1072.

Bearman, M., & Ajjawi, R. (2023). Learning to work with the black box: Pedagogy for a world with artificial intelligence. *British Journal of Educational Technology*, *54*(5), 1160–1173.

Bećirović, S., Polz, E., & Tinkel, I. (2025). Exploring students' AI literacy and its effects on their AI output quality, self-efficacy, and academic performance. *Smart Learning Environments*, *12*(1). Advance online publication. DOI: 10.1186/s40561-025-00384-3

Beerkens, M. (2020). Evidence-based policy and higher education quality assurance: progress, pitfalls and promise. In *Impact evaluation of quality management in higher education* (pp. 38–53). Routledge.

Behera, S. K., Ibrahim, A. H., & Romdhani, F. (Eds.). (2024). *Inclusive educational practices and technologies for promoting sustainability*. IGI Global.

Belay, S., & Dejene, W. (2024). Testing and validating the Collaborative for Academic, Social, and Emotional Learning (CASEL) model in the context of Ethiopian secondary schools: Factorial analysis. *Social Sciences & Humanities Open*, *10*, 101128. DOI: 10.1016/j.ssaho.2024.101128

Benevides, T. W., Shore, S. M., Andresen, M. L., Caplan, R., Cook, B., Gassner, D. L., & Wittig, K. (2020). Interventions to address health outcomes among autistic adults: A systematic review. *Autism*, *24*(6), 1345–1359. DOI: 10.1177/1362361320913664 PMID: 32390461

Benjamin, R. (2019). *Race after technology: Abolitionist tools for the new Jim code*. Polity Press.

Binns, R. (2018, January). Fairness in machine learning: Lessons from political philosophy. In *Conference on fairness, accountability and transparency* (pp. 149-159). PMLR, DOI:DOI: 10.48550/arXiv.1712.03586

Bircan, T., & Özbilgin, M. F. (2025). Unmasking inequalities of the code: Disentangling the nexus of AI and inequality. *Technological Forecasting and Social Change*, *211*, 123925.

Birhane, A., Kasirzadeh, A., Leslie, D., & Wachter, S. (2023). Science in the age of large language models. *Nature Reviews. Physics*, 1–4.

Bozdağ, A. A. (2024). The AI-mediated intimacy economy: A paradigm shift in digital interactions. *AI & Society*, •••, 1–22.

Bozkurt, A., Junhong, X., Lambert, S., Pazurek, A., Crompton, H., Koseoglu, S., & Romero-Hall, E. (2023). Speculative futures on ChatGPT and generative artificial intelligence (AI): A collective reflection from the educational landscape. *Asian Journal of Distance Education*, *18*(1), 53–130.

Bozkurt, A., Xiao, J., Farrow, R., Bai, J. Y., Nerantzi, C., Moore, S., Dron, J., Stracke, C. M., Singh, L., & Crompton, H. (2024). *The manifesto for teaching and learning in a time of generative AI: A critical collective stance to better navigate the future* (Vol. 16). International Council for Open and Distance Education Oslo.

Bridewell, W., Bello, P. F., & Bringsjord, S. (2024). The Technology of Outrage: Bias in Artificial Intelligence. arXiv preprint arXiv:2409.17336.

Broadbent, J., & Lodge, J. (2021). Use of live chat in higher education to support self-regulated help seeking behaviours: A comparison of online and blended learner perspectives. *International Journal of Educational Technology in Higher Education*, *18*(1), 1–20. PMID: 34778522

Burgstahler, S. (2009). *Universal Design in Education: Principles and Applications*. DO-IT.

Burke, K., & Leben, S. (2024). Procedural fairness: A key ingredient in public satisfaction. *Ct. Rev.*, *60*, 6.

Burrell, J. (2016). How the machine 'thinks': Understanding opacity in machine learning algorithms. *Big Data & Society*, *3*(1). Advance online publication. DOI: 10.1177/2053951715622512

Busch, F., Adams, L. C., & Bressem, K. K. (2023). Biomedical ethical aspects towards the implementation of artificial intelligence in medical education. *Medical Science Educator*, *33*(4), 1007–1012. PMID: 37546190

Butler-Ulrich, T., Hughes, J., & Morrison, L. (2024). Creativity and Generative AI for Preservice Teachers. In *Contemporaneous Issues about Creativity*. IntechOpen.

Calma, A., Cotronei-Baird, V., & Chia, A. (2022). Grammarly: An instructional intervention for writing enhancement in management education. *International Journal of Management Education*, *20*(3), 100704. DOI: 10.1016/j.ijme.2022.100704

Calonia, J. T., Pagente, D. P., Jane, D., Capio, R. T., Tembrevilla, A. P., Guzman, C. A., & Jay, A. (2023). Time management and academic achievement: Examining the roles of prioritization, procrastination and socialization. *International Journal of Innovative Science and Research Technology*, *8*(6), 766–775. DOI: 10.5281/zenodo.8115965

Cameron, F. R. (2021). *The future of digital data, heritage and curation: in a more-than-human world*. Routledge.

Cant, C., Muldoon, J., & Graham, M. (2024). *Feeding the machine: The hidden human labor powering AI*. Bloomsbury Publishing USA.

Capel, T., & Brereton, M. (2023, April). What is human-centered about human-centered AI? A map of the research landscape. In *Proceedings of the 2023 CHI conference on human factors in computing systems* (pp. 1-23).

Carolus, A., Augustin, Y., Markus, A., & Wienrich, C. (2023). Digital interaction literacy model – Conceptualizing competencies for literate interactions with voice-based AI systems. *Computers and Education: Artificial Intelligence, 4*, 100114. https://doi.org/https://doi.org/10.1016/j.caeai.2022.100114

CASEL. (2024). What is the CASEL framework? *Collaborative for Academic, Social, and Emotional Learning*. https://casel.org/fundamentals-of-sel/what-is-the-casel-framework/

Cassez, F., Fuller, J., Ghale, M. K., Pearce, D. J., & Quiles, H. M. (2023). Formal and executable semantics of the ethereum virtual machine in dafny. In *International Symposium on Formal Methods* (pp. 571-583). Cham: Springer International Publishing.

CAST. (n.d.). *Artificial Intelligence & UDL*. Retrieved from https://www.cast.org/what-we-do/artificial-intelligence/

Chakraborty, O. (2024). Role of AI in special education in India. In *Advances in Educational Technologies and Instructional Design* (pp. 279–324). IGI Global.

Challoumis, C. (2024). The dawn of artificial intelligence. In *XIX International Scientific Conference*. London. Great Britain (pp. 169-205).

Chan, C. K. Y. (2024). Exploring the factors of "AI guilt" among students – Are you guilty of using AI in your homework? *arXiv*. https://doi.org//arxiv.2407.10777DOI: 10.48550

Chan, C. K. Y. (2023). A comprehensive AI policy education framework for university teaching and learning. *International Journal of Educational Technology in Higher Education*, *20*(1), 38.

Chatterjee, S., & Bhattacharjee, K. K. (2020). Adoption of artificial intelligence in higher education: A quantitative analysis using structural equation modeling. *Education and Information Technologies*, *25*(5), 3443–3463. DOI: 10.1007/s10639-020-10159-7

Chedrawi, C., Kazoun, N., & Kokkinaki, A. (2024). The role of AI agents in fostering inclusivity for HEIs' students with special needs against backdrops of the accreditation trend. *Quality Assurance in Education*, *32*(4), 582–596.

Chen, B., Cheng, J., Wang, C., & Leung, V. (2025). Pedagogical Biases in AI-Powered Educational Tools: The Case of Lesson Plan Generators. *Social Innovations Journal, 30*.

Chen, Y. (2024). Generative Artificial Intelligence Empowering Translation: Current Status, Challenges, and Prospects. The Educational Review, USA, 8(12).

Chen, Y., Jensen, S., Albert, L. J., Gupta, S., & Lee, T. (2023). Artificial intelligence (AI) student assistants in the classroom: Designing chatbots to support student success. *Information Systems Frontiers*, *25*(1), 161–182.

Chi, N., Lurie, E., & Mulligan, D. K. (2021, July). Reconfiguring diversity and inclusion for AI ethics. In Proceedings of the 2021 AAAI/ACM Conference on AI, Ethics, and Society (pp. 447-457).

Chinta, S. V., Wang, Z., Yin, Z., Hoang, N., Gonzalez, M., Quy, T. L., & Zhang, W. (2024). FairAIED: Navigating fairness, bias, and ethics in educational AI applications. arXiv preprint arXiv:2407.18745.

Choi, S. P., Lam, S. S., Li, K. C., & Wong, B. T. (2018). Learning analytics at low cost: At-risk student prediction with clicker data and systematic proactive interventions. *Journal of Educational Technology & Society*, *21*(2), 273–290.

Christanti, M. F., Mawangir, M., Arevin, A. T., Ramadhan, I., & Limijadi, E. K. S. (2024). The digital divide in education: Bridging gaps in the era of online learning. *Migration Letters : An International Journal of Migration Studies, 21*(S4), 1070–1079.

Clance, P. R., & Imes, S. A. (1978). The impostor phenomenon in high-achieving women: Dynamics and therapeutic intervention. *Psychotherapy (Chicago, Ill.), 15*(3), 241–247. DOI: 10.1037/ h0086006

Coldwell, W. (2024). *"I received a first but it felt tainted and undeserved": inside the university AI cheating crisis.* The Guardian. https://www.theguardian.com/technology/2024/dec/15/i-received-a-first-but-it-felt-tainted-and-undeserved-inside-the-university-ai-cheating-crisis

Cooper, G. (2023). Examining Science Education in ChatGPT: An Exploratory Study of Generative Artificial Intelligence. *Journal of Science Education and Technology, 32*(3), 444–452. DOI: 10.1007/s10956-023-10039-y

Costanza-Chock, S. (2020). *Design justice: Community-led practices to build the worlds we need.* The MIT Press.

Creely, E., & Carabott, K. (2025). Generative AI and New Pedagogies in Times of Change. Posthumanist and Phenomenological perspectives. *Posthumanist and Phenomenological perspectives* (April 01, 2025).

Cukurova, M., Kent, C., & Luckin, R. (2019). Artificial intelligence and multimodal data in the service of human decision-making: A case study in debate tutoring. *British Journal of Educational Technology, 50*(6), 3032–3046. DOI: 10.1111/bjet.12829

Darvishi, A., Khosravi, H., Sadiq, S., Gašević, D., & Siemens, G. (2023). Impact of AI assistance on student agency. *Computers & Education, 210*, 104967. DOI: 10.1016/j.compedu.2023.104967

Darwish, D. (2024). Human-AI Collaboration in Industry 5. In Human-Machine Collaboration and Emotional Intelligence in Industry 5.0 (pp. 44–70). IGI Global.

Daugherty, P. R., & Wilson, H. J. (2024). *Human+ Machine, Updated and Expanded: Reimagining Work in the Age of AI.* Harvard Business Press.

Davis, K., Christian, D. D., Hammett, R., Low, G., & Seagraves-Robinson, T. (2022). Social Emotional Learning: A case for appreciative inquiry to develop TEI/SEL skills. *AI Practitioner, 24*(2), 81–100. DOI: 10.12781/978-1-907549-51-9-16

Davood, A. (2023). EQUAL AI: A framework for enhancing equity, quality, understanding, and accessibility in liberal arts through AI for multilingual learners. *Language, Technology, and Social Media, 2*(1), 15–29.

Deckker, N. D., & Sumanasekara, N. S. (2025). Systematic review on AI in emotional intelligence and psychological education. *EPRA International Journal of Research & Development (IJRD)*, 400–414. https://doi.org/DOI: 10.36713/epra21351

Dede, C., Saxberg, B., & Richards, J. (2018). *Learning engineering for online education* (Vol. 95). Routledge.

Diamond, A. (2007). Interrelated and interdependent. *Developmental Science*, *10*(1), 152–158. PMID: 17181714

Dignum, V. (2019). *Responsible Artificial Intelligence: How to develop and use AI in a responsible way*. Springer.

Dinker, N. (2024). Artificial intelligence and inequality: examining the social divides created by technological advancements. International Journal of Innovations in Science, Engineering And Management, 228-236.

Dlamini, R., & Ndzinisa, N. (2025). Towards a critical discourse on artificial intelligence and its misalignment in sub-Saharan Africa: Through an equality, equity, and decoloniality lens. *Journal of Education (University of KwaZulu-Natal)*, (98), 42-61.

Domingo, M. A. (2025). Investigating the influence of AI-driven tools in ESL students' experience of AI-induced impostor syndrome and academic confidence. [AJELS]. *Asian Journal of English Language Studies*, *13*(1), 98–125. DOI: 10.59960/13.1.a5

Domingo, N. J., & Lintao, R. B. (2025). ChatGPT's Usability in Expository Writing in AI-Enabled Classrooms: Perceptions of Tertiary students and teachers. *JPAIR Multidisciplinary Research*, *60*(1), 81–101. DOI: 10.7719/jpair.v60i1.931

dos Santos, A. D. P., Ferrari, A. L. M., Medola, F. O., & Sandnes, F. E. (2022). Aesthetics and the perceived stigma of assistive technology for visual impairment. *Disability and Rehabilitation. Assistive Technology*, *17*(2), 152–158. DOI: 10.1080/17483107.2020.1768308 PMID: 32501732

Eden, C., Adeleye, O., & Adeniyi, I. (2024). A review of AI-driven pedagogical strategies for equitable access to science education. Magna Scientia Advanced Research and Reviews. 10. 044-054. DOI: 10.30574/msarr.2024.10.2.0043

El Arab, R. A., Abu-Mahfouz, M. S., Abuadas, F. H., Alzghoul, H., Almari, M., Ghannam, A., & Seweid, M. M. (2025, March). Bridging the gap: From AI success in clinical trials to real-world healthcare implementation—A narrative review. In *Healthcare, 13(7), 701*. MDPI.

Elsayed, A. R., & Alfawzan, S. K. (2025). A proposed vision for the use of artificial intelligence in education by teachers of students with intellectual disabilities. *International Journal of Innovative Research and Scientific Studies*, *8*(4), 1270–1281. DOI: 10.53894/ijirss.v8i4.8055

Ersoy, C. (2025). Inclusive transformation with artificial intelligence. In *Advances in Computational Intelligence and Robotics* (pp. 275–296). IGI Global.

Escalante, J., Pack, A., & Barrett, A. (2023). AI-generated feedback on writing: Insights into efficacy and ENL student preference. *International Journal of Educational Technology in Higher Education*, *20*(1). Advance online publication. DOI: 10.1186/s41239-023-00425-2

Essa, H. (2024). *The Consciously Unbiased Educator*. ASCD.

Evmenova, A. S., Borup, J., & Shin, J. K. (2024). Harnessing the Power of Generative AI to Support ALL Learners. *TechTrends*, *68*(4), 820–831. DOI: 10.1007/s11528-024-00966-x

Faisal, R., Chong, A. L., & Yee, A. S. V. (2017). Systematic review of the sustainable knowledge transfer process in government-industry-academia consortium. *Asian Journal of Innovation and Policy*, *6*(3), 295–312.

Farhah, N. S., Wadood, A., Alqarni, A. A., Uddin, M. I., & Aldhyani, T. H. H. (2025). Enhancing Adaptive Learning with Generative AI for Tailored Educational Support for Students with Disabilities. *Journal of Disability Research*, *4*(3), 1–17. DOI: 10.57197/JDR-2025-0012

Faulconbridge, J., Sarwar, A., & Spring, M. (2025). How professionals adapt to artificial intelligence: The role of intertwined boundary work. *Journal of Management Studies*, *62*(5), 1991–2024.

Fawns, T. (2023). Postdigital Education. In Jandrić, P. (Ed.), *Encyclopedia of Postdigital Science and Education* (pp. 1–11). Springer Nature Switzerland. DOI: 10.1007/978-3-031-35469-4_52-1

Fitas, R. (2025). Inclusive Education with AI: Supporting Special Needs and Tackling Language Barriers. *arXiv preprint arXiv:2504.14120*.

Fitch, E., McKenzie, C., Janke, T., & Shul, A. (2023, November 30). The new frontier: Artificial intelligence, copyright and Indigenous culture. *Terri Janke and Company*. https://www.terrijanke.com.au/post/the-new-frontier-artificial-intelligence-copyright-and-indigenous-culture

Fjeld, J., Achten, N., Hilligoss, H., Nagy, A., & Srikumar, M. (2020). Principled artificial intelligence: Mapping consensus in ethical and rights-based approaches to principles for AI. SSRN Electron. J.

Floridi, L., & Cowls, J. (2019). A unified framework of five principles for AI in society. *Harvard Data Science Review, 1*(1). Advance online publication. DOI: 10.1162/99608f92.8cd550d1

Fontanillas, T. R., Carbonell, M. R., Catasús, M. G., & Quemada, P. B. (2025). Challenges of generative Artificial Intelligence in higher education: Promoting its critical use among students. *Revista Iberoamericana de Educación a Distancia, 28*(2), 209–228. DOI: 10.5944/ried.28.2.43535

Ford, B., Bernholz, L., Landemore, H., & Reich, R. (2021). Technologizing democracy or democratizing technology? A layered-architecture perspective on potentials and challenges. Digital technology and democratic theory, 274-321.

Francis, J., Jones, M., & Smith, A. (2025). Generative AI in higher education: Balancing innovation and integrity. Retrieved from https://pubmed.ncbi.nlm.nih.gov/39850144

Fraser, N. (2020). From redistribution to recognition?: Dilemmas of justice in a'postsocialist'age. In *The new social theory reader* (pp. 188–196). Routledge.

Fricker, M. (2007). *Epistemic injustice: Power and the ethics of knowing*. Oxford University Press.

Fu, B., Hadid, A., & Damer, N. (2025). Generative AI in the context of assistive technologies: Trends, limitations and future directions. *Image and Vision Computing, 154*(November 2024), 105347. https://doi.org/DOI: 10.1016/j.imavis.2024.105347

Funda, V., & Cilliers, L. (2024). AI chatbots and the future of academic writing: Insights from the University of Fort Hare [Research study announcement]. University of Fort Hare. Retrieved June 26, 2025, from https://shorturl.at/zgeXr

Funda, V., & Francke, E. (2024). Benefits and challenges of AIOPS adoption and usage in HEIS in developing countries. *South African Journal of Higher Education, 38*(6), 56–78.

Funda, V., & Mbangeleli, N. B. A. (2024). Artificial Intelligence (AI) as a tool to address academic challenges in South African higher education. *Int. J. Learn. Teach. Educ. Res, 23*, 520–537.

Fu, Y., & Weng, Z. (2024). Navigating the ethical terrain of AI in education: A systematic review on framing responsible human-centered AI practices. Computers & Education. *Artificial Intelligence*. Advance online publication. DOI: 10.1016/j.caeai.2024.100306

Gadekallu, T. R., Yenduri, G., Kaluri, R., Rajput, D. S., Lakshmanna, K., Fang, K., Chen, J., & Wang, W. (2025). The role of GPT in promoting inclusive higher education for people with various learning disabilities: A review. *PeerJ. Computer Science, 11*, e2400. DOI: 10.7717/peerj-cs.2400 PMID: 40062249

Gallagher, M., Breines, M., & Blaney, M. (2021). Ontological Transparency, (In)visibility, and Hidden Curricula: Critical Pedagogy Amidst Contentious Edtech. *Postdigital Science and Education, 3*(2), 425–443. DOI: 10.1007/s42438-020-00198-1 PMID: 40477160

Geesa, R. L., Rose, M. A., Stith, K. M., Lowery, K., & Caniglia, J. (2021). Equity, diversity, and inclusion within integrative STEM education. *Leadership in Integrative STEM Education: Collaborative Strategies for Facilitating an Experiential and Student-Centered Culture*, 51.

Gevher, M., Öncü, S. E., & Erdoğdu, E. (2025). Exploring the potential use of generative ai for learner support in ODL at scale. *Journal of Educational Technology and Online Learning, 8*(1), 80–99. DOI: 10.31681/jetol.1559442

Ghimire, A. (2025). Utilizing ChatGPT to integrate world English and diverse knowledge: A transnational perspective in critical artificial intelligence (AI) literacy. *Computers and Composition, 75*, 102913.

Giansanti, D., & Pirrera, A. (2025). Integrating AI and Assistive Technologies in Healthcare: Insights from a Narrative Review of Reviews. *Health Care, 13*(5), 556. DOI: 10.3390/healthcare13050556 PMID: 40077118

Gimmler, A. (2024). Exploring the Possibilities of Dramatic Rehearsal as a Framework for the Evaluation of Digital Technologies in Education. In *Framing Futures in Postdigital Education: Critical Concepts for Data-driven Practices* (pp. 163–179). Springer Nature Switzerland.

Giray, L. (2024). AI humanizer as a cheating tool in academic writing among Filipino ESL students. *ResearchGate*. https://www.researchgate.net/publication/381843271_AI_Humanizer_as_a_Cheating_Tool_in_Academic_Writing_among_Filipino_ESL_Students

Glazko, K. S., Yamagami, M., Desai, A., Mack, K. A., Potluri, V., Xu, X., & Mankoff, J. (2023). An Autoethnographic Case Study of Generative Artificial Intelligence's Utility for Accessibility. In *ASSETS 2023 - Proceedings of the 25th International ACM SIGACCESS Conference on Computers and Accessibility* (Vol. 1, Issue 1). Association for Computing Machinery. https://doi.org/DOI: 10.1145/3597638.3614548

Gligorea, I., Cioca, M., Oancea, R., Gorski, A. T., Gorski, H., & Tudorache, P. (2023). Adaptive learning using artificial intelligence in e-learning: A literature review. *Education Sciences*, *13*(12), 1216.

Global, S. I. S. (2024). *University of the Free State launches multilingual AI-powered chatbot to enhance student engagement.* https://sisglobal.com/university-of-the-free-state-launches-multilingual-ai-powered-chatbot

Goktas, P., & Grzybowski, A. (2025). Shaping the future of healthcare: Ethical clinical challenges and pathways to trustworthy AI. *Journal of Clinical Medicine*, *14*(5), 1605.

Goos, M., & Savona, M. (2024). The governance of artificial intelligence: Harnessing opportunities and mitigating challenges. *Research Policy*, *53*(3), 104928.

Graham, O., & Milan, Y. (2025). The Influence of AI Tools on the Student Writing Process and Compositional Fluency.

Greenwald, E., Krakowski, A., Hurt, T., Grindstaff, K., & Wang, N. (2024). It's like I'm the AI: Youth sensemaking about AI through metacognitive embodiment. In *IDC '24: Proceedings of the 23rd Annual ACM Interaction Design and Children Conference* (pp. 789–793). https://doi.org/DOI: 10.1145/3628516.3659395

Gross, N. (2023). What chatGPT tells us about gender: A cautionary tale about performativity and gender biases in AI. *Social Sciences*, *12*(8), 435.

Guadu, A., Dibelkulu, D., & Menberu, A. W. (2025). Artificial Intelligence in African Higher Education: Uses, Misuses, and Ethical Dilemmas. *Advances in Artificial Intelligence and Machine Learning. RE:view*, *5*(3), 4196–4221.

Guettala, M., Bourekkache, S., Kazar, O., & Harous, S. (2024). Generative Artificial Intelligence in Education: Advancing Adaptive and Personalized Learning. *Acta Informatica Pragensia*, *13*(3), 460–489. DOI: 10.18267/j.aip.235

Gulson, K. N., Sellar, S., & Webb, P. T. (2022). *Algorithms of education: How datafication and artificial intelligence shape policy.* U of Minnesota Press.

Gurevich, E., El Hassan, B., & El Morr, C. (2023, March). Equity within AI systems: What can health leaders expect? [Sage CA: Los Angeles, CA: SAGE Publications.]. *Healthcare Management Forum*, *36*(2), 119–124.

Gustilo, L., Ong, E., & Lapinid, M. R. (2024). Algorithmically-driven writing and academic integrity: Exploring educators' practices, perceptions, and policies in the AI era. *International Journal for Educational Integrity*, *20*(1), 2. Advance online publication. DOI: 10.1007/s40979-024-00153-8

Hamad, W. (2022). Understanding the foremost challenges in the transition to online teaching and learning during COVID-19 pandemic: A systematic literature review. *Journal of Educational Technology and Online Learning*, *5*(2), 393–410. DOI: 10.31681/jetol.1055695

Haoyang, D. L., & Towne, J. (2025). *How AI and human teachers can collaborate to transform education, World Economic Forum*. Available at: https://www.weforum.org/stories/2025/01/how-ai-and-human-teachers-can-collaborate-to-transform-education/ (Accessed: 27 June 2025).

Haraway, D. (2020). Situated knowledges: The science question in feminism and the privilege of partial perspective. In *Feminist Theory Reader* (pp. 303–310). Routledge.

Haraway, D. J. (2013). *Science fiction, speculative fabulation, string figures, so far*.

Haraway, D. J. (2016). Staying with the trouble: Making kin in the Chthulucene. In *Staying with the Trouble*. Duke University Press.

Harden, P., & Fanfarelli, J. R. (2023). Boundaries, Informed Consent, and Learning. In Ethical Considerations of Virtual Reality in the College Classroom (pp. 293-304). Routledge.

Harding, S., & Mendoza, B. (2020). Latin American decolonial feminist philosophy of knowledge production. In Crasnow, A., & Intemann, K. (Eds.), *The Routledge Handbook of Feminist Philosophy of Science* (1st ed., pp. 13–28). Routledge. DOI: 10.4324/9780429507731

Haroud, S., & Saqri, N. (2025). Generative AI in higher education: Teachers' and students' perspectives on support, replacement, and digital literacy. *Education Sciences*, *15*(4), 396. DOI: 10.3390/educsci15040396

Heffernan, N. T., & Heffernan, C. L. (2014). The ASSISTments ecosystem: Building a platform that brings scientists and teachers together for minimally invasive research on human learning and teaching. *International Journal of Artificial Intelligence in Education*, *24*(4), 470–497.

Helsper, E. (2021). The digital disconnect: The social causes and consequences of digital inequalities.

Helvie, F. C. (2025). *Ghost in the Classroom: A Practical Guide to AI, Pedagogy, and Possibility*. Forrest C. Helvie.

Holman, K., Marino, M., Vasquez, E., Taub, M., Hunt, J., & Tazi, Y. (2024). Navigating AI-Powered Personalized Learning in special education: A guide for preservice teacher faculty. *Journal of Special Education Preparation*, *4*(2), 90–95.

Holmes, W. (2020). Artificial intelligence in education. In *Encyclopedia of education and information technologies* (pp. 88–103). Springer International Publishing.

Holzinger, A., Zatloukal, K., & Müller, H. (2025). Is human oversight to AI systems still possible? *New Biotechnology*, *85*, 59–62. PMID: 39675423

Howard, S., & Mozejko, A. (2015). Teachers: technology, change and resistance.

Hughes, L., & Malik, T. Dettmer, Al-Busaidi, A. S., & Dwivedi, Y. K. (2025). Reimagining Higher Education: Navigating the Challenges of Generative AI Adoption. *Information Systems Frontiers*. Advance online publication. DOI: 10.1007/s10796-025-10582-6

Hutson, J. (2024). Rethinking plagiarism in the era of generative AI. *Journal of International Communication*, *3*(2), 20–31. DOI: 10.54963/jic.v3i2.220

Jain, R., Garg, N., & Khera, S. N. (2023). Effective human–AI work design for collaborative decision-making. *Kybernetes*, *52*(11), 5017–5040.

Jantanukul, W. (2024). AI and human synergy: Utilizing AI to enhance teaching and learning. *Journal of Education and Learning Reviews*, *1*(4), 1–12.

Ji, Y., Zhong, M., Lyu, S., Li, T., Niu, S., & Zhan, Z. (2025). How does AI literacy affect individual innovative behavior: The mediating role of psychological need satisfaction, creative self-efficacy, and self-regulated learning. *Education and Information Technologies*. Advance online publication. DOI: 10.1007/s10639-025-13437-4

Johnsen, M. (2024). *AI Alignment*. Maria Johnsen.

Kaisara, G., & Bwalya, K. J. (2022). Trends in Mobile Learning Research in Sub-Saharan Africa: A Systematic Literature Review. *International Journal of Education and Development Using Information and Communication Technology*, *18*(2), 231–244.

Kaisara, G., Mare, A., & Peel, C. (2021) Haven't we been here before? A critical analysis of the fourth industrial revolution, in the *2021 Conference on Information Communications Technology and Society, ICTAS 2021 - Proceedings*. Durban: IEEE, pp. 67–72. Available at: https://doi.org/DOI: 10.1109/ICTAS50802.2021.9395028

Kalmus, J., & Nikiforova, A. (2024). Generative AI adoption in higher Education: Exploring educator resistance in Estonian universities. *AIS Electronic Library (AISeL)*. https://aisel.aisnet.org/sigdsa2024/13

Kalniņa, D., Nīmante, D., & Baranova, S. (2024). Artificial intelligence for higher education: Benefits and challenges for pre-service teachers. *Frontiers in Education*, *9*, 1501819. DOI: 10.3389/feduc.2024.1501819

Kang, B., Ma, X., Du, C., Pang, T., & Yan, S. (2023). Efficient diffusion policies for offline reinforcement learning. *Advances in Neural Information Processing Systems*, *36*, 67195–67212.

Kaplan, J. (2024). *Generative Artificial Intelligence: What Everyone Needs to Know*. Oxford University Press.

Karadağ, N. (2023). The impact of artificial intelligence on online assessment: A preliminary review. *Journal of Educational Technology and Online Learning*, *6*(4), 822–837.

Kaur, D., Uslu, S., Rittichier, K. J., & Durresi, A. (2022). Trustworthy artificial intelligence: A review. *ACM Computing Surveys*, *55*(2), 1–38.

Kay, J., Bartimote, K., Kitto, K., Kummerfeld, B., Liu, D., & Reimann, P. (2022). Enhancing learning by Open Learner Model (OLM) driven data design. *Computers and Education: Artificial Intelligence*, *3*, 100069.

Kayyali, M. (2025 A). The Future of AI in Education: Predictions and Emerging Trends. Next-Generation AI Methodologies in Education, 367-406.

Kayyali, M. (2025 B). AI in Higher Education: Revolutionizing Curriculum and Administration. In AI Adoption and Diffusion in Education (pp. 31-62). IGI Global Scientific Publishing.

Kayyali, M. (2025 C). Ethical Implications of Generative AI in Education: Privacy, Bias, and Integrity. In Transformative AI Practices for Personalized Learning Strategies (pp. 185-218). IGI Global Scientific Publishing.

Kayyali, M. (2025a). Ethical Implications of Generative AI in Education: Privacy, Bias, and Integrity. In Transformative AI Practices for Personalized Learning Strategies (pp. 185-218). IGI Global Scientific Publishing.

Kayyali, M. (2025b). Generative AI and Education: Transforming Teaching and Learning Through Collaborative Intelligence. In Humans and Generative AI Tools for Collaborative Intelligence (pp. 25-52). IGI Global Scientific Publishing.

Kayyali, M. (2025c). The Future of AI in Education: Predictions and Emerging Trends. Next-Generation AI Methodologies in Education, 367-406.

Kayyali, M. (2025d). AI in Higher Education: Revolutionizing Curriculum and Administration. In AI Adoption and Diffusion in Education (pp. 31-62). IGI Global Scientific Publishing.

Kayyali, M. (2025e). Ethical Implications of Generative AI in Education: Privacy, Bias, and Integrity. In Transformative AI Practices for Personalized Learning Strategies (pp. 185-218). IGI Global Scientific Publishing.

Kayyali, M. (2026). AI in Education: Learning Platforms for Personalized Learning. In Advanced Interdisciplinary Applications of Large Language Models and AI Agents (pp. 83-108). IGI Global Scientific Publishing.

Kayyali, M. (2026). The Impact of AI on Classroom Dynamics in Higher Education: Shifting Roles for Professors and Students. In Responsible AI Integration in Education (pp. 151-180). IGI Global Scientific Publishing.

Kayyali, M. (2022). Equity, Equality, Diversity, and Inclusion as Key Performance Indicators in Higher Education. *Online Submission*, *3*(5), 1–3.

Kayyali, M. (2024). A). Future directions towards sustainable educational equity: Policies and practices. In *Exploring Educational Equity at the Intersection of Policy and Practice* (pp. 81–100). IGI Global Scientific Publishing.

Kayyali, M. (2024). Future possibilities and challenges of AI in education. In *Transforming education with generative AI: Prompt engineering and synthetic content creation* (pp. 118–137). IGI Global Scientific Publishing.

Khosravi, H., Shum, S. B., Chen, G., Conati, C., Tsai, Y. S., Kay, J., ... & Gašević, D. (2022). Explainable artificial intelligence in education. *Computers and education: artificial intelligence, 3*, 100074.

Kılınç, S. (2024). Comprehensive AI assessment framework: Enhancing educational evaluation with ethical AI integration. Journal of Educational Technology and Online Learning, 7(4-ICETOL 2024 Special Issue), 521-540.

Kılınç, S. (2024). Comprehensive AI assessment framework: Enhancing educational evaluation with ethical AI integration. *Journal of Educational Technology and Online Learning, 7*(4-ICETOL 2024 Special Issue), 521–540. https://doi.org/DOI: 10.31681/jetol.1492695

Kim, J. H., Moldavan, A. M., Terry, R., & Massey, C. C. (2025). Enhancing Student Engagement With Generative AI. In *Transformative AI Practices for Personalized Learning Strategies* (pp. 69–106). IGI Global Scientific Publishing.

Klaassen, G. (2024). Confronting bias in artificial intelligence: building transparent, diverse, and ethical AI systems.

Knibbe, J., Peschl, R., & Osiyevskyy, O. (2024). Unleashing Creative Potential: The Role of Generative AI in Business Education. In Impacts of Generative AI on Creativity in Higher Education (pp. 399-422). IGI Global.

Korseberg, L., & Elken, M. (2025). Waiting for the revolution: How higher education institutions initially responded to ChatGPT. *Higher Education, 89*(4), 953–968. DOI: 10.1007/s10734-024-01256-4

Kuerban, Y., Oyelere, S. S., & Sanusi, I. T. (2025). ReadSmart: Generative AI and Augmented Reality solution for supporting students with dyslexia learning disabilities. *International Journal of Technology in Education and Science, 9*(1), 159–176.

Kumar, A.. (2023). Managing healthcare supply chain through artificial intelligence (AI): A study of critical success factors. *Computers & Industrial Engineering, 175*. Advance online publication. DOI: 10.1016/j.cie.2022.108815

Kumashiro, K. K. (2024). *Against common sense: Teaching and learning toward social justice*. Routledge.

Kunjumuhammed, S. K. (2024). Artificial Intelligence in Addressing Educational Inequality Dimensions in Higher Education Institutions (HEIs): A Critical Review. *Risks and Challenges of AI-Driven Finance: Bias, Ethics, and Security*, 146-164.

Kuriakose, B., Shrestha, R., & Sandnes, F. E. (2022). Tools and Technologies for Blind and Visually Impaired Navigation Support: A Review. *IETE Technical Review (Institution of Electronics and Telecommunication Engineers, India), 39*(1), 3–18. https://doi.org/DOI: 10.1080/02564602.2020.1819893

Latham, A., & Goltz, S. (2019). A survey of the general public's views on the ethics of using AI in education. In *Lecture Notes in Computer Science* (pp. 194–206). Springer International Publishing.

Lee, J., Hicke, Y., Yu, R., Brooks, C., & Kizilcec, R. F. (2024). The life cycle of large language models in education: A framework for understanding sources of bias. *British Journal of Educational Technology*, *55*(5), 1982–2002.

Lee, S., & Lee, K. (2024). Smart teachers in smart schools in a smart city: Teachers as adaptive agents of educational technology reforms. *Learning, Media and Technology*, *49*(3), 456–477.

Lin, Z. (2024). Beyond principlism: Practical strategies for ethical AI use in research practices. *AI and Ethics*, •••, 1–13.

Lipovec, A. (2024). Charting the Path Forward: Effective Didactic Approach for Teaching AI Literacy in K-12 Education. *2022 11th Mediterranean Conference on Embedded Computing (MECO)*, 1–4. https://doi.org/DOI: 10.1109/meco62516.2024.10577894

Lopez-Gazpio, I. (2025). Integrating Large Language Models into Accessible and Inclusive Education: Access Democratization and Individualized Learning Enhancement Supported by Generative Artificial Intelligence. *Information (Basel)*, *16*(6), 473. DOI: 10.3390/info16060473

Luckin, R., & Holmes, W. (2016). Intelligence unleashed: An argument for AI in education.

Luckin, R. (2025). Nurturing human intelligence in the age of AI: Rethinking education for the future. *Development and Learning in Organizations*, *39*(1), 1–4.

Madaio, M., Blodgett, S. L., Mayfield, E., & Dixon-Román, E. (2022). Beyond "fairness": Structural (in)justice lenses on ai for education. In The ethics of artificial intelligence in education (pp. 203-239). Routledge.

Mahabeer, P., & Pirtheepal, T. (2019). Assessment, plagiarism, and its effect on academic integrity: Experiences of academics at a university in South Africa. *South African Journal of Science*, *115*(11-12), 1–8.

Maimela, C., & Mbonde, P. (2025). Artificial Intelligence (AI) in South African Universities: Curriculum Transformation and Decolonization–Aid or Obstacle? *Frontiers in Sociology*, *10*, 1543471.

Malcolm, D. (2021). Post-truth society? An Eliasian sociological analysis of knowledge in the 21st century. *Sociology*, *55*(6), 1063–1079.

Maphalala, M. C., & Ajani, O. A. (2025). Leveraging artificial intelligence as a learning tool in higher education. *Interdisciplinary Journal of Education Research*, *7*(1), a01–a01.

Marino, M. T., Vasquez, E., Dieker, L., Basham, J., & Blackorby, J. (2023). The future of Artificial Intelligence in special education technology. *Journal of Special Education Technology, 38*(3), 404–416.

Marrero, A. (2024). In the Crosshairs: Navigating Political Pressures as a New Leader. In Pursuing Equity and Success for Marginalized Educational Leaders (pp. 101-117). IGI Global.

Martiniello, N., Eisenbarth, W., Lehane, C., Johnson, A., & Wittich, W. (2022). Exploring the use of smartphones and tablets among people with visual impairments: Are mainstream devices replacing the use of traditional visual aids? *Assistive Technology, 34*(1), 34–45. DOI: 10.1080/10400435.2019.1682084 PMID: 31697612

Mathai, A. (2024). *Enhancing Education for Underprivileged Children Through AI-Powered Native Language Learning Inclusive Education Through AI-Powered Native Language Learning. SSRN.* https://papers.ssrn.com/sol3/papers.cfm?abstract_id=4899553

Mbangeleli, N. B. A., & Funda, V. (2024). Mapping the Evidence Around the Use of AI-Powered Tools in South African Universities: A Systematic Review. *In Proceedings of the International Conference on Education Research.* (149-158). Academic Conferences and Publishing Limited. DOI: 10.34190/icer.1.1.3180

McAfee, A., & Brynjolfsson, E. (2017). *Machine, platform, crowd: Harnessing our digital future.* WW Norton & Company.

McDermid, J. A., Jia, Y., Porter, Z., & Habli, I. (2021). Artificial intelligence explainability: The technical and ethical dimensions. *Philosophical Transactions of the Royal Society A, 379*(2207), 20200363. PMID: 34398656

Meenakshi Dwivedi. (2021). *Creating inclusive classrooms.*

Mehling, S., & Kolleck, N. (2019). Cross-sector collaboration in higher education institutions (HEIs): A critical analysis of an urban sustainability development program. *Sustainability, 11*(18), 4982.

Meijer, A., & Wessels, M. (2019). Predictive policing: Review of benefits and drawbacks. *International Journal of Public Administration, 42*(12), 1031–1039.

Melo-López, V.-A., Basantes-Andrade, A., Gudiño-Mejía, C.-B., & Hernández-Martínez, E. (2025). The Impact of Artificial Intelligence on Inclusive Education: A Systematic Review. *Education Sciences, 15*(5), 539. DOI: 10.3390/educsci15050539

Ménard, A. D., & Chittle, L. (2023). The impostor phenomenon in post-secondary students: A review of the literature. *Review of Education, 11*(2), e3399. Advance online publication. DOI: 10.1002/rev3.3399

Mergen, A., Çetin-Kılıç, N., & Özbilgin, M. F. (2025). Artificial intelligence and bias towards marginalised groups: Theoretical roots and challenges. In *AI and Diversity in a Datafied World of Work: Will the Future of Work be Inclusive?* (Vol. 12, pp. 17–38). Emerald Publishing Limited.

Miao, F., & Holmes, W. (2021). *AI and education: A guidance for policymakers.* Unesco Publishing.

Mickelsen, S. B. (2025). Exploring the Role of AI and Educators in Shaping Student Creativity.

Milan, S. (2020). Techno-solutionism and the standard human in the making of the COVID-19 pandemic. *Big Data & Society*, *7*(2), 2053951720966781. DOI: 10.1177/2053951720966781

Mitchell, M., Wu, S., Zaldivar, A., Barnes, P., Vasserman, L., Hutchinson, B., & Gebru, T. (2019, January). Model cards for model reporting. In *Proceedings of the conference on fairness, accountability, and transparency* (pp. 220-229).

Mogoale, P. D., Pretorius, A., Mogase, R. C., & Segooa, M. A. (2025). Integrating artificial intelligence within South African higher learning institutions. *South African Journal of Information Management*, *27*(1), 1939.

Mohammed, R. R. (2025). Generative AI in the Academy: Analysis of Stakeholders' Experiences in US Higher Education Organizations (Doctoral dissertation, Arizona State University).

Mohammed, S. J., & Khalid, M. W. (2025). Under the world of AI-generated feedback on writing: Mirroring motivation, foreign language peace of mind, trait emotional intelligence, and writing development. *Language Testing in Asia*, *15*(1), 10. Advance online publication. DOI: 10.1186/s40468-025-00343-2

Molaudzi, A. I., & Marutha, N. (2024). Contributory factors to attitudes towards the adoption of artificial intelligence technology in public academic libraries in South Africa. *Information Development*, •••, 02666669241304704.

Moustaghfir, S., & Brigui, H. (2024). Navigating critical thinking in the digital era: An informative exploration. International Journal of Linguistics. *Literature and Translation*, *7*(1), 137–143.

Mukhtarkyzy, K., Smagulova, L., Tokzhigitova, A., Serikbayeva, N., Sayakov, O., Turkmenbayev, A., & Assilbayeva, R. (2025). A systematic review of the utility of assistive technologies for SEND students in schools. *Frontiers in Education*, *10*(February). Advance online publication. DOI: 10.3389/feduc.2025.1523797

Mungai, B. K., Omieno, P. K. K., Egessa, M., & Manyara, P. N. (2024). AI chatbots in LMS: A pedagogical review of cognitive, constructivist, and adaptive principles. *Engineering And Technology Journal*, *9*(8), 4709–4715.

Murtiningsih, S., & Sujito, A. (2024). Reimagining the future of education: Inclusive pedagogies, critical intergenerational justice, and technological disruption. *Policy Futures in Education*, 14782103251341406.

Mutambara, A. G. (2025). *Artificial Intelligence: A driver of inclusive development and shared prosperity for the Global South*. CRC Press.

NAKAMURA, T. M. (2025). ETHICAL AI IN US NEWSPAPER COVERAGE: MEDIA FRAMING AND CORPORATE ACCOUNTABILITY.

Napitupulu, M. F., & Dalimunte, A. A. (2025). A study of students' perception of character AI in practicing English speaking fluency. Celtic: A Journal of Culture, English Language Teaching. *Literatura y Lingüística*, *12*(1), 384–404.

Nasim, S. S., Pranav, P., & Dutta, S. (2025). A systematic literature review on intrusion detection techniques in cloud computing. *Discover Computing*, *28*(1). Advance online publication. DOI: 10.1007/s10791-025-09641-y

Navales, G. (2024). ChatGPT as a writing aid: English teachers' perceptions on its usefulness and ethical acceptability. *Asian Journal of English Language Studies*, *12*(2), 27–50. DOI: 10.59960/12.2.a2

Nazzaro, A., Santini, C., & Nazzaro, L. (2025). LSTM-driven CLIL: Cybersecurity vocabulary learning with AI. *Journal of Educational Technology and Online Learning*, *8*(3), 313–329. DOI: 10.31681/jetol.1685183

Nesru, S. R. K. (2023). The Ethics of AI Use in Special Education Settings. *Multidisciplinary Science Journal*, *1*(01), 34–40.

Nguyen, A., Ngo, H. N., Hong, Y., Dang, B., & Nguyen, B. P. T. (2023). Ethical principles for artificial intelligence in education. *Education and Information Technologies*, *28*(4), 4221–4241. PMID: 36254344

Nixon, N., Lin, Y., & Snow, L. (2024). Catalyzing equity in STEM teams: Harnessing generative AI for inclusion and diversity. *Policy Insights from the Behavioral and Brain Sciences*, *11*(1), 85–92. PMID: 38516055

Nongqwenga, M., & Funda, V. (2024). A model to integrate Generative Artificial Intelligence to improve student academic performance in South African universities. In *International Conference on Emerging Technology and Interdisciplinary Sciences* (pp. 46-53).

Norman-Major, K. (2023). Balancing the four Es; or can we achieve equity for social equity in public administration? In *Social Equity in the Public Administration Classroom* (pp. 27–46). Routledge.

Noviandy, T. R., & Maulana, A., Idroes Ghazi Mauer and Zahriah, Z., Paristiowati, M., Emran, T. B., Ilyas, M., & Idroes, R. (2024). Embrace, don't avoid: Reimagining higher education with generative artificial intelligence. *J. Educ. Manag. Learn.*, *2*(2), 81–90.

Nyahodza, L., & Higgs, R. (2017). Towards bridging the digital divide in post-apartheid South Africa: A case of a historically disadvantaged university in Cape Town. *South African Journal of Library and Information Science*, *83*(1), 39–48.

O'Leary, E. S., Shapiro, C., Toma, S., Sayson, H. W., Levis-Fitzgerald, M., Johnson, T., & Sork, V. L. (2020). Creating inclusive classrooms by engaging STEM faculty in culturally responsive teaching workshops. *International Journal of STEM Education*, *7*(1), 32. PMID: 32647597

Oberle, E., Domitrovich, C. E., Meyers, D. C., & Weissberg, R. P. (2016). Establishing systemic social and emotional learning approaches in schools: A framework for schoolwide implementation. *Cambridge Journal of Education*, *46*(3), 277–297.

OECD. (2024). The potential impact of Artificial Intelligence on equity and inclusion in education. *OECD Artificial Intelligence Papers*, (23). Advance online publication. DOI: 10.1787/15df715b-en

Omodan, B. I. (2024). Redefining university infrastructure for the 21st century: An interplay between physical assets and digital evolution. *Journal of Infrastructure. Policy and Development*, *8*(4), 3468.

Opesemowo, O. A. G., & Adekomaya, V. (2024). Harnessing artificial intelligence for advancing sustainable development goals in South Africa's higher education system: A qualitative study. *International Journal of Learning. Teaching and Educational Research*, *23*(3), 67–86.

Ormond, E. (2022). *Global to Local: South African Perspectives on AI Ethics Risks.* https://papers.ssrn.com/sol3/papers.cfm?abstract_id=4240356

Ortiz, E. A., Vergara, N. C., Pabón, T. F., Gambi, G. D. N., Giambruno, C., Alfaro, M. P., & Segura, D. R. (2025). AI and Education: Building the Future Through Digital Transformation.

Paglialunga, A., & Melogno, S. (2025). The Effectiveness of Artificial Intelligence-Based Interventions for Students with Learning Disabilities: A Systematic Review. *Brain Sciences*, *15*(8), 806. DOI: 10.3390/brainsci15080806 PMID: 40867139

Pagliara, S. M., Bonavolonta, G., Pia, M., Falchi, S., Zurru, A. L., Fenu, G., & Mura, A. (2024). The integration of Artificial Intelligence in inclusive education: A scoping review. In *Preprints*.

Palid, O., Cashdollar, S., Deangelo, S., Chu, C., & Bates, M. (2023). Inclusion in practice: A systematic review of diversity-focused STEM programming in the United States. *International Journal of STEM Education*, *10*(1), 2.

Pan, J. (2024). AI-driven English language learning program and academic writing integrity in the era of intelligent interface. *English Language Teaching and Linguistics Studies*, *6*(4), 120.

Paris, D., & Alim, H. S. (2017). *Culturally sustaining pedagogies: Teaching and learning for justice in a changing world.* Teachers College Press.

Patel, S., & Ragolane, M. (2024). The implementation of artificial intelligence in South African higher education institutions: Opportunities and challenges. *Technium Education and Humanities*, *9*, 51–65.

Paul, M., Sunil, M. N., & Neena, P. (2024). The silent struggle—Imposter syndrome and its influence on self-efficacy and academic performance: A study on MBA students in a private university. *International Journal for Multidisciplinary Research*, *6*(3), 20790. Advance online publication. DOI: 10.36948/ijfmr.2024.v06i03.20790

Pazmino-Maji, R., Conde, M. Á., & García-Peñalvo, F. (2021). Learning analytics in Ecuador: A systematic review supported by statistical implicative analysis. *Universal Access in the Information Society*, *20*(3), 495–512.

Pedrazas, M. A., Hahm, W. J., Huang, M. H., Dralle, D., Nelson, M. D., Breunig, R. E., ... & Rempe, D. M. (2021). The relationship between topography, bedrock weathering, and water storage across a sequence of ridges and valleys. Journal of Geophysical Research: Earth Surface, 126(4), e2020JF005848.

Pendy, B. (2023). Artificial Intelligence: The future of education. Jurnal Indonesia Sosial Sains, 2(11).

Perkmen, S. (2024). The role of self efficacy and school climate in motivation for technology integration in education. *Journal of Educational Technology and Online Learning, 7*(4-ICETOL 2024 Special Issue), 358–366. https://doi.org/DOI: 10.31681/jetol.1557095

Perrotta, C., Selwyn, N., & Ewin, C. (2022). Artificial intelligence and the affective labour of understanding: The intimate moderation of a language model. *New Media & Society, 14614448221075296*. Advance online publication. DOI: 10.1177/14614448221075296

Petrachenko, J. (2024). Dwelling in the In-Between: A Self Study of Moving into a Classroom with Unconventional Learners.

Pettitt, J. (2023). How Exemplary Female Executive Leaders in Higher Education Use Five Principles of Grit—Courage, Conscientiousness, Long-Term Goals, Resilience, and Excellence Versus Perfection—to Accomplish Extraordinary Results in Their Organizations (Doctoral dissertation, University of Massachusetts Global).

Pierrès, O., Christen, M., Schmitt-Koopmann, F. M., & Darvishy, A. (2024). Could the use of AI in higher education hinder students with disabilities? A scoping review. *IEEE Access : Practical Innovations, Open Solutions*, *12*, 27810–27828.

Pierrès, O., Darvishy, A., & Christen, M. (2025). Exploring the role of generative AI in higher education: Semi-structured interviews with students with disabilities. *Education and Information Technologies*, *30*(7), 8923–8952. DOI: 10.1007/s10639-024-13134-8

Polverini, G. (2022). Exploring interdisciplinarity between physics and mathematics: the design of a linguistic and an epistemological tool for analysing texts about the parabolic motion (Doctoral dissertation, Master thesis in Physics, Alma Mater Studiorum–University of Bologna).

Popenici, S. A., & Kerr, S. (2017). Exploring the impact of artificial intelligence on teaching and learning in higher education. *Research and Practice in Technology Enhanced Learning*, *12*(1), 22. PMID: 30595727

Prangon, N. F., & Wu, J. (2024). AI and computing horizons: Cloud and edge in the modern era. *Journal of Sensor and Actuator Networks*, *13*(4), 44.

Pratschke, B. M. (2024). *Generative AI and education: Digital pedagogies, teaching innovation and learning design*. Springer Nature.

Puplampu, R. (2024). *What Everyone Should Know About the Rise of AI: AI Transparency, Privacy, and Ethics Best Practices*. Puplampu Books.

Purwanto, & Hendrawan, J. H. (2024). Smart collaboration: Improving learning achievement with Artificial Intelligence. Icasse, 1(1), 335–341.

Radanliev, P. (2024). Artificial intelligence: Reflecting on the past and looking towards the next paradigm shift. *Journal of Experimental & Theoretical Artificial Intelligence*, •••, 1–18.

Ragolane, M. (2025). Teaching Artificial Intelligence and Teaching with Artificial Intelligence in South African Higher Education Institutions.

Rahimi, Z., & Azadmanesh, S. (2025). Educational Justice in the Age of Artificial Intelligence through the Lens of Deconstruction Theory. It is under consideration.

Rainie, L., & Anderson, J. (2024). Experts imagine the impact of artificial intelligence by 2040. Imagining the Digital Future Center. *Retrieved*, (December), 15.

Raja, R., & Nagasubramani, P. C. (2018). Impact of modern technology in education. Journal of applied and advanced research, 3(1), 33-35.

Rane, N., Choudhary, S., & Rane, J. (2023). Education 4.0 and 5.0: Integrating artificial intelligence (AI) for personalized and adaptive learning. *Journal of Artificial Intelligence and Robotics*, *1*(1), 29–43.

Rashid, S. F., Duong-Trung, N., & Pinkwart, N. (2024). *Generative AI in education: Technical foundations, applications, and challenges*. Artificial Intelligence and Education-Shaping the Future of Learning.

Rasul, T., Nair, S., & Kalendra, D., Balaji, De Oliveira Santini, F., Ladeira, W. J., Rather, R. A., Yasin, N., Rodriguez, R. V., Kokkalis, P., Murad, M. W., & Hossain, M. U. (2024). Enhancing academic integrity among students in the GenAI era: A holistic framework. *International Journal of Management Education*, *22*(3), 101041. DOI: 10.1016/j.ijme.2024.101041

Reddy, K. J. (2025). Accessibility and Affordability of Technologies. In *Innovations in Neurocognitive Rehabilitation: Harnessing Technology for Effective Therapy* (pp. 285–304). Springer Nature Switzerland.

Rizos, I., Foykas, E., & Georgakopoulos, S. V. (2024). Enhancing mathematics education for students with special educational needs through generative AI: A case study in Greece. *Contemporary Educational Technology*, *16*(4), ep535.

Roscoe, R. D., Salehi, S., Nixon, N., Worsley, M., Piech, C., & Luckin, R. (2022). Inclusion and equity as a paradigm shift for artificial intelligence in education. In *Artificial Intelligence in STEM Education* (pp. 359–374). CRC Press.

Rose, D. H., & Meyer, A. (2002). *Teaching every student in the digital age: Universal design for learning*. Association for Supervision and Curriculum Development, 1703 N. Beauregard St., Alexandria, VA 22311-1714 (Product no. 101042: $22.95 ASCD members; $26.95 nonmembers).

Rostami, M., & Longo, V. (2024). Teachers' narratives on implementing AI-based learning tools for students with severe disabilities. *The Psychological Research in Individuals with Exceptional Needs*, *2*(2), 20–27.

Rout, B. (2024). SEL and Technology: The Role of Digital Tools in Promoting Emotional and Social Skills. *International Journal for Research in Applied Science and Engineering Technology*, *12*(12), 1584–1589. DOI: 10.22214/ijraset.2024.66086

Sahebi, S., & Formosa, P. (2025). The AI-mediated communication dilemma: Epistemic trust, social media, and the challenge of generative artificial intelligence. *Synthese*, *205*(3), 1–24.

Sakubu, D. (2025). *Challenges of Artificial Intelligence today and future implications for society and the world*. World Journal of Advanced Research and Reviews.

Saleela, D., Oyegoke, A. S., Dauda, J. A., & Ajayi, S. O. (2025). Development of AI-Driven Decision Support System for Personalized Housing Adaptations and Assistive Technology. *Journal of Aging and Environment*, *0*(0), 1–24. DOI: 10.1080/26892618.2025.2534956

Samadi, M., Faculty of Educational Sciences, Psychology University of Isfahan, I., Ghamarani, A., Department of Psychology, of Children with Special Needs, F. of E. S., Psychology University of Isfahan, I., Faramarzi, S., Department of Psychology, of Children with Special Needs, F. of E. S., & Psychology University of Isfahan, I. (2020). Role of PASS cognitive processes in explaining the ability of word reading and text comprehension in children with dyslexia. *Q. J. Child Ment. Health*, *7*(2), 268–279.

Saman, H. M., Noor, S. M., Isa, C. M. M., Lian, O. C., & Narayanan, G. (2024). Embracing Artificial Intelligence as a Catalyst for Change in Reshaping Malaysian Higher Education in the Digital Era: A Literature Review. In *International Conference on Innovation & Entrepreneurship in Computing, Engineering & Science Education (InvENT 2024)* (pp. 633-643). Atlantis Press.

Santhana Hari, S., Harine Rajashree, R., Dharani, J., & Santhiya, C. (2025). AI-enabled learning ecosystems. In *Driving Quality Education Through AI and Data Science* (pp. 165–192). IGI Global.

Santos, S. M. A. V., Da Silva, C. G., De Carvalho, I. E., De Castilho, L. P., Meroto, M. B. das N., Tavares, P. R., Pires, R. dos R., & Moniz, S. S. de O. R. (2024). The art of personalization of education: Artificial Intelligence on the stages of special education. CONTRIBUCIONES A LAS CIENCIAS SOCIALES, 17(2), e4971.

Sapkota, R., Roumeliotis, K. I., & Karkee, M. (2025). Ai agents vs. agentic ai: A conceptual taxonomy, applications and challenges. arXiv preprint arXiv:2505.10468.

Saragih, R. I. E. (2024). AI-Powered Education: Transforming Learning through Personalized and Scalable Solutions. *International Journal of Information Systems and Innovative Technology*, *3*(2), 1–9.

Schreffler, J., Vasquez, E.III, & Chini, J.. (2019). Universal Design for Learning in postsecondary STEM education for students with disabilities: A systematic literature review. *International Journal of STEM Education*, *6*, 8. DOI: 10.1186/s40594-019-0161-8

Schuster, N. (2023). The skill model: A dilemma for virtue ethics. *Ethical Theory and Moral Practice*, *26*(3), 447–461.

Sebihi, A., Schoelen, L., & Uwamwezi, B. (2025). Unveiling AI's impact in Rwandan higher education: Navigating trends, challenges, and imperatives at the University of Rwanda. *Discover Education*, *4*, 166. DOI: 10.1007/s44217-025-00576-6

Secl, M. J. (2025). The Educational Perspective of At-Risk Students: How Standards-Based Grading Affects Students in Alternative Education.

SELVI, B. (2024). Artificial Intelligence in Higher Education: Transforming Internationalization at Home. Shanlax Publications Book Chapters, 1-17.

Senjam, S. S., Manna, S., & Bascaran, C. (2021). Smartphones-based assistive technology: Accessibility features and apps for people with visual impairment, and its usage, challenges, and usability testing. *Clinical Optometry*, *13*, 311–322. DOI: 10.2147/OPTO.S336361 PMID: 34866955

Sharma, L. (2023). *Building Culture: A handbook to harnessing human nature to create strong school teams.*

Sharma, U., Loreman, T., & Forlin, C. (2012). Measuring teacher efficacy to implement inclusive practices. *Journal of Research in Special Educational Needs*, *12*(1), 12–21.

Singh, S., & Jain, P. (2024). AI in special education. In *Advanced Intelligence Systems and Innovation in Entrepreneurship* (pp. 56–75). IGI Global.

Singh, V. (2025). AI-Powered Assistive Technologies for People with Disabilities: Developing AI Solutions that Aid Individuals with Various Disabilities in Daily Tasks. *Journal of Engineering Research and Reports, 27*(2), 292–309. DOI: 10.9734/jerr/2025/v27i21410

Skinner, E. A., Kindermann, T. A., & Furrer, C. J. (2008). A motivational perspective on engagement and disaffection. *Educational and Psychological Measurement, 69*(3), 493–525. DOI: 10.1177/0013164408323233

Sliwka, A., Klopsch, B., Beigel, J., & Tung, L. (2024). Transformational leadership for deeper learning: Shaping innovative school practices for enhanced learning. *Journal of Educational Administration, 62*(1), 103–121.

Smith, L. T. (2021). *Decolonizing methodologies: Research and indigenous peoples*. Bloomsbury Publishing.

Smit, M., Bond-Barnard, T., & Wagner, R. F. (2025). Artificial Intelligence in South African Higher Education: Survey Data of Master's Level Students. *Data in Brief*, •••, 111813.

Souval, D. H., Haber, Y., Tal, A., Simon, T., Elyoseph, T., & Elyoseph, Z. (2025). Transforming Perceptions: Exploring the Multifaceted Potential of Generative AI for People With Cognitive Disabilities. *JMIR Neurotechnology, 4*, 1–11. DOI: 10.2196/64182

Sridhar, A., Pesala, B., Radhakrishnan, G., Niezgoda, J., & Gopalakrishnan, S. (2025). Evolution of Artificial Intelligence. In *Artificial Intelligence and Biological Sciences* (pp. 26–37). CRC Press.

Stracke, C. M. (2024). Artificial Intelligence and education: Ethical questions and guidelines for their relations based on human rights, democracy, and the rule of law. In *Lecture Notes in Educational Technology* (pp. 97–107). Springer Nature Singapore.

Suliman, Z., Mohale, N. E., Maphoto, K. B., & Sevnarayan, K. (2004). The interconnectedness between Ubuntu principles and generative artificial intelligence in distance higher education institutions. *Discover Education, 3*. Advance online publication. DOI: 10.1007/s44217-024-00289-2

SWARGIARY. (2024). *K*. Addressing Maladaptive Behaviors from AI Integration in Learning. EdTech Research Association.

Syaidina, M. O., Fahrudin, R., & Mutiara, I. A. (2024). Implementation of ethics of using Artificial Intelligence in the education system in Indonesia. *B-FronT, 4*(1), 63–71.

Syed, W. (2025). Advancing Accessibility and Social Inclusion through Generative AI and Machine Learning-Powered Multi-Modality on Mobile Platforms. *International Journal of Scientific Research in Computer Science. Engineering and Information Technology, 11*(1), 475–483. DOI: 10.32628/cseit25111254

Tang, K. H. D. (2024). Implications of artificial Intelligence for teaching and learning. *Acta Pedagogia Asia, 3*(2), 65–79.

Taylor, C., Dewsbury, B., & Brame, C. (2022). Technology, equity, and inclusion in the virtual education space. In *Technologies in Biomedical and Life Sciences Education: Approaches and evidence of efficacy for learning* (pp. 35–60). Springer International Publishing.

Tilak, S., Lincoln, J., Miner, T., Christensen, N., Jankowski, J., & Kennedy, K. (2024). A participatory, qualitative analysis of the use of MagicSchool AI for course design. *J. Sociocybernetics, 19*(1).

Tonbuloğlu, B. (2023). An evaluation of the use of artificial intelligence applications in online education. *Journal of Educational Technology and Online Learning, 6*(4), 866–884.

Topol, E. (2019). *Deep medicine: how artificial intelligence can make healthcare human again.*

Tripathi, A., Yadav, V., & Kumar, S. (2025). Leveraging artificial intelligence for rural education: A systematic review of transforming learning opportunities and bridging the urban-rural divide.

UNESCO, E. S. (2020). Distance learning strategies in response to COVID-19 school closures. *Nota informative, 2*(1), 1-8.

Ungar, M., Theron, L., & Höltge, J. (2023). Multisystemic approaches to researching young people's resilience: Discovering culturally and contextually sensitive accounts of thriving under adversity. *Development and Psychopathology, 35*(5), 2199–2213. PMID: 37128831

University of Cape Town. (2024, July 31). *GRIT introduces an AI chatbot to UCT staff and students. UCT News.* https://news.uct.ac.za news.uct.ac.za+10news.uct.ac.za+10iol.co.za+10

Veletsianos, G., & Koseoglu, S. (2022). *Feminist Critical Digital Pedagogy.*

Viberg, O., & Kizilcec, R. F., Wise Alyssa Friend and Jivet, I., & Nixon, N. (2024). Advancing equity and inclusion in educational practices with AI-powered educational decision support systems (AI-EDSS). *British Journal of Educational Technology, 55*(5), 1974–1981.

Villena, F., Véliz, C., García-Huidobro, R., & Aguayo, S. (2024). Generative artificial intelligence in dentistry: Current approaches and future challenges. arXiv preprint arXiv:2407.17532.

Voss, A. (2024). The Future We're Building: How Today's Innovations Will Shape Tomorrow's World. eBookIt. com.

Wamba, S. F., Queiroz, M. M., Randhawa, K., & Gupta, G. (2025). Generative artificial intelligence and the challenges to adding value ethically. *Technovation, 144*, 103235.

Wan, Y., Pu, G., Sun, J., Garimella, A., Chang, K.-W., & Peng, N. (2023). "Kelly is a Warm Person, Joseph is a Role Model": Gender Biases in LLM-Generated Reference Letters. *arXiv preprint arXiv:2310.09219.*

Wang, Q. (2024). Mutual theory of mind for human-AI communication in AI-mediated social interaction (Doctoral dissertation, Ph. D. Dissertation. Georgia Institute of Technology).

Wang, S., Xu, T., Li, H., Zhang, C., Liang, J., Tang, J., . . . Wen, Q. (2024). Large language models for education: A survey and outlook. arXiv preprint arXiv:2403.18105.

Wang, C., & Si, L. (2024). The intersection of public policy and public access: Digital inclusion, digital literacy education, and libraries. *Sustainability*, *16*(5), 1878.

Waterfield, D. A., Coleman, O. F., Welker, N. P., Kennedy, M. J., McDonald, S. D., & Cook, B. G. (2025). IEPs in the age of AI: Examining IEP goals written with and without ChatGPT. *Journal of Special Education Technology.*

Williams, C., Pease, A., Warnes, P., Harrison, S., Pilon, F., Hyvarinen, L., West, S., Self, J., Ferris, J., Goodenough, T., Watanabe, R., Clark, R., Evans, M., Osborne, D., Edwards, E., Billington, C., Hunn, R., & Matharu, G. (2021). Cerebral visual impairment-related vision problems in primary school children: A cross-sectional survey. *Developmental Medicine and Child Neurology*, *63*(6), 683–689. DOI: 10.1111/dmcn.14819 PMID: 33533021

Williamson, B. (2023). Governing through infrastructural control: Artificial intelligence and cloud computing in the data-intensive state. *Digital Society : Ethics, Socio-Legal and Governance of Digital Technology*, 521.

Williamson, B., Celis, C. V., Sriprakash, A., Pykett, J., & Facer, K. (2024). Algorithmic futuring: Predictive infrastructures of valuation and investment in the assetization of edtech. *Learning, Media and Technology*, 1–15.

Williamson, B., & Eynon, R. (2020). Historical threads, missing links, and future directions in AI in education. *Learning, Media and Technology*, *45*(3), 223–235.

Wiredu, J. K., Abuba, N. S., & Zakaria, H. (2024). Impact of Generative AI in academic integrity and learning outcomes: A case study in the Upper East Region. *Asian J. Res. Com. Sci.*, *17*(8), 70–88.

Woolf, B. P. (2010). *Building intelligent interactive tutors: Student-centered strategies for revolutionizing e-learning*. Morgan Kaufmann.

Xulu, H. H., Hlongwa, N. S., & Maguraushe, K. (2024, December). Unlocking the Potential of AI in Higher Education: A Multi-Dimensional Study of ChatGPT Adoption at a South African University. In *The Focus Conference (TFC 2024)* (pp. 516-532). Atlantis Press.

Xu, Y., Wen, F., Zuo, B., & Rhodes, M. (2023). Social essentialism in the United States and China: How social and cognitive factors predict within-and cross-cultural variation in essentialist thinking. *Memory & Cognition*, *51*(3), 681–694. PMID: 35419740

Yahya, S. I., Alameri, B. M., Jamshidi, M., Roshani, S., Chaudhary, M. A., Ijemaru, G. K., & Roshani, S. (2022). A new design method for class-E power amplifiers using artificial intelligence modeling for wireless power transfer applications. *Electronics (Basel)*, *11*(21), 3608.

Yakobi, K., & Yakobi, S. (2025). Online learning support as a pedagogical strategy for student learning in the developing universities in South Africa: A literature review. *Cogent Education*, *12*(1). Advance online publication. DOI: 10.1080/2331186X.2025.2464310

Yambal, S., & Waykar, Y. A. (2025). Future of Education Using Adaptive AI, Intelligent Systems, and Ethical Challenges. In Effective Instructional Design Informed by AI (pp. 171-202). IGI Global Scientific Publishing.

Yang, X., Yeo, K. J., Lee, S.-H., & Handayani, L. (2024). A systematic review of impostor syndrome in higher education. [IJERE]. *International Journal of Evaluation and Research in Education*, *13*(6), 3884–3892. DOI: 10.11591/ijere.v13i6.30726

Yousefi, F., Dehnavieh, R., Laberge, M., Gagnon, M. P., Ghaemi, M. M., Nadali, M., & Azizi, N. (2025). Opportunities, challenges, and requirements for Artificial Intelligence (AI) implementation in Primary Health Care (PHC): A systematic review. *BMC Primary Care*, *26*(1), 196.

Youvan, D. C. (2024). Amplification Through Progression: From Analog Signals to Artificial Intelligence.

Yu, P., Lu, S., Long, Z., Chen, Y., Qian, J., & Shah, Z. A. (2024). Exploring ethical considerations in utilizing generative AI for global knowledge sharing in higher education. In *Advances in Higher Education and Professional Development* (pp. 1–27). IGI Global.

Yu, Z. (2021). The effects of gender, educational level, and personality on online learning outcomes during the COVID-19 pandemic. *International Journal of Educational Technology in Higher Education*, *18*(1), 14. PMID: 34778520

Zawacki-Richter, O.. (2019). Systematic review of research on artificial intelligence applications in higher education – where are the educators? *International Journal of Educational Technology in Higher Education*, *16*(1). Advance online publication. DOI: 10.1186/s41239-019-0171-0

Zawacki-Richter, O., Marín, V. I., Bond, M., & Gouverneur, F. (2019). Systematic review of research on artificial intelligence applications in higher education–where are the educators? *International Journal of Educational Technology in Higher Education*, *16*(1), 1–27.

Zembylas, M. (2023). The resilience of racism and affective numbness: Cultivating an aesthetics of attention in education. *Critical Studies in Education*, *64*(5), 411–427. DOI: 10.1080/17508487.2023.2171452

Zhai, C., Wibowo, S., & Li, L. D. (2024). The effects of over-reliance on AI dialogue systems on students' cognitive abilities: A systematic review. *Smart Learning Environments*, *11*(1), 3. Advance online publication. DOI: 10.1186/s40561-024-00316-7

Zhai, X., Chu, X., Chai, C. S., Jong, M. S. Y., Istenic, A., Spector, M., & Li, Y. (2021). A Review of Artificial Intelligence (AI) in Education from 2010 to 2020. *Complexity*, *2021*(1), 8812542.

Zhang, L., Carter, R. A., Liu, Y., & Peng, P. (2024). Let's CHAT About Artificial Intelligence for Students With Disabilities: A Systematic Literature Review and Meta-Analysis. *Review of Educational Research*, *XX*(X), 1–43. DOI: 10.3102/00346543241293424

Zhang, S., Zhao, X., Zhou, T., & Kim, J. H. (2024). Do you have AI dependency? The roles of academic self-efficacy, academic stress, and performance expectations on problematic AI usage behavior. *International Journal of Educational Technology in Higher Education*, *21*(1), 19. Advance online publication. DOI: 10.1186/s41239-024-00467-0

Zhao, X., Cox, A., & Chen, X. (2025). The use of generative AI by students with disabilities in higher education. *Internet and Higher Education, 66*(June 2024), 101014. https://doi.org/DOI: 10.1016/j.iheduc.2025.101014

Zhou, Q. (2023). How does dyslexia influence academic achievement? In *Proceedings of the 2022 2nd International Conference on Modern Educational Technology and Social Sciences (ICMETSS 2022)* (pp. 861–868). Atlantis Press SARL.

Zulvi, J. D., & Abidin, Z. (2025). Coping strategies of high-achieving students in boarding excellence high schools: A Case study. *The International Journal of Science in Society*, *7*(1), 31–41. DOI: 10.54783/ijsoc.v7i1.\1357

Zunaidah, A., Wiharja, C. K., & Febriantono, M. A. (2023). Dependency on AI-Based Writing Tools in English Learning: Implications for Human-Computer Interaction. *2022 International Conference on Information Management and Technology (ICIMTech)*, 1–6. https://doi.org/DOI: 10.1109/icimtech59029.2023.10278054

About the Contributors

Gürhan Durak is currently a visiting scholar at The Open University (UK) and serves as the president of the International Conference on Educational Technology and Online Learning (ICETOL). His research interests include Generative Artificial Intelligence, Learning Analytics, Instructional Design, and Mixed Research Methodologies. Gürhan Durak serves as the Editor-in-Chief for several international journals, including the Journal of Innovations in Learning and Technology (JILT), Journal of Educational Technology and Online Learning (JETOL), Journal of Online Learning Studies (Jour-OLS), and Journal of Innovations in Learning and Technology (JILT). He holds a PhD in Distance Education from Anadolu University, one of the leading global institutions in distance education.

Serkan Çankaya is an Associate Professor at İzmir Demokrasi University, Faculty of Economics and Administrative Sciences, and the director of the university's Distance Education Center. He holds a PhD in Distance Education from Anadolu University, with research focusing on educational technology, special education technology, online course design, and interactive learning environments. He serves as Editor-in-Chief of the International Journal of Computers in Education (IJCE) and the Journal of Online Learning Studies (Jour-OLS), and as an editor for the Journal of Educational Technology and Online Learning (JETOL). Serkan has contributed significantly to research and practical projects aimed at improving educational experiences through technology.

***

Masud Ahmmed is a Lecturer and researcher in education at Victoria University, Melbourne. His work focuses on inclusive education, teacher development, and intercultural pedagogy. He has contributed to teacher education reform both in Australia and internationally, particularly in South Asia. Masud's research explores the intersections of social justice, education policy, and culturally responsive teaching. He is committed to advancing equity in education through critical and practice-based inquiry. ORCID: 0009-0007-2783-8558

Janine Arantes is a Senior Lecturer and Research Fellow at Victoria University in Melbourne, Australia. With over 25 years in secondary, TAFE and tertiary education, Janine explores how teachers negotiate emergent technologies through the field of AI for Education. Her research critically examines AI governance, digital poverty, automation's impact on educator rights, and data-driven inequalities in education.

Sulaiman Olusegun Atiku is a Professor of Human Resources and Director of Research at Harold Pupkewitz Graduate School of Business (HP-GSB), Namibia University of Science and Technology, Namibia. He is a pragmatic researcher specializing in Strategic Human Resource Management. His current research area of interest includes Human Capital Formation for Industry 5.0, and People Management Practices for Promoting Sustainability. He has over 16 years' experience in Higher Education. A native of Lagos, Sulaiman graduated from the University of KwaZulu-Natal with a PhD degree in Human Resource Management. His Master of Science degree was awarded in Human Resources and Industrial Relations at Lagos State University, Nigeria. His Bachelor of Science (Honours) degree was also awarded at Lagos State University in the field of Industrial Relations and Personnel Management. He has lectured several courses in his field home/abroad and published many scholarly articles in international journals. He is a member of International Labour and Employment Relations Association (ILERA), Nigerian Institute of Management (NIM), and Institute of People Management (IPM) South Africa.

Swetha C. B. is an Assistant Professor at the Alliance School of Advanced Computing, Alliance University, Bengaluru, India. She holds a B.Tech in Computer Science and Engineering from Mahatma Gandhi University, Kerala, and an M.Tech in Information Systems Security from IGNOU. Currently pursuing her Ph.D. in Federated Learning, her academic and research interests span compiler design, cryptography, system software, Unix programming, data communication, artificial intelligence, and cybersecurity. With a strong commitment to academic excellence and innovation, Mrs. Swetha focuses on integrating secure and intelligent computing practices into modern education and research.

Maria Arjie T. Domingo is a permanent faculty member under the Institute of Arts and Sciences at Bulacan Agricultural State College in Bulacan and a part-time academic staff at the University of Santo Tomas in Manila, the Philippines. She is interested in exploring topics related to discourse analysis and corpus linguistics.

Tary Hadani is a motivated Information Systems student at Esa Unggul University who is passionate about harnessing digital tools to improve organizational workflows and decision-making. During her studies, Tary has engaged in academic writing and contributed to collaborative research projects, showcasing her dedication to learning and innovation. She thrives in environments that challenge her analytical thinking and creativity, and she is committed to using data-driven solutions to address real-world problems. Tary aspires to develop impactful technologies that enhance efficiency, support strategic goals, and bring sustainable value to businesses.

Pavithra K is an Assistant Professor in the Department of Computer Science, renowned for her extensive following and profound expertise in the fields of Data Mining and Reinforcement Learning. She has completed her Ph.D. in Computer Science from Dr.G.R. Damodaran College of Science, Bharathiar University, Coimbatore, Tamil Nadu. Ranked 2nd in her post-graduation and with over a decade of experience in academia, she has honed her teaching skills to excellence. She actively participates in various professional associations, including the International Association of Engineers & Computer Scientists (IAECS) & the Indian Academicians and Researchers Association (IARA). Her research journey is well-documented through publications, notably in Elsevier, SCOPUS, SCI, and Web of Science-indexed journals. She has also presented her work at numerous International Conferences, National Conferences, International and National Seminars, and International and National Workshops. Her areas of interest include Data warehousing and Mining, Artificial Intelligence, Machine Learning, Mobile Applications, Augmented and Virtual Reality.

Godwin Kaisara (PhD) is a Research Fellow at the Harold Pupkewitz Graduate School of Business, at the Namibia University of Science and Technology. Godwin previously worked at various institutions in South Africa, where he was lecturer and a team member of a National Research Foundation project on Information Systems effectiveness evaluation, and was a co-leader of the sub-project on e-Government evaluation. His research interests span the domain areas of artificial intelligence, knowledge management, e-government, e-learning, mobile learning, and ICT4D evaluation. Godwin has published several book chapters, conference papers and articles in international journals.

Asha Kurian is an academic and researcher with over 13 years of experience in teaching and mentoring students. Deeply passionate about education, she specializes in artificial intelligence, deep learning, computer vision, and generative modeling. Currently, she serves as a faculty member at Alliance University, Bangalore, where she is actively involved in teaching, curriculum development, and research supervision. Dr. Asha has an illustrious academic background, having held positions at esteemed institutions such as PES University, Bangalore, and Dr. M.G.R. University, Chennai. She has authored several papers in Scopus-indexed journals and has contributed as a reviewer for various conferences. Her research spans AI applications in healthcare and human-centered computing, with contributions to international conferences and workshops on topics such as sentiment analysis and social robotics. In addition to her research pursuits, she has played key roles in academic administration, conference organization, and student mentoring. Driven by a strong commitment to academic excellence and impactful research, Dr. Asha Kurian brings valuable expertise in the fields of AI and emerging technologies.

K. Lalitha is an Assistant Professor in the Department of Computer Science and Engineering at Santhiram Engineering College, Nandyal, Andhra Pradesh, India. She received her Master of Technology in Computer Science and Engineering from Vaagdevi Institute of Technology & Science, Proddatur, Andhra Pradesh, India. Her research interests include machine learning, data mining, and healthcare informatics. She has published multiple research articles in reputed journals.

Rashmi Mothkur working as Associate Professor in the Department of Alliance School of Advanced Computing at Alliance University, Bangalore. She has completed her Ph.D from Visweswaraya Technological University, Belgaum. Her research work is based on the medical image processing, deep learning and bioinspired techniques. She has completed her M.Tech degree from M.S.Ramiah Institute of Technology, Bangalore. She has completed her B.Tech degree from Bapuji Institute of Engineering and Technology, Davangere. She has total of 11 years of teaching experience. Her research interest include Artificial Intelligence, Medical Image Processing, Computer Vision. She has published various conference papers and journal papers.

O. Bhaskaru is an Assistant Professor in the Department of Computer Science and Engineering at Vignan's Foundation for Science, Technology & Research, Guntur, Andhra Pradesh, India. He received his Ph.D. in Computer Science and Engineering from KL University, Vijayawada, Andhra Pradesh, India. His research interests include machine learning, data mining, and artificial intelligence. He has published several papers in national and international journals.

Aarthi S is a dedicated Assistant Professor in Computer Science with over six years of teaching experience. She is currently pursuing her Ph.D. at Marwadi University, Gujarat, and holds an M.Phil. and MCA from Bharathiar University, Tamil Nadu. Throughout her academic career, Aarthi has specialized in programming languages such as C++, Java, and C, and contributed to research in recommender systems and AI-related data privacy. She has published journal articles, contributed to book chapters, and actively participated in technical workshops. Known for her student mentorship and engagement in academic events, Aarthi remains committed to fostering innovation and excellence in computer science education.

S. Prabagar, Associate Professor at the Alliance School of Advanced Computing, Alliance University, Bengaluru, India, holds a Ph.D. in Information and Communication Engineering from Anna University, Chennai, along with Master's degrees in Computer and Information Technology from Manonmaniam Sundaranar University and Computer Applications from Madurai Kamaraj University, as well as a B.Sc. in Computer Science from VHNSN College, Virudhunagar. With over 22 years of teaching and administrative experience, he specializes in computer networks, IoT, cryptography, steganography, and machine learning, with his doctoral research focusing on designing security protocols and algorithms for protecting medical images transmitted over the internet. He has published extensively in reputed journals including Scopus, Elsevier, and IJEECE, presented research at leading IEEE conferences, and holds multiple patents in IoT-based healthcare and safety systems. An active contributor to academia, he serves as a reviewer for journals such as ASTESJ and has been on advisory committees like the International Conference on Data Science & Big Data Analytics (IDBA-ACMWIR 2023). He teaches diverse subjects including Computer Networks, Artificial Intelligence, Machine Learning, IoT, Operating Systems, Generative AI, NLP, Programming Languages, Computer Graphics, and Distributed Systems, emphasizing the integration of theoretical knowledge with practical applications, while mentoring students and researchers in emerging fields. His career reflects a strong balance between teaching, research, innovation, and academic leadership, with continued engagement in publications, collaborations, and knowledge-sharing activities at national and international levels.

Binastya Anggara Sekti has been a lecturer at the Faculty of Computer Science, Esa Unggul University, Jakarta, since 2016. He is actively involved in the Artificial Intelligence and Information Security Study Group. He holds a Bachelor's degree in Informatics Engineering from the Bandung Institute of Technology and a Master's degree in Information Systems Management from Trisakti University, Jakarta. Prior to entering academia, he accumulated over 25 years of professional experience as an IT practitioner in various companies across Jakarta. His work focused on developing data centers for internet service providers and delivering IT solutions for the manufacturing and oil & gas sectors. His research interests include artificial intelligence, cybersecurity, and the development of IT infrastructure.

Chrisella Natasia Tanujaya is a dedicated Information Systems student at Esa Unggul University, with a strong passion for digital innovation and business process optimization. Throughout her academic journey, Chrisella has authored a book and contributed to a scientific journal, reflecting her enthusiasm for research and continuous learning. She is eager to apply her expertise in leveraging data and technology to design impactful solutions that drive organizational growth and operational excellence.

Khulekani Yakobi (PhD) is a senior lecturer at Mangosuthu University of Technology in the department of Office Technology possessing more than 10 years experience in academics. He holds a PhD in Information Systems from Nelson Mandela University, South Africa. His research interests and activities are based in the fields of Social Media, Social Media Analytics (SMA), Social Media Intelligence (SOCMINT), Big Data Analytics (BDA), Citizens Relationship Management (CzRM), Information and Communication Technology (ICT) in Education and Entrepreneurship. He is recently appointed as a Honorary Research Associate by the Durban University of Technology. He attended, presented, and published conference proceedings in both international and national conferences/symposiums including Malaysia, Peru, UK, Cyprus and South Africa.

Index

A

AI Ethics 23, 29, 39, 58, 76, 192, 214, 228, 236, 255
AI-Induced Impostor Syndrome 237, 238, 239, 241, 243, 256, 260, 265
AI in Education 15, 17, 18, 21, 23, 24, 25, 33, 38, 39, 44, 47, 48, 50, 56, 82, 88, 97, 116, 123, 199, 200, 201, 202, 227, 232, 233, 256
Algorithmic Bias 30, 61, 63, 64, 70, 91, 95, 97, 99, 108, 114, 122, 125, 133, 134, 171, 173, 189, 190, 193, 197, 206, 208, 214, 222, 231, 236
Apartheid 56, 70, 71, 76, 78
Artificial intelligence (AI) 1, 23, 24, 25, 26, 29, 48, 49, 51, 52, 53, 55, 56, 72, 73, 74, 75, 76, 77, 78, 80, 90, 99, 100, 101, 102, 103, 105, 106, 112, 114, 116, 122, 131, 137, 139, 140, 141, 142, 167, 168, 169, 171, 172, 173, 174, 177, 182, 189, 190, 191, 193, 197, 199, 200, 201, 202, 203, 206, 213, 214, 230, 231, 232, 233, 234, 235, 236, 237, 238, 248, 252, 260
Assistive Technology 140, 141, 142, 151, 152, 153, 154, 155, 157, 158, 165, 167, 168, 169, 208, 223, 236
Authorship 61, 95, 107, 112, 115, 237, 241, 242, 244, 246, 247, 248, 249, 251, 252, 254, 255, 257, 258, 259, 260, 261, 262

C

Cultural Sensitivity 14, 15, 17, 18, 22

E

Educational Equity 3, 4, 6, 50, 65, 71, 115, 155, 181, 197, 260
Educational Innovation 47, 192, 260
Educational Policy 72, 99, 196
Emotional Resilience 185, 237
Epistemic Justice 79, 80, 85, 93, 94, 96
Equitable education 22, 29, 66, 78, 148, 154
Equity in Education 30, 152, 157, 207, 228
ESL learners 237, 238, 247, 248, 250, 252, 255
Ethical AI Integration 40, 168, 201, 206

G

Generative AI 1, 2, 3, 4, 5, 6, 7, 11, 14, 15, 16, 21, 22, 23, 24, 25, 29, 30, 31, 33, 34, 37, 47, 48, 50, 56, 74, 75, 79, 80, 91, 92, 96, 98, 100, 105, 106, 110, 112, 114, 115, 116, 117, 118, 119, 120, 122, 123, 125, 126, 127, 128, 129, 130, 132, 133, 134, 135, 137, 142, 147, 150, 157, 159, 161, 163, 165, 166, 167, 169, 170, 171, 172, 173, 174, 184, 186, 187, 199, 200, 202, 205, 206, 207, 208, 209, 210, 211, 212, 213, 214, 215, 217, 219, 220, 221, 222, 223, 224, 225, 226, 227, 228, 230, 231, 232, 233, 234, 235, 236, 260, 264, 265

I

Inclusive Education 1, 2, 22, 73, 75, 78, 80, 81, 82, 87, 93, 96, 97, 139, 140, 141, 142, 143, 147, 148, 150, 151, 152, 154, 155, 156, 159, 161, 162, 163, 164, 165, 166, 168, 173, 181, 186, 201, 203, 208, 209, 210, 213, 214, 215, 219, 227, 233, 236, 261, 263
Inclusive Learning 92, 106, 120, 126, 130, 140, 142, 143, 148, 150, 153, 158, 159, 171, 176, 186, 207, 214, 219, 248
Inclusive Pedagogy 127, 132, 134, 198, 205

L

Liberal Arts 105, 106, 107, 108, 109, 110, 111, 112, 113, 114, 115, 116, 117, 118, 119, 120, 121, 122, 123, 124, 125, 126, 127, 128, 129, 130, 131, 132, 133, 134, 135, 136, 137

P

Personalized Learning 1, 20, 24, 25, 50, 57, 59, 65, 66, 99, 105, 106, 114, 117, 118, 119, 124, 125, 130, 134, 139, 141, 142, 174, 175, 177, 178, 179, 182, 197, 200, 203, 208, 214, 216, 226, 233, 260
Policy Frameworks 1, 2, 29, 62, 66, 82, 196, 197, 225

S

Science Education 77, 80, 85, 99, 100, 105, 107, 108, 109, 110, 111, 112, 113, 116, 118, 119, 120, 123, 125, 126, 127, 128, 129, 130, 131, 133, 134, 135, 137
Social-Emotional Learning 221, 237, 238, 239, 241, 244, 251, 252, 260
Special Education 171, 172, 173, 174, 175, 176, 177, 178, 179, 182, 183, 187, 189, 190, 191, 193, 194, 195, 196, 197, 198, 201, 203, 205, 206, 207, 208, 209, 211, 212, 214, 216, 220, 221, 222, 223, 224, 225, 226, 227, 228, 229, 230, 231, 232, 233, 234, 235, 236
Speculative Fabulation 79, 86, 101
STEM Education 79, 81, 83, 84, 85, 86, 90, 91, 93, 94, 96, 97, 98, 101, 102, 120, 121, 137
Sustainable Development 56, 76, 78

T

Teacher Education 23, 79, 83, 85, 86, 88, 89, 90, 91, 92, 93, 95, 96, 99, 192

U

Ubuntu 66, 69, 70, 77, 78
Universal Design for Learning (UDL) 27, 105, 106, 108, 109, 114, 116, 118, 120, 121, 124, 127, 130, 133, 134, 137, 154, 155, 173, 176, 179, 194, 199, 202, 203, 205, 206, 208, 209, 214, 222, 236

www.ingramcontent.com/pod-product-compliance
Ingram Content Group UK Ltd.
Pitfield, Milton Keynes, MK11 3LW, UK
UKHW052003051026
15624UKWH00003B/541

9 798337 337456